BEETHOVEN

BEETHOVEN

William Kinderman

UNIVERSITY OF CALIFORNIA PRESS

Berkeley   Los Angeles

University of California Press
Berkeley and Los Angeles, California

Published by arrangement with Oxford University Press.

Library of Congress Cataloging-in-Publication Data
Kinderman, William.
Beethoven / William Kinderman.
p.   cm.
Includes bibliographical references and indexes.
ISBN 0-520-08796-8
1. Beethoven, Ludwig van, 1770-1827—Criticism and interpretation.
I. Title.
ML410.B4K56   1995

780'.92—dc20   94-4813

Printed in the United Kingdom

9   8   7   6   5   4   3   2   1

For Eva,
and for
Daniel and Laura

PREFACE AND
ACKNOWLEDGMENTS

This book examines the main lines of Beethoven's creative development, from his formative years at Bonn to the last string quartets written near the end of his life. The investigation is set in the context of Beethoven's biography, but gives priority to representative musical works in the major genres: the piano sonata and variation set; the duo sonata, trio, string quartet, and other types of chamber music; the concerto, overture, and symphony; and the forms of vocal music such as the art song, opera, cantata, and sacred mass. Not to be overlooked is Beethoven's contribution to patriotic programme music, of which the 'Battle Symphony' *Wellingtons Sieg* is the best-known example.

Beethoven scholarship has never been more active than in recent years, and I have attempted to absorb some new research findings into a relatively comprehensive critical context. Primary sources such as Beethoven's conversation books and his diary from 1812–18 have become available in reliable editions, and the vast legacy of his musical sketchbooks has begun to be explored in rich detail. A more convincing psychological portrait of Beethoven has emerged, in part through re-examination of the conventional heroic myths that attached themselves to the composer in the nineteenth century. The falsifications of unreliable but influential witnesses, particularly Anton Schindler, have been exposed. And some recent analytical studies have shown healthy signs of a shift towards a more integrated approach that avoids sacrificing artistic sensibility to systematic method. Analysis at its best is not an end in itself but a means to an end: it enables us to hear more in the music. In this sense, an analysis resembles an inward performance; it depends vitally on our imagination of the sound, and it needs to be verified by the reader: how does it feel?

Since the primary focus of the present study is aesthetic rather than biographical, some familiarity with the musical works has to be presupposed in the analytical discussions. The reader is invited to use the book in several ways: as an analytical guide to individual pieces, which can readily be located in the text by consulting the Index of Beethoven's Compositions; as a study placing these pieces into the context of Beethoven's life and his response to philosophical and political currents of his time; and as a reassessment of Beethoven's creative development and his cultural importance. Other relevant topics recur throughout the book like ever new variations on a theme: Beethoven's verbal and musical humour, for instance, is explored in chapters 2, 3, 8, 9, and 12, whereas his evolving treatment of narrative design is discussed in chapters 3–5, 9–10, and 12, among others.

The introductory chapter, 'Overture', sets out the main philosophical and aesthetic argument. Like Beethoven's second and third *Leonore* overtures, this one presents important themes that are later exemplified in detail. Readers with little interest in philosophy are urged to begin with chapter 1 and return later to the introduction. Like the 'overture', some of the later chapters are relatively self-sufficient essays as well as stations in the larger chronological narrative. Many threads connecting the chapters derive from the subject itself; the numerous comparisons between the musical works discussed, for instance, manifest the deep continuity in Beethoven's creative development. The problem of Beethoven's 'creative periods' is addressed in part through the chapter organization; the issue of periodization is discussed in chapter 8. The emphasis given in this book to Beethoven's later music reflects the growing recognition now accorded to works whose early performances often provoked scepticism if not disfavour.

*   *   *

The research and writing of this book has taken a decade, and the project could not have been completed without the support of several institutions. I am grateful to the Social Sciences and Humanities Research Council of Canada and to the Alexander von Humboldt Foundation for their generous and indispensable assistance at different times during the last seven years. During 1986–7 I worked at the Beethoven-Archiv at Bonn; since 1990 my time has been divided almost equally between the Hochschule der Künste, Berlin, and the University of Victoria, Canada. The sustained writing was begun in Berlin in 1992, largely completed at Victoria in early 1993, and finished and revised in Berlin that summer with the assistance of a grant from the German Academic Exchange Service.

Several archives and libraries kindly provided illustrative material for this volume. These include the Staatsbibliothek Preussischer Kulturbesitz, Berlin; Hochschule der Künste, Berlin; Beethoven-Archiv, Bonn; Bibliothèque Nationale, Paris; Österreichische Nationalbibliothek, Vienna; Historisches Museum, Vienna; and the McPherson Library, University of Victoria. Thanks are also due to the private owner in Brussels of the little-known Beethoven portrait by Waldmüller from 1823 that preceded his famous picture for Breitkopf and Härtel (see Plate 21). Helmut Hell and Hans-Günter Klein kindly allowed me access to manuscripts in the Staatsbibliothek Preussischer Kulturbesitz at Berlin, and Sieghard Brandenburg and Michael Ladenburger offered helpful assistance at the Beethoven-Archiv at Bonn.

I am grateful to the following individuals for offering helpful comments during my work on the book: Vilhjálmur Árnason, Michael Benedikt, Elmar Budde, Barry Cooper, John Daverio, Werner Grünzweig, Sylvia Imeson,

Pierre Jasmin, Paul Kling, John Kongsgaard, Kevin Korsyn, Harald Krebs, Gary Le Tourneau, and Albrecht Riethmüller. Our music librarian at Victoria, Sandra Acker, deserves credit for her resourceful acquisition of Beethoven materials. I am thankful as well for the stimulating input of the students in several courses on Beethoven that I have taught at the University of Victoria, the University of British Columbia, and the Hochschule der Künste, Berlin.

Special thanks go to Hans-Werner Küthen, who generously shared material on Beethoven's puns. Sieghard Brandenburg made a number of factual corrections and valuable suggestions for the improvement of my working draft, as well as drawing my attention to the source of Plate 13 and transcribing Beethoven's inscription. My student assistant, Lynn Matheson, helped diligently with the preparation of the typescript and music examples, Malcolm Gerratt, formerly of J. M. Dent, offered much encouragement for the project, and Julia Kellerman has skilfully seen it through to publication.

My profoundest gratitude is to Alfred Brendel and Maynard Solomon, both of whom read the entire typescript and offered valuable detailed comments and critique. They are, of course, in no way responsible for remaining infelicities.

To my wife, Eva Solar-Kinderman, I am indebted in a hundred ways. Not only her work as research assistant, but her musical insight as pianist and her mastery of languages have contributed to the book. One small example of her input is the new clarification of Beethoven's puns on the name of his friend Zmeskall as 'dearest dirt hauler' in chapter 2; Jürgen May and Johann Knobloch are also to be thanked for their careful subsequent research into this rare instance of Beethoven's plays on words relating to the Czech language. I should beg forgiveness here from family and friends for my own numerous bad puns made during the writing of this book—I have become infected by Beethoven's example.

Portions of this book have appeared in different forms in *19th Century Music, Zu Beethoven, Nineteenth-Century Piano Music,*[1] and *Beethoven Forum.* Chapter 10 intersects with my published studies of *Beethoven's Diabelli Variations* and of the Ninth Symphony in *Beethoven's Compositional Process,* and the discussion of the last sonatas and the quartet op. 127 overlaps with my contributions to *Beethoven: Interpretationen seiner Werke.*[2] I am grateful to the editors and publishers for their permission to republish these materials.

---

[1] From my essay 'Beethoven'. Excerpted and adapted with permission of Schirmer Books, an imprint of Macmillan Publishing Company, from *Nineteenth-Century Piano Music,* edited by R. Larry Todd. Copyright © 1990 by Schirmer Books.

[2] Ed. Carl Dahlhaus, Albrecht Riethmüller, and Alexander Ringer (Laaber: Laaber Verlag, 1994).

Most of the music examples are taken from the standard collected edition, *Beethovens Werke: Vollständige kritische durchgesehene Gesamtausgabe*, 25 vols (Leipzig: Breitkopf & Härtel, 1862–5; 1888); examples 79–84 and 94–5 were first published in my article 'Beethoven's Symbol for the Deity in the *Missa solemnis* and the Ninth Symphony', *19th Century Music*, ix (1985), pp. 102–18. I have had the benefit of coordinating work on this book with three ongoing recording projects for Philips Classics Productions: the symphonies, conducted by Colin Davis; the quartets, performed by the Guarneri Quartet; and the piano sonatas, played by Alfred Brendel; and I rehearsed some ideas contained in the book in a three-day workshop with Brendel on Beethoven held at Carnegie Hall in May 1993. The experience of writing notes for these distinguished performers has helped me in my attempt to convey a sense of engagement with this remarkable music.

Berlin
July 1994

CONTENTS

LIST OF PLATES

LIST OF MUSIC EXAMPLES AND FIGURES

Music examples

Figures

Overture

No composer occupies a more central position in musical life than Beethoven. Changes in taste and in the role of art in society have in no way blunted the appeal of his music on many levels—from ubiquitous popularization in television advertising to the most exemplary professional performances. If the fascination Beethoven exerted in the nineteenth and early twentieth centuries was tied to his heroic, revolutionary image, the last half-century has increasingly demonstrated the universal scope of his legacy. Beethoven's deep roots in the Enlightenment lent qualities to his art that cannot be adequately understood in terms of a merely personal or national style. His restless, open vision of the work of art reflects a modern and essentially cosmopolitan aesthetic attitude. Flexible principles and not fixed preconceptions guided Beethoven's artistic process, as is minutely documented in the thousands of pages of his surviving musical sketches.

There is no short-cut to discerning these principles: only detailed critical engagement with the music offers a tenable basis for interpretation. Still, it is helpful to recall Beethoven's own professed convictions about his general artistic aims. In a letter of 29 July 1819 to his patron and student the Archduke Rudolph, he wrote characteristically about the need for 'freedom and progress . . . in the world of art as in the whole of creation'.[1] To refer to his own artistic goal in this context Beethoven coined the term *Kunstvereinigung*, or 'artistic unification', a notion that is connected to the ageing composer's intense assimilation of Handel and Bach during his last decade. A striving towards *Kunstvereinigung* is in no way confined to his later years, however, and Beethoven's entire career may be viewed as embodying just such a progressive unification of artistic means.

[1] My translation. For a translation of the entire letter and a brief commentary, see Thayer-Forbes, pp. 741–2.

The central task of the present study is to trace the formation and evolution of this process through analysis of works from all periods of Beethoven's life. A necessary prerequisite of any such undertaking is the examination of the historical, aesthetic, and biographical context of Beethoven's style. Great works of art may seem to transcend their historical setting, absorbing its conventions into an aesthetic object in which, in Friedrich Schiller's words, 'the idea of self-determination shines back to us'. But it would be a serious error to confuse the apparent autonomy of the 'absolute music' of the Viennese Classics with modern notions of a merely abstract structural matrix, lifted out of history. For Beethoven, as for Schiller, the idea of artistic self-determination meant something quite different, whereby the autonomy manifested in the work by no means insulates it from the world according to the ideal of 'l'art pour l'art', but, on the contrary, enables the work to display a 'representation of freedom' as a goal for human striving.[2] A proper consideration of Beethoven's musical legacy thus entails not only an assessment of his impact on the musical traditions and characteristic styles of his day, but also an evaluation of the latent symbolism investing so many of his works.

Susanne Langer once described the successful artwork as presenting 'an unconsummated symbol' through a 'process of articulation'.[3] Crucial to her formulation is the word 'unconsummated', which points to the capability of the work to transcend the bounds of direct representation, so encasing the symbol within the artistic medium that its full meaning cannot be unpacked or reduced through analysis. It is revealing in this respect that many works of a superficial, conventional cast are all too explicit or unmediated in their symbolic content. In Beethoven's music, this principle is illustrated by the series of patriotic compositions written around 1813–14, the Congress of Vienna period. Beethoven's battle symphony *Wellingtons Sieg* ('Wellington's Victory') and his cantata *Der glorreiche Augenblick* ('The Glorious Moment') marked a summit of his outward, public acclaim but a nadir of his artistic achievement.

What the bundle of processional anthems and cannonades in *Wellington's Victory* lacks is a compelling internal artistic context. In this work a literal, external programme assumes priority, whereas in the *Eroica* Symphony or the 'Lebewohl' Sonata, by contrast, symbolic elements are absorbed into new and original musical designs, creating a whole greater than the sum of the parts. To express the same point differently, we could say that in *Wellington's Victory* Langer's requirement of a 'process of articulation' is inadequately developed; as in most popular and commercial music, the symbolic content is not truly integrated into an artistic structure. This touches in turn on the problem of

---

[2] This and the preceding quotation are from Schiller's correspondence with Körner, cited in Chytry, *The Aesthetic State*, pp. 81, 82.

[3] *Philosophy in a New Key*, p. 204.

'absolute music' that has been so much debated in connection with Beethoven's works since the nineteenth century.

As some insightful earlier critics from E. T. A. Hoffmann to Walter Riezler have argued, Beethoven's music represents a supreme embodiment of an art that had finally emancipated itself, through a long historical process, from its traditional dependence on words, dance, or ritual. Its status as 'absolute music' was thus bound up with a sense of autonomy whereby the work seemed to follow not convention or external models but its own inner laws, achieving a qualitatively new realization of the tonal language in works of highly individualized character. Beethoven increasingly transformed the rhetorical models and conventional formal gestures of the music of his day. He was prepared thereby to strain the expectations of the aristocratic patrons who nourished his career but towards whom he showed a fierce independence. More than any previous composer Beethoven contributed to a reversal of the perceived relation between artist and society: instead of supplying commodities for use, like a skilled tradesman, the successful artist could now be regarded as an original genius in the Kantian sense, revealing an unsuspected higher order in nature, and giving voice thereby to the unconditioned, or even paradoxically to the infinite or the inexpressible.

This idealistic outlook, which reinforced the myth of Beethoven as revolutionary prophet or 'deaf seer', in Wagner's words, risks obscuring some essential aspects of the music and must be complemented by a dose of empirical realism. We are now more aware of the problematic character of evolutionary historicism, as well as the pitfalls of overemphasizing the allegedly unconditioned nature of the aesthetic object. In fact, a popularized version of the new aesthetic of expression, together with the cult of genius and a strong appetite for programmatic interpretations and titles, were all associated with a change in taste that was already becoming evident in Vienna during Beethoven's lifetime, a change that in some important respects must be reckoned a decline. The palaces where Beethoven established himself in the 1790s and Mozart worked just a few years earlier supported a more refined audience than the general concert public that came into existence a few decades later. Lost to the new aesthetic, for instance, was the dry, rationalistic spirit that inspired the comic instrumental works of Haydn and Beethoven—music with few parallels before the twentieth century. The Romantic composers tended to take themselves too seriously to partake in the ironic play of incongruity that remained a lifelong interest of Beethoven.

Beethoven's legacy cast a long shadow over the nineteenth century, a shadow covering both sides of the famous aesthetic controversies that raged around Liszt and Wagner on the one hand, and Brahms and Hanslick on the other. These controversies illustrate how difficult it was to maintain the Beethovenian balance between tradition and innovation. For many, it seemed unavoidable to take sides for or against the 'Music of the Future' through commitment to either the expressive or formalistic aesthetic, and the duality has continued to exert influence up to the present. Yet the choice is invidious and unnecessary, since neither perspective rules out the other.

A major challenge to criticism of Beethoven's music consists precisely in the need to sustain a balance between these dimensions, which have been described as 'the two classic elements that rub against one another in every work: expressive, fallible substance on the one hand, and determined, inexorable structure on the other'.[4] Critics and analysts have often emphasized one or other of these aspects without grasping the synthesis on which Beethoven's art vitally depends. The danger of a programmatic approach is that an objective, verifiable relationship with the work may be shortchanged in favour of the impressionistic response of the critic. Many such interpretations have been offered: two examples are Arnold Schering's *Beethoven und die Dichtung* and Wilfrid Mellers's *Beethoven and the Voice of God*. Schering saw the key to interpretation in dramas by Shakespeare, Schiller, and Goethe, and freely underlaid themes from Beethoven's works with texts by these authors. Mellers, on the other hand, discerned in the emergent lyricism of Beethoven's music a 'hidden song' with divine connotations. Despite occasional insights, the work of both authors is gravely compromised by their tendency to oversimplify the artistic phenomenon, interpreting its symbolism in a too explicit and arbitrary fashion. Consequently, the dialogue of the critic with the artwork and its historical context often collapses into a monologue, revealing far more about the writer than about the object of discourse.

Equally serious difficulties undermine approaches based narrowly on aspects of musical structure whose aesthetic qualities are ignored. In Allen Forte's book *The Compositional Matrix*, devoted to Beethoven's Piano Sonata in E major op. 109, for instance, any reference to the aesthetic character of the music is conspicuously avoided as if unworthy of consideration. Some analyses, especially in English-speaking countries, continue to reflect inhibitions or even embarrassment about those aspects of the artistic experience that seem less accessible to systematic methodologies. Just as in Anglo-American philosophy of the post-war period, in which perennial issues of ethics and metaphysics were cast aside in favour of an intense yet often myopic probing of the logic of language, so has musical analysis too frequently limited its attention to quantifiable entities, cutting short the inquiry into artistic meaning.

How, then, can we address Beethoven's music in its proper aesthetic terms, while maintaining the necessary balance between subjectivity and objectivity? It is helpful in this connection to reassess some of the aesthetic ideas that emerged out of Enlightenment thought. To be sure, the leading thinkers of

[4] Richard Kramer, 'Ambiguities in *La Malinconia*', p. 29.

the age, such as Kant, Schiller, and Goethe, often showed insufficient awareness of the potential of musical art, and it is usually not their explicit pro-
nouncements about music but their more comprehensive insights that most
richly reward our attention. Most crucial is the concept of human experience
as a synthesis of sense perception and understanding regulated by the faculty
of reason (*Vernunft*). The classic statement of this argument, which has been
reformulated and elaborated many times up to the present day, is the first of
Kant's three great critiques, the *Kritik der reinen Vernunft* ('Critique of Pure
Reason'), first published in 1781. Beethoven's enthusiasm for one of Kant's dic-
tums is recorded in his conversation-book notation of February 1820: '"The
moral law within us, and the starry heavens above us" Kant!!!'[5] By the same
token, Beethoven declined to attend lectures on Kant held at the University
of Vienna, and it is unlikely that he studied many of Kant's works at first
hand. Maynard Solomon has described Beethoven's position as 'superficial
Kantianism'.[6] It is possible, however, that Beethoven's affinity with Kant lies
not in any direct philosophical engagement but rather in his response,
through his art, to the same underlying experiential issues.

Still more important are the ideas of another creative artist who strove to
integrate Kant's theory with an elevated concept of the artwork—Schiller,
whose letters *Über die aesthetische Erziehung des Menschen* ('On the Aesthetic
Education of Mankind') first appeared in 1795, to be warmly if not uncritically
appreciated by the philosopher at Königsberg. Schiller's *Aesthetic Letters* are
underestimated today, but the core of his argument remains viable and
provocative. One difficulty lies in his reliance on the term 'beauty' (*Schönheit*)
instead of 'work of art', since beauty is clearly not a necessary or sufficient criterion for art, as Schiller sometimes implies. His basic argument nevertheless
allows for the substitution of 'artwork' for 'beauty', a substitution which
strengthens the connection between the ontological and ethical aspects of his
theory. For Schiller, the inborn faculty of the senses, comprising our perception of manifold impressions in a temporal continuity, is regarded as a 'sensuous drive' (*Sinntrieb*). Our rational nature, on the other hand, which seeks to
annul time by imposing categories on experience, is the 'form drive'
(*Formtrieb*). The profound significance accorded to art in Schiller's theory
derives from its synthesis of the sensuous and rational in the 'play drive'
(*Spieltrieb*), which brings 'life' and form (*Gestalt*) into conjunction as 'living
shape' (*lebende Gestalt*).[7]

This tensional synthesis of sensuous intuition and rational understanding
should be distinguished from the dialectical speculations of Hegel and later
idealistic thinkers. For Schiller or Kant, unlike the Romantic idealists, the
recognition of limits is crucial. The limits imposed by the 'critique of reason'

---

[5] *Ludwig van Beethovens Konversationshefte*, i, p. 235.   [6] *Beethoven*, p. 38.

[7] Cf. Chytry, *The Aesthetic State*, p. 82.

hold ideological speculation in check, while moral and ethical issues emerge through the idea of freedom. Hegel's philosophy of spirit oversteps, but does not escape, the Kantian critique by systematically dissolving fixity of thought. The rhythm of Hegel's speculative dialectic strives to overcome the gap between subjectivity and objectivity by means of an 'expressive pantheism', infusing philosophy with aesthetics, just as art in turn, in his view, can transcend its own sphere by becoming religion or *Kunstreligion*. Hegel ultimately elevates speculative thought to a kind of mysticism that supersedes religion while allegedly preserving its essential content. His closest musical counterpart is Wagner, who embraced Hegel's commitment to a sweeping, evolutionary historicism and whose final work became the most controversial modern embodiment of *Kunstreligion*: *Parsifal*.

If Beethoven was no Hegelian, some of his aesthetic convictions do parallel those of Friedrich Schelling, a pivotal figure in the circle at Jena in the 1790s that included both Hölderlin and Hegel. As Joseph Chytry recently observed, these three colleagues pursued a 'philosophical quest for an intuition prior to the distinction between subject and object', a project with strong social, political, and religious implications, since what was sought was a unity with all being (*Vereinigung*).[8] The attempt to advance beyond Kant's *Kritik der Urteilskraft* ('Critique of Judgment') of 1790 and Schiller's *Aesthetic Letters* was a perilous one, and Schelling ultimately succumbed to the dismal attractions of political romanticism. The Schellingian position in his *System of Transcendental Idealism* of 1800, however, deserves attention for the exalted role it grants the artwork in displaying this original harmony of object and subject, unconscious and conscious, nature and freedom. Schelling's concept of the natural world, like Goethe's, was organicist; for him, mind itself was seen as emanating from the unending activity of nature. We are reminded here of Beethoven's own nature worship, so richly documented in his heavily annotated copy of Christian Sturm's *Reflections on the Works of God in Nature*. That Beethoven's feelings had a philosophical core is implied as well by the inscriptions from ancient Egyptian monuments that he kept under glass on his work table. The second of these appeared as a footnote in Kant's *Critique of Judgment* together with the following commentary:

Perhaps nothing more sublime was ever said and no sublimer thought ever expressed than on the Temple of Isis (Mother Nature): 'I am all that is and that was and that shall be, and no mortal hath lifted my veil'.

The dictum characterizes nature as infinite, timeless and beyond comprehension, much the same message as conveyed in the Kantian quotation about the 'starry heavens above'—an image Beethoven absorbed into an entire series of musical works. Noteworthy in this connection is Schelling's argument that

[8] *The Aesthetic State*, pp. 109–10, 135–47.

since philosophy is reflection, it must wait for art to produce a consciousness of the unity of nature and freedom. In effect, Schelling offered a philosophical justification for the claim, attributed apocryphally to Beethoven, that the revelation of art was 'higher than all wisdom and philosophy'. And it is perhaps in light of the struggle of the Jena circle to transcend the limits of Kantian and Schillerian aesthetics that we may best view the artistic enterprise that Beethoven himself provocatively dubbed *Kunstvereinigung*.

What is the character of this unity of object and subject, or nature and freedom? The subsequent history of aesthetics shows clearly the temptation to oversimplify the issue, or even whiten it into abstraction. Sensationist or formalistic theories of art, for instance, isolate one side of Schiller's triadic configuration, giving too little attention to the interaction of the sensuous and rational. Analogous problems underlie the shortcomings of many musical analyses, as we have seen. Ultimately, the meaning of a pair of concepts such as 'subjective' and 'objective' proves provisionary if not vague when tested against concrete experience. The polarity of nature and freedom, however, touches abiding issues that were tackled in different ways by all the thinkers we have mentioned, and have lost none of their relevance in the ongoing philosophical debate.[9] One pole centres on the 'sublime' in nature, our experience of the infinite and awe-inspiring in the phenomenal world; the other revolves around the possibility of 'freedom', that autonomy of the individual that is the prerequisite of moral action or creativity.

The philosophical dilemma that has often impoverished aesthetics is lodged precisely at the nexus prior to the distinction between subject and object that Schelling contemplated in 1800. Schelling posited that the artwork displays the synthesis of nature and freedom 'as the most perfect unity', treating the aesthetic experience as a medium of reconciliation in a manner looking back to Kant and forwards to Hegel. The problem is that it is the aesthetic of beauty, not the sublime, that offers itself as an embodiment of reconciliation. Schiller's vision of the artwork also involves a mediating synthesis, as we have seen, but the dynamic, tension-laden elements that are undervalued in too much aesthetic theory, including Kant's *Critique of Judgment*, are fully recognized by Schiller. Unlike Kant, Schiller did not embrace the somewhat abstract notion of art as a 'disinterested pleasure'; he persisted, despite all obstacles, in seeking an objective definition for art that would underscore its ethical character. Furthermore, Schiller located a conflict at the heart of the artwork, since in his view the synthesis of the rational and sensuous is problematic and can never be fully achieved. In this respect, his vision of the work of art belongs to what we may broadly describe as the aesthetic of the sublime

---

[9] Vilhjálmur Árnason has recently claimed, for instance, that 'philosophy must recover the notion of *nature* as it enters into the history of human development' in order to provide 'an adequate account of human morality' ('Morality and Humanity', p. 3).

rather than the aesthetic of the beautiful. The sublime, in Schiller's formulation, fuses disparate elements, and its power is bound up with the *irreconcilability* of reason and sensibility. The ultimate aim of art, in this sense, is inevitably left unfulfilled, but the task is all the more compelling for its apparent impossibility.

The ascendancy of the aesthetic of beauty and the related decline of the aesthetic of the sublime in the nineteenth century arose from a different line of interpretation. Kant saw in beauty a harmonious relationship between the imagination and understanding; in his view, a beautiful object is brought into accordance with unknown laws that govern a higher unity in nature. The sublime, however, entails a relationship between the imagination and reason that resists the ideal of reconciliation; for Kant, as for Schiller, the structure of the sublime is characterized by an unresolvable conflict. Consequently, Kant could not clearly incorporate the sublime into the comprehensive system of his philosophy. Beauty, being unburdened by any such fundamental conflict, offered a more serene model for art seemingly grounded in universal natural phenomena. Not surprisingly, systematic thinkers such as Hegel neglected the sublime, and tended to domesticate art under the category of beauty. The influence of German neo-Classicism, as mediated by Johann Winckelmann, who discovered in the art of Greece a spirit of 'noble simplicity and quiet grandeur', contributed to this trend, which was reflected for instance in the reduction of Mozart to Schumann's 'floating Greek gracefulness' or Wagner's 'genius of light and love'. Despite some countervailing tendencies, the nervous, disturbing, conflict-ridden aspects of Mozart—not to mention his wit—were often underestimated by an age predisposed to hear in his music a tranquil beauty comparable to the works of painters such as Raphael or Watteau.

If the classicizing ideal of beauty proved too abstract to encompass the artistic reality of Mozart, its application to Beethoven seemed questionable from the beginning. For as E. T. A. Hoffmann stressed in his famous review of the Fifth Symphony, Beethoven's music is permeated by the sublime. An aesthetic of the beautiful, whereby the artwork acts as a medium of reconciliation, is exemplified far more in a composer like Johann Strauss. The 'Blue Danube', not the Ninth Symphony, has settled deeply into the general social consciousness without forfeiting its integrity. Whereas the waltzes of Strauss invite easy assimilation, the meaning of even the popular melodic emblem of Beethoven's 'Joy' theme is rendered conditional by the internal context of the symphony, placing further demands on the listener; only in relation to the earlier movements can the choral finale be fully understood.

The challenges of a work like Beethoven's Ninth conform to the aesthetic analysis by Hans-Georg Gadamer, for whom 'not only the cognition of meaning is involved . . . something else is always awakened, whereby we recognize ourselves'. Gadamer proposes that only when the listener 'fills out' the work of art, going beyond its immediate sensuous appearance in the direction of its implied meanings, does the work really come into existence. 'Only then does all conflict disappear between intention and being, and every difference vanish between that which the artist wishes to say and what the interpreter makes of it. They have become one . . . This is the reason why works of art bring about a true self-encounter in all those who come to grips with them.'[10] Like Schiller, Gadamer thus stresses both the moment of aesthetic identification and the ethical character of this process, whereby the individual is freed from a purely sensuous relationship with the work. Ultimately, of course, this process embraces much more than just the sublime: humour, defined by Jean Paul Richter as 'the sublime in reverse', or gaiety, pathos or tragedy all surface in Beethoven's dramatic style, emerging out of the configuration of relationships forming the unconsummated symbol.

Beethoven's music often displays a provocatively open relationship with the world that forces us to reconsider the nature of aesthetic experience itself. In its original sense as *episteme aisthetike*, aesthetics refers not only to art or beauty but to sensible awareness more generally; the opposing complement to this concept is the anaesthetic, involving a loss or deadening of feeling.[11] One reason for the scope of Beethoven's achievement may lie in his ability to navigate between these two realms, ironically granting the anaesthetic its place beside the aesthetic. Beethoven expands the boundaries of art through his absorption of trivial, commonplace material, as in the Diabelli Variations, or through symbolic intrusions into a work from without, as in the 'terror fanfare' in the finale of the Ninth Symphony or the war-like episodes in the *Missa solemnis*. His use of severe contrasts becomes a means of welding sections or movements into a larger narrative sequence with symbolic implications, as in the last piano sonatas, with their open cadences pointing into the silence beyond. In the dualistic finale of the Sonata in Ab major op. 110, the resolution at the end of the second fugal section is affirmed yet endangered; it proves barely sufficient to outweigh the preceding *Arioso dolente*. Like the close of the *Missa solemnis*, this resolution is poised at the edge of an abyss. Walter Riezler wrote accordingly about the presence of the 'world background' in Beethoven's works, the sense that despite all their density of internal unifying relations these pieces are not self-contained but strive to confront the outer world of common existence.[12] It is precisely this quality that invites and even demands of the listener the kind of self-encounter described by Gadamer.

This need for the listener to grasp the latent artistic content—in its uneasy blending of object and subject, conscious and unconscious, nature and freedom—harbours ethical and even political implications. The work of art, in

[10] This and the preceding quotation come from 'Ende der Kunst?', pp. 31–2.
[11] Cf. Welsch, *Ästhetisches Denken*, pp. 9–40. [12] *Beethoven*, pp. 108–9, 198.

the sense described above, arises in a realm beyond the reach of political power and social conformity, and its very existence potentially confirms the democratic ideal of personal freedom. For Schiller or Beethoven, the glorification of freedom through art was coupled with discontent about actual political conditions. Schiller remained justifiably sceptical about the attainment of 'freedom and progress' in the political sphere, maintaining that 'art is the daughter of freedom' and that 'in order to solve the political problem, one must take the route of aesthetics, since it is through beauty that the way is made to freedom'.[13] Moreover, as Chytry has pointed out, Schiller explicitly distinguishes his approach from the premises motivating 'the most perfect Platonic republic', exposing the fallacy behind the standard argument of German Romantics advocating subordination of the individual to the state based on the metaphor of the formal artwork.[14]

With historical hindsight we can acknowledge the continuing validity of Schiller's position: the work of art, if it is to represent the highest human potential, must embody the principle of self-determination while avoiding ideological determination from without. In this sense Schiller's revised Enlightenment perspective remains more viable than later idealistic, romantic, formalist, structuralist, or socialistic views of the relationship of art and society. The danger of political romanticism, with its impending retrogression into nationalism or fascism, arises from inadequate recognition of the individual human being as a potentially autonomous and creative agent, the grounds of whose self-determination constitute freedom. As soon as our concept of the human being is dominated or consumed by his or her relationship with state, people, class, gender, background, formative experiences, or any other contextual factors, this principle of freedom is violated by ideology, that is, by premature and illegitimate generalization about human nature. An assumption of potential autonomy on the part of other human beings, then, is an indispensable means of curbing the intrusion of a limiting ideological bias. The open universe of Beethoven's *Fidelio*, *Missa solemnis*, and Ninth Symphony, with its rejection of materialism, de-emphasis on received doctrine, and glorification of freedom, is not merely one ideological statement in preference to others but rather an artistic embodiment of ideas intrinsically resistant to ideology.

Any such claim about specific works by Beethoven can of course be properly supported only through detailed analysis. But these preliminary observations already begin to indicate how close Beethoven's aesthetic attitudes come to the ideas articulated by Schiller. The claims of 'freedom and progress', innovation and fantasy, were ingrained so deeply into Beethoven's creative method that he could say about the last string quartets in 1826 that 'You will

---

[13] *Aesthetic Letters*, letter 2.   [14] *The Aesthetic State*, p. 86.

find a new manner of voice treatment, and thank God there is less lack of fantasy than ever before'.[15] He could have added that there is also less lack of
integration and structural control than ever before. Beethoven's innovative
quest is merged here with all those qualities of sovereign concentration that
E. T. A. Hoffmann described as self-possession (*Besonnenheit*).

The astonishing understatement of this comment about 'less lack of fantasy' is characteristic of Beethoven, and carries the same implication as
Schiller's tenet about the unfulfilled nature of the artwork. Already 25 years
earlier Beethoven had expressed dissatisfaction with his previous works, and
according to Carl Czerny, stated his intention to seek a 'new way', a claim
borne out by the series of pathbreaking compositions from around 1802, the
threshold of his so-called 'second period'. Beethoven's conviction that in art
one 'cannot stand still' is best understood not merely as a personal idiosyn-
crasy, or as an expression of the problematic romantic notion of originality, but
rather in terms of a universal experiential duality whose reconciliation is an
ever-challenging task of art.

The possibility of an artistic resolution to the division in human nature
between the sensuous and rational accords a special role to the productive
imagination, and raises fundamental aesthetic questions. A work of musical
art is not an abstract entity, but needs to be realized in sound and time. The
implications of that fact were probed by Theodor W. Adorno, who, like
Gadamer, viewed the work itself as 'a copy of a non-existent original'—for,
paradoxically, there is no work as such—it must become.[16] At the same time,
in Adorno's view, the true performance or analysis does not possess the work
ontologically—in its essential being—though it must convey it. For, as with
any creative act, the product cannot be predicted or fully envisaged in advance
but represents rather an imaginative synthesis consisting of elements that are
intimately known.

This concept of the musical work of art thus eschews relativism and struc-
turalism by placing analytic criticism in the service of aesthetic categories in
an immanent relationship with the music, which remains ever unknown in its
totality, waiting for its true realization. Built into this concept is the necessary
dynamic relation: 'What is only and surely right', in Adorno's formulation,
'isn't right'. The underlying principle is thus analogous to the arguments
stated above concerning the possibility of human freedom: only through an
acknowledgment of limits to categorial understanding can we approach a
truly integrated internal sound-image of the work and a balanced appreciation
of its blend of the sensuous and rational. The point needs stressing in view of
the overemphasis on systematic methodology characteristic of some musical
analysis, as well as recent polemical attacks on the notion of artistic unity by

---

[15] Thayer-Forbes, p. 982 (translation amended).
[16] *Ästhetische Theorie*, Gesammelte Schriften, vii, p. 32.

critics innocent of the underlying issues. If a primary condition for the appearance of a true work is its unity, this is to be understood not as an abstract, tautological concept, or even an organic whole, but rather that totality of concrete elements and relationships that demand realization in sound. What is meant is a unity that is synthetic in nature, and entirely compatible with tension, contrast, diversity, and the individuality of a work.

Ultimately, of course, an apprehension of unity or integration is wholly dependent on our internal sound-image, or *Klangvorstellung*, of the music. Without this key ingredient, analysis is empty and criticism blind. It follows that analysis, properly considered, must engage the immanent temporality of the work, not merely the visual notation of the score, nor a structural matrix posited by *a priori* theoretical constructs. Unlike most earlier music, which unfolds in a successive, linear fashion, and much later music, which returns to the continuous pulse characteristic of the Baroque, the Viennese Classical style cultivates structures whose internal shapes and symmetries seem to hold back or modify the unidirectional passage of time by joining the musical events together in complex ways. This process corresponds to the annulment of time Schiller attributed to the 'form drive'. In recognition of this phenomenon, some scholars have distinguished between 'temps espace', or measured, divisible, quantitative time, and 'temps durée', a musical time-concept contesting the transience of experience through anticipation of the future and memory of the past.[17] The configuration of such durational time typically involves a forward-directed tension, a field of culmination, and a resolving, past-orientated phase—all three of which taken together comprise the sense of the gesture.

Beethoven's complex use of thematic foreshadowing and reminiscence contributes a dimension to his music that transcends a linear temporal unfolding. And his special interest in techniques of parenthetical enclosure, whereby contrasting passages are heard as an interruption within the larger context, further enriches the temporality of his musical forms, helping to open up narrative possibilities rare in instrumental music. Beethoven tended increasingly to tighten the cyclic relationship between movements of his larger works, de-emphasizing their genre character while enhancing the individuality of the whole. Examples of this practice stem from Haydn and Mozart, but the unification of the Classical sonata cycle reached new phases of development in Beethoven, often absorbing a symbolic component. In the Fifth Symphony, for instance, he thoroughly interweaves the formal and motivic content, compromising the autonomy of the four movements. Their individuality of character nevertheless remains more distinct than in comparable works by Berlioz, Schumann, or Bruckner, where shared thematic material is also spread across successive movements. The later practice is often more

---

[17] These concepts, which are indebted to the philosophy of Henri Bergson, are convincingly applied to music in Uhde and Wieland, *Denken und Spielen*.

prose-like and analogous to literary practice,[18] and more diffuse in its larger rhythmic movement. These factors tend to undermine the narrative possibilities of the intrinsic musical design, by softening the hard contrasts and concentrated movement characteristic of Beethoven into a more static, less highly determined idiom.

Of course, the programmatic designates favoured in the nineteenth century often condition a more explicit narrative design than is characteristic of Beethoven (apart from aberrations such as *Wellington's Victory*). In Beethoven, we typically encounter associations that 'overflow the musical scenario, lending a sense of extramusical narrativity to otherwise untranslatable events', to quote Solomon's description of the Ninth Symphony.[19] The narrative design involved is not externally imposed, and it eludes reductionistic interpretations in programmatic or structuralist terms. Far from being exhausted through analysis, these pieces seem more fully integrated than any single hearing, and better than any single performance, as Artur Schnabel liked to claim.

The discernment in Beethoven of narrative designs of symbolic import—as opposed to merely literal, programmatic narratives—requires extensive discussion of the works in question. But we should note even at this early stage that the recognition is not new but builds on older insights. In his letter of 19 July 1825 Beethoven responded enthusiastically to the critical writings about his music by Adolf Bernhard Marx, expressing his 'fervent hope that Marx would continue to reveal the higher aspects of the true realm of art' as an antidote to 'the mere counting of syllables'—one example among others of an abstract mode of criticism incapable of grasping the essential artistic content. Marx, by contrast, addressed Beethoven's works using the criteria of 'organic wholeness and coherence' and perceived in them a 'dramatic narrative' containing 'deep psychological truth'.[20]

Beethoven's path towards progressive integration, narrative design, and a deepened symbolic expression is perhaps encapsulated most succinctly in the following lines of the Schiller poem glorified in the choral finale of the Ninth Symphony:

> Freude, Tochter aus Elysium!
> Deine Zauber binden wieder,
> was die Mode streng geteilt.
>
> Joy, daughter from Elysium!
> join again with your magic
> what custom strictly divided.

---

[18] For a discussion of 'musical prose' from Berlioz to Mahler and Schoenberg, see Danuser, *Musikalische Prosa*.

[19] *Beethoven Essays*, p. 10.

[20] Beethoven's letter and Marx's reviews are cited in Burnham, 'Criticism, Faith, and the *Idee*', esp. pp. 183–4, 188, 191.

The term 'Mode' invites a broader interpretation here than 'custom' or 'fashion', especially when we recall Schiller's quest, begun well before the composition of the Ode in 1785, for a 'transformational force' (*Mittelkraft*) to merge the rational side of the human being with the sensuous. Only years later, after Schiller's move to Weimar in 1787 and his subsequent engagement with the thought of Wilhelm von Humboldt and Kant, did this ambition receive its philosophical expression in the *Aesthetic Letters*, and its highest artistic expression in his final play, *Wilhelm Tell*. Nevertheless, a gap remained in Schiller's achievement between the ideal and the historical, as has often been observed. In the recent formulation of Chytry, 'Ultimately, Schiller's praxis confirms the implicitly pessimistic conclusion of the *Aesthetic Letters*: the theory of the aesthetic state, at least in Schiller's version, cannot transcend an esoteric circle of initiates'.[21]

In this sense Beethoven succeeded where Schiller did not. Already in 1793 Schiller's friend at Bonn, Bartholomäus Ludwig Fischenich, had written to Charlotte Schiller that Beethoven would set the *Ode to Joy* 'strophe by strophe'. In the end, the project waited more than three decades for its fulfilment, by which time historical events had cast new meaning on the poem. It is remarkable that the *Ode to Joy*, almost repudiated by its author in 1802, became the poem through which Schiller's 'effigy of [the] ideal' has had its most profound impact, delivered through a sonorous medium more eminently suited to the blending of the sensuous and rational than spoken drama.

[21] *The Aesthetic State*, p. 101.

I

The Bonn Years

I N retrospect, there is something fitting and almost inevitable about Beethoven's passage from Bonn to Vienna in 1792. The elector, or *Kurfürst*, at Bonn from 1784 was Maximilian Franz, the youngest son of Empress Maria Theresia of Austria, brother of Marie-Antoinette in Paris and the Emperor Joseph II in Vienna. Max Franz's assumption of the post was the product of intrigues and negotiations, part of an effort to extend the influence of the Habsburg monarchy into the Rhineland while limiting Prussian influence. As a result of this circumstance, the most intimate connections linked the small city on the Rhine with the distant capital on the Danube, ten times its size. For the arts and sciences the appointment had a beneficent effect. Max Franz continued the reforms initiated by his predecessor, the Elector Maximilian Friedrich, reforms that paralleled those of his brother Joseph II in Vienna. The clerics and especially the Jesuits were curbed; musical, literary, and theatrical institutions were reorganized and supported. In 1785 the Bonn Academy was elevated to the rank of a university. Johannes Neeb was engaged to teach Kantian philosophy, and men like the later revolutionary Eulogius Schneider and Schiller's friend Fischenich lectured on Greek literature, ethics, and law. By the 1780s Bonn was recognized as a centre of the Enlightenment, that fragile yet immensely productive movement whose liberal reforms were imposed from above, not in response to revolutionary strivings of the suppressed classes. Bonn might have become another Weimar except for the upheavals brought about through the French occupation, which was to sweep away the government of Max Franz in 1794, less than two years after Beethoven's departure. But no-one could have anticipated these events a few years earlier.

Otto Jahn, in his biography of Mozart, speculated that with a slightly different turn of events Mozart might have been offered employment at Bonn.

Max Franz had known Mozart for many years and evidently valued him more highly than did his brother, Joseph II ('for him there is nobody but Salieri', Mozart is supposed to have exclaimed).[1] Already in 1787 Beethoven made a brief, abortive journey to Vienna to see Mozart. And in 1792, one year after the great composer's death, Max Franz's friend Count Ferdinand Waldstein depicted Mozart as Beethoven's guardian spirit in his famous entry in the young composer's album:

You are going to Vienna in fulfillment of your long-frustrated wishes. The Genius of Mozart is mourning and weeping over the death of her pupil. She has found a refuge but no occupation with the inexhaustible Haydn; through him she wishes to form a union with another. With the help of assiduous labor you shall receive *Mozart's spirit from Haydn's hands . . .*[2]

But if the association between Bonn and Vienna was natural and expected, the presence of another key influence on the young Beethoven—his most important teacher, the composer and court organist Christian Gottlob Neefe—was a fortunate stroke of luck. Neefe was a 'foreigner'—from Chemnitz in Saxony—and a Protestant as well (see Plate 2). For these reasons he was at first considered expendable when reorganization of the musical institutions at Bonn was begun under the new elector. Beethoven's first salary as organist, in fact, was taken out of Neefe's income. It was Neefe who grounded Beethoven in the musical forms of the Classical style, who presumably introduced him to the theoretical works of Marpurg and C. P. E. Bach, and who arranged for Beethoven's adolescent publications, the 'Dressler' Variations and three *Kurfürsten* Sonatas for piano. Yet entirely apart from his competent professional guidance and early recognition of his pupil's creative potential, Neefe made further contributions that exercised fruitful influence on the young Beethoven.

One of these consisted in Neefe's knowledge of and enthusiasm for the music of J. S. Bach. Very little of the elder Bach's music had appeared in print by the 1780s, and one would not have expected *The Well-Tempered Clavier* to serve as the cornerstone of instruction, as it did in fact for Beethoven. Neefe, however, had studied in Leipzig, where his musical mentor had been Johann Adam Hiller, the director of the Gewandhaus Concerts and later Bach's successor as Kantor of the Thomaskirche. By the time he came to Bonn in 1779 to work for the Grossmann theatrical company, Neefe was an avid Bach admirer eager to pass on the legacy. He summed up the situation in his notice in Cramer's *Magazin der Musik* dated 2 March 1783, the very first printed statement about Beethoven:

Louis van Betthoven, son of the tenor singer mentioned, a boy of eleven years and of most promising talent. He plays the clavier very skillfully and with power, reads at

---

[1] Cf. Thayer-Forbes, p. 77.   [2] Ibid., p. 115.

sight very well, and—to put it in a nutshell—he plays chiefly *The Well-Tempered Clavier* of Sebastian Bach, which Herr Neefe has put into his hands. Whoever knows this collection of preludes and fugues in all the keys—which might almost be called the *non plus ultra* of our art—will know what this means. So far as his duties permitted, Herr Neefe has also given him instruction in thorough-bass. He is now training him in composition and for his encouragement has had nine variations for the pianoforte, written by him on a march—by Ernst Christoph Dressler—engraved at Mannheim. This youthful genius is deserving of help to enable him to travel. He would surely become a second Wolfgang Amadeus Mozart were he to continue as he has begun.[3]

Like Haydn and Mozart before him, Beethoven was to be exposed during his first Vienna years to works of Handel and J. S. Bach at the musical gatherings of the venerable connoisseur Baron Gottfried van Swieten, who had developed his taste for Bach in Berlin before moving to the Austrian capital. Unlike his predecessors, however, Beethoven's formative musical direction was already shaped by the Leipzig master. From an early stage Bach's music counterbalanced for Beethoven the pervasive presence of the *galant*, the elegant but superficial manner that had threatened to submerge Mozart's individuality during the 1770s. So thorough was Beethoven's assimilation of Bach, in fact, that Erwin Ratz was able to base an illuminating study of musical form precisely on the comparison of Bach's inventions and preludes and fugues with Beethoven's sonatas and quartets.[4]

Neefe's own published compositions included operettas as well as songs, keyboard sonatas, and even a Piano Concerto in G major published in 1782. He also translated many opera librettos from French and Italian, including Mozart's *Don Giovanni*. Beethoven's early acquaintance with the music of C. P. E. Bach, Haydn, and especially Mozart owed much to Neefe. And although Neefe's purely musical achievement remained within the sphere of solid professional competence, his works must have posed a stimulating challenge to his young assistant. Among Neefe's larger compositions from the 1770s, for instance, were 12 settings of odes by Klopstock. In 1782, three years after his arrival at Bonn, Neefe set another such ode, *Dem Unendlichen*, for four choral voices and orchestra; it was performed at first privately and then, during Holy Week, in the Fräuleinstiftskirche. This piece forms part of the context out of which was to emerge Beethoven's most weighty single composition from his years at Bonn: the *Cantata on the Death of Joseph II* written eight years later, in 1790.

For Beethoven, Neefe presumably became an important role model, helping to fill the void opened by Beethoven's difficult relationship with his father

---

[3] Thayer-Forbes, p. 66. The spelling 'Betthoven' appears in the original source: Beethoven was actually twelve years old at the time in question.

[4] *Einführung in die musikalische Formenlehre* (Vienna, 1968).

Johann. Neefe was the most crucial but by no means the only source of personal support and cultural nourishment for the young musician; another was Beethoven's friendship with the von Breuning family. The widow Frau von Breuning befriended Beethoven after the death of his mother in 1787, assuming a protective, motherly attitude: as Beethoven later recalled, 'She knew how to keep the insects off the flowers'. To a great extent, then, the roles of both his natural parents were taken over by others by the time of Beethoven's adolescence. Stefan von Breuning remained one of Beethoven's closest friends during later years in Vienna, although their relationship was strained by occasional quarrels and misunderstandings.

Before we consider Beethoven's intimate family constellation, it is essential to address one more aspect of Neefe's contributions to Bonn cultural life: his role in the *Orden der Illuminaten*, and later in the *Lesegesellschaft* (Literary Society), organizations closely tied to the Enlightenment and not without links to freemasonry. The Freemasons' Lodge founded at Bonn in 1776 soon disappeared in response to Maria Theresia's suppression of the order, but its role was largely filled during the 1780s by the two aforementioned societies. The Bonn chapter of the *Orden der Illuminaten*, founded in 1781, included among its members many who stood close to Beethoven, including the horn player (later a publisher) Nikolaus Simrock, and Franz Ries, father of Beethoven's student and friend Ferdinand Ries. Neefe was one of the leaders of the group. In 1784–5 the *Orden der Illuminaten* was suppressed at its headquarters in Ingolstadt, Bavaria; the Bonn circle continued their activities in following years in the *Lesegesellschaft*. Although there is no evidence that Beethoven belonged to the *Lesegesellschaft*, many of the key players surrounding him during his last years in Bonn were members, including not only Neefe and Ries but also Count Waldstein. One reflection of its importance for Beethoven is the fact that it commissioned the *Joseph* Cantata.

If some of Beethoven's loftiest ideals can be associated with the cultural milieu in Bonn during his second decade, his relationship to his family reveals the other side of the coin: it is troubled and difficult to assess. A probing evaluation of the conditioning role of Beethoven's early experiences on his personality was undertaken by Maynard Solomon in his 1977 biography. Solomon builds on documented facts of Beethoven's life to construct a suggestive psychological model that attempts to pinpoint some of the driving sources of his creativity. Unlike many earlier biographers, Solomon does not hesitate to confront the more disturbing aspects of Beethoven's character or actions, but neither does his work dwell on demythologizing critique. Deep psychological conflicts have, of course, been experienced by many persons without a trace of the miraculous artistic after-effects these experiences helped produce in Beethoven, but this fact neither compromises Solomon's insights nor confines their relevance strictly to the biographical sphere. The link between biography and the analysis of works of art is delicate, but it can sometimes prove tangible and illuminating.

Solomon identifies a complex of conflicts and delusions in Beethoven's psychological make-up whose underlying sources relate to Beethoven's relationship to his parents, and especially to his father. Beethoven's deceased elder brother Ludwig Maria, who lived only six days, was not forgotten but lived a posthumous existence in Beethoven's psyche. What Solomon describes as Beethoven's 'birth year delusion'—his lifelong tendency to deny the plain evidence that he was born in December 1770—involves much more than a simple misunderstanding based on Johann's falsification of his son's age. Psychologically, this behaviour may reflect Beethoven's response to the unhappy resignation of his beloved mother, while also revealing an impulse to deny or disown his father. Within the family Beethoven's role was to parallel that of his admired grandfather and namesake, the elder Ludwig van Beethoven, successful Kapellmeister at the Bonn court from 1761 until his death in 1773. The curse of the Beethoven family, on the other hand, was alcoholism: the Kapellmeister's wife Maria Josepha was removed to a cloister on account of severe drunkenness, and the steep decline of Beethoven's father into helplessness took the same form. (On hearing of Johann van Beethoven's death, the elector spoke coldly about the loss to the liquor excise.) Beethoven's ambivalence towards his father probably stemmed not only from Johann's increasing addiction to drink, however, but from the severe and arbitrary discipline he suffered as a child.

For the creative artist, nourished by dreams, fantasies, and aspirations toward a higher, more beautiful or perfectible world, a relationship with an ordinary, banal, depraved existence can become strained, even broken. Solomon argues convincingly that, in Beethoven's case, one response to this schism took the form of what Freud and Otto Rank termed the 'Family Romance'—the replacement of one or both parents by suitably elevated personages. Beethoven's nobility pretence may be understood at least partly in these terms (the 'van' in his name did not designate nobility). But Solomon also suggests the relevance of this constellation—involving the search for an ideal, loving father-figure—to passages in the finale of the Ninth Symphony, and he identifies the mythic component of Beethoven's musical works as a possible link between the apparently discrete realms of the biographical and artistic.[5]

In some respects, the challenge to analytic criticism is greatest when we confront the immature work of an artist, in which an authentic, original voice is not yet heard, or not clearly heard. Many of the piano pieces, songs, and chamber works that Beethoven composed at Bonn show relatively little of the

---

[5] Cf. 'The Ninth Symphony: A Search for Order', *Beethoven Essays*, pp. 309–26.

skill and power that distinguish his mature music. When did the young composer first assemble the elements out of which his creative enterprise was to
be shaped? Until 1884, almost a century after he left Bonn for Vienna, this
question could not have been answered, since only then did the score of the
Joseph Cantata come to light. Even now, few recordings are available, and the
piece remains virtually unknown to the general public. It never reached performance in 1790, possibly because its technical challenges overtaxed the performers; according to Simrock, 'all the figures were completely unusual,
therein lay the difficulty'. This was the score that Beethoven probably showed
to his future teacher Haydn at their first meeting, when the latter passed
through Bonn. Beethoven could have been justly proud of the piece, since it
is the most prophetic single composition of his entire Bonn period. After the
cantata's rediscovery, Johannes Brahms wrote enthusiastically that 'Even if
there were no name on the title page none other could be conjectured—it is
Beethoven through and through!'[6]

A glance at the score suffices to show why Beethoven never revised or published the cantata, for two of the most memorable passages in his opera *Fidelio*
were adapted from its material! The passages in question represent more than
thematic borrowings, and neatly illustrate sharply contrasting aspects of
Beethoven's musical symbolism. They could be described as *topoi*, or basic
rhetorical archetypes, with their roots in the conventions of figurative musical expression of the eighteenth century. Beethoven's continuing development
of these rhetorical models is by no means confined to *Fidelio*; it touches on a
broader dimension of symbolic expression in his music in general. For that
reason we shall examine the cantata in some detail. Our concern is not to offer
exhaustive description, however, but to indicate the work's broader importance for the evolution of Beethoven's musical language.

The first of the prophetic passages begins and closes the cantata:
Beethoven rounds off the design of the whole piece with a varied repetition of
its opening chorus. The registral and textural dissociation of sonorities in the
solemn orchestral ritornello is especially striking (see Ex. 1). A low unison C
in the strings in the first bar is repeated more emphatically two bars later; pitted against these deep octave unisons are harmonized woodwind sonorities in
a higher register. The first unison is answered by a C minor triad, the second
by a dissonant diminished-seventh chord that is dynamically inflected, played
mezzoforte instead of *piano*. The intensification is not merely harmonic, since
the melodic implications of these paired sonorities allow us to hear the rising
tenth C–E♭ as growing into a tritone with octave displacement, C–F♯, when
the gesture is restated. In bar 5 the diminished-seventh chord is resolved to
the C minor tonic triad that marks the beginning of a two-bar harmonized

6 Thayer-Forbes, p. 120.

Ex. 1 *Joseph* Cantata WoO 87

segment for the winds, featuring a prominent flute. The ritornello is completed by the return of the unharmonized strings, which assume a lamenting, declamatory character. At the repetition of the striking opening chords, the high woodwind sonorities are set to the words 'Todt! Todt!' ('Dead! Dead!') in the chorus, now making explicit the music's desolate expressive connotations.

The rhetorical devices employed here were not of course invented by Beethoven, but he combined them so as to make a strongly original impression. The most revealing factor, however, is neither the genuine pathos that the 20-year-old composer evoked here, nor the shortcomings in technique or sensibility that prevented him from sustaining the opening tension effectively. The beginning of the *Joseph* Cantata confronts us with a characteristic phenomenon in Beethoven's creative process: the deepening of musical conceptions in a seemingly continuous process which was to stretch over decades of his life. To evaluate the significance of this piece in Beethoven's artistic development we must glimpse ahead 15 years, to around 1805, when he completed his opera in its first version, then entitled *Leonore*, soon after incorporating a startling late-minute revision into what was then the largest of all his piano sonatas, the *Waldstein* op. 53.

Most obviously related to the cantata is the orchestral ritornello marked *Grave* that opens the last act of the opera, set in Florestan's prison cell (Ex. 2). The low unison Fs in the strings are juxtaposed with penetrating woodwind chords in the high register—the gesture taken as a whole represents a direct transposition of the 'death' *topos* from the cantata into the even more dismal, F minor gloom of Pizarro's dungeon. But most instructive are this changes Beethoven makes as regards the musical continuation. He now exploits a variety of means—rhythmic, harmonic, linear, and motivic—to give to this music a powerful dramatic coherence that was beyond his ability in 1790.

In *Leonore* Beethoven discards the *fermate* that prolonged each sonority in the opening of the cantata. He endows the music with a new rhythmic energy bound up with his characteristic device of foreshortening: the metric emphasis on two-bar units allows us to hear the three repeated chords in bar 5 as a diminution of the rhythmic shape of the entire opening gesture, with its slow articulation of three impulses spread over five bars. This process propels the music forwards, generating a gradual increase in tension. The larger harmonic progression, on the other hand, is controlled by a descending bass, reaching the first significant phrase division at bar 11 on the dominant of F minor. Here Beethoven injects declamatory motifs in the strings into the texture, motifs strongly reminiscent of the unharmonized string phrases in the *Joseph* Cantata. But unlike the cantata, this music seems constantly to be listening to itself. The expressive gesture in bar 11 highlights the semitone Db–C, and Beethoven's rhythmic and dynamic nuances underscore the poignant tension

Ex. 2 *Fidelio*, Act II, no. 11

of the dissonance. This motif, in turn, is joined to a higher, answering inflection in the winds, with both elements combined into a sequential progression building in intensity to the climactic dissonant sonority in bar 15. But that is not all: the D♭–C semitone figure is not only an expressive figure but a *structural* intensification—only in the merging of both functions does it take on its full aesthetic force. For the voice-leading of the opening woodwind chords—the gestures set ominously to 'dead' in the cantata—had already exposed the interval C–Db in a conspicuous way. The string motif is racked with the painful dissonance already heard at the very outset of the *Grave*.

Such aesthetic relationships need to be conveyed in any adequate performance but are passed over by many. A merely literal rendering in sound of the appearance of the score is inadequate here, since an essential part of the meaning of this gesture in the strings is connected to its dramatic derivation from the opening chords in the winds. The connection can be made palpable through the combination of clarity of execution and expressive nuance, a matter to which we shall return. This example scratches only the smallest surface of the requirements of a successful performance, but it does point to the kinds of relationships that take us beyond the mere surface of the sound into the true content of the work seen as an unconsummated symbol.

Once Beethoven had seen past the merely figurative level of this *topos*, other possibilities occurred to him that lend themselves eminently well to instrumental music. Characteristic is his use of a variant of the same *topos* in the substitute slow movement of the *Waldstein* Sonata op. 53, written a year earlier, in 1804. The original slow movement was an expansive, luxurious *Andante favori* in rondo form that Beethoven is supposed to have removed for reasons of overall length. That there were other, more intrinsic reasons for the change speaks for itself. The substitute movement is an extended introduction to the finale, to which it is directly linked; at the same time it makes a much stronger effect of contrast in relation to the outer movements than did the original slow movement. At stake in Beethoven's decision to substitute the *Introduzione* were issues of balance and integration in the sonata cycle as a whole.

This substitution marked a turning-point in Beethoven's practice. There are, to be sure, other slow introductions leading into finales in his earlier works—'La Malinconia' in the Quartet in Bb major op. 18 no. 6, for instance. But after the *Waldstein*, the principle of a contrasting slow movement linked to the finale in a three-movement design becomes a mainstay of his style for about six years, until 1810. Examples include the *Appassionata* and *Lebewohl* sonatas, the Violin Concerto, and the last two piano concertos.

By juxtaposing the contrasting slow movement directly with the finale, Beethoven brings their moods into a closer relationship, setting the moment of transition to the finale into sharp relief. Many later masterpieces, from the *Archduke* Trio to the C♯ minor Quartet, follow this pattern. But most revealing in comparison with the *Joseph* Cantata is the way Beethoven achieves that quality of gigantic simplicity that marks the slow interlude of the *Waldstein* (Ex. 3). The *topos* from the cantata—with a low tonic pedal in unharmonized octaves answered first by tonic harmony and then by a dissonant harmony with ascending voice-leading—is replicated in the sonata. The harmonic resolution of the dissonant sonority, however, is not to the tonic, as in the can-

Ex. 3 *Waldstein* Sonata op. 53/II

tata, but to an E major chord, which lends a more directional impetus to the phrase, bridging the evocative silence at the start of the second bar. Furthermore, the ascending seventh in the bass, from F to E, is treated by Beethoven as the starting-point for a long stepwise *descending* progression, even more relentless than the one in *Fidelio*.

The form of the *Adagio molto* is based on a twofold statement of this progression drawn from the *topos* from the cantata, blended with an expressive idiom suggestive of recitative and thematic dualism. Following the opening nine-bar phrase, Beethoven restates the initial motif in the right hand which unfolds in a declamatory fashion, with rising echoes in a polyphonic texture. After only six bars, however, the passage dissipates into a hushed, enigmatic return of the beginning of the *Introduzione*. The recitative-like phrases posit an alternative to the sombre, static character of the opening music that recalls the cantata. This brighter, more consoling voice cannot be sustained, however; the music settles even more deeply into the pensive mood generated by the falling-bass progression and countervailing ascent in the right hand. Only after an arresting climax on a widely spaced diminished-seventh sonority and the convergence onto the dominant seventh of C do we reach a miraculous turning-point: the descending bass movement is reversed as G rises to G#, clearing the way for a cadential progression in C major that underscores the luminescent texture and vast spacing at the beginning of the finale.

Perhaps most remarkable here is the severe economy of the thematic material and tight coherence of its development. In the *Waldstein*, the structural model of the solemn chord progression that opens this youthful work was sufficient to ground the entire structure of the slow introduction. At the same time, the dark-hued, mysterious character of this music creates an expressive polarity that places the brilliant C major world of the outer movements of the sonata in a new light.

The aspiring, affirmative side of Beethoven's symbolic art is adumbrated just as clearly in the *Joseph* Cantata. The emblematic theme heard in the aria with chorus 'Da stiegen die Menschen ans Licht' ('There the people ascended into the light') is not only quoted in *Fidelio* but became a prototype for other Beethovenian melodies carrying analogous expressive connotations. The melodic shape in the cantata, featuring two initial rising fourths and further upward extension in the following phrases, reflects the venerable practice of word-painting motivated in the text by the idea of the ascent of humanity toward illumination. In *Fidelio*, this *Humanitätsmelodie* emerges at the moment in the second-act finale when Leonore releases Florestan from his chains. Beethoven re-uses the theme here to symbolize what language cannot convey. For after it is first sounded in the oboe, Florestan himself doubles the melody heard in the winds to the words 'O unaussprechlich süsses Glück!' ('Oh unspeakable sweet happiness!'). And when this hymn-like theme is repeated in the chorus, it is linked to the Deity and to a higher moral authority: 'Gerecht, o Gott! gerecht ist dein Gericht. Du prüfest, du verlässt uns nicht' ('Just, oh God, just is your judgment! You test us, you abandon us not').

If the symbolism of this theme in the *Joseph* Cantata can be adequately grasped in terms of traditional musical rhetoric, its role in *Fidelio* is far more complex. The key of F major and soloistic role of the oboe in the setting of Florestan's 'unspeakable happiness', for instance, recall his earlier aria in the dungeon, culminating in his delirious vision of Leonore as an angel leading him into the 'heavenly realm of freedom'. Appeals to freedom, of course, infiltrate the dark landscape of *Fidelio* at every turn, from the symbolic trumpet calls of the *Leonore* overtures to the prisoners' chorus in Act I.

As a harbinger of Beethoven's mature style, 'Da stiegen die Menschen ans Licht' is at least as portentous as its antipode, the grim C minor opening of the cantata. Its hymn-like character with prominent rising perfect fourths prefigures a whole category of Beethovenian themes, from the *Adagio cantabile* of the *Sonate Pathétique* to the 'Dona nobis pacem' of the *Missa solemnis*. Most revealing, however, is how both these symbolic musical elements from Beethoven's ambitious early composition were eventually absorbed into the mainstream of his creative enterprise. Beethoven's symbolic homage to the enlightened emperor reminds us that his art was from the beginning no abstract occupation. At the same time, his subsequent use of borrowings from the cantata underscores the fundamental compatibility between symbolic rhetoric and the rigorous musical processes so indispensable to the expressive power of his art.

The *Joseph* Cantata is not the only weighty composition from Beethoven's Bonn years, nor the only prophetic one. The 24 Variations on *Venni amore* by Righini for piano WoO 65 from 1791 is equally rich in ideas and devices used in Beethoven's later music. In their imaginative skill and formal ingenuity the 'Righini' Variations are perhaps the finest of all Beethoven's independent variation sets up to 1802, when he wrote his important variations in F major and Eb major, opp. 34 and 35 respectively. Other works from the Bonn period were revised at Vienna—salvaged, like the cantata, for material used in new pieces—or simply forgotten. For in spite of exceptional cases like the 'Righini' Variations, the music Beethoven composed at Bonn is of interest less for artistic than for historical and biographical reasons. His coming-of-age as an artist may be placed around 1795, on the basis of his impressive piano sonatas from that year, and our first detailed analyses of works will focus on these pieces. In reality, however, Beethoven's creative development was a continuous, ongoing process that resists easy categorization but to which the works themselves bear witness in abundant measure. The formative influence of Bonn on Beethoven was profound, but its deepest artistic expression belonged to another time and place.

2

The Path to Mastery

1792–1798

B EETHOVEN could hardly have imagined when he left Bonn in late
1792 that he would never again see his birthplace, or that the reign of
the elector would be swept away in the wake of the French occupation
less than two years later. The conditions of his entry into Vienna were auspi-
cious; he immediately came under the wing of music-loving aristocrats who
supported him generously. Although he never held an official court position
at Vienna, his success was dependent on the patronage of noble benefactors
including Count Karl von Lichnowsky, Baron van Swieten, the Count and
Countess von Browne, and in later years Prince Lobkowitz and Prince
Kinsky, among others. Soon after his arrival in Vienna, Beethoven moved in
for a time with Lichnowsky, who had patronized Mozart a few years earlier
and whose private string quartet, led by Ignaz Schuppanzigh, assumed special
importance for Beethoven. The patronage of the Count and Countess
Browne is reflected in Beethoven's dedications of several important works,
including the string trios op. 9 and piano sonatas op. 10. Beethoven received
valuable presents from his patrons, including a quartet of string instruments
from Lichnowsky and a horse from Count Browne in response to his dedication to the Countess of the Twelve Variations for Piano on a Russian Dance
WoO 71 in 1797.

One of Beethoven's most lasting friendships dating from these years was
with the amateur cellist Nikolaus Zmeskall von Domanovecz, who attended
the musical performances held on Friday mornings at Lichnowsky's house.
Zmeskall carefully preserved his correspondence with Beethoven from this
period when the latter was not yet famous; the letters richly display
Beethoven's sense of humour and his indulgence in extravagant plays on

words. One note, addressed to 'My dearest Baron Muckcart-driver' (or 'dirt-driver') contains an elaborate pun based on the mixing-up or transposition of the last three letters of 'baron'. Beethoven delights himself here by linking the noun *Versatzamt* ('pawnshop') with the verb *versetzen* ('to transpose'—in this case, words, letters, or notes), and he throws in for good measure a reference to his Duet for Viola and Cello WoO 32, a piece he dubbed a 'duet with two eyeglasses obbligato' and apparently performed with Zmeskall.[1] Zmeskall worked at the Hungarian Court Chancellery, but his name is Czech (or Slovakian); 'zmeškal' literally means 'missed' in the sense of being late due to wasted time; another Czech word that sounds similar, *zmetek*, means 'misfit'. Zmeskall presumably explained these meanings to the composer, who fancifully blended the connotations in addressing his friend as 'dearest dirt hauler' or 'garbage man'. Further examples of Beethoven's puns from about this time surface in his correspondence with the horn player and publisher Nikolaus Simrock in Bonn in which Beethoven plays on the word *stechen*, meaning 'to sting or stab', as well as 'to engrave'.

Beethoven composed little music during his first year in Vienna. This situation led to embarrassment when Haydn sent to the elector at Bonn a letter of recommendation for an increase in Beethoven's stipend, accompanied by copies of pieces, most of which Beethoven had already written before his departure. The sting of the elector's reply—with its assertion that Beethoven had learnt little and would bring back to Bonn nothing but debts—cannot have helped endear Haydn to Beethoven. Their relationship was somewhat stiff and reserved, though it remained cordial. There is little doubt that Beethoven owed less to formal instruction with Haydn than to the inspiring model of the older man's compositions. The creative achievements of Haydn and Mozart were fully recognized for the first time during the 1790s, and no-one was better situated to build on their legacy than Beethoven.

During his first Vienna years Beethoven composed primarily for solo piano or combinations of instruments including piano. He devoted attention as well to the medium of the string trio, as represented by the divertimento-like Trio in E♭ op. 3 and the accomplished set of three trios op. 9, and composed occasional songs, including the famous *Adelaide*, published years later as op. 46. The proud designation of op. 1 was granted, however, to the three Trios for Piano, Violin, and Cello in E♭ major, G major, and C minor, which were performed at a private concert at Count Lichnowsky's residence in late 1793 or early 1794 and painstakingly revised before their eventual publication in 1795. Beethoven's pupil Ferdinand Ries reported that Haydn expressed reservations about the C minor Trio—remarks not well received by Beethoven, who considered it the best of the three. Haydn embarked around this time on his

---

[1] Cf. Thayer-Forbes, pp. 221–2.

second triumphant journey to London. Beethoven, meanwhile, supple-mented his instruction with Haydn by diligent study with others: the composer Johann Schenk and the systematic theorist Johann Georg Albrechtsberger.

Beethoven's independent artistic stance was thus fully compatible with his determination to master the traditional methods of composition; the imagi-native flights of the virtuoso pianist gained thereby in solidity, depth, and con-structive power. By the time he had finished his First Symphony and the String Quartets op. 18 in 1800, Beethoven had written 13 piano sonatas (up to and including op. 22 and the two sonatas op. 49), the first two concertos, and more than a dozen sets of independent piano variations. Other piano works of the 1790s include the Rondo in C op. 51 no. 1, the four-hand Sonata in D op. 6, various bagatelles and miscellaneous pieces, and the *Rondo à Capriccio* in G, published posthumously as op. 129. Contemporary reports described his extraordinary abilities in improvisation. In view of his formidable mastery of the instrument, we need hardly marvel that Beethoven's piano music remained a vehicle for his most advanced ideas throughout his career.

It would be a serious error to underestimate Beethoven's sonatas from the 1790s. Whereas his first published examples of the concerto, quartet, and symphony are generally inferior to Haydn's and Mozart's masterpieces in those genres, the same cannot be said of his early sonatas, especially those for solo piano. It was in the piano sonata that Beethoven first revealed the full expressive range and power of invention that he was to demonstrate only years later in some other musical forms. In their broad scale and structural grandeur, his early sonatas and chamber music with piano show signs of a symphonic ambition. Characteristic, for instance, is his use of the four-move-ment form then associated more with symphonies or quartets than with these more intimate genres; each of the three piano trios of op. 1 and sonatas of op. 2 adds a minuet or scherzo to the conventional three-movement plan. In the case of the big Piano Sonata in E♭ op. 7, Beethoven incorporated a dance-like *Allegro* with *Minore* as the penultimate movement, a piece he had originally sketched as a 'bagatelle' independent from the sonata.[2] In the three violin sonatas of op. 12 written in 1797–8, he retained the three-movement frame-work, but he employed four movements in two later works in this genre—the C minor Sonata op. 30 no. 2 of 1802 and the final violin sonata, op. 96 of 1812.

Our examination of the music from Beethoven's early Vienna years will focus primarily on his piano sonatas, beginning with the three works in F minor, A major, and C major published with a dedication to Haydn as op. 2 in 1795. The first movement of the very first sonata serves as well as any to illustrate Beethoven's thorough and original mastery of the Viennese classical

---

[2] Nottebohm, *Zweite Beethoveniana*, pp. 508–11.

style. This *Allegro* is dominated even more than usual by his favourite practice of increasing structural compression—a device sometimes described as 'fragmentation' and which Alfred Brendel has more suitably termed 'foreshortening' and described as '*the* driving force of his sonata forms and a basic principle of his musical thought'.[3] In a foreshortening process phrases are divided into progressively smaller units: the effect is to drive the music forwards with a nervous intensity quite alien to the relaxed rococo elegance of the *ancien régime*. The opening theme of op. 2 no. 1 (Ex. 4) juxtaposes two-bar phrases on tonic and dominant, using a version of the 'Mannheim rocket' figure with a rising staccato arpeggiation peaking first on Ab and then Bb in the treble, while staccato chords on the weaker beats in the left hand provide the accompaniment.

Ex. 4 Piano Sonata op. 2 no. 1/I

The vitality of this theme is sustained from within, through constant re-examination of the ongoing musical discourse. Bar 5 is an intensification of bar 2, cutting the initial phrase to half its length; 6 similarly curtails the second phrase to a single bar. All the dynamic markings are structural: they emphasize the melodic peaks of the opening phrases as well as the isolation of those pitches through *sforzandi*, while the crescendo to *fortissimo* at the broken chord in bar 7 reinforces both the upper linear motion to the fifth degree, C, and the growing intensity of the process of rhythmic diminution. The last bars of the theme are also controlled by consistent foreshortening in the harmonic structure: the tonic chord in bar 7 is sustained for only a half-bar, whereas the shift from tonic to dominant in the last bar of the theme is compressed into successive beats. The very silence at the fermata after the turn-figure in this bar seems generated by the intensity of the drive toward

---

[3] 'Form and Psychology in Beethoven's Piano Sonatas', *Musical Thoughts and Afterthoughts*, p. 43; also see Brendel's essay 'The Process of Foreshortening in the First Movement of Beethoven's Sonata Op. 2, No. 1' in the same volume, pp. 154–61.

concision, resulting in virtual liquidation of the basic thematic material. In this arresting theme the initial two-bar units are thus reduced to single bars, half-bars, and single beats before the music abruptly confronts that silence out of which it came into being. One senses in the opening rhetorical accents of Beethoven's first sonata a more aggressive variant of Haydn's exquisitely delicate play with silence in some movements of his op. 33 quartets.

Ex. 5 Piano Sonata op. 2 no. 1/I
(*a*) sketch   (*b*) final version

Beethoven's rough draft of this *Allegro* shows how concerned he was to tighten its thematic and harmonic relations. Compare, for instance, his sketch for the beginning of the second subject with the final version (Exx. 5*a* and *b*).[4] In the finished work Beethoven has changed his sketch into a free inversion of the shape of the first subject, designating a crescendo and *sforzando* to make the correspondence clear. But that is not all: he has also shifted the second subject into the minor mode, so that the flat sixth degree of A♭ minor—F♭— is emphasized in two registers, harmonically as part of a dissonant minor ninth chord on the dominant. This stress on F♭ in the second theme sounds much like an intensification of the emphasis on the minor third (A♭), in the opening theme.

Beethoven's procedure of foreshortening is a flexible means of intensification that is especially appropriate to the development section of the sonata design. In this movement the development starts with a varied restatement of the opening theme beginning in A♭ major but passing through the pivotal harmony of a German augmented sixth to the second subject, now in B♭ minor (Ex. 6). Beethoven thereby telescopes the entire first half of his exposition, deleting a dozen of its bars while dramatically juxtaposing the two subjects he had devised as inversions of one another. The energy produced by this accelerated plunge into the second subject is sustained in turn through a new process of foreshortening. First, the eight-bar model of the second theme leads through a new augmented-sixth chord into C minor. Then the basic phrase is shifted into the bass, and descending sequences carry the music progressively lower in pitch as the thematic structure breaks up into smaller units. The prominent accented dissonances thus fall from A♭ to G♭ and F♭, before Beethoven takes the crucial step of stripping away the melodic material while preserving the descending linear motion and syncopated rhythmic energy in

4 Nottebohm transcribed the sketch in *Zweite Beethoveniana*, p. 565.

Ex. 6 Piano Sonata op. 2 no. 1/I, bars 42–60

the circle-of-fifths progression that follows. These deeper musical processes are the very life-blood of the music. The falling series of syncopated bass notes reaches Eb, Db, and C (pitches echoed a fourth higher in the treble), and the energy of this impressive passage is finally released at a powerful half-cadence on the dominant of F minor (Ex. 7). The rhythmic articulation or structural downbeat at this juncture is marked by the ensuing dominant pedal, presaging the recapitulation 21 bars later.

The following passage on the dominant pedal is no longer driven by the impetus of rhythmic compression and modulation; it assumes a more static, retrospective character. This music echoes the climactic cadence that had preceded it, particularly the semitone fall F–E and the associated harmonic resolution of the diminished-seventh chord, now heard over the pedal. There is

Ex. 7 Piano Sonata op. 2 no. 1/I, bars 73–82

a close kinship here with the second subject, with its similar dominant pedal and harmonic support; the relationship is easily audible in the recapitulation, when the second subject appears at the same pitch level. The gradually subsiding effect of the end of the development is conveyed by the decrescendo to *pianissimo* as the last cadential echo dissipates, reducing the music to a substratum of softly pulsating Cs in the left hand. This too is part of the process of foreshortening in its broadest sense: the lively eight-bar unit of the second subject has undergone a dramatic development so exhaustive that its material literally dissolves.

Beethoven now uses the turn-figure drawn from the opening theme to signal the imminent recapitulation, which is enhanced through more forceful placement of the accompanying chords of the main theme. Even more striking is his treatment of the closing theme of the exposition and his reinterpretation of this music at the close of the *Allegro*. He marks these passages 'con espressione'; they are imbued with declamatory rhetoric recalling the opening theme (Ex. 8 shows the passage from the end of the movement). The staccato chords resemble its chordal accompaniment, while the basic motivic shape—except for the ascending leap to the dominant, C—derives from rhythmic augmentation of the turn-figure. What sticks out curiously is the upward leap and accented stress on the dominant note, an inflection that soon delivers an astounding punch. The gesture at first sounds odd, but harmless; only on its third appearance does Beethoven make his point. He repeats the motif an octave higher and drastically reinterprets the sensitive dominant note *fortissimo* with full harmonic support, prolonging it fourfold, through an entire bar. So emphasized, this pitch becomes the surprising penultimate chord of the cadence that closes the exposition.

When Beethoven returns to this passage at the end of the movement, he retains not the same formula but his instinct for surprise. This time the emphatic 'closing' chord is reharmonized to pass deceptively to the subdomi-

Ex. 8 Piano Sonata op. 2 no. 1/I

nant, evading a tonic cadence. A pause and descending sequence follow, carrying the progression down a tone to the mediant. Then Beethoven resorts for the last time to rhythmic diminution, as faster sequences of accented chords drive to the close in F minor. The brief coda traces a linear descent from dominant to tonic—thereby echoing gestures like the climax of the opening theme or the 'con espressione' phrases—while gathering rhythmic energy through foreshortening to lead into the terse, emphatic cadence.

This tight, concise movement shows that by 1795 Beethoven was capable of achieving a thematic integration and formal coherence which, though comparable to Haydn's, are quite individual in quality. Particularly noteworthy is Beethoven's almost obsessive use of rhythmic foreshortening as a means of musical development. Douglas Johnson's comparison with Haydn, claiming that 'the old man's models are lean and taut, while the young man's copies are overweight and longwinded'[5] does not apply here, though it is true of certain other works from this period. In op. 2 no. 1 that criticism could perhaps be levelled at the second movement, a florid *Adagio* in F major, although its lyrical repose does bring welcome contrast after the terse drama of the *Allegro*. Like the opening *Allegro con brio* of op. 2 no. 3, this *Adagio* uses material from Beethoven's earlier Piano Quartet WoO 36 no. 3, a work he wrote in Bonn at the age of 15, while duteously emulating one of Mozart's violin sonatas. We shall return to the issue of Beethoven's use of Haydnesque and Mozartian models. More important in connection with op. 2 is actually to acknowledge how boldly independent Beethoven had already become.

The opening *Allegro vivace* of op. 2 no. 2 offers further testimony to Beethoven's audacity in its extraordinary treatment of the second subject-group. After a brilliant play of scalar figures and falling leaps in the opening theme the music settles mysteriously onto the dominant E minor, with slow tremolos in the left hand and a legato, *espressivo* phrase in the treble (Ex. 9). The lyrical phrase outlines the falling semitones E–D#–D, while the bass rises step by step, facilitating a modulation to G. Sequential intensification of these bars extends the rising bass movement, bringing the music to the remote key of B♭. Beethoven now exploits his procedure of foreshortening to bring matters to breaking-point: instead of employing a stable thematic configuration, he devises his second subject as a dramatic series of modulations that are strictly controlled by the long ascent of the bass through a full octave. Once this progression has re-attained the original pitch an octave higher, the impact of foreshortening has stripped away all but the semitone E–D# in the melody.

Now comes the real crux of the matter: after the virtual disappearance of the second subject, the falling scalar figure of the opening theme returns *fortissimo* to fill the void! Beethoven adds a touch of the grotesque by

⁵ '1794–95: Decisive Years in Beethoven's Early Development', p. 26.

Ex. 9 Piano Sonata op. 2 no. 2/I, bars 57–85

juxtaposing the soft, enigmatic high semitone E–D♯ with the insistent bass figure outlining a tritone. He then dwells on the semitone in the high register, pausing on an ambiguous diminished-seventh chord. The silence that follows magnifies the complex quality of this moment, preparing a triumphant *reversal* of the resolution of the semitone, as the diminished seventh containing D♯ is finally resolved into cascades of figuration elaborating the long-awaited E major triad.

Dramatically, the entire passage is posited on the notion of a controlled postponement of the dominant key, building suspense that makes the eventual discovery of that goal all the more satisfying. The dynamic thrust so evident in the development of the *Allegro* of op. 2 no. 1 is transplanted here into the exposition of the sonata form. The idea is original and the execution flawless, demonstrating that by 1795 Beethoven had already transcended an imitative style of composition, at least in this genre. But many other aspects of his art can be properly appreciated only in the broader context of an entire piece or opus. To that end, we turn for an example to the remarkable trilogy of piano sonatas in C minor, F major, and D major that Beethoven published three years later, in 1798, as op. 10.

The sharply profiled individuality of the op. 10 sonatas nevertheless admits some common features among them, such as the presence of comic music abounding in sudden contrasts and unexpected turns. A whimsical, unpredictable humour surfaces in the finales of all three pieces, and most strikingly in the opening *Allegro* of the second sonata, in F major. The sonatas are nonetheless admirably contrasted in character, particularly in their first movements: the terse, dramatic idiom of the C minor sonata sets into relief the relaxed, mischievous spirit of the F major, whereas the dynamic brilliance of the third sonata, in D major, expands the formal design from within. Like Beethoven's four earlier sonatas, op. 10 no. 3 also has four movements, incorporating a minuet before the finale. The first two sonatas of op. 10 employ the more usual Classical design of three movements, with a slower movement sandwiched between an opening *Allegro* and a finale in a still faster tempo.

Op. 10 no. 1 marks the first appearance in the piano sonatas of Beethoven's celebrated 'C minor mood', the tempestuous, strife-ridden character reflected in pieces such as the string trio op. 9 no. 3, the *Pathétique* Sonata, the Fifth Symphony, and the very last sonata, op. 111. This idiom was forged by Beethoven out of an artistic context reaching back to Mozart, Haydn, and Bach. Mozart's piano works in this key, such as the Sonata K457 and the Concerto K491, particularly impressed Beethoven: he reportedly commented to J. B. Cramer about the concerto that 'we shall never be able to do anything like that!'[6] The rhetorical contrasts of these works often juxtapose a forceful, dramatic expression invested with rhythmic tension and dissonance on the one hand, with the emergence of a plaintive or lyrical voice on the other. Mozart's C minor pieces, such as K491, frequently project a sense of fatalistic resignation that arises through the objective, even impersonal character of their pathetic chromaticism, implying a subordination of subjectivity to objectivity; Beethoven, by contrast, tends to subsume such contrasts into an all-encompassing subjective dynamic.

The first movement of op. 10 no. 1 distils these contrasts with utmost concentration. The powerful opening C minor chord, with its jagged, rising rhythmic inflections, yields to a quiet transformation of the same sound, while the ensuing motivic fall from C to B in bar 4 sets up reiteration of the forceful opening gesture, now intensified through use of the dissonant diminished-seventh chord (see Ex. 10). The following phrases build the climax of the opening theme through a threefold stress on the dominant, G, before the line

---

[6] Thayer-Forbes, p. 209.

Ex. 10 Piano Sonata op. 10 no. 1/I

descends stepwise through an octave and breaks off mysteriously into silence. Here, as elsewhere in Beethoven, the pauses are no less important than the notes: the rapport of sound with silence imparts tension to the end of the opening thematic period, before the head of the theme is reasserted with even greater vehemence.

Most of what follows is related to this opening theme. Variants of the stepwise descending motif lurk in the tranquil transition passage, whereas the more lyrical second subject in E♭ major utilizes the falling semitone figure of the opening theme while also hinting at its rhythm. The new melody that emerges in the development section brings together motifs from both principal themes, carrying the music through minor keys. The approach to the recapitulation, on the other hand, reshapes the descending line from the opening theme, the passage that had been broken off initially into silence. Now the pause is filled in, supplanting the mysterious interruption by a sonorous connection to the reprise—the symmetrical turning-point in the movement as a whole.

Another climax occurs later in the recapitulation, where the brighter second subject is drawn into the sphere of C minor, with an effect of pathos. Beethoven does not merely transpose it according to convention but first elaborates it in a major key, F, re-entering the tonic minor only at the point where the second subject is decorated with rising staccato scales. Thereafter the tonic remains unchallenged; the movement closes laconically, with stark cadential chords. The terse, concentrated expression of this movement would be misconstrued if taken as the effusion of a youthful, emotional *Sturm und Drang*. As the other movements make still clearer, the Beethoven that emerges here is as much a clearsighted rationalist as a romantic visionary.

As is usual in Beethoven's C minor works, the slow movement, an *Adagio molto*, is in the key of the flat sixth, A♭ major. Its grand lyrical expression relies much on decorative variation, especially in the quiet second subject, in which each phrase is reshaped into rapid, delicate figuration. This movement is a sonata form with a single, emphatic dominant-seventh chord standing in place of a development, but there is an extended coda, in which the reflective main theme is given a new continuation and a new outcome. Its characteristic falling melodic thirds are extended here to reach the dominant, E♭, before being softly resolved to the tonic in a gesture of thematic completion and liquidation.

Out of the stillness at the end of the *Adagio* emerges the lean, shadowy opening of the *prestissimo* finale, in which motifs from the first movement—such as the semitone C–B—reappear in a new context. Still more surprising is the way the principal motif is absorbed, with comic effect, into the second subject-group of this compact sonata form. Riotous humour erupts in the cadential theme: as if the drastic contrasts of dynamics and register and the hammering, 'telegraphic' rhythms were not enough, Beethoven wickedly inserts a 'wrong' chord on C♭, *fortissimo*, just before the cadence!

Following the brief development and a recapitulation hardly less amusing than the exposition, despite its turn to the minor, the coda gradually slows the tempo to *adagio*. Beethoven lingers here over his second subject, transforming its jaunty character into a more reflective expression, while bringing the music to rest on a seventh chord of A♭ at the first *tenuto* marking (Ex. 11).

Ex. 11 Piano Sonata op. 10 no. 1/III

What is the meaning of this striking gesture? The sound is familiar, being enharmonically equivalent to the first vertical harmony in the shadowy main theme of the movement. The point is that this sound *contains* the tonic sonority of the A♭ major of the slow movement and can thereby serve both as a harmonic threshold to the finale and, later, as a subtle means of reference to the *Adagio molto*. Without making a direct thematic allusion, Beethoven thus evokes the aura of the slow movement, effectively setting off his final plunge into the *prestissimo*, which quickly dissolves into a silence of pregnant irony.

The second sonata, in F major, takes its point of departure from the comic strain already present in the finale of op. 10 no. 1. Though a favourite of Beethoven's, the piece has been regarded disapprovingly by some commentators, who have pointed accusingly to loose, meandering features in the opening *Allegro* while remaining deaf to their aesthetic quality. Brendel has recently observed how easily such comic music can be spoilt in performance, or misunderstood by listeners 'expecting the celebration of religious rites'.[7] Beethoven felt no such constraints: like Laurence Sterne's character Tristram Shandy, he could revel in the unexpected, the incongruous, and the grotesque, and, as in this movement, exhibit a coyish, good-natured capacity for just getting lost. In comparison with op. 10 no. 1 the form is anti-teleological; the music appears to progress in fits and starts, sometimes driven by feverish outbursts of impatience. One cul-de-sac occurs in the second subject-group after the first cadence in the dominant, C major, in bar 41 (Ex. 12). The ensuing phrase loses its grip on the cadence, and the *pianissimo* chord in bar 46 suggests raised eyebrows of puzzled confusion. Another such passage is the false recapitulation, which begins innocently enough in D major. Remarkably, it is not the harmonized chords forming the head of the theme but rather its little ornamental turn whose repetitions stabilize the true recapitulation in F, conveying a sense of the tail wagging the dog.

Ex. 12 Piano Sonata op. 10 no. 2/I, bars 38–50

The second movement is an *Allegretto* with trio in F minor, the focus of gravity in this otherwise lighthearted work. Its seriousness of character stands as complementary to the comic fugal burlesque that forms the *presto* finale. This relationship can be vividly projected in performance through rhythmic means, if the steady motion in quarter-notes in the *Allegretto* yields to a subdivision of these beats into eighth-notes in the shorter bars of the *Presto*, thereby giving the effect of an acceleration to double-time in the finale. The beginning of the *Presto* also reshapes the same registral ascent that had begun the meditative *Allegretto*, transforming its structural aspects in an atmosphere of unbuttoned wit and musical laughter that 'inverts the sublime', according to one of Jean Paul Richter's insightful definitions of humour.

The design of the D major Sonata op. 10 no. 3 is unusual in that Beethoven

---

[7] 'Must Classical Music be Entirely Serious?', *Music Sounded Out*, p. 35.

maintains the tonic major or minor throughout all four movements. One reason for this tonal plan is found in the expressive relationship between the
inner movements—an extended *Largo e mesto* of tragic character in D minor,
whose solemn darkness is broken by the beginning of the gentle *Minuetto* in
the major, marked *dolce*. This wonderfully sensitive and gradual effect of light
dispelling darkness depends crucially on the use of a common tonality. A different sort of complementation holds between the bold and energetic first
movement, marked *Presto*, and the grave slow movement in the minor.

The very opening of the sonata, in unharmonized octaves, presents material that in itself is not particularly distinctive: its initial descending fourth,
D–A, and subsequent ascent through tonic triads of D major represent commonplace elements of Classical tonality (Ex. 13). The sparse, elemental nature
of this opening lends itself well to reinterpretation and reworking, however, as
is soon evident in the exposition, where extended passages are given over to
developmental processes. The sudden interruptions and contrasts characteristic of this movement are carefully coordinated with a logical, progressive
unfolding and development of the basic thematic material. Only after a contrasting episode in B minor and a brilliant transition passage does Beethoven
present the main part of his second subject-group, in A major. He incorporates here a new version of the opening motif in smaller note values, with the
descending fourth D–A given three times in the major and three times in the
minor before the music dissolves into silence. The motif is then absorbed into
a contrapuntal phrase leading into an exciting developmental continuation of
modulating sequences and persistent syncopations. The cadential themes are
just as clearly based on the initial phrase of the movement, notably on the thematic motto of the descending fourth. The exposition of this *Presto*, as well as
the remainder of the movement, shows an intense internal dynamism that
strains the formal framework of the Classical sonata and expands it from
within—a hallmark of Beethoven's forceful early style.

Ex. 13 Piano Sonata op. 10 no. 3/I

In the following *Largo e mesto* in D minor Beethoven exploits the contrast between thick, dark chords (with frequent use of the diminished-seventh sonority) and a more transparent, recitative-like voice in the upper register. This slow movement is one of the great tragic utterances in early Beethoven, and it displays a sense of abortive struggle and resignation in his treatment of the sonata form. The mood of brightness and hope at the beginning of the F major development is soon negated by the *fortissimo* diminished-seventh chords that lead back into the minor, while their register and motifs recall the movement's opening theme. Especially powerful is the coda, in which a statement of the principal theme in the lowest register leads to a dramatic, chromatic ascent through an entire octave in the bass. The movement ends with references to fragments from the opening theme and allusions to the registral disparities between its low chords and the extracted motif of a semitone in the highest register.

If the ensuing transparent *Minuetto* leaves behind the gloomy depths of the slow movement, the concluding rondo is characterized by an unpredictable humour. Here the dynamic stops and starts from the *Presto* become a game of hide-and-seek for the theme itself (Ex. 14). Indeed, is the theme ever found? The rondo seems to suggest a process of seeking, doubting, and evasion. Its prominent deceptive cadence on B minor (bar 7) is later developed in an entire central episode built upon a more jarring deceptive cadence on B♭. This episode, in turn, leads to a false recapitulation in that key, and to a transition based on the crucial interval of the fourth—no less important in this movement than in the *Presto*. The final episode is like a quest for a more substantial but unattainable goal, and its sequences rise ecstatically into the highest register of the piano before falling back in a short cadenza. In a peculiar way we seem not to have left the original ground: the opening motif returns yet

Ex. 14 Piano Sonata op. 10 no. 3/IV

again, now assuming the minor mode and reminding us of the tragic slow movement. A series of chords based on the rhythm of the initial motif follows, and the sonata ends quietly with repetitions of the motif in the bass, heard beneath chromatic scales and arpeggios in the right hand. Like op. 10 no. 1, this D major sonata has an open, dissolving conclusion, as befits its commitment to emerging process and ongoing development, as well as the deft circumspection of its wit.

*   *   *

If Beethoven had already by the 1790s achieved a consummate mastery in the piano sonata, his compositional struggles are more clearly reflected in other genres, in works like the Piano Concerto in B♭, the surviving torso of the C major Symphony he abandoned in 1796, and in some of the six string quartets of op. 18. Beethoven himself expressed dissatisfaction with the concerto in his letter to Breitkopf & Härtel of 22 April 1801:

> . . . I wish to add that one *of my first concertos* and therefore *not one of the best of my compositions*, is to be published by *Hofmeister*, and that Mollo is to publish *a concerto which*, indeed *was written later*, but which also does *not* rank among *the best of my works in this form*.[8]

The earliest of these concertos was the work in B♭ eventually published as op. 19; the second concerto, in C major, received the lower opus number 15. The history of the B♭ Concerto mirrors Beethoven's growing compositional powers, since it was revised or overhauled repeatedly between 1790 and 1801. Its origins go back to the Bonn years; at that stage it probably had an entirely different finale, the movement now known as the Rondo for Piano and Orchestra WoO 6. The rondo was modelled in turn on the finale of Mozart's Piano Concerto in E♭ K271, a work whose influence also left traces in Beethoven's first movement. It was the D minor and C minor concertos of Mozart, however, together with the opening *Allegro maestoso* of the C major K503, that most deeply impressed Beethoven.

Beethoven's sketches for a Symphony in C major occupied him in Vienna in 1795 and again during his concert tour to Prague and Berlin the next year. Douglas Johnson has speculated that Beethoven may have expected a performance of the piece at Berlin that did not materialize. Johnson convincingly places the piece in the context of Beethoven's frustrated ambition to match Haydn's towering symphonic achievements, and he points as well to parallels between Beethoven's fragment and Haydn's Symphony no. 97 in the same key.[9] Characteristically, some thematic material from the abandoned work

---

[8] Thayer-Forbes, p. 275.

[9] Johnson's full discussion of the unfinished symphony is found in the part of his PhD dissertation entitled 'The Unfinished Symphony of 1795–96', pp. 785–1037; he summarizes his findings in *Beethoven's Early Sketches*, i, pp. 461–9.

eventually came to light five years later in the finale of Beethoven's First
Symphony in C major op. 21, a piece that owes little to the fragment but still
falls short of Haydn's lofty standards. The full power of Beethoven's symphonic style first emerges in the Second Symphony op. 36, one of a series of
pathbreaking works from the watershed year of 1802.

Beethoven's pieces for winds and for winds and strings stem almost entirely
from his Bonn period and first Vienna years, and often show Mozart's
influence. They include the Octet in Eb, which Beethoven reworked as the
String Quintet op. 4, the Rondino WoO 25, the Sextet for two horns and
strings, and the Trio for two oboes and English horn. The Octet, Sextet, and
Trio were all eventually published with deceptively high opus numbers: 103,
81b, and 87, respectively. Beethoven wrote the Serenade op. 25 and Sextet for
Wind op. 71 during 1796; the minuet of the Sextet quotes the opening of
Mozart's String Quintet in Eb K614, as Denis Matthews pointed out.[10] A
more obvious parallel exists between Beethoven's Quintet in Eb for piano and
winds op. 16, also from 1796, and Mozart's great work for the same combination of instruments K452. The most famous of all Beethoven's chamber works
featuring winds is the Septet in Eb op. 20, from 1800. This attractive six-
movement divertimento is scored for bassoon, clarinet, horn, string trio, and
double bass. Its extreme popularity irked Beethoven, who did not regard his
pieces for wind ensemble too seriously; he claimed to have written the wind
sextet 'in a single night'. After 1800 the evolution of his resourceful writing for
winds can be followed in his greater symphonic works.

The early performance history of the Trio in Bb for clarinet, cello, and
piano op. 11 of 1798 is bound up with Beethoven's colourful competitive
encounter with the flamboyant virtuoso pianist Daniel Steibelt in 1800.
According to Ferdinand Ries, Steibelt responded to a performance of
Beethoven's trio with polite condescension, offering in turn a showy improvisation on a popular theme drawn from Joseph Weigl's opera L'Amor mari-
naro—the same tune chosen by Beethoven for the variations forming the
finale of his trio. Beethoven retaliated by seizing the cello part of a quintet by
Steibelt: after placing it upside down on the music stand, he poked out a
theme with one finger from its opening bars. Offended, Steibelt walked out
during Beethoven's ensuing improvisation, and refused any further association
with him.[11] The use of a fashionable operatic tune as the basis for the variation finale of op. 11 is reminiscent of Beethoven's practice in many independent piano variations of the 1790s, which employ themes by such composers
as Dittersdorf, Haibel, Paisiello, Grétry, Salieri, Süssmayr, and Winter,
among others. Years later, Beethoven is supposed to have talked about substituting another finale for the variations on Weigl's tune in op. 11, which would

[10] *Beethoven*, p. 150.   [11] Thayer-Forbes, p. 257.

have distanced this charming work from its original topical context. After the 1790s, he preferred to use original themes as the basis for variations in his greater works, and in the rare exception of the Diabelli Variations he transcended the pre-existing theme in unprecedented fashion.

Unlike his occasional works for wind ensemble, Beethoven's contributions to the duo sonata for piano with cello or violin became an important abiding part of his career. While he was in Berlin in 1796 he composed two innovative sonatas for cello and piano op. 5, and probably also wrote his sets of variations for these instruments on Mozart's 'Ein Mädchen oder Weibchen' op. 66 and on a theme from Handel's *Judas Maccabaeus* WoO 45. In the two sonatas, in F major and G minor, the pianist assumes an essential, virtuoso role for the first time in the history of the genre. The older continuo practice in cello sonatas is thereby discarded; a dramatic interplay of the two instruments is made possible. Beethoven himself performed the two sonatas at the Berlin court, presumably with the famous cellist Jean Louis Duport; they are dedicated to King Friedrich Wilhelm II. Especially prominent are their extended slow introductions. In the G minor Sonata the introduction takes on almost the weight of a slow movement. The serious, even pathetic character of this *Adagio sostenuto ed espressivo* is maintained in the following *Allegro*, before a joyous mood emerges in the G major rondo finale.

The importance of the G minor Sonata to Beethoven's artistic development has been underestimated. In its sombre rhetoric and dramatic dialogue the slow introduction of op. 5 no. 2 is prophetic. It points toward the harrowing climax of the development in the slow movement of the Piano Sonata in E♭ op. 7 and to 'La Malinconia' in the last of the op. 18 quartets. Its most familiar successor, however, is another slow introduction, the *Grave* of the *Sonate Pathétique* in C minor op. 13, largely composed in 1798 and published the following year. The *Pathétique* is one of those celebrated works whose revolutionary aura so excited artists like the young pianist Ignaz Moscheles, who secretly copied it as a student at Prague in 1804, in defiance of his teacher. Moscheles related that

The novelty of its style was so attractive to me, and I became so enthusiastic in my admiration of it, that I forgot myself so far as to mention my new acquisition to my teacher, who reminded me of his injunction, and warned me not to play or study any eccentric productions until I had based my style upon more solid models. Without, however, minding his injunctions, I seized upon the pianoforte works of Beethoven as they successively appeared, and in them found a solace and a delight such as no other composer afforded me.[12]

The *Sturm und Drang* pathos of pieces like the *Pathétique* was often overestimated in the nineteenth century but has been dismissed too readily in the

[12] Thayer-Forbes, pp. 242–3.

twentieth as self-indulgent posturing. A more promising approach is offered by Schiller's 1793 essay *Über das Pathetische*; its lucid discussion of tragic art contains a conceptual framework that applies well to Beethoven. Schiller stresses that the depiction of suffering *as such* is not the purpose of art; such depiction is properly regarded as but a means to an end. Pathos or tragedy arises when unblinkered awareness of suffering is counterbalanced by the capacity of reason to resist these feelings. In such resistance to the inevitability of pain or despair is lodged the principle of freedom. Schiller thus regards tragic art as founded on the intersection of suffering nature on the one hand, and moral resistance to this reality on the other.

Beethoven's Schillerian tendencies ran so deep that tragic resignation appears relatively rarely in his works, at least as a primary determinant of artistic character. In his C minor pieces, unlike Mozart's, resignation is typically supplanted by a resistance tending to revolution; this subjective principle in Beethoven often involves a quest for an alternative vision that banishes, or at least delimits, the sway of strife. We shall return to this idea in connection with the narrative design of the Fifth Symphony. More germane to the *Sonate Pathétique* is Schiller's basic concept of tragic pathos as a resistance to suffering. What is it about Beethoven's treatment of textural dialogue or contrast and the development of musical tension that seems to convey an existential conflict encoded in the very structure of the sound?

In the introductory *Grave* of this sonata, like the *Largo e mesto* of op. 10 no. 3, Beethoven stresses the contrast between an aspiring, transparent lyricism and darker, dissonant chords in the bass. But in the *Pathétique* these aspects are merged at the outset; the sense of resistance implied in the upward melodic unfolding is pitted against the leaden weight of the C minor tonality, with its emphasis on diminished-seventh chords. While penetrating the higher pitch registers, the melodic ascent becomes both poignant and fragile, since it is dependent on the unyielding harmonic underpinning of the bass. The recitative-like phrases near the end of the *Grave* are harmonically parenthetical, poised on a deceptive cadential inflection that delays the imminent resolution to the tonic C minor until the beginning of the ensuing *Allegro di molto e con brio*.

At this moment of transformation Beethoven freely reshapes the rising chordal progression from the *Grave* above a rumbling bass pedal of tremolo octaves. The bass shows a powerful inclination to ascend, eventually forcing the music out of the tonic C minor to the dominant of E♭. Here, at the threshold of the second subject-group, he resorts to a variant of his innovation from op. 2 no. 2: he avoids entering the key of E♭ and remains instead on its minor dominant, creating thereby a large-scale tension underlying an immense passage 40 bars long. The tension is reflected motivically in a dramatic dialogue exploiting registral contrast, in a manner reminiscent of the slow introduction, while also foreshadowing the first movement of Beethoven's 'Tempest' Sonata op. 31 no. 2 of 1802.

Most striking is how the *Grave* returns to preface the development and the coda. Beethoven thereby underscores the juxtaposition of tempos as the germinal idea of the movement, and he gradually deepens this conception. In the development he quotes phrases from the *Grave* in the ensuing *Allegro*, confirming their relationship, whereas at the climax just before the recapitulation he heightens the registral contrast first exposed in the slow introduction. It is in the coda, however, that the dramatic core of the movement is encapsulated in a single gesture. The opening *Grave* phrases resolve here, for the first time, to bare octaves on C. This hint of resigned capitulation is abruptly negated by Beethoven's intensified closing reinterpretation of the *Allegro di molto e con brio*. The leverage, as so often in Beethoven, is rhythmic: foreshortening of the closing phrase of the recapitulation propels the music into the final accented chords, ending the movement with the precise sonority with which it had begun.

The basic expressive tension is not laid to rest here but only disclosed: the cycle of suffering and resistance could continue indefinitely. This demands a response from the following movements if they are to be linked psychologically with the first; and in fact the *Sonate Pathétique* displays the outlines of a narrative sequence on which Beethoven was to build in subsequent compositions. The ensuing *Adagio cantabile* offers the fundamental contrast of hymnic serenity, set in Beethoven's characteristic key for lyricism within a C minor context—the flat sixth, A♭ major. Characteristic too is the registral correspondence between the end of the first movement and the beginning of the *Adagio*: the same C is reharmonized as the point of transition into a new region of consciousness and feeling. Accordingly, any extended pause or break of concentration between the movements is destructive to the artistic effect. The form of the *Adagio* is that of a slow-movement rondo, with two varied repetitions of the broad, lyrical subject separated by episodes touching on minor keys. The design is rounded off by a coda echoing the cadential phrase of the theme. Beethoven avoids an unambiguous close by ending in the middle of the bar; and he extends the final chord with a fermata, implying an immediate continuation into the C minor finale.

The rondo finale is clearly linked to each of the preceding movements. The head of its main theme, for instance, is derived from the beginning of the second subject in the *Allegro di molto e con brio*. The relationship between the rondo and the preceding *Adagio* is more involved. The role of the *Adagio* as lyrical complement to the turbulent outer movements is bound up with the tonal relationship of A♭ major to C minor, and the rondo draws heavily on this association. Thus the sonority of the German augmented-sixth chord built on A♭ appears conspicuously in the accompaniment to the rondo theme, whereas the central episode of the formal design is actually in the key of A♭ major. In the coda, moreover, Beethoven recaptures this tonal relationship with a concentrated sense of summation. The last appearance of the head of the rondo theme (bar 203) appears in A♭ major, in the same register as the main theme of the *Adagio cantabile*; Beethoven even strips away the flowing left-hand accompaniment to enhance the similarity.

Although this last-minute departure into a remote key might seem to disturb seriously the formal equilibrium, in fact Beethoven uses the technique as a means of formal integration and resolution of tensions. For in the final bars, the German augmented-sixth chord on A♭ serves as the pivot for the return to C minor, while the final cadence, with its powerful descending scale in triplets from high F, assumes a structural significance evidently overlooked in the analytical literature. A cardinal principle of Classical sonata procedure entails the ultimate resolution to the tonic of material originally heard in secondary keys. In this instance, the downward-rushing triplets recall earlier musical gestures, for example, descents from high F above the dominant-seventh chord of C minor (bars 58–60, 117–20), or, in the coda, above the dominant seventh of A♭ (bars 198–201). Only at the very end of the finale is the sweeping downward run directed emphatically into the C minor triad. The trick of delaying resolution of such a gesture until the final bar was a speciality of Haydn, but never before Beethoven had it assumed such dramatic force and significance.[13]

The rondo finale of the *Pathétique* does more than allude to the preceding movements; it welds these allusions into the intrinsic musical design. Important in this respect is the detached, serene character of the central episode; its contrapuntal subject is built on the interval of the fourth—the motivic hallmark of the hymn-like main theme of the *Adagio*. This initially calm episode stands apart from the rest of the movement in its texture, rhythm, key, and even its form—it unfolds as a series of variations. Variation procedure is the most static and unified of musical forms, since it revolves around repetition of a basic thematic shape. And although Beethoven is clearly indebted here to the venerable tradition of variation writing, he achieves a qualitatively new realization of artistic possibilities by leading his chain of variations on an abstract contrapuntal formula into a resumption of the strife-ridden music in C minor.

Beethoven's main resources here are rhythmic diminution and a rise in register. The registral starting-point of the theme is identical with the beginning of the *Adagio cantabile*, whereas the first variation of the eight-bar theme ascends an octave in pitch, while subdividing the basic rhythmic motion from

[13] For an example of this practice in Haydn, see the first movement of the String Quartet in C op. 33 no. 3, in which a last-minute adjustment enables Haydn to close the movement with its opening phrase.

half- to quarter-notes. After a four-bar interlude Beethoven brings in the second variation up another octave and then fills out the tonal space through a further diminution in rhythm to eighth-notes (Ex. 15). The configuration of fourths still heard in the original form in the right hand is 'composed out' in inversion in the long falling scale into the bass. The structure of falling fifths Ab–Db–G–C–F–Bb is unravelled and bodied-out in the scale, gaining sinuous strength reflected in the crescendo to *forte* when the descending scale-pattern begins in the right hand. This process of elaboration generates energy for the ensuing transition in character, as Beethoven leaves Ab major for the dominant of C minor, building toward a dramatic climax through further rhythmic foreshortening.

This passage thus embodies on a larger scale the same relations as does the coda: a calm, detached oasis of sound in Ab dissipates into C minor pathos. What Beethoven does here is to incorporate a 'foreshortening' or compressed

Ex. 15 *Pathétique* Sonata op. 13/III, bars 73–107

formulation of the progression *between movements* into the finale proper. The rondo responds to its context in the work as a whole, twice making itself transparent to the *Adagio cantabile*. The resulting progression, as often in Beethoven, is from contemplation to action, and harbours an unmistakable hint of narrative strategies in works to come. This contrapuntal *topos* in A♭ major is the departure-point of a creative journey leading ultimately to the fugue of op. 110; the short series of variations on it is a much more distant prototype for the slow movement of the *Appassionata* or even for the Arietta movement of the last sonata, op. 111. Seeds for many of Beethoven's greatest works were sown in the impressive piano sonatas from his first decade in Vienna.

3

Crisis and Creativity

1799–1802

THE years around the turn of the century saw an important transition in Beethoven's artistic development, accompanied by a biographical crisis of major proportions. No one category of analysis can adequately describe these complex events. The tension between consolidation and innovation, between retrospective and progressive tendencies, is particularly conspicuous in the music up to 1801, when, according to Czerny, Beethoven told his friend Wenzel Krumpholz that 'I am only a little satisfied with my previous works. From today on I will take a new path'.[1] Beginning in 1802, we can indeed discern a 'new path' in works like the piano sonatas of op. 31, the piano variations opp. 34 and 35, and the Second Symphony op. 36. But close examination of the music reveals deep continuities with Beethoven's earlier and later works. The new path was not entirely new, and it was long—the expression attributed to Hippocrates, 'ars longa, vita brevis', was a favourite dictum of Beethoven's which he repeatedly set as a canon many years later.

The claim about the 'new path' that Czerny attributed to Beethoven, and even the similar documented comment from the composer himself in 1802 concerning the variations opp. 34 and 35, need to be interpreted cautiously, with due attention to other historical evidence. With the passage of time, a simplified retrospective order tends to be imposed on the rich disorder of complex events, which are easily distorted thereby. In particular, we should avoid assuming, on the basis of verbal reports alone, that Beethoven set out to be more original at any one particular moment in time. As Hans-Werner Küthen has observed, Beethoven's claim about the innovative quality of his opp. 34 and 35 variations was evidently connected to his irritation with a recent

---

[1] *On the Proper Performance of All Beethoven's Works for the Piano*, p. 13; translation amended. This remark supposedly followed the completion of the Sonata in D, op. 28, the autograph score of which is dated '1801'. See Sonneck, ed., *Beethoven: Impressions of Contemporaries*, p. 31.

publication of music by his old friend from Bonn, the flautist and composer Anton Reicha, in which reference was made to a 'new method of writing fugues'.[2] Beethoven's letter to Gottfried Christoph Härtel in December 1802 refers to '. . . all the commotion about a new method of v[ariations], as would be made by our neighbours, the Gallo-Franks, as for instance how a certain French composer offers fugues according to a new method [*après une nouvelle méthode*], which consists in the fact that the fugue is no longer a fugue, etc.'.[3] The term 'French composer' was Beethoven's replacement for the name 'Reicha', but it also fits the context of his allusion here to the German idiom 'Da kommt einem ja die Galle hoch!' Beethoven found Reicha's claim unjustified and therefore 'galling' and responded verbally with one of his characteristic puns. His own similar allusion to a 'new manner' in his variations of 1802 may represent his ironic response to, or 'persiflage' of, Reicha's statement, but in Beethoven's case the innovative presumption is actually confirmed by the musical content. Beethoven's claim cannot be discounted, but it needs to be understood in context.

There is a special biographical background to Beethoven's creative development during these years, but we shall attempt here to re-evaluate the facts of his life in the light of the music, thus inverting the traditional procedure of artistic biography. His composing activities are documented in much more detail than his biography, and their sources are less familiar. My strategy is therefore to examine Beethoven's personal crisis primarily in the light of his compositional preoccupations. His stylistic development, on the other hand, can be assessed only on the basis of a substantial selection of works in different genres. Attention will be given in this chapter not only to solo piano works but to three other genres: the quartet, concerto, and symphony.

In 1799, despite his formidable accomplishments and increasing stature, Beethoven still remained cautious and even somewhat insecure when tackling those musical genres in which Haydn and Mozart reigned supreme. In opera and the piano concerto, a comparison with Mozart's great legacy was inevitable; for the symphony and string quartet, Haydn's model was perhaps even more intimidating, and more recent. Beethoven showed a particular self-consciousness about his early works in these genres, and he exerted a tireless will to match the accomplishments of his great predecessors on their own ground.

One of the first significant works in which the brilliant young pianist-composer staked claim to the universal musical legacy of the Viennese Classical style was his Symphony in C major op. 21, completed in 1800.

<hr />

[2] 'Beethovens "wirklich ganz neue Manier"—Eine Persiflage'; also see Küthen's essay 'Pragmatic instead of Enigmatic: "The Fifty-First Sonata" of Beethoven', *The Beethoven Newsletter*, vii (1992), p. 73 note 14.

[3] Anderson, ed., *The Letters of Beethoven*, L. 67; translation amended.

Stylistically, the First Symphony is firmly rooted in the eighteenth century, especially the graceful *Andante cantabile con moto* in F major, with its rococo rhetoric, and the playfully humorous, Haydnesque finale. Bolder and more progressive are the first movement, with its impressive slow introduction and resourceful orchestration highlighting the woodwinds, and especially the dance movement, in the penultimate position. Beethoven entitled the movement *Menuetto*, but that designation is contradicted by his indication 'Allegro molto e vivace' and by the swift metronome marking, not to mention the sharp rhythmic accents of the opening section. The dynamic tension is evident from the very first phrase, in which a rising scale pattern in iambic rhythm drives with a crescendo to an emphatic cadence in the dominant. The trio retains the tonic key of C major and develops the contrasts in timbre from the first movement in a delightful dialogue of pulsing woodwind phrases and swirling string figuration. More than other movements of the symphony, this *Allegro molto e vivace* breaks free from the burden and the anxiety of influence; it displays a striking stylistic originality, while foreshadowing the scherzos in some of Beethoven's later symphonies.

It is in the context of this ambitious struggle with the legacy of Haydn and Mozart that we may view Beethoven's biggest single compositional project of the first decade at Vienna: the set of six Quartets op. 18, written during 1798–1800. The very number of pieces in the opus recalls the practice of Beethoven's predecessors: Haydn's quartets opp. 20 and 33 and Mozart's famous 'Haydn' quartets were all published in groups of six. In certain of Beethoven's op. 18 quartets the influence of these earlier pieces is direct and tangible. Op. 18 no. 2, in G major, is Haydnesque in spirit, reminding us of the older master's quartet in the same key from his op. 33, as Joseph Kerman observed.[4] And Beethoven's A major Quartet op. 18 no. 5 shows a still closer kinship with Mozart's quartet in this key from his 'Haydn' set, K464, parts of which Beethoven even copied out in score. According to Czerny, Beethoven once exclaimed about Mozart's K464: 'That's what I call a work! In it, Mozart was telling the world: "Look what I could do if you were ready for it!"'[5]

In view of the size of the project, and Beethoven's inexperience in the medium, it is not surprising that the op. 18 quartets are more uneven in quality than some of his earlier piano sonatas or the three string trios op. 9 of 1798, which Beethoven had described as 'la meilleure de [mes] œuvres'. Like the First Symphony, these quartets have shortcomings that Beethoven soon redressed in his later pieces in these forms; for this reason, an awareness of the historical context becomes an especially important part of the critical enterprise. Beethoven frankly acknowledged his struggle with op. 18 no. 1, in F major. This quartet was actually the second of the pieces composed;

[4] *The Beethoven Quartets*, pp. 44–5.   [5] *On the Proper Performance*, p. 8.

Beethoven presumably placed it at the head of the set because it is the grandest and most immediately impressive. It exists in a version that Beethoven presented to his friend Karl Ferdinand Amenda in 1798—not just a draft, but a set of parts then intended as the finished work. Two years later, however, after completing his *magnum opus* of the first Vienna decade, Beethoven cautioned Amenda to keep the manuscript to himself, since 'he had only now learned how to write quartets properly'.

Many of Beethoven's revisions involved refinements in scoring, but one far-reaching change was the decrease in motivic saturation in the opening *Allegro con brio* movement, reducing the number of occurrences of the opening turn-figure from 130 to 104.[6] The number of accents was similarly curtailed, although one striking new rhetorical feature was added—the two unison *fortissimo* scale figures that mark the beginning of the coda in this sonata-form movement. Even in the movement's published form Beethoven exploits the turn-figure with concentrated single-mindedness. The opening theme is permeated with it, and the transition begins with sequences of it leading to accented diminished harmonies. In the ensuing passage, and again near the end of the exposition, the cello takes it up as an ostinato figure, which generates a whole chain of turns in rapid figuration. In the development section Beethoven is obsessed more than ever with the figure. He resourcefully exploits its rhythm in the agitated retransition to the *fortissimo* recapitulation: the characteristic threefold upbeat pulse is detached from the turn, rhythmically augmented, and syncopated as well in this striking if somewhat blatant passage.

The slow movement in D minor, marked *Adagio affettuoso ed appassionato*, is somewhat reminiscent of the *Largo e mesto* in this key in Beethoven's great Piano Sonata in D op. 10 no. 3. A specific poetic association is known for this *Adagio*. Amenda reported that Beethoven wrote it while thinking of the burial-vault scene in Shakespeare's *Romeo and Juliet*. The connection is confirmed by one of Beethoven's sketchleaves, which contains the inscription 'les derniers soupirs' over a passage emphasizing the interval of the diminished seventh. Such dissonances, together with an intense dramatic rhetoric, effective dynamic contrasts, and an evocative use of silences, all support the expression of pathos in this *Adagio*, the centre of gravity in the quartet as a whole. The following scherzo and finale are less weighty in tone and substance, though they offer some captivating passages, such as the humorous trio, with its striking rhythmic and textural contrasts.

The opening *Allegro* of the G major Quartet op. 18 no. 2 shows a thorough assimilation of Haydn's comedy of manners merged with an occasional dramatic thrust that is unmistakably Beethovenian. The beginning of the

---

[6] Cf. Kerman, *The Beethoven Quartets*, p. 32, and the detailed comparison of the two versions in Levy, *Beethoven's Compositional Choices*.

recapitulation, for instance, is rhythmically charged by accented octaves, casting the theme in a new light. The following *Adagio cantabile* employs a curious formal design, with a dance-like *Allegro* interpolated between the slow lyrical theme and its decorated recapitulation. In the scherzo and the finale Beethoven employs a rhetoric bristling with Haydnesque devices. The false recapitulation in the closing *Allegro molto quasi Presto* steals in quietly in A♭ major, and then suspiciously repeats the rising scale-pattern from the theme, conveying a character of puzzlement. Haydn typically handles such tricks with finesse; Beethoven makes his point more bluntly, by restating the ascending motif in doubled note values in a broad spacing, and with a crescendo as well. Not infrequently, a tension can be felt in these early quartets between a refined, courtly rhetoric and a powerful directness of expression that is typical of Beethoven.

Another striking parallel with Haydn is offered by the *Andante* and variations in C major forming the middle movement of Beethoven's G major Piano Sonata op. 14 no. 2, a work completed shortly before the quartets, in 1799. The artless simplicity of Beethoven's *Andante* tune is underscored by repetitions of its opening phrase; one eminent critic was even provoked into describing the movement as 'stupid'. Yet the expressive heart of the piece lies in the tension between the apparent naïveté of the theme and its reinterpretation through the addition of syncopations and dissonances in Beethoven's variations. This tension is sustained until the very end of the coda, with Beethoven's humorous intent confirmed once and for all in the surprising *fortissimo* outburst of the final chord! In these variations, Beethoven enlarges on the famous musical joke contained in another *Andante* movement in C—the slow movement of Haydn's 'Surprise' Symphony (no. 94). Instead of placing the shocking chord in immediate juxtaposition to a soft and harmless theme, as Haydn did, Beethoven reserves the disruptive gesture until the close, challenging the sober listener to question the seriousness of the entire musical discourse, while also forging a transition to the finale—a playfully humorous rondo bearing the unusual designation 'scherzo'.

The third quartet of op. 18, in D major, opens with an *Allegro* of rather relaxed, even somewhat bland character, but Beethoven resourcefully experiments with the listener's expectations. Once again the moment of recapitulation receives special reinforcement. Whereas the movement begins quietly with unaccompanied whole-notes on the dominant-seventh chord in the first violin, Beethoven later supports this sonority harmonically with a chromatic ascent reaching C♯ at the end of the exposition. This pitch in turn becomes the focus for a huge *fortissimo* climax concluding the development, with the C♯ resolved into the delicate continuation of the main theme. The following *Andante con moto* in B♭ major is characterized by warmly lyrical canonic textures and contains one of the early instances in Beethoven of a coda in which the basic thematic material is gradually stripped away and virtually dissolved into silence. Beethoven labelled the penultimate dance movement neither 'scherzo' nor 'minuet' but merely 'Allegro'. It relies heavily on motivic development of the appoggiatura or turn-figure from the first phrase of the theme; the trio, or 'minore', is based on the descending linear configuration from the beginning of the *Allegro*, now heard in longer note values. The *presto* finale further develops the motivic turn D–C♯–D from the preceding *Allegro* in an expansive sonata form spiked with canonic episodes. The piece ends in a gesture of Haydnesque wit, as Beethoven reduces the music to the turn alone, heard *pianissimo* in all four instruments.

The quartet in C minor op. 18 no. 4, and especially its opening *Allegro ma non tanto*, is one of the most controversial of Beethoven's compositions. Hugo Riemann speculated that it was based on older material, perhaps even dating back to the Bonn period; and Kerman has followed up this line of thought, concluding that 'the C-minor first movement is more crudely written than anything in the other op. 18 quartets'.[7] Ferdinand Ries related a conversation in which he pointed out to Beethoven a case of parallel fifths in this work, to which Beethoven replied 'Now, and who has forbidden them?' To Ries's answer, that this grammatical failing was forbidden by Marpurg, Kirnberger, Fuchs, and other theorists, Beethoven defiantly declared 'And so I allow them!'[8]

More recently Richard Kramer has analysed the parallel fifths which occur at the transition to the development in this first movement, a passage in which strong chords preface a new statement of the main theme in G minor (Ex. 16).[9] The bald unison progression from C♮ through C♯ to D overlaps here with the upper-voice ascent from A♭ (= G♯) to A. It is difficult to explain this particular irregularity in voice-leading as being required by artistic necessity. Beethoven's protest to the contrary, a lapse in technique is indicated; nor is it an isolated failure. In fact, Beethoven's earlier String Trio in this key, op. 9 no. 3, is a considerably more polished work than the C minor Quartet. Suspicions are rightly aroused about the piece being of early origin, but studies of the manuscript sources have not lent much support to such speculation.

Ultimately, the roughness of this movement seems to arise from an imbalance between the passionate force of Beethoven's 'C minor mood' and his ability to mediate or control this idiom in the artistic form as a whole. A comparison with another C minor piece, the first movement of the *Sonate Pathétique* op. 13, is revealing. The beginning of the *Pathétique* slow introduction is extremely close to the opening of the quartet in its rhythm, register, and

[7] Riemann's analysis appears in his 1917 German edition of the first volume of Thayer's biography, pp. 188–90; the passage is translated and commented on by Kerman in *The Beethoven Quartets*, pp. 65–71.

[8] Sonneck, ed., *Beethoven: Impressions of Contemporaries*, pp. 49–50.

[9] 'Counterpoint and Syntax: On a Difficult Passage in the First Movement of Beethoven's String Quartet in C minor, Opus 18 No. 4', p. 116.

Ex. 16 String Quartet op. 18 no. 4/I, bars 76–96

rhetoric, with a parallel placement of expressive appoggiaturas in each work. The *Pathétique* relies on the repeated juxtaposition of its *Grave* introduction with the *Allegro con brio*, however; it does not depend so heavily on the vehement but rather simplistic gestures that sustain the quartet. Least convincing in the *Allegro ma non tanto* of the quartet is perhaps the succession of *fortissimo* chords alternating between tonic and dominant at the end of the main theme and at other junctures, including the passage with the parallel fifths. To be sure, Beethoven is exposing in these bars an important rhythmic configuration, one that is implicit within the main theme itself. But that is not quite enough to justify these powerful outbursts, nor to resolve suspicions about the somewhat overblown rhetoric of the movement.

The other movements as well may not always convince according to the lofty standards set by Beethoven's greater works, but they do contain unusual and striking ideas. For the finale, for example, Beethoven employed a kind of rustic gypsy melody in the first violin which is accelerated to *prestissimo* in the coda. At the close, Beethoven first separates the head of this theme from its continuation of six repeated notes, and then allows the latter motif to soar quietly into the very highest register, before ending the piece with arresting *fortissimo* strokes.

As we have seen, Mozart's Quartet in A major K464 was an inspiring influence on Beethoven's op. 18 no. 5, in the same key. The impact of Mozart is also felt in several of Beethoven's piano sonatas of these years, including the two little sonatas in G minor and G major that he wrote between 1795 and 1798 and eventually published as op. 49, the two sonatas of op. 14 from 1799, and the Sonata in B♭ major op. 22 from 1800. In the opening *Allegro* of the E major Sonata op. 14 no. 1 the Mozartian influence is reflected in the skilful arrangement of distinct yet related musical figures. Beethoven's familiar technique of using a single dominating rhythmic motif is not in evidence. Instead, he devises the three phrases of the main theme as a network of thematic variations stressing the interval of a rising fourth. There is a Mozartian flavour as well to the chromatic touches in the main subsidiary theme, and perhaps also to the transparent contrapuntal textures so evocative of chamber music. Op. 14 no. 1 is the only sonata Beethoven ever arranged for string quartet, and his decision to undertake the transcription in 1802 was surely motivated by the special affinity of this sonata with the quartet medium.

In Beethoven's A major Quartet, on the other hand, the Mozartian influence is centred on the third movement—like Mozart's a set of variations. At the same time, Beethoven's five variations on his *Andante cantabile* theme mark a significant moment in his lifelong fascination with this form; there is a distant foreshadowing here of the slow movements of the *Appassionata* Sonata and *Archduke* Trio, among other works. As in these pieces, the theme has a quality of elemental simplicity, and it serves as an effective point of departure for a series of transformations based on progressively faster rhythmic figuration—a venerable device in the history of variation writing. The opening phrases of the melody do little but spell out the interval of the sixth A–F♯, both ascending and descending. This basic structure is elaborated in increasingly intricate textures and figuration as far as Variation 4, a still, mysterious, chromatic version of the theme. Then the rhythmic development reaches its climax in the high spirits of the last variation, in which a new version of the theme in the inner voices is glorified by trills in the first violin and accented leaps in the cello. The movement ends with a soft, reflective reminiscence of the theme in a form close to its original.

Of the other movements, the *Allegro* finale is nearest to Mozart. Near the end of the development Beethoven even borrows thematic material from K464, and he demonstrates mastery in handling the transparent counterpoint characteristic of the older master. A problem here, however, as elsewhere in the A major Quartet, is that the process of modelling has muted something of Beethoven's own individual voice. Kerman concluded that 'it must be counted the least personal of the quartets'.[10]

---

[10] *The Beethoven Quartets*, p. 64.

The opening *Allegro con brio* of the final quartet of op. 18, in B♭ major, shows a humorous spirit and lightness of tone. The delicately ornamented *Adagio ma non troppo* that follows shares with it a certain economy in form and expression. The most innovative and challenging movements are the energetic, syncopated scherzo and, above all, the finale, with its juxtaposition of radically contrasting material. The finale is a highly original conception that does not suggest the influence of Haydn or Mozart. Beethoven labels its opening *Adagio* section 'La Malinconia', and he recalls the *Adagio* in the midst of the following dance-like *Allegretto quasi Allegro*. We are reminded here of his abiding preoccupation with composite movements embracing strongly contrasting ideas. An earlier work in this vein is the *Sonate Pathétique*, which twice recalls the slow introduction in the context of the *Allegro con brio*. Later, more complex examples include the interweaving of scherzo and *Allegro* in the Fifth Symphony, and of arioso and fugue in the late piano sonata op. 110. Beethoven's integration of powerful contrasts within a larger continuity is also a conspicuous feature in some of his last quartets, such as the first movements of op. 130 in B♭ and op. 132 in A minor.

Extraordinary in 'La Malinconia' are the mysterious chromatic progressions, which for all their effect of harmonic disorientation are masterfully shaped into an integrated dramatic progression. After this enigmatic harmonic labyrinth, the following dance in 3/8 time provides an effective contrast and resolution of tension; and it also reshapes the falling third and rising steps from 'La Malinconia' in a new context, suggesting a rejection of melancholy

Ex. 17 String Quartet op. 18 no. 6/IV

LA MALINCONIA.
Questo pezzo si deve trattare colla più gran delicatezza.

Ex. 17 *cont.*

(Ex. 17). Typically for Beethoven, however, this optimistic transformation is not permanent but conditional. He later brings back ten bars of the *Adagio* juxtaposed with four of the *Allegretto*, and then two further bars of the *Adagio*, before the dance finally reasserts itself, shaking off the memory of 'La Malinconia'. The intimate facing of these contrasting modalities represents perhaps the most single arresting idea in all the op. 18 quartets.

*   *   *

Up to now our narrative has traced Beethoven's increasing but still imperfect mastery of the legacy of Haydn and Mozart; the fulfilment of Waldstein's prophecy was actually a lifelong task for Beethoven, an occupation that ceased to be a problem by 1809 but which left traces even in the last quartets of 1824–6. The evocative juxtaposition of gaiety and melancholy in the finale of op. 18 no. 6 may be seen to signal a more profound conflict, with multiple implications. For it is around this time that Beethoven was forced to confront a demon from within: a progressive deterioration in his hearing that could no longer be ignored. His increasing deafness plunged him into despair at the very time when his outward success seemed assured. A pair of letters to Franz

Wegeler and Amenda from 29 June and 1 July 1801 respectively document Beethoven's response to his disability. To Wegeler he wrote:

For almost two years I have ceased to attend any social functions, just because I find it impossible to say to people: I am deaf.

And to Amenda he confided:

You will realize what a sad life I must now lead, seeing that I am cut off from everything that is dear and precious to me . . . I must withdraw from everything; and my best years will rapidly pass away without my being able to achieve all that my talent and my strength have commanded me to do. Sad resignation, to which I am forced to have recourse. Needless to say, I am resolved to overcome all this, but how is it going to be done?[11]

As Beethoven makes clear, the onset of his deafness predates these letters by a considerable period; what precipitated his anguish was a growing recognition of both the incurable nature of his condition and the implications for his social and artistic life. The most important written documentation of Beethoven's personal crisis is the *Heiligenstadt Testament*, dated 6 October 1802, well over a year after his letters to Wegeler and Amenda (we shall return to it below in connection with the *Eroica* Symphony). Its references to suicide, contemplated and then rejected in favour of stoical acceptance of his condition, show a deepening of the attitudes expressed in his letters of the preceding year. It appears from these documents that Beethoven came to terms with his infirmity only very gradually. The crisis of his deafness forced him to reconsider the most fundamental assumptions about his life and art. For, as Beethoven put it to Amenda, he was consumed by doubts not only about his social life but about his 'being able to achieve all that [his] talent and strength commanded [him] to do'. One of his worst fears may have been that his deafness would stifle realization of his artistic potential.

The relationship between Beethoven's deafness and his artistic development is fascinating. Despite his initial fears, and now discredited attempts to characterize his late style as a degeneration resulting from a lack of hearing, his art actually became richer as his hearing declined. Whereas the evolution of his so-called heroic style closely paralleled the personal crisis articulated in his *Heiligenstadt Testament*, the emergence of his late style, or 'third period', was marked by the complete erosion of his hearing many years later, around 1818. The parallel between Beethoven's stylistic development and his increasing deafness is more than coincidental, and it has not escaped notice. For instance, Solomon assesses the period around 1801–2 as follows: 'one begins to suspect that Beethoven's crisis and his extraordinary creativity were somehow related, and even that the former may have been the necessary precondition of the latter'.[12]

---

[11] Anderson, L. 51 (to Wegeler), L. 53 (to Amenda).   [12] *Beethoven*, p. 115.

In the very same letters to Wegeler and Amenda lamenting his condition Beethoven wrote: 'I live entirely in my music, and hardly have I completed one composition when I have already begun another'. He even added: 'Why, at the moment I feel equal to anything. Since your departure I have been composing all types of music, except operas and sacred works'. Beethoven's expressions of confidence are fully justified by the works of this period, and not only by those for piano but increasingly in 'all types of music'. The consciously innovative thrust to his music from this time can be confirmed by analysis, lending general support to the notion of a 'new path', though not to the fixation of this pathbreaking trend to any particular point in time.

The relationship between the biography of an artist and his works is a delicate one. But however difficult it may be to establish the precise nature of the relationship, the connection cannot be severed in principle. It is pointless and unnecessary to isolate works of art from their biographical and historical context. At the same time, the successful artwork, if regarded in the sense of Langer's 'unconsummated symbol', cannot be reduced to an expression of the artist's personality or regarded merely as a historical artefact. These alternatives simplify or evade the critical challenge posed by the phenomenon of creativity. As Solomon has written:

creativity is a threatening subject . . . the artist himself is a dangerous child . . . Little wonder that he arouses extremes of ambivalent feeling—hostility and adoration, rage and awe, hate and love. Little wonder that those critics who speak for their own timidities, as well as for fearful social orders, have undertaken to neutralize him and his work by every conceivable strategy.[13]

We are now in a position to gain new perspective on Beethoven's creative achievement from sources that were not available, or not fully available, to earlier commentators. The most important of these is the rich legacy of manuscripts that Beethoven left at his death in 1827, including a large number of autograph scores and more than 8000 pages of musical sketches. The Beethoven sketchbooks and loose sketchleaves represent the richest documentation of the creative process available for any composer of the first rank. Yet because of the large-scale dispersal of these sources during the decades following Beethoven's death, and the upheaval of the two World Wars in our century, a proper overview of them became available only in 1985, about a century after Gustav Nottebohm's pioneering surveys of the sketchbooks that were then accessible for study.[14] A significant body of analytical work has now been produced on the Beethoven sketches, and their significance for our understanding of the music has become clearer, although much still remains to be done.

[13] *Beethoven Essays*, pp. 110–11.
[14] *The Beethoven Sketchbooks* by Douglas Johnson, Alan Tyson, and Robert Winter.

When we contemplate this massive legacy of sketchbooks, a correspondence soon emerges between Beethoven's response to his deafness and his ever-deepening commitment to his art. Although Beethoven had made sketches in earlier years, his first use of a bound sketchbook was in mid-1798, in connection with the op. 18 quartets. The process of rigorous self-criticism so richly documented in his sketches mirrors something of the increasing complexity and density of his style. The genesis of the *Eroica*, for instance, is documented in a long series of drafts, famous since Nottebohm. Much less familiar are the copious sketches from Beethoven's last decade. For works like the *Missa solemnis* or the C♯ minor Quartet op. 131 Beethoven made hundreds of pages of sketches in multiple formats before writing out the autograph scores, which themselves were often subject to far-reaching revisions necessitating new bouts of sketching.

Thus, long before Beethoven would have been forced to abandon composition at the piano because of his increasing deafness he had already adopted a method of composition specially designed to support his ambition to follow a 'new path'. The sketches are fixed improvisations, preserving a partial record of those sounds Beethoven heard while his works progressed towards their final shape. The availability of these sources not only provides a remarkably detailed record of the chronology of his works, it also reveals important principles that guided his creative method. Many aspects of composition from melodic refinement to large-scale formal continuity are clarified in them. It is doubtful whether these documents have yet received the recognition they deserve. Their ontological status is nebulous, poised as it is between the biographical and the aesthetic, and this tension poses special challenges to interpretation.

A popular notion of Beethoven's sketching and compositional process would have it that he laboured long and hard on unpromising motifs and themes that some other composers, such as Mozart or Schubert, would not have penned at all. The problem with this view is its tendency to identify the part of the creative process that was captured on paper with Beethoven's artistic intention, without giving sufficient heed to the full aesthetic context. In Beethoven's sketches much and sometimes most of this context is not yet written down. Beethoven's 'movement plans' for works in progress reflect his attempt to envisage the whole even before the motifs, themes, and individual sections had been realized. Further evidence comes from his reported comment to Neate, 'I have always a picture in my mind, when I am composing, and work up to it', and by his comment to Treitschke, 'For my custom when I am composing even instrumental music is always to keep the whole in view'.[15] This characteristic but paradoxical procedure was recognized by

---

[15] Cited in Solomon, 'Beethoven's Creative Process: A Two-Part Invention', *Beethoven Essays*, pp. 127–8, which demonstrates that the famous account of Beethoven's creative process by Louis Schlösser is untrustworthy.

Ernest Newman (in his book *The Unconscious Beethoven*), who wrote of the first movement of the *Eroica*:

From the Sketch Books, we get the impression that in some queer subconscious way the movement possessed him as a whole before he began to think out the details; and the long and painful search for the themes was simply an effort, not to find workable atoms out of which he could construct a musical edifice according to the conventions of symphonic form, but to reduce an already existing nebula, in which that edifice was implicit, to the atom, and then, by the orderly arrangement of these atoms, to make the implicit explicit.[16]

We shall return to the subject of Beethoven's compositional process in connection with individual works. Important here is the recognition that beginning in 1798 Beethoven expanded his practice of making preliminary musical sketches to that of using bound books; in subsequent years the nature of his creative project tended to demand more and more sketching. There can be no doubt that this practice somehow mirrored the complex ramifications of Beethoven's aesthetic project. Whereas Mozart had resorted to sketches especially to work out contrapuntal passages, and Haydn made the greatest use of them in connection with the special demands of 'The Depiction of Chaos' in *The Creation*, for Beethoven they became an absolute necessity. The attitude they reflect is instructive, for it turns the conventional dichotomy of 'inspiration' and 'calculation' on its head. We often find that Beethoven's relentless self-criticism in his sketchbooks has cleared the way for original and powerful ideas that emerge late in the compositional process. With Beethoven, it was not generally a matter of spontaneous ideas that were subsequently worked out with rational calculation, but, rather, a blend of the rational and sensuous achieved in a prolonged process of critical reflection. Ultimately Beethoven's deafness may have aided this process, by insulating him from the outside world and by forcing him to abandon activities that competed with his composing, such as his public performances as a keyboard virtuoso.

*   *   *

The Piano Concerto in C minor op. 37 is the first of Beethoven's great works in a genre closely associated with Mozart. Beethoven's admiration for Mozart's C minor Concerto is reflected in some details of the first movement. Thus the motif C–E♭–A♭ at the outset of K491 appears as counterpoint in the bass in bar 9 of Beethoven's concerto. The continuing presence of the piano after the cadenza is probably also inspired by Mozart's concerto. The opening of Beethoven's *Allegro con brio*, on the other hand, contains a succession of unison string and harmonized wind phrases followed by the orchestral tutti, a procedure reminiscent of the beginning of Mozart's C major Concerto K467.

[16] pp. 115–16.

1 View of Bonn from the
  Kreuzberg. Copper
  engraving by Johann
  Ziegler based on Lorenz
  Janscha, 1798.

2 Christian Gottlob Neefe,
  unsigned painting.

3 Engraving by Johann
Neidl, after a drawing
of Beethoven by
Gandolph Ernst
Stainhauser von
Treuberg of 1800
(Vienna: Giovanni
Cappi, 1801).

4 Vienna: Graben,
towards Kohlmarkt.
Coloured engraving by
C. Schütz. Around
1800 Beethoven lived
nearby in the Tiefer
Graben.

5 Autograph score of the Third Piano
Concerto in C Minor op. 37, first
movement, last bars of the development.
This heavily revived MS shows two
main layers of writing, in brown and
black ink. (Staatsbibliothek Preussischer
Kulturbesitz, Berlin, Beethoven mus.
autogr. 14, fol. 36ʳ).

6 Ludwig van Beethoven, 1803. Miniature
on ivory by Christian Hornemann.

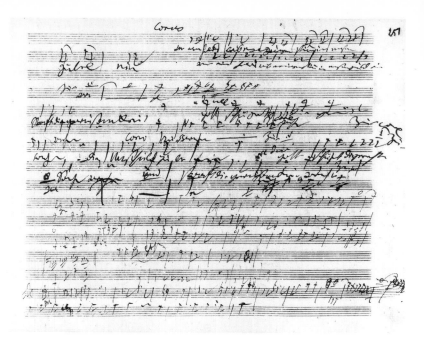

7 A page from the Mendelssohn 15 Sketchbook containing sketches for the finale of the last act of *Fidelio* in the 1805 version, now no. 18. Beethoven wrote 'Corus' at the top, and continued with the text 'Wer ein holdes Weib errungen . . .' drawn from Schiller's *An die Freude*, lines that also appear in the finale of the Ninth Symphony. The first two entries on the sketchleaf are transcribed by Nottebohm, *Zweite Beethoveniana*, p. 445. (Staatsbibliothek Preussischer Kulturbesitz, Musikabteilung, Berlin, Mus. ms. autogr. Mendlessohn-Stiftung 15, p. 251).

8 The Palais Kinsky in Vienna, an der Freyung. Drawing by Salomon Kleiner.

The compositional origins of the C minor Concerto reach back to Beethoven's journey to Berlin in 1796, when he made the notation 'To the Concerto in C minor kettledrum at the cadenza'. As Küthen has observed, the timpani motif has a military flavour that harks back to Mozart's example;[17] in Beethoven's hands this motif becomes an important compositional element throughout the opening *Allegro con brio*. He may have originally intended to play this concerto at his benefit concert on 2 April 1800, but the piece seems not to have been completed in time; Beethoven probably performed a revised version of the older C major Concerto op. 15. The C minor Concerto was apparently played for the first time on 5 April 1803, with Beethoven as soloist, but aspects of the basic conception considerably predate the completion of the autograph score.

The date on the autograph manuscript of the concerto (Staatsbibliothek Preussischer Kulturbesitz, Berlin, Beethoven ms. autogr. 14) has been disputed. Leon Plantinga has read the last digit of the apparent entry '1800' as a '3' turned on its side, and has argued consequently for a later chronology for the work.[18] The thoroughgoing compositional changes in the score, however, lend more support to the older view that the concerto was revised after an interval. As with previous works in this genre, Beethoven subjects his own style to incisive critique of a kind that might imply a temporal gap, though no proof may be forthcoming on this matter. The solo part was left in an unfinished state in the autograph. The earlier layer of writing in the score, in brown ink, shows the rondo theme of the finale with syncopated chords in the left hand in place of the melodic accents of the finished work; the sixteenth-note figuration in the left hand was not originally part of Beethoven's conception at all. In other passages, such as the end of the development in the first movement, shown in Plate 5, Beethoven's revisions suppress gestures of an excessively showy pianistic virtuosity in favour of a more organic and logical development of the musical material. His revisions to the wind parts in the upper systems were entered in the older, brown ink, whereas his reworking of the solo piano part was made in darker ink. He originally notated a long rising chromatic scale in the piano, beginning one bar before the excerpt shown in Plate 5 and extending to the measured trill on high G and F♯ in the second bar.

Beethoven's seminal notion of highlighting the kettledrum in the first movement is noteworthy in view of his later practice, in several important orchestral works, of exposing an important motif in the timpani. One thinks of the opening drum taps in the Violin Concerto, or the transition to the

---

[17] *Ludwig van Beethoven. Klavierkonzert Nr. 3 in c, op. 37*, preface, p. v.

[18] Cf. Johnson, *Beethoven's Early Sketches*, pp. 389–93, and Plantinga, 'When Did Beethoven Compose His Third Piano Concerto?'; Plantinga argues that the main work on the concerto began only in 1802.

finale in the Fifth Symphony, not to mention the prominent timpani in the finale of the Seventh Symphony or in the scherzo of the Ninth. In the C minor Concerto the drum passage takes on a mysterious intensity in association with the solo cadenza, which Beethoven may have finalized as late as 1809. He strips away much of the thematic material and the orchestral texture here to isolate the dotted rhythm on tonic and dominant in the timpani, delaying the imminent cadence and redefining at one stroke the customary relationship between solo and tutti at this point in the form.

The end of the cadenza had already taken an extraordinary turn. Some moments before, the pre-cadential trill on the supertonic, D, was prolonged in the right hand without being resolved (Ex. 18). Against this trill, a rising chromatic scale in the left hand merges into a simultaneous trill on B, the leading-note. Beethoven extends the double trill for six bars, while the motif

Ex. 18 Piano Concerto no. 3 op. 37/I, bars 469–82

from the second bar of the opening theme is played in imitation above and below the trill on the harmony of the dominant seventh. Then G joins the trill, and the entire dominant triad is set ablaze through this unmeasured pulsation. The A♭–G semitone at the top of this multiple trill is derived from the last two notes of the thematic fragment heard one bar before. The triple trill was a speciality of Beethoven's piano playing: it also appears in the longest of the three cadenzas to the C major Concerto, near the conclusion of the virtuoso piano sonata in this key, op. 2 no. 3, and in the cadenza preceding the recapitulatory variation in the last movement of the final sonata, op. 111. Here, in op. 37, the 'Beethoven' trill stabilizes into a triple appoggiatura chord whose A♭ harmony resolves onto the dominant triad; a series of repetitions and sequences of this figure leads once again to the dominant-seventh chord with a trill on the supertonic.

The entire passage has been poised at the threshold of the expected cadence and represents an immense internal expansion within the structural framework of the concerto cadenza. But now Beethoven again avoids resolution with an even more impressive effect. For the trill on the supertonic does not resolve to C; instead, it *ascends* chromatically, reaching not the tonic triad of C minor but an unstable seventh chord. This is the moment Beethoven may have imagined as early as 1796, 'the kettledrum at the cadenza'. The drum taps out the third to fourth bars of the opening theme four times in all, accompanied softly by the strings and answered by figuration in the piano outlining diminished harmonies. The passage is *pianissimo* and still suspended tonally, since the tonic cadence has not yet been affirmed.

Beethoven's treatment of his opening theme in the cadenza as a whole displays a vast architectural logic. After the opening 'lead-in' and canonic imitations on the head of the theme, he dwells at length on the rising third from its first bar, as brilliant arpeggiations carry the music into distant tonal regions. Much later, near the conclusion of the cadenza, Beethoven resumes this thread, developing the second bar of the theme in the passage with the double trill, as we have seen. What remains is the tail of the theme—the last two bars with their characteristic dotted rhythm. This is what Beethoven gives to the timpani, while wrapping the motif in an uncanny veil of harmonic ambiguity. A guiding idea of the cadenza is thus the successive treatment of the three component parts of the main theme, culminating in the mysterious drum passage. Strictly considered, the cadenza embraces not only the solo but also the timpani statements, and ends only with the long-delayed C minor cadence in the last bar of the example, where a new dialogue between the piano and strings leads to the terse close of the movement.

The climax of Beethoven's cadenza at the triple trill with A♭ as highest note foreshadows a relationship of surpassing importance in the movements to come. The slow movement is a reflective *Largo*, whose expressive contrast to the pathos of the outer movements is heightened by Beethoven's choice of E major as the tonic key. Consequently, the first and third degrees of the new tonic, E and G♯, are raised a semitone above the triadic degrees of C minor; this relationship contributes, along with many details of texture and orchestration, to the magical shift to a brighter tonal colour that sets the *Largo* apart from the framing movements. That very contrast, in turn, poses a challenge to the finale, whose task it becomes to integrate the luminescent, lyrical E major sphere with the darker C minor idiom.

Only in this light can we understand the E major chord with G♯ as highest note that is played in the full orchestra to close the *Largo* (Ex. 19). The dynamic emphasis on this *fortissimo* chord, in conjunction with its weak rhythmic position, makes it into the most disruptive element in the movement—so disruptive, in fact, that conductors need to take care not to overemphasize the sudden increase in volume or the detached articulation of the sonority. The unstable, unfitting chord sets up the ensuing rondo finale, the main theme of which provides a tonal pivot from E major into the tonic of the work as a whole, C minor. The pivotal sound is, of course, the reinterpretation of G♯ as A♭, and the motif that accomplishes the transition is built into the rondo theme as its most conspicuous melodic element: the emphasis on the semitone G–A♭ at the beginning is re-emphasized by the rising scale in bars 4–5. This striking melodic feature of the rondo theme will eventually be resolved in the coda. But long before that, Beethoven seizes the opportunity to recall the slow movement within the central episode of the rondo, a procedure comparable to (though more complex than) that in the finale of the *Sonate Pathétique*.

As in the *Pathétique*, Beethoven begins the middle episode with a more placid section in A♭ major employing variation; in the concerto the theme is marked *espressivo* and *dolce*, and offers a medium for lyrical exchange between the clarinet and solo piano. What ensues is an orchestral fugato based on the main subject; this developmental section converges onto the dominant of C minor with strong reinforcement from the trumpets and timpani. Beethoven now reduces the content of the music to two bars of bare octave Gs followed by reiterated octaves on A♭: the music now re-examines the figure that had launched the rondo finale and was so conspicuous in its main theme—the semitone G–A♭, which is made gigantic—and the dramatization of this motif in the tutti sets the stage for a fundamental reinterpretation by the piano soloist (Ex. 20).

For the soloist *withdraws* here into the tranquillity of the slow movement. Its first bars receive the A♭ octaves from the orchestra with a descrescendo; the next two have softened to *pianissimo*, and take on a liquidity of sound indicated by Beethoven's pedal marking, corresponding to the slow movement. Beethoven does not indicate that the pedal be lifted two bars later, when the miracle occurs: the hands of the pianist are now resting over the precise spacing of the beginning of the *Largo*, and the most crucial aspect of interpretation here is to convey in sound the enharmonic shift of Ab into G# as the E octave emerges in the bass. Unfortunately, even the best available editions suggest a change of pedal at this point; convincing performances are rare

Ex. 19 Piano Concerto no. 3 op. 37/II–III

Ex. 19 *cont.*

because of lack of comprehension of the full import of the passage. A 'clear' performance of the change in harmony is not to the point here, and only betrays a lack of poetic sensibility. Essential, on the other hand, is the veiled effect of the softening A♭s, the sound of which is enveloped in pedal and then gradually mixed with the E octave in the left hand. This quiet sound represents the *a priori* condition of the slow movement, a tonal space not yet filled

Ex. 20 Piano Concerto no. 3 op. 37/III, bars 252–70

out. Moments later, a new transparent variant of the rondo theme is heard in the piano, *pianissimo* in E major; it is accompanied delicately in the strings but soon tails off into hushed legato phrases converging onto a quiet unison E in the violins. This is a vision of the slow movement seen through the veil of the rondo theme itself, and it shows how capable Beethoven is of such allusion even in the absence of direct thematic recall. In turn, this ethereal episode admirably prepares the ensuing transition to C minor for the following statement of the rondo theme in its original form, which takes on in this context the quality of a return to reality after the dream-like aura of the E major episode.

One more phase remains: the final resolution of the crucial Ab as G#, this time not in E major but in the major mode of the tonic, C. Beethoven's solo cadenza before the coda meaningfully recaptures and reinterprets the rising figuration that previously led to various statements of the rondo theme: the tempo gradually slows to *adagio*, the dynamic level thins to *pianissimo*. The piano pauses on G in the same register as the beginning of the rondo. The last transformation comes as G# is carried upwards to A in the C major *Presto*, and the coda revels in the resolution of A to the keynote C, both ascending and descending. The expressive atmosphere of the coda is unmistakably that of the *opera buffa* finale; comic wit and jubilation crown the dénouement of this drama in tones.

*   *   *

The years spanning the intended performance and eventual completion of the C minor Concerto, 1800 to 1803, were especially fruitful for Beethoven; in 1802 in particular his productivity was awesome. As usual, a considerable number of his pathbreaking works were for piano solo or were duo sonatas with piano. The hastily written Sonata for Piano and Horn op. 17, from April 1800, is rather lightweight, but Beethoven was quite proud of the big Piano Sonata in Bb major op. 22, from the end of that year, claiming that the sonata 'hat sich gewaschen'—that it had turned out splendidly. In 1801 he finished two impressive violin sonatas: a terse, concentrated work in A minor, op. 23, and the lyrically expansive 'Spring' Sonata in F major op. 24. Beethoven conceived these sonatas as a contrasting pair and originally planned to have them appear under the single opus number 23. Two years earlier he had paired together the two charming piano sonatas in E major and G major as op. 14, but the violin sonatas offer the first notable instance of Beethoven's juxtaposition of drastically opposing characteristics in a pair of works in the same genre, one in the major and one in the minor. Later examples include the *Waldstein* and *Appassionata* Sonatas, and the Fifth and Sixth Symphonies.

Another genre that occupied Beethoven at this time was the string quintet. Already in 1795–6 he had arranged and revised his then unpublished Octet for Winds as the String Quintet op. 4, as we have seen. In 1801 he composed the attractive C major String Quintet op. 29, a work whose unexpected and faulty publication by Artaria the following year led to bitter accusations of piracy from the composer and to a confused and messy lawsuit. To the irascible composer, Artaria & Co. were 'rascals', guilty of the '*biggest swindle* in the world'; yet Artaria was exonerated by the court, which requested in vain a retraction of Beethoven's accusations against the firm. Beethoven's only other original work for the string quintet medium was to be the Fugue in D major from 1817, published posthumously as op. 137, although he made sketches for another string quintet in C on his deathbed.

A series of piano sonatas completed by Beethoven in 1801 and 1802 shows a variety of innovative approaches to the genre and, specifically, to the problem of welding successive movements into a unified continuity. The Sonata in A♭ op. 26 begins with a variation movement (as had Mozart's A major Sonata K331) and dispenses entirely with movements in sonata form, whereas the two works of op. 27 are each specifically described by Beethoven as 'Sonata quasi una fantasia'. The popular C♯ minor Sonata op. 27 no. 2 is one of Beethoven's few works in which the finale is of unremittingly tragic character; the title 'Moonlight', invented by the poet and critic Ludwig Rellstab, is quite inappropriate. The sonata is dedicated to Countess Giulietta Guicciardi, who was incorrectly regarded in the nineteenth century as the likely recipient of Beethoven's letter to the 'Immortal Beloved'. In light of this, the opening slow movement was sometimes misconstrued as a kind of love-song without words. No other sonata by Beethoven has been so abused as kitsch; sentimental images of lovers adrift on a moonlit lake have clung to the opening *Adagio sostenuto*. Much more suggestive and true to the music is Franz Liszt's description of the middle movement as 'a flower between two abysses'.

A central idea of this sonata concerns the transformation of the gently ascending arpeggios of the *Adagio sostenuto* in the *Presto agitato* finale, where surging arpeggios lead to emphatic syncopated chords in the highest register, supported by a descending bass progression similar to that at the beginning of the first movement. The second subject of the finale also recalls the principal theme of the opening movement in its use of dotted rhythms, while still other passages of the finale, such as the end of the development and the elaborate cadenza in the coda, bear marked thematic and textural similarities to the *Adagio sostenuto*. The middle movement, a minuet and trio in D♭ major, represents a kind of interlude that connects the almost static opening movement with the rapid, agitated finale. Some 25 years later, in his great String Quartet op. 131 in the same key, Beethoven returned to this conception of a series of interconnected movements leading, in the finale, to a fully developed sonata form; and in op. 131, as in op. 27 no. 2, the clear return of thematic material from the opening movement helps to confirm the role of the finale as a culmination to the entire work.

The next piano sonata, op. 28 in D major ('Pastoral'), and each of the three violin sonatas of op. 30 are highly individual and polished works. The title 'Pastoral' is not unfitting for op. 28: one can find pedal points in the first and last movements and occasional bagpipe fifths, whereas the cadential theme in the first movement, internal episode of the slow movement, and scherzo are all rustic in character. The *Andante* in D minor has a processional, ballade-like atmosphere: the melodic inflections of its main theme seem suggestive of speech. In the coda Beethoven juxtaposes the first phrases of the main theme with a disturbing, dissonant transformation of the innocent contrasting subject—a glimpse of the abyss, followed by a close in bleak resignation. In the other movements of op. 28, Beethoven often employs static textures with repetitive figures, yet the development of the opening *Allegro* is dominated even more than usual by a process of foreshortening. Appropriately, this developmental passage is set apart from its context: the music comes firmly to rest on a protracted F♯ major harmony before phrases drawn from the cadential theme are played in B major and minor to preface the recapitulation. Beethoven used an identical modulation through the submediant to introduce the climactic ninth variation of the 'Joy' theme in the choral finale of the Ninth Symphony.

The C minor Violin Sonata op. 30 no. 2 is perhaps the most powerful of Beethoven's works in this key up to 1802; one of its many inspired ideas is the terse rhythmic motif linked to a German augmented sixth harmony that begins the finale. The G major Violin Sonata op. 30 no. 3, on the other hand, is one of his wittiest contributions to the high comic style forged by Haydn, and its finale is a worthy successor to the humorous rondo finales in the D major Violin Sonata op. 12 no. 1 (with its clownish main theme) and the G major Piano Sonata op. 14 no. 2 (marked 'Scherzo'). This *Allegro vivace* is studded with appearances of the flowing contrapuntal theme in contrasting keys: we hear a robust version in C major, a gentle 'false' return in B major, and yet another statement of the rondo theme in E♭ major preceding the coda. At the close Beethoven heightens the humour by deriving a string of syncopated accents in the deepest bass register from the rustic trills of the original subject.

Impressive as they are, these sonatas may be regarded as works of consolidation. Beethoven's innovative tendencies surface more clearly in the three piano sonatas of op. 31, also from 1802. These three sonatas, in G major, D minor, and E♭ major, are notable landmarks along Beethoven's so-called 'new path', boldly exploring artistic territory that he soon consolidated in the *Eroica* Symphony.

An aggressively original thrust emerges at the beginning of the G major Sonata op. 31 no. 1. The initial gestures are syncopated; the two hands seem unable to play together. Swift falling passagework yields to repeated tonic chords that reach the dominant at the end of the first phrase. Then, surprisingly, Beethoven shifts the following phrase down a whole step into F major. Such treatment of the nearer keys 'as if they were mere local chords', in Donald Francis Tovey's words,[19] expands the tonal and dramatic range of the

---

[19] *A Companion to Beethoven's Piano Sonatas*, p. 115.

music. Beethoven introduced similar harmonic departures at the outset of his *Waldstein* and *Appassionata* sonatas. Both of the other op. 31 sonatas, in D minor and E♭ major, also begin with striking harmonic ambiguities and tensions—a hallmark of his innovative approach.

Unlike these pieces, the G major Sonata proceeds with an air of paradox and comedy, with a touch of the bizarre that is no longer Haydnesque but distinctively Beethovenian. As Brendel writes, 'the character that emerges is one of compulsive, but scatterbrained, determination'.[20] Such a work cannot be taken at face value, but solemn commentators who would deny humorous possibilities to music have maligned op. 31 no. 1 as inferior and slipshod.[21] A key to understanding the opening *Allegro vivace* lies in Beethoven's ironic attitude to the unbalanced, somewhat commonplace nature of his basic material: what unfolds in the development with startling vehemence later dissolves into coyish, understated accents in the coda, where a new point emerges in the business at hand. In these last moments of the *Allegro vivace*, Beethoven introduces a turn-figure foreshadowing the head motif of the rondo finale, while he correspondingly recalls the opening movement in the last moments of the rondo, thereby casting unifying threads across the piece as a whole.

The second movement, *Adagio grazioso*, displays an atmosphere of operatic elegance slightly overdone. The trills and ornate decorations, the serenade-like flavour, and the exaggerated rhetoric convey a hint of sophisticated mockery. In the following rondo finale, Beethoven's ingenious demands on the musical tradition take yet another form. He renders the expected repetitions of the main theme in the rondo design unpredictable through variations in texture and rhythmic intensification, but reserves the most extraordinary events for the coda. Here, once more, he sees through, and beyond, the surface of his thematic material, exposing an underlying substratum of musical meaning. First, the head of the rondo theme is broken off into silence; the ensuing phrase is then broadened into an *Adagio*. Beethoven extends the series of interrupted phrases without allowing the music to close in the tonic, building suspense (Ex. 21). He then plunges into an exciting *Presto* coda, with the thematic turn emancipated from its earlier context. Beethoven caps his sonata by allowing the rapid turn-figure to migrate into the low bass register, as sharp repeated rhythms recalled from the opening movement dissipate into a paradoxical close of soft chords and pregnant silences.

The Sonata op. 31 no. 2, the so-called 'Tempest', is Beethoven's only sonata in the key of D minor. A chief innovation of this work is its use of an opening theme that embraces two diametrically opposed tempos and characters: a hovering, ambiguous unfolding of dominant arpeggios in first inversion, marked *largo*; and a turbulent continuation stressing a rising bass and expres-

---

[20] *Music Sounded Out*, p. 28.
[21] See, for instance, Blom, *Beethoven's Pianoforte Sonatas Discussed*, pp. 125–6.

Ex. 21 Piano Sonata op. 31 no. 1/III, bars 219–48

sive two-note sigh figures or appoggiaturas, marked *allegro*. The harmonically ambiguous opening allows Beethoven to delay the first strong cadence in D minor until the beginning of the apparent transition, where the initially suspended, arpeggiated motif is incarnated in the driven, propulsive *Allegro* (Ex. 22). The long series of ascending sequences in the bass is balanced against expressive gestures in the treble, creating a dramatic dialogue. From a variant of this passage Beethoven derives much of the development section, leading towards the climax of the movement at the beginning of the recapitulation. Here the mysterious arpeggios return, a kind of temporal oasis removed from the strife of the *Allegro*, and their expressive implications are now made explicit through passages of unaccompanied recitative.

This recitative was the passage that influenced Beethoven, consciously or unconsciously, when he conceived the famous baritone recitative 'O Freunde, nicht diese Töne!' in the choral finale of the Ninth Symphony, also in D minor. The thematic similarity amounts almost to quotation, and the analogous expressive function of the two recitative passages invites close compari-

Ex. 22 Piano Sonata op. 31 no. 2/I

(a) opening   (b) bars 21-2

(c) recapitulation, bars 142-8

son.[22] In a sense, Beethoven seized on and exploited this moment of inter-nalization and reflection as embodied in the gesture of recitative in the sonata to provide a gateway to the utopian plane of the *Ode to Joy* as the basis for the choral finale of the Ninth.

The ensuing *Adagio* in the 'Tempest' Sonata transforms elements from the first movement in a brighter, warmer context: the opening arpeggio now rests on the stable tonic sonority of Bb major, and the following, double-dotted motifs in the high register are reminiscent of the recitative. The broadly lyri-cal periods of this *Adagio* are linked by mysterious drum-rolls in the bass. The close of the movement exposes this registral gap in the most striking way, as a final, cadential version of the high motif is answered by a single Bb in the cavernous low register. In the *Allegretto* finale, in D minor, Beethoven devel-ops the arpeggiated chords throughout, as an all-encompassing, *perpetuum mobile* rhythm sweeps away the rhetoric of dialogue characteristic of the pre-ceding movements. Intimate, speech-like accents are left behind here. As Jürgen Uhde pointed out, the temporal drive of this finale opens a new and strangely distanced dimension, suggestive not of spontaneous human expres-sion but of engagement with objective phenomena beyond our control.[23]

Even more than the D minor Sonata, the opening of op. 31 no. 3 in Eb major sounds like a continuation of music that had already begun. Its initial 'call' figures have no stable harmonic support; Beethoven's characteristic

[22] Certain aspects of this relationship are noted by Kolodin in *The Interior Beethoven*, pp. 128–30.
[23] *Beethovens Klaviermusik*, iii, pp. 78–9.

device of rhythmic acceleration, together with asymmetrical phrasing and a fluctuation in tempo, all lend tension to the gracious opening theme. The initial impression of holding back, of hesitation, stands as complementary to the irrepressible rhythmic energy characteristic of this sonata as a whole. When the opening theme of this *Allegro* closes, it sets into operation a steady eighth-note motion; later, in the second theme, the figuration is rendered in still faster sixteenth-notes. The comic atmosphere of these passages is heightened in the development, when a prominent motif derived from the main theme is reiterated with amusing insistence in the bass.

Particularly innovative is the following *Allegretto vivace* in A♭ major, labelled 'Scherzo' by Beethoven. It is a typical scherzo neither in its metre (2/4) nor in its form, a sonata design without a trio. The defining quality, of course, lies in its general character of humorous wit and rhythmic verve. As in the first movement, a meaningful hesitation is built into the opening. After the initial phrases, a hushed, unharmonized staccato continuation reaches C and then D♭, before Beethoven reinterprets this pitch as part of the dominant seventh of A♭ major. Later, after repetition of both the opening theme and the quiet deflection to C, Beethoven replaces the move to D♭ with jarring, almost explosive *fortissimo* chords, decisively carrying the music away from the tonic. By contrast, the ensuing closing theme of the exposition is delicately transparent, staccato, and *pianissimo*.

The development unfolds around appearances of the main theme in new keys—F major and C major. Beethoven extends the C major statement melodically to lead to D♭, and in the following passage forges the climax of the whole scherzo. D♭ is stressed in all the pitch registers, and the supporting diminished-seventh harmony is altered to a dominant seventh as Beethoven 'composes out' an enormous linear descent from the highest D♭ to the lowest A♭ marking the beginning of the recapitulation (Ex. 23). But the D♭, we recall, is not new: Beethoven's curious dwelling on this pitch at the outset, and his brilliant stroke of placing the *fortissimo* eruption in the recapitulation on D♭, can only be fully appreciated if the climax of the development has made its mark. Here, as elsewhere, Beethoven's treatment of dissonant sonorities is discriminate but potent and far-reaching: the tension of the climax on D♭ overflows, as it were, into a network of related passages.

The third movement, a minuet with trio, is the focus of lyricism in the sonata. A darker, mysterious dimension surfaces through a persistent emphasis on C♭, the lowered sixth degree in E♭ major. In the second half of the minuet this sensitive pitch occurs twice, but in the middle of the trio it appears no fewer than seven times, as part of a diminished-ninth chord on the dominant. For a few moments the music is frozen on this static dissonance, before the graceful melodic character is re-established. In the coda Beethoven recalls these darker inflections, casting shadows over the *pianissimo* conclusion.

Ex. 23 Piano Sonata op. 31 no. 3/II, bars 97–107

In the finale Beethoven recaptures with a vengeance the comic, grotesque, even parodistic tone of the opening movements of this sonata and of the G major Sonata. There is something almost mechanical about the opening figuration, which sets in motion a tarantella rhythm that dominates the wide expanses of this sonata form. Like the finale of the *Tempest* Sonata, this *Presto con fuoco* is practically a *perpetuum mobile*, but Beethoven takes special care to hold back the momentum in the last few bars: twice the music halts on *fortissimo* arpeggiated diminished-seventh chords, before he reinterprets the jocular opening motif as a series of rising sequences leading to the powerful full close.

Immediately after completing the op. 31 sonatas Beethoven wrote his first big sets of piano variations on original themes: the Six Variations in F op. 34, and the Fifteen Variations and Fugue in E♭ op. 35. In his often-cited letter from October 1802, whose background we have considered above, Beethoven described them as having been written in 'quite a new style and each in an entirely different way'.[24] Both works introduce features that overcome the basically static and additive nature of Classical variation technique. The tonal plan of op. 34, for example, is unusual and wide-ranging. The successive variations do not remain in the expected tonic but appear in keys forming a chain of descending thirds, leading from the tonic, F major, through D major, B♭ major, G major, E♭ major, and C minor; a short extension to the fifth variation elaborates the dominant seventh on C, preparing the F major cadence at the beginning of the final variation, which closes the circle of falling thirds. This variation reminds us of the original theme in more compelling terms than the intervening ones (highly individualized and marked by strong contrasts, with frequent changes of metre); the set concludes with an ornately decorated reprise of the theme, marked *Adagio molto*.

The op. 35 Variations represent a larger and even more original conception

[24] Anderson, L. 62.

than op. 34 and assume a special significance by serving as a model for the finale of the *Eroica* Symphony, the seminal movement of that great work, as Lewis Lockwood has shown.[25] In op. 35, as in the *Eroica* finale, the bass of the theme is presented first alone and then in a series of introductory variations, with two, three, and four voices. The subsequent appearance of the actual theme, together with its bass, thus represents in a sense the fourth variation, but Beethoven's numbering begins only after this statement of the composite theme. (In its fully harmonized form the theme was used earlier as the seventh of the Contredances for Orchestra WoO 14 and in the *Prometheus* ballet op. 43.) Opening with the *basso del tema* enables Beethoven to emphasize its comic aspects, particularly the three *fortissimo* B♭ octaves in its second half, which are surrounded by rests, creating a humour of expressive silences. In the ninth and especially the thirteenth variations, this stress on B♭ is developed as a pedal throughout the first half, with amusing effect. The *Minore*, the 14th variation, and *Maggiore*, the 15th—a majestic, decorated *Largo*—represent a new section in the overall formal progression, which culminates in the powerful fugal finale. In its structural grandeur and comprehensive range of expression this set anticipates the greatest of Beethoven's works in this genre, the 33 Variations on a Waltz by Diabelli op. 120.

In a relatively short period Beethoven had completed the six sonatas of opp. 30 and 31 and the variations of opp. 34 and 35, in addition to several other pieces; he capped his work of 1802 with the Second Symphony in D major op. 36. In this symphony, especially in its outer movements, Beethoven brought the full scope of his imagination to bear on the orchestral genre for the first time. A link with the legacy of Haydn and Mozart is still tangible, to be sure: certain features of the slow introduction to the first movement are reminiscent of Mozart's 'Prague' Symphony in the same key K504, whereas the coda of the finale has Haydnesque touches. Unlike the famous off-tonic opening of the First Symphony, Beethoven begins here with a deep unison D sounded across all the pitch registers. The unison figure is analogous to the opening of Mozart's symphony, yet more forceful, since Beethoven begins not on the downbeat but with a thirty-second-note upbeat to the sustained unison, and marks the gesture *fortissimo*. Such upbeats are characteristic of his dynamically propulsive style, of which this movement is a particularly telling example.

The contrast between forceful unison octaves and more intimate, lyrical, harmonized phrases is a *topos* to which Mozart gave unforgettable expression; the beginning of the C minor Piano Sonata K457 must have particularly impressed Beethoven in this respect. Beethoven's own development of this *topos* in the first movement of op. 36 is brilliant, because it discloses a remote and almost forbidding character lurking behind the playful action and high

---

[25] Cf. 'The Compositional Genesis of the Eroica Finale', esp. pp. 84–5.

spirits of the *Allegro con brio* and thereby lends much dramatic weight to the whole. Haydn frequently deepens the character of his symphonic allegro movements through a slow introduction, but nowhere in his symphonies do the expressive implications of an introduction impress themselves so powerfully on the following *Allegro* as in Beethoven's D major Symphony.

Crucial to Beethoven's conception is the association of the stark, unharmonized unison gesture with the minor mode of D. The opening phrases of the *Adagio molto* employ this gesture to preface a pair of lyrical antecedent and consequent phrases in the wind and strings, respectively. Much else happens in the introduction, whose elaborate orchestral textures again invite comparison with Mozart's 'Prague' Symphony. But the climax and turning-point of the entire introduction comes as Beethoven reaffirms and develops the unison gesture, with its double-dotted upbeat rhythm, as the music plunges into D minor. He enlarges the seminal rhythmic motif to form a broad, imposing arpeggiation that comes to rest on the dominant pedal, which is sustained in turn over the next ten bars, up to the beginning of the *Allegro con brio* (Ex. 24).

This is one of the moments in Beethoven's earlier music that reminds us forcefully of the Ninth Symphony. The main theme of the later work's first movement, in all its stark grandeur, is implicit in the dark undercurrent in the first movement of this early symphony in the major mode of D. For the *fortissimo* outburst in the slow introduction is by no means an isolated gesture. The second subject-group is fashioned so as to absorb the conflict exposed in the slow introduction, and the triumphant character of the movement as a whole, culminating in the chorale-like climax of the coda, is balanced against this large-scale tension. The second subject is a march-like theme employing a rising arpeggio and double-dotted rhythm. As in op. 2 no. 2, its development brings an increase in excitement, leading to a crisis that disrupts the organic musical development and opens a void that is filled by opposing forces. The *fortissimo* gesture from the slow introduction, now harmonized, punctuates the passage that prepares an expected cadence in the dominant at bar 100, but Beethoven breaks off the cadence deceptively, and silence ensues (Ex. 25).

This rip in the form is filled by an interpolated passage. The turn-figure from the main theme is recalled *pianissimo* in a series of rising sequences, reaching the cadence in the dominant in bar 112. Then comes one of those brilliant strokes that so utterly demolish the conventional gentility of courtly manners, transforming the very notion of sectional closure in this style. For as the music moves toward a further, necessary cadential articulation, Beethoven restates, in slightly varied form, the entire arpeggiated climax in D minor from the slow introduction, complete with the ensuing dominant pedal on A in the horns. The gesture is repeated, and the pedal derived from it resounds through the closing moments of the exposition.

Ex. 24 Second Symphony op. 36/I, bars 23–47

Ex. 24 *cont.*

Ex. 25 Second Symphony op. 36/I, bars 96–105

The intense energy from this thematic and modal conflict infuses the following cadential passages based on syncopated augmentation of the turn-figure from the main theme; it also generates the scintillating arpeggiation of A major in the wind that is mirrored in rhythmic diminution in the strings across all the pitch registers. The excitement of passages like these was new to music, and it points toward some of the most intoxicated moments in the third *Leonore* Overture and the finales of the Fifth and Seventh symphonies. Yet, in all these cases, the impression of unbridled power is inextricably linked with conflict, or set into relief through powerful contrasts. Genuine triumph cannot be easily won.

Some early critics had difficulty with the Second Symphony, preferring the milder manners of the First. Exasperated denunciation of the music as bizarre, confused, or incomprehensible was directed especially at the finale, an *Allegro molto* in sonata form. The style is clearly Haydnesque, but it is even more audaciously impertinent than Haydn would have allowed. Immediately provocative is the opening theme, with its huge gap of one and a half octaves between the upbeat semitone F#–G and the following trill figure on C#. Only in the massive coda, however, are the full implications of this startling gesture realized. The semitone figure rises chromatically to C, as a chain of turns and trills around this pitch releases an almost frightening energy in *fortissimo* outbursts for the full orchestra. Earlier, a surprising dramatic bluster had surfaced, only to be incorporated paradoxically into the comic character of the movement as a whole. The *Allegro molto* of Beethoven's Second Symphony is a heightened comedy, capable of absorbing disruptive elements and even an excessiveness bordering on the absurd. This is the comedy of the sublime.

4

The Heroic Style I

1803–1806

EIGHTEEN hundred and three was the main year of composition of the *Eroica* Symphony, the centrepiece of the great stylistic transition that emerged out of Beethoven's personal and artistic crisis of 1802, a crisis precipitated above all by his incurable loss of hearing. In the Third Symphony Beethoven's 'new path' ascended to a lofty summit with a commanding position in the history of the symphonic genre. The historical and biographical terrain surrounding the *Eroica* has not yet been exhaustively explored, despite the fame and irresistible fascination of Beethoven's intended dedication of the work to Napoleon Bonaparte and his angry destruction of that dedication after Napoleon had himself crowned emperor. It is a commonplace of criticism that the *Eroica* inaugurates or consolidates Beethoven's 'heroic' style. In approaching the symphony, however, we should reconsider some of the familiar but questionable assumptions that have linked the work with heroism of the Napoleonic variety. Beethoven's attitude towards Bonaparte was ambivalent, but he contemplated a possible move to Paris around this time, and he might have had some entirely pragmatic reasons for dedicating the symphony to the French leader—reasons that vanished when he remained in Vienna. The deepest importance of the *Eroica* in Beethoven's creative development may lie in its symbolic or mythic qualities, which shape not only the individual movements but also their relationship to one another. This work is neither simply a homage to Bonaparte nor a 'programmatic' symphony in the conventional manner, whereby the music follows a literal narrative sequence. The continuity between movements in the *Eroica* is sufficiently compelling to force us to give it critical recognition. But what really counts here is not the imposition of associations from outside the work, but rather the recognition that the music itself embodies these associations in its structure, rhythmic movement, orchestration, and character. For want of a better formulation, we may refer to this phenomenon as an intrinsically musical narrative.

The explication of these relationships demands detailed musical analysis. But the biographical context is intriguing as well. The *Heiligenstadt Testament*, in particular, deserves renewed attention in relation to the symbolism of the *Eroica*. Solomon has offered an insightful analysis of Beethoven's testament, shrewdly observing that 'this neatly written document is a carefully revised "fair copy" which has been scrubbed clean of much of its original emotion'. Solomon argues that

one remains unpersuaded by the references to suicide: 'I would have ended my life— it was only *my* art that held me back'; 'Thanks to [virtue] and to my art, I did not end my life by suicide.' It is as though Beethoven were being deliberately laconic in order to avoid reviving distressful feelings.[1]

This histrionic element, suggesting the symbolic enactment of the artist's own death in order that he might start anew—in short, the notion of a 'rebirth'— is also implied by Beethoven's references from about this time to a 'new path' or 'a completely new manner' in reference to his art. More evidence comes from the oratorio *Christus am Oelberge* op. 85 that Beethoven wrote in late 1802 and early 1803 and which served as the final work at his concert of 5 April 1803. As Alan Tyson and Barry Cooper have pointed out, the libretto has much in common with the *Heiligenstadt Testament*, concerning ideas of undeserved suffering, intense struggle, terror, imminent death, love of mankind, and eventual triumph over adversity.[2]

Further indications of Beethoven's psychological realignment at around this time come from the immediate background of the *Eroica* Symphony. Its genesis is bound up with the now obscure ballet music to *Die Geschöpfe des Prometheus* ('The Creatures of Prometheus') op. 43, written by Beethoven in collaboration with the dance master Salvatore Viganò. The *Prometheus* music was Beethoven's first major work for the stage and one of his earliest public successes, with more than 20 performances given at Vienna during 1801 and 1802. After the initial run, the choreography was lost. There have been practically no attempts to revive the ballet; concert performances of the music are rare. According to an anecdote preserved by Alois Fuchs, Haydn is supposed to have told Beethoven in 1801 that 'I heard your ballet yesterday and it pleased me very much!', whereupon Beethoven replied: 'O, dear Papa, you are very kind; but it is far from being a *Creation!*' Surprised and almost offended,

---

[1] *Beethoven*, pp. 118–19. Canisius argues that some passages of the *Heiligenstadt Testament* paraphrase Goethe's *The Sorrows of Young Werther* (*Beethoven*, pp. 158–64).

[2] Cf. Tyson, 'Beethoven's Heroic Phase', p. 140; Cooper, *Beethoven and the Creative Process*, p. 48.

Haydn retorted: 'That is true; it is not yet a *Creation* and I can scarcely believe that it will ever become one'.[3] This story seems entirely characteristic and credible; it once again illustrates Beethoven's strong attraction to puns, a matter to which we shall return. Haydn's great oratorio *The Creation* had just recently been performed. The agreement of both composers that the ballet music was 'far from being a *Creation*' is significant. The *Prometheus* ballet is of course a creation myth in its own way, but what Beethoven produced in his op. 43 is illustrative, programmatic music that follows a scenario imposed from without. There is no real attempt here to achieve an 'unconsummated symbol' in Langer's sense. It is not the ballet music but the *Eroica* Symphony that embodies an achievement of Promethean stature, a work eminently worthy of being regarded as a 'creation'. Nevertheless, the symphony owes more to the earlier work than has often been recognized.

Because of the unfamiliarity of the ballet music, the extent of its relationship to the *Eroica* Symphony has remained obscure, in spite of the obvious reuse of an important theme from the ballet in the symphonic finale. Complicating matters further is the fact that Beethoven first elaborated some ideas derived from the ballet in a work for piano: the Fifteen Variations and Fugue in Eb op. 35 from 1802. Together with its companion work, the F major Variations op. 34, this innovative variation set helped to launch Beethoven's so-called 'new way'. But behind both the piano variations and the symphony lies an inspiring mythic source that until recently had been largely forgotten. Only in the 1970s did Constantin Floros succeed in largely reconstructing the choreography and related symbolism of the ballet from Beethoven's surviving musical sketches.[4] Since Beethoven made notations about the stage action in these sketches, the association of music and dance can be largely reestablished.

Floros's work has shown that the links between the ballet and the symphony are more substantial than has usually been assumed. Floros traces various rhetorical and formal parallels between the opening *Allegro con brio* of the symphony and, in particular, the eighth piece of the *Prometheus* music, the 'Danza eroica'. Still more important is the affinity of the two following pieces of the ballet, the 'Tragica scena' (no. 9) and 'Giuocosa scena' (no. 10, in which the dead Prometheus is restored to life), to the progression from the *Marcia funebre* to the scherzo in the symphony. This part of the *Eroica* has often proven a stumbling-block for commentators: Paul Bekker even suggested that the work would be more effective if the inner movements were interchanged, with the scherzo preceding the slow movement.[5] The symbolism of the 'heroic-allegorical' ballet—as it was described in the programme at the pre-

[3] Thayer-Forbes, pp. 272–3.

[4] *Beethovens Eroica und Prometheus-Musik*; see especially chapters 4 and 6.

[5] *Beethoven*, p. 223.

mière—can help here to supply a more convincing basis for analysis of the symphony.

The version of the Prometheus myth that Beethoven and Viganò tackled reinterprets the ancient tale of the defiant champion of humanity in a manner compatible with the spirit of the Enlightenment. Prometheus ennobled humankind through his gifts of knowledge and art fashioned from fire that he stole from the gods. In all versions of the myth Prometheus is severely punished in reprisal for his actions on behalf of humanity. In the original version, Prometheus is chained to a rock, where an eagle descends to devour his liver. After long years of suffering he is eventually freed by Hercules, a descendant of Io, who had come to Prometheus in the shape of a goat many years earlier. Variants of the legend exist in the ancient Greek sources, but all agree that the titan refuses to yield or compromise. Though physically in chains, Prometheus is spiritually free. In the world of myth, there is perhaps no more telling symbol of resistance to the arbitrary exercise of authority.

In the version that Beethoven set to music, Prometheus's suffering on the rock is deleted, but his punishment is rendered more decisive, since he is put to death. Another important change consists in the role of the two 'creatures', the *Urmenschen*, or archetypal man and woman. In the Greek sources the struggle of Prometheus occurs even before the creation of woman, whereas in the ballet the story is revised to embrace all humanity as potential beneficiaries of the Promethean sacrifice. Prometheus's long trials and agonies are replaced here by a progression of death and rebirth, since Prometheus is subsequently restored to life. The ballet concludes with the apotheosis of Prometheus as he is celebrated by his two creatures, who at last begin to display a true understanding of the significance of his heroic deed.

This version of the myth thus shifts the dramatic emphasis from the defiant martyr to the reception by humankind of the Promethean gift of culture. In the ballet the cultural gifts of the titan are not initially understood or appreciated by his two 'creatures'; consequently, Prometheus's agony comes to parallel the plight of the misunderstood artist. Ultimately, a reconciliation is achieved in that final section of the ballet that has always been understood as a link to the *Eroica* Symphony. The shared material is the lively tune that Beethoven employed as the seventh of his 12 German contredances WoO 14. He recycled the contredance three times: in the ballet, the E♭ Piano Variations, and the *Eroica* finale. The original audience for the symphony would surely have recognized this theme in the finale, but that is not all they are likely to have recognized.

The dramatic and symbolic elements incorporated from the Prometheus myth are by no means confined to the finale. The overall narrative progression of the four movements of the symphony outlines a sequence—struggle, death, rebirth, apotheosis. The parallel with Beethoven's own despair, thoughts of suicide, and discovery of his new artistic path is scarcely accidental. But the heroic symbolism of the *Eroica* is too deeply embodied in the artwork to be adequately interpreted in terms of Beethoven's biography, or in relation to any other historical figure such as Napoleon. What Beethoven explores in the *Eroica* are universal aspects of heroism, centring on the idea of a confrontation with adversity leading ultimately to a renewal of creative possibilities. Variants of this narrative sequence surface again and again in Beethoven's music up to his very last years.

The immense scope of Beethoven's first movement is reflected in his open, continuously evolving treatment of the basic thematic material. Elements of dramatic tension are exposed from the outset. After the powerful opening chords and the following triadic turning figure, the melody descends to a mysterious, low C♯, with syncopations heard above this pitch in the violins (Ex. 26). The full implications of the mysterious C♯ are explored only at the begin-

Ex. 26 *Eroica* Symphony op. 55/I

ning of the recapitulation, when Beethoven reinterprets this pitch as D♭, with a new downward resolution leading to an extended solo for horn in F major. Beethoven's most striking formal innovation in the opening *Allegro con brio* is his expansion of the development section and coda. With its 245 bars the development dwarfs the exposition, whereas the coda approaches the length of the recapitulation. The climax of the development is generated by an intense rhythmic process involving accented, syncopated dissonances; so unrelenting is this rhythmic fragmentation and compression that the thematic material is virtually dissolved into nothing at about that point when the recapitulation would normally be expected. Here Beethoven introduces an apparently new theme in the remote key of E minor, a theme that is later resolved to the tonic key in the coda.

The formal expansion created by this infusion of new material in the development thus arises as a consequence of unprecedented dramatic tension, and particularly from Beethoven's techniques of rhythmic foreshortening. His use of such fragmentation culminating in dramatic silence is characteristic; we have discussed one such example in the exposition of the first movement of the Piano Sonata in A major op. 2 no. 2. There the device has the effect of comic wit; in the *Eroica*, by contrast, it yields one of the most shattering climaxes in all music. The sense of scale is vastly expanded: a long series of registrally enhanced motivic syncopations leads into massive syncopated chords, with a dissonant collision of the A minor and F major triads marking the peak of intensification. The strongest rhythmic impulse or structural downbeat in the entire movement falls on the empty beat in bar 280, four bars before the E minor theme (Ex. 27). In this first movement, then, the pivotal crux of the entire dramatic structure is anchored in a temporal moment that is, paradoxically, *soundless*. This enables Beethoven to discharge the almost unbearable tension of the dissonant syncopations while preparing the new formal episode that is to fill the remainder of the development.

Beethoven's pupil Ferdinand Ries related an incident at a rehearsal of the symphony in which he mistook the premature horn entry just before the recapitulation as an error in performance. The unfortunate Ries said to Beethoven 'Can't the damned horn player count?—it sounds infamously false!', a remark that enraged the composer. The device is not well regarded as a 'mischievous whim' or a 'primitive banana skin', as described by Ries or Martin Cooper, respectively.[6] Beethoven's music is elsewhere rich in humour, but this passage can hardly be reckoned comic, though it severely dislocates the instrumental parts. The effect is of a bold expansion and diffusion of the structural moment of recapitulation over a broader temporal span. The second horn anticipates the reprise four bars before it occurs in the full orchestra, and brings about a

---

[6] Thayer-Forbes, p. 350; *Judgements of Value*, p. 150.

Ex. 27 *Eroica* Symphony op. 55/I, bars 272–92

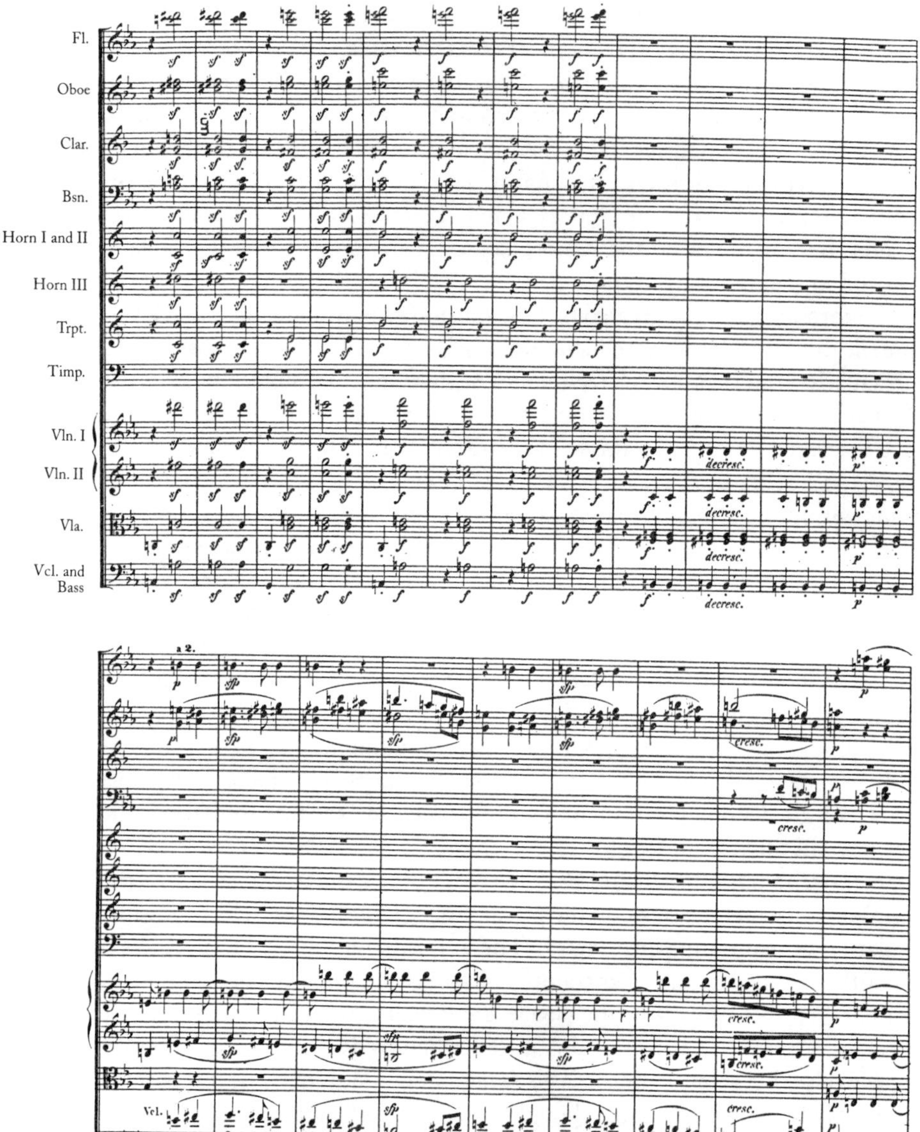

superimposition of tonic and dominant harmonies. The resulting dissonance is acute, despite the soft dynamic level, and this helps motivate the powerful *fortissimo* outburst that ushers in the 'true' recapitulation. Nevertheless, the reprise fails to follow a familiar path: the mysterious C♯ is now reinterpreted as D♭, and its resolution to C opens up the key of F major for the solo of the first horn. The two horn passages are related; both infuse excitement and unpredictability into the music at just that moment when concerns of formal symmetry would seem to be paramount.

The coda is expanded to almost the length of the exposition and recapitulation. Here, the 'new' theme from the development is resolved to the tonic key of E♭ major. Thus the coda serves to recapitulate those musical passages that did not appear in the exposition or recapitulation. But it also presents the exciting last chapter in the story of the triadic turning theme that opens the movement. This main theme is joined with a contrasting rhythmic subject, recalling a thematic combination from the development section, and Beethoven gradually intensifies the passage by means of orchestration and dynamics. As the music reaches its climax he reinterprets the theme to lead to a full authentic cadence in E♭ major: the resolution of this primary theme is inseparably bound up with the tonal closure of the movement as a whole. Another reminder of the vast scale of this *Allegro con brio* comes in the emphatic closing chords, which correspond to the two great E♭ chords at the beginning of the work. As Beethoven's sketches show, these initial chords were an afterthought: they anticipate the majestic power of the movement to follow, but their echo in Beethoven's final cadence also serves to cast unifying threads over this immense symphonic structure.

Beethoven was particularly drawn to the genre of the *Marcia funebre* during the transitional period that gave rise to his 'new path'; other examples besides the slow movement of the *Eroica* include the C minor variation in op. 34 and the funeral march 'on the death of a hero' in the A♭ Piano Sonata op. 26, from 1801. The sonata 'with the funeral march' was one of the most popular of all Beethoven's works in the nineteenth century. Its *Marcia funebre* was performed during Beethoven's own funeral procession in Vienna in 1827; it is the only movement in his sonatas that he arranged for orchestra. It thus takes on unusual interest not just for its orchestral rhetoric but for the part it played in the evolution of Beethoven's posthumous reputation as artistic hero, a mythic role still very potent today.

In its epic grandeur and dramatic power, the *Marcia funebre* in C minor in the *Eroica* goes far beyond the more conventional march in the piano sonata. The transparent orchestration gives special prominence to the woodwinds, particularly the oboe. Especially impressive is Beethoven's reinterpretation and development of the opening processional theme, as well as his incorporation of contrasting episodes. At the heart of this *Adagio assai* he introduces a subject of triumphant character in C major, with very full orchestration, which leads into a dramatic fugato based on the main theme in the minor. The melodic climax of the processional march had been on A♭, a pitch that assumes special importance throughout. Now, immediately after the luminous C major climax with trumpets and drums, the music falls onto a mysterious unharmonized A♭, and hence into the darkness of the minor, with the sense of a gaze into the abyss. Later, following the fugato, Beethoven restates the head of the processional theme softly in the dominant before pausing on a high A♭ in the violins, with the effect of a question posed against an indifferent sky. The ensuing silence is broken by an emphatic answering A♭ in the low register, and a powerful 'composing out' of this harmony leads to a varied reprise of the processional march. Equally striking is the fragmentation of the basic thematic material into hushed, broken inflections in the final passages of the coda. Beethoven had already effected such a disintegration of his main theme at the close of the *Largo e mesto* of his Piano Sonata op. 10 no. 3, and he was to use the device again in his *Coriolan* Overture.

The subtle opening of the scherzo—which begins *pianissimo* and in the dominant instead of the tonic—is presumably connected with the symbolic 'rebirth' of Prometheus, as Floros has suggested.[7] A more obvious heroic note is sounded in the trio, with its soloistic use of three horns—a special feature in the orchestration of the symphony. The musical character here is animated, even joyous, making a convincing psychological transition to the comedy and high spirits that emerge in the finale. But Beethoven also incorporates into the scherzo a specific thematic reference to the outset of the first movement which clarifies the narrative sequence of the work as a whole. Just moments before the close, the rising motivic progression D♭–D♮–E♭ is played twice in the high register in the winds (Ex. 28). In a sketch, Beethoven labelled the rising figure as 'a strange [or unfamiliar] voice' ('eine fremde Stimme').[8] This is, of course, an inversion, and resolution, of the mysterious downward shift E♭–D–D♭(C♯) that was heard in bars 6–7 of the *Allegro con brio* (cf. Ex. 26). That dissonant inflection in the first movement is the first hint in the work of strife and dramatic tension; the syncopations in the first violins emerge in response to the downward chromatic figure, already foreshadowing the unprecedented rhythmic force of passages to come. At the end of the scherzo, by contrast, this breach in the E♭ major tonality is closed; the wound is healed. The struggle embodied in the first movement has been transcended.

In the finale the association with Prometheus becomes explicit through the re-use of the theme from the ballet. As in the op. 35 Variations Beethoven first develops just the bass of the theme—with its grotesque humour of expressive

---

[7] *Beethovens Eroica und Prometheus-Musik*, p. 98.

[8] Nottebohm transcribes this sketch in *Ein Skizzenbuch von Beethoven aus dem Jahre 1803*, p. 44.

Ex. 28 *Eroica* Symphony op. 55/III, bars 419–31

silences—before joining it to the upper-line melody. We thereby witness the
gradual creation of a composite theme out of its component elements, a
notion that took deep hold on Beethoven and which surfaces again in more
radical form in the *scherzando* movement of the F major Quartet op. 59 no. 1,
from 1806. The variations that follow in the *Eroica* finale are resourcefully
blended with fugato passages, an *alla marcia* section, and an extended *andante*
featuring wind solos to create a unique formal design. As Lewis Lockwood
has observed, 'The *Eroica* finale emerges as the generating movement for the
whole work and as the most fully original symphonic finale that Beethoven or
anyone else had written up to its time'.[9]

*   *   *

Beethoven's other instrumental works from the period of the *Eroica* are few in
number but great in their dimensions and demands on performers and instruments. One landmark is the Sonata for Violin and Piano op. 47, from 1803,
dedicated to the violinist Rodolphe Kreutzer. This is the most celebrated of
Beethoven's violin sonatas, and the very name 'Kreutzer' gradually assumed
mysterious connotations which Tolstoy's novel served to intensify. (In his
book Tolstoy ascribed uncanny seductive power to the first movement of the
sonata.) Beethoven described the piece as 'written in a very concertante style,

    [9] 'The Compositional Genesis of the *Eroica* Finale', p. 100; *Beethoven: Studies in the Creative
Process*, p. 166.

like that of a concerto'. The *Kreutzer* Sonata is a grand and ambitious duo-sonata, a counterpart among the violin sonatas to works such as the *Waldstein* and *Appassionata* sonatas for piano alone. The first movement begins with a weighty slow introduction, marked *Adagio sostenuto*, protean in character and tonally unstable after its first four bars for unaccompanied violin in A major. This modulatory introduction gradually isolates the germinal motif of a rising second, which becomes a crucial element in all the themes of the ensuing *Presto*, in A minor. The relentless rhythmic drive of the *Presto* abates momentarily at the chorale-like second theme, marked *dolce*, a passage linked thematically to the introduction. Beethoven briefly recalls the *Adagio*, furthermore, in his coda. A central idea in this movement, as in the first movement of the 'Tempest' Sonata, is the relationship and contrast between the slow introduction and the faster, intensely dramatic material in the minor that forms the main body of the movement. The second movement, an *Andante con variazioni* in F major, consists of four increasingly florid variations followed by an extended coda. The finale is a rondo in tarantella rhythm, in A major, originally conceived as the finale of op. 30 no. 1, composed in 1802. Beethoven regarded it as too 'brilliant' for the earlier work, but it is perfectly in keeping with the other movements of the *Kreutzer*, his most brilliant violin sonata.

A remarkably original yet somewhat neglected piece from this period is the Piano Sonata in F major op. 54, of 1804, the first movement of which is above all a study in contrasts. Richard Rosenberg dubbed it 'La Belle et la Bête', and Brendel has described how its two contrasting themes—a gracious, dignified 'feminine' theme resembling a minuet, and a stamping, assertive, 'masculine' theme employing accented octave triplets—gradually influence one another in the course of the movement, until they become thoroughly integrated and combined in the final passages.[10] Here the music resembles the conventional form of minuet and trio only very superficially, and the point of the dissonant outburst immediately preceding the final cadence is to remind us—through the diminished-seventh harmonies, triplet rhythm, and the use of register—of the contrasting thematic complex that has gradually become absorbed into the minuet while transforming it. In this movement Beethoven thus explores a directional process and an ongoing synthesis of experience—qualities he further developed in many later works.

The ensuing *Allegretto* in a *perpetuum mobile* rhythm is already the finale—op. 54 is the first of Beethoven's major sonatas for piano to compress the formal plan into a pair of movements. This sonata form unfolds with an irresistible momentum in long ascending lines punctuated by syncopated pedal notes. The two-voice texture is reminiscent of Bach, but the dramatic

---

[10] *Die Klaviersonaten*, ii, p. 282; *Musical Thoughts and Afterthoughts*, pp. 47–50.

power is unmistakably Beethovenian. In the development Beethoven inverts the ascending linear motion so that it sinks chromatically into the depths of the bass, preparing a modulation into C minor. The coda then accelerates the perpetual motion in a furious *più allegro*. We can discern in this rhythmic drive a key to the relationship between the two strongly contrasting movements of op. 54. The initial minuet had proceeded in halting fashion, stopping every two or four bars in cadences set off by rests, but the assertive contrasting theme of that movement infused the music with an energy that in the finale becomes an all-encompassing force. The discovery, integration, and celebration of this rhythmic energy is a guiding idea of the sonata as a whole.

In the wake of the *Eroica* Beethoven showed a strong inclination to reshape his sonatas and quartets on a grand scale, introducing innovations in texture, sonority, register, and colour. Also essential is a sense of deepened contrast or conflict—a quality present in op. 54 but largely absent in the contemporaneous Triple Concerto in C major op. 56, with its superficially brilliant yet rather conventional rhetoric. Wilhelm von Lenz once described the *Waldstein* Sonata in C major op. 53, of 1804, as 'heroic pianistic deeds' ('Klavierheldenthaten') with a 'symphonic essence' ('symphonistischen Wesen').[11] In its opening *Allegro con brio* Beethoven goes beyond the harmonic experiments of earlier sonatas such as op. 31 no. 1 to create an enlarged sense of tonal space. The quietly pulsating tonic chords with which the sonata begins lead up a third to the dominant; moments later, a restatement of the opening phrase beginning a step lower carries the music to the subdominant. Within this broadened tonal spectrum it is natural that Beethoven should choose the remote key of E major for his second subject-group, which begins with a serene, chorale-like subject marked *dolce e molto legato*. He develops this lyrical subject through variation, embroidering its sustained notes in a rhythmic texture of triplets that gradually reasserts the brilliant pianistic textures so characteristic of this sonata.

The scale of conception of the *Waldstein* is impressive, yet Beethoven substantially reduced the length of the piece when he resolved to cut the original slow movement, a luxurious rondo in F major, and have it published separately, while substituting a brief but profound *Introduzione* in this key. As we have seen, the pensive substitute movement is linked, in its structure and character, to Beethoven's setting of 'Dead! Dead!' at the beginning of his *Joseph* Cantata, as well as to the orchestral introduction to the dungeon scene in *Fidelio*, composed the following year. To be sure, the symbolic connotations of the contrast between movements in the *Waldstein* are latent rather than explicit, and hardly comparable with, for instance, the drastic juxtaposition of the third and fourth Gellert songs 'Vom Tode' ('Of Death') and 'Die Ehre

---

[11] *Kritischer Katalog sämtlicher Werke Ludwig van Beethovens mit Analysen derselben*, ii, p. 273.

Gottes aus der Natur' ('The Glory of God from Nature'), op. 48, from 1801–2, where gloomy F♯ minor music associated with death yields to a resounding C major setting marked 'majestic and sublime'. In the sonata, the new slow movement is admirably calculated to set into relief the luminous C major world of the longer outer movements. Its guiding structural idea—a descending bass progression with a countervailing ascent in the right hand—is so devised that resolution and closure cannot be achieved within the *Introduzione* but only at the threshold of the ensuing finale. Only after an arresting climax on a widely spaced diminished-seventh sonority do we reach a miraculous turning-point at the emergence into the rondo, which is marked *Allegretto moderato*.

The high G that acts as pivot from the *Introduzione* into the finale serves also as the crucial peak of the main theme of the rondo. Beethoven glorifies this pitch through sustained trills as the theme migrates into the stratosphere with the left hand encompassing the lower registers with rapid scales (Ex. 29). Pianistic textures like these were unprecedented in 1804; they foreshadow some of the most visionary moments in Beethoven's last sonatas. Impressive as well are the episodes of the rondo (the first of which has a 'Russian' flavour, in A minor) and the central development section, an imaginative fantasy based on the rhythm of the head of the main theme. The *prestissimo* coda doubles the tempo, turning the main theme into an ethereal parody of itself. But that is not all: Beethoven recaptures here the developmental fantasy, and connects that passage to a series of octave *glissandi* in both hands culminating in the sustained trills. Now, however, the main theme is written in longer note

Ex. 29 *Waldstein* Sonata op. 53/III, bars 49–64 (and 331–46)

values; it reassumes its original shape before the closing passages of this great sonata reassert first the urgency of the thematic compression and then the magnificent breadth of Beethoven's rhythmic conception.

The contrasting companion work to the *Waldstein* is the *Appassionata* Sonata in F minor op. 57. This work is overcast with dark foreboding and represents an antipode to the luminous C major Sonata. Tovey once observed that the F minor Sonata is Beethoven's only work to maintain a tragic solemnity throughout all its movements.[12] The title *Appassionata*, though not from Beethoven, is not inappropriate (though Czerny was surely correct in observing that the work is 'much too magnificent' for the title.)[13] In its poetic power and richness of allusion, and in the gigantic simplicity of its structural foundation, this sonata represents a profound achievement, outstanding even for Beethoven.

The opening *Allegro assai* begins with a phrase of four bars, whose two halves embody contrary tendencies. The first two, unharmonized, bars consist of a triadic figure in gapped octaves, with the bass reaching the lowest F (Ex. 30). The second half of the phrase, in contrast, presents an imploring, plaintive, harmonized gesture around an expressive trill. The tension implicit in this motivic juxtaposition is heightened in the following phrase, which is placed by Beethoven up a semitone, so that it closes on the dominant harmony of the Neapolitan, Db. Subsequently, through his technique of foreshortening, Beethoven compresses the four-bar phrases into shorter units, beginning with the plaintive gesture of the trill, at which point we hear a four-note motif in the bass—Db–Db–Db–C—a motto that tersely encapsulates the harmonic tension.

Ex. 30 *Appassionata* Sonata op. 57/I, bars 1–4

A crucial dramatic event in the movement centres on the appearance in the development of the lyrical second theme in Db major. Already in the exposition this theme had employed a bass-line rising stepwise through a fifth. Now, in the development, the bass continues to rise, carrying the music through a series of modulations. After the ascent has spanned two octaves the theme

---

[12] *A Companion to Beethoven's Pianoforte Sonatas*, p. 169.
[13] *On the Proper Performance of All Beethoven's Works for the Piano*, p. 12.

dissolves, and the music becomes, in Tovey's words, 'inarticulate'.[14] All that remains of the thematic material is a rhythmically charged texture of diminished-seventh arpeggios, and the music descends, in a free fall of four octaves, until impact is made on the low D♭. In a brilliant stroke Beethoven introduces at this point the four-note motto from the outset of the movement, the motif that so resembles the so-called Fate motif of the Fifth Symphony. The recapitulation follows, as the accumulated energy of the development is unleashed in an ostinato bass pedal.

Other passages, such as the end of the exposition and conclusion of the coda, trail off into a mysterious *pianissimo*, while opening a vast gap in register between the two hands. As Martha Frohlich has observed, Beethoven actually sketched a powerful *fortissimo* conclusion, only to reject that idea in favour of a hushed, open-ended cadence.[15] The mysterious ending connects more effectively with the ensuing slow movement, implying the unresolved character of the dramatic tensions exposed in the *Allegro assai*—tensions that must carry over into the remaining movements.

In the overall design of the *Appassionata* Beethoven exploits a relationship between serene lyricism in D♭ major and the tempestuous idiom in F minor such as is exposed in the first movement. Important are the parallels in character between the opening *Allegro assai* and the finale, *Allegro ma non troppo*, and especially the contrasting role of the slow movement, a set of variations in D♭ major on an almost static, hymn-like *andante* theme. The course of these variations seems predetermined by the quietly reflective nature of the theme, which consists initially of stationary pedal notes and which repeatedly closes harmonically on the tonic triad. The variations embellish the theme through a series of progressive rhythmic subdivisions, coordinated with a gradual ascent in register; yet the entire process is contemplative and dreamlike, to be abruptly shattered, as Tovey observed, by the first hint of action. That confrontation occurs at the harmonic substitution of an arpeggiated diminished seventh beneath the cadential D♭, in the treble which might, under other circumstances, have closed the movement (Ex. 31). The arpeggiated chord returns an octave higher and then is reiterated 13 times in the original register at the outset of the *Allegro ma non troppo*, now intensified rhythmically and dynamically. The rhythm of the *Andante* theme is extracted and accelerated in these chords, which build the threshold into the finale. The 'self-sufficiency' of the variation movement is thus annihilated, as its tonic, D♭, now becomes a crucial dissonance in the context of F minor, recalling a similar treatment in the first movement. Indeed, from those 13 repeated chords Beethoven derives the main theme of the finale by 'composing out' the diminished-seventh chord as a sinuous figuration that carries over into the passagework of the *Allegro ma non troppo*.

---

[14] *Beethoven*, p. 44.   [15] *Beethoven's 'Appassionata' Sonata*, pp. 97, 108–9.

Ex. 31 *Appassionata* Sonata op. 57/II–III

According to Ries, Beethoven conceived this passage, and much that follows it, during and immediately after a long walk in the countryside near Döbling, a small town outside Vienna where he spent part of the summer of 1804. Ries wrote that during the walk,

in which we went so far astray that we did not get back to Döbling, where Beethoven lived, until nearly 8 o'clock, he had been all the time humming and sometimes howling, always up and down, without singing any definite notes. In answer to my question what it was he said: 'A theme for the last movement of the sonata has occurred to me' [in F minor, op. 57]. When we entered the room he ran to the pianoforte without taking off his hat. I took a seat in the corner and he soon forgot all about me. Now he stormed for at least an hour with the beautiful finale of the sonata. Finally he got up, was surprised still to see me and said: 'I cannot give you a lesson today, I must do some more work'.[16]

What preoccupied Beethoven on that summer day in 1804 was one of his most unrelenting finales, a movement 'whose tragic passion is rushing downwards', in Tovey's words (if 'rushing' is the right expression for a measured *Allegro ma non troppo*). Beethoven gives unusual weight to the later portions of the finale by prescribing a repetition of the development and recapitulation, a direction unfortunately ignored by some pianists, at the recommendation of Hans von Bülow.[17] No-one who has seen the inscription 'la seconda parte due volta' written in large letters in Beethoven's autograph, however, would be likely to ignore it. After the repetition we hear a *presto* coda, beginning with an ecstatically stamping dance which dissolves into a final, frenzied

[16] Thayer-Forbes, p. 356.
[17] Notes in his edition of the sonatas (New York: Schirmer, 1894), p. 473.

intensification of the turbulent rhetoric from the *Allegro ma non troppo*. Uhde has rightly pointed to the dissociated, even shocking effect of the coda's beginning:[18] it seems to represent a valiant yet futile attempt to break out of the downward rush of music burdened with a sense of tragic doom.

*   *   *

The antipodal tonal worlds of the *Waldstein* and *Appassionata* mirror something of the central schism in *Fidelio*, Beethoven's only opera and the greatest problem-child of all his works. Beethoven's labours over *Fidelio*, or *Leonore*, to use the title he would have preferred, were protracted over a decade and involved two major revisions of the entire opera and the composition of no fewer than four overtures. The models for the libretto and indeed also for aspects of the music were French; Beethoven was attracted at this time by the grand rhetorical manner of the operas and overtures of Luigi Cherubini. *Fidelio* is the only example of the genre of French Revolutionary 'rescue' opera that has remained in the active repertory. Its text was adapted from J. N. Bouilly's *Léonore* of 1798, a libretto based in turn on an actual episode from the Reign of Terror. In *Fidelio* themes of unjust imprisonment at the hands of a tyrant and heroic valour in the name of freedom are given expression in a manner not merely realistic but deeply symbolic and archetypal in import. Ironically, the première of *Fidelio* in November 1805 was spoilt by the military occupation of Vienna by the French. Many Viennese aristocrats fled the city; some of those who did hear the sparsely attended performances were French officers. Beethoven soon undertook a revision of the opera, compressing the original three acts into two. After only two performances of this version in the spring of 1806 he withdrew the opera, disgruntled over the financial return. Not until 1814 was *Fidelio* successfully revived in the form that is familiar today.

Fidelio can almost be regarded as two operas: a drama centred on noble, elevated personages—the unjustly imprisoned Florestan and his loyal, courageous wife Leonore, who works at the prison disguised as a man—inlaid into a more humble, *opéra comique* plot inhabited by the commonplace characters of Rocco the jailor, his daughter Marzelline, and her jealous boyfriend Jaquino. As in Mozart's *Zauberflöte*, things are not as they seem at the beginning. Doubtless the transformation of Bouilly's libretto into the more exalted, ethically inspired drama of *Fidelio* is no more perfect, even in its final version, than was the somewhat analogous reworking of the original fairy-tale plot of *The Magic Flute* into a richly symbolic drama of a rather different kind.

The discrepancy between these dramatic levels has always been regarded as the most problematic aspect of *Fidelio*. Beethoven was captivated by the great,

---

[18] *Beethovens Klaviermusik*, iii, p. 214.

over-reaching themes of freedom and tyranny, life and death, and he wedded them to music of surpassing power. In the tonal symbolism of the opera the antipodes are F minor, the key of Florestan's aria in the dungeon, and C major, that of the three *Leonore* overtures and the finale of the last act, which culminates in the arrival of the minister of state and the release of Florestan and the other political prisoners held by the tyrant Pizarro (see Plate 7). As in the *Appassionata* Sonata, the F minor music of the dungeon scene particularly emphasizes the dissonant semitone D♭–C. Noteworthy in this connection is Beethoven's use of D♭ major as the first change of key, 21 bars into the orchestral introduction. There are few direct thematic correspondences between *Fidelio* and either of the great piano sonatas, apart from the *Introduzione* of op. 53. Nevertheless, there is an unmistakable and characteristic kinship in their key symbolism. If Florestan's 'God!—what darkness here!' might serve as commentary on the conclusion of the *Appassionata*, the choral text 'Hail to the day! Hail to the hour!' at the end of *Fidelio* might almost be the motto for the jubilant coda of the *Waldstein* finale. In comparison with *Fidelio*, of course, the *Waldstein* coda is more rarefied and ethereal: the sonata does not confront the world in the same direct, encompassing way as does the opera.

The trouble with the great overtures to *Fidelio*—the second and third *Leonore* overtures—is that they distil the overriding dramatic themes with such powerful concentration as to overshadow, if not annihilate, the homely opening scenes of the first act. Beethoven recognized this problem, and finally in 1814 substituted the shorter *Fidelio* overture, a piece that only hints at the deeper issues that lie concealed at the outset of the dramatic action. Significantly, he decided to change the key of the overture to E major, dominant of the opening duet between Marzelline and Jaquino at the beginning of Act I. The very choice of C major as tonic for the *Leonore* overtures had been connected with Beethoven's intention to anticipate the most weighty events to follow—these are foreshadowed not only in a direct quotation from Florestan's aria and in the trumpet calls, but no less importantly in the ecstatic climax in the coda of *Leonore* no. 3 on a dominant minor ninth chord, where the musical intensity equals that of the most gripping of the later staged dramatic events. No amount of revision, including even the compression of the original three acts to two, could resolve the fundamental conflict between the overture and the ensuing Act I. Beethoven had spectacularly overindulged his characteristic practice of musical foreshadowing. Paradoxically, the greatest of all dramatic overtures, *Leonore* no. 3, had to be cut from the opera to which it is inextricably bound. It is no wonder that Beethoven claimed in 1814 to have earned a 'martyr's crown' for his labours on the revision of *Fidelio*!

In the *Adagio* introduction of *Leonore* no. 3, a descent into darkness is embodied in the tonal shift from C major to B minor—from a stepwise falling scale emerging out of the initial *fortissimo* unison G to the hushed F♯ octaves

reached in bar 5. Then, following the quotation of Florestan's 'In des Lebens
Frühlingstagen' ('In the springtime of life') in A♭ major, with its mood of
hopeful reminiscence, Beethoven modulates through the major mode of B to
release astonishing energies in the A♭ major tutti outburst of bar 27. The
dynamic and rhythmic power exposed here in the introduction reaches its culmination only in the coda of the sonata form. Dizzying chains of syncopations
lead into a rising, chromatic linear ascent through a tenth to high A, a note
corresponding to the peak of the initial motif of the main *Allegro* theme. In
the ensuing climactic minor ninth chord, with its reversal of the linear motion
through the downward shift to a dissonant A♭, Beethoven absorbs the darker
tensions once and for all into the triumphant accents of the conclusion.

Despite the problems of dramatic imbalance between the opera and its
overtures, and the awkwardness of Marzelline's infatuation with the disguised
Leonore, *Fidelio* draws much power from a collision of perspectives in which
the commonplace characters such as Rocco play an essential role. It is under-
standable that Beethoven, after having removed Rocco's 'Gold' aria from the
first revision, restored it in the final version. We all know people like Rocco:
his is a materialistic ideology that rejects higher values and fills the void
through the embrace of money. He is not free, but is obliged to serve the
tyrant Pizarro. Rocco's integrity is severely compromised by his complicity in
oppressive criminal activities. While not inherently evil, he is a collaborator,
guilty because he lacks the conviction or courage to stand by higher, ethical
principles.

The political dimension of *Fidelio* operates on a collective as well as an individual level. The finale of Act I centres on the prisoners' chorus. At Fidelio's
insistence, the prisoners are allowed brief access to the warmth and light of
the outside. Their appeal 'O freedom, will you come?' is juxtaposed with whis-
pered warnings that the guards are listening; the atmosphere is that of a concentration camp. The same basic dramatic progression, with a sustaining
vision of freedom maintained against formidable physical odds, is repeated in
more drastic form in Florestan's aria. It is revealing that the death-wish of the
prisoner in Bouilly's French text was deleted in *Fidelio*. Close to death,
Florestan is consoled by the knowledge that his action in seeking to expose
Pizarro's wrongdoing was virtuous and necessary: 'I have done my duty!' The
music of Florestan's aria embodies a complex psychological progression: the
dismal, death-haunted atmosphere is reflected in unusual aspects of harmony
and orchestration, such as the drumstrokes on pitches a tritone apart, while
his reminiscence of past happiness is conveyed in a *dolce* theme for winds in
A♭ major—the subject foreshadowed at the outset of the second and third
Leonore overtures. Concluding the aria is Florestan's delirious vision of
Leonore as an angel leading him to freedom, a passage added to the work in
1814. In this F major section Beethoven uses an oboe melody soaring into the

high register to symbolize the angel Leonore (Ex. 32). The association is made explicit at Florestan's words 'ein Engel, Leonore' ('an angel, Leonore'), which mimic the preceding oboe phrase.

Nowhere else in the opera are the boundaries between imagination and reality so challenged as here. The 'heavenly realm' of freedom—is it to be

Ex. 32 *Fidelio*, Act II, no. 2, bars 82–98

Ex. 32 cont.

realized in life, or only in death? The final section of this aria is one of
Beethoven's most significant monuments to the Romantic tenet that the current of subjectivity, of spiritual activity, of the individual's apprehension of
value, is more real than external reality. Florestan's aria is among those parts
of the opera that most deeply impressed Wagner; and traces of its influence
are felt in Tristan's 'delirium' scene in the last act of *Tristan und Isolde*.

The corresponding psychological moment for Leonore—exposing the
underlying, nourishing source of her courageous determination—occurs in
her aria 'Komm, Hoffnung' ('Come, Hope') in Act I. The principle of hope
had occupied Beethoven in another context at about this time. In late 1804
and early 1805 he was infatuated with the Countess Josephine Brunsvik
Deym; the first of his two song settings of Tiedge's *An die Hoffnung* op. 32 was
written for her. His passion went unrequited; he soon had to retreat into a
more distanced relationship with Josephine, and by the time the song was
published, in September 1805, her name had been removed from the dedication. Some years later Beethoven produced a more elaborate, through-
composed setting of *An die Hoffnung* that was published in 1816 as op. 94.
Tiedge's poem takes the form of an ode, like Schiller's *An die Freude*. As Hans
Boettcher observed, such texts articulate an objective, conceptual awareness of
an entity beyond the self.[19] Similarly, in 'Come, Hope' in *Fidelio*, Leonore's
vision of hope taps hidden archetypal energies that sustain her struggle
against adversity.

The three horns used in Leonore's aria are reminiscent of those in the
Eroica Symphony. In the *Allegro con brio* of the aria, in particular, the rising
triadic horn fanfare invites comparison with the ascending horn gestures in
the trio of the *Eroica*. But this is not the only point of contact between these
two major monuments of Beethoven's heroic style. Both works reflect his

[19] *Beethoven als Liederkomponist*, p. 46.

artistic response to serious issues of life and his determination to maintain an open, optimistic perspective despite setbacks and apparently insurmountable obstacles. The rescue of Florestan, or the rehabilitation of Prometheus, each stands for a generative process with universal human relevance, aspects of which are embedded in the 'unconsummated symbol' of Beethoven's music. As we have seen, the symbolization involved here is no mere programmatic illustration; the difference is well indicated by setting the Prometheus ballet music alongside the far greater achievement of the *Eroica* Symphony. The enhancement of the narrative and mythic dimension in some of Beethoven's works after 1801 resulted from a confluence of historical, artistic, and personal factors, but above all from his deepening appreciation of the almost unlimited potential of musical expression. The apparent failure of his opera after 1806 in no way dampened the energy he brought to this task.

5

The Heroic Style II

1806–1809

AFTER he put *Fidelio* aside, Beethoven's major artistic preoccupation became the set of three 'Razumovsky' string quartets in F major, E minor, and C major of op. 59, composed mainly between April and November 1806. This trilogy stands at the centre of a splendid series of masterpieces from that year, including the Fourth Piano Concerto op. 58, the Fourth Symphony op. 60, and the Violin Concerto op. 61. An orchestral ambition surfaces in the imaginative sonorities and enhanced scale of some movements of the 'Razumovsky' quartets, from the broad opening *Allegro* of the F major Quartet to the nervously emphatic finale of the C major. At the request of the Russian ambassador, Count Razumovsky, who commissioned the pieces, Beethoven incorporated Russian folk-songs into the finale of op. 59 no. 1 and the third movement of op. 59 no. 2. The third quartet contains no obvious quotations, but, as Riezler and Marion Scott have suggested, its melancholy slow movement may harbour a more elusive relationship with Russian style.[1]

The first two quartets were coolly received when first performed; only the C major was warmly appreciated. Time has reversed that judgment, however: the F major and E minor quartets are now placed among Beethoven's surpassing essays in this genre, overshadowing op. 59 no. 3. Alan Tyson's study of the genesis of these works indicates that the C major Quartet was composed swiftly, perhaps even hastily: the evidence comes from water-stains on Beethoven's manuscripts for the quartets and his *Appassionata* Sonata (which

---

[1] Riezler, *Beethoven*, p. 172; Scott, *Beethoven*, pp. 256–7; Czerny, *On the Proper Performance*, p. 13. Lini-Hübsch, in her study *Ludwig van Beethoven: Rasumowsky-Quartette*, pp. 90–3, identifies a Russian melody beginning at bar 23.

was finished only in 1806, though begun two years earlier).[2] In late October 1806 Beethoven travelled from a country retreat in Silesia to Vienna with his manuscripts packed in a trunk. On the way he encountered a storm with pouring rain that penetrated the trunk, so that the manuscripts were wet when he reached Vienna. Thanks to this leaky trunk and the resulting water-stains on his manuscripts, we know that by this point he had finished in score only the first two movements of the E minor quartet and had sketched just the first movement of the C major. This left little time for the completion of op. 59 no. 3. The smaller scale of this work, the apparent absence of a Russian theme, and Beethoven's use in the minuet of material sketched years earlier are all factors that may connect with a certain haste in the process of composition.

The opening *Allegro* of the F major Quartet bears comparison with the corresponding movement of the *Eroica* Symphony. Like the *Eroica*, it is on an immense scale, with a development much longer than the exposition and studded in this case by a big double fugue. The quartet movement relies, as does the symphony, on far-reaching reinterpretation of the main theme at important junctures of the sonata form. Beethoven places the main subject in the cello, under the pulsating accompaniment; only after the second phrase does the theme pass to the violin two octaves higher. The guiding motivic idea is a series of ascending steps in quarter-notes that becomes gigantic when this rising pattern is augmented to whole-notes at the cadence of the theme. Especially important in the opening melody is the pitch G, which closes the second and third phrases in the cello and first violin. When Beethoven restates this subject at the opening of the development, the G has become G♭, forcing a new harmonic continuation. Even more conspicuous is the shift at the recapitulation to a G♭ that is sustained over ten bars to support a powerful climax. As Kerman has observed, two further reinterpretations of the opening theme occur in the coda.[3] First, its harmonic ambiguity is purged when Beethoven restates the melody *fortissimo* in the upper instruments, while the cello (for once!) supplies the solid harmonic foundation that was previously withheld. Later in the coda the first violin carries the rising steps from the theme into the stratosphere, as the highest C is sounded against G and then F in the cello.

The *scherzando* movement that follows is an astonishingly original conception. Beethoven experiments here, as in the *Eroica* finale and its model, the op. 35 piano variations, with the notion that a piece may be conceived as a search for its own thematic material. He begins with a mere abstract of a seminal rhythm, tapped out softly in the cello on a single stationary pitch. Motivic

[2] 'The "Razumovsky" Quartets: Some Aspects of the Sources'; the water-staining can be seen in the facsimile editions of the quartets edited by Tyson.

[3] *The Beethoven Quartets*, pp. 95–7.

fragments are juxtaposed long before they are eventually assembled as the 'completed' theme. Only in bar 29 is the bare rhythm from the outset filled out harmonically and dynamically, and only near the end of the first subject-group is this harmonized rhythm to be combined with an upper-line melody (Ex. 33). The overall design is a modified sonata form with a sombre second subject in the minor that foreshadows the character of the following slow movement. Beethoven dovetails the end of the development with the passage from his exposition leading to the harmonized *fortissimo* statement of the seminal rhythm, and it is again with this gesture that the *scherzando* movement ends. Immediately before the final cadence he mischievously interpolates a striking dissonant G♭ in the first violin, reminding us thereby of disruptive earlier passages based around this sensitive note.

The *Adagio molto e mesto* is a lament of tragic character that directly connects, through a florid violin cadenza, with the finale in sonata form. The main subject is a Russian tune that Beethoven found in a contemporary anthology. Here, as in the E minor quartet, he showed little regard for the stately character and moderate tempo of the pre-existing theme, as Philip

Ex. 33 String Quartet op. 59 no. 1/II, bars 1–34

Radcliffe has pointed out.[4] The theme is effective in the brisk tempo chosen by Beethoven; it also lends itself well to development. In its rising stepwise motion it has an obvious motivic parallel with the main subject of the opening *Allegro*.

Whereas the F major Quartet is spacious and grand in its overall character, the E minor Quartet is more concentrated, at least in its first movement. The introductory gesture of chords and silences is terse and arresting; the initial tonic sonority then unfolds as a broken chord, and, after another striking pause, Beethoven restates the idea on the Neapolitan, a semitone higher. Most of the movement's thematic material is derived from these opening bars. According to Czerny, the following *Molto adagio* in E major occurred to Beethoven while he was 'contemplating the starry heavens and thinking of the music of the spheres'.[5] This is indeed music of sublime contemplation, foreshadowing later works, such as the Benedictus of the *Missa solemnis* and the celestial central variation in E major in the slow movement of the first of the late quartets, op. 127. It is in the trio of the third movement, marked *Allegretto*, that Beethoven cites the second of the Russian folk-songs used in op. 59, the same melody used by Mussorgsky in the Coronation Scene in *Boris Godunov*. The theme is stripped of its solemn, ecclesiastical associations and treated in a parodistic fugal medley that is repeated in full after the return of the *Allegretto*. The *presto* finale employs a main theme that begins in the 'wrong' key of C major instead of the tonic E minor. In its rhythmic character this movement strongly anticipates the finale of the later Quartet in C# minor op. 131.

The characteristic tonal relationships of the second 'Razumovsky' Quartet may be connected in part with its central position in op. 59. Its first and third movements are closely related in their structure and expression, sharing an emphasis on the Neapolitan degree of F in an E minor context; no less striking is the persistent C major beginning of the rondo theme in the finale. Whereas the Neapolitan emphasis can be heard in relationship to the tonic key of the preceding quartet, the main theme of the finale may be linked to the tonality of the following quartet.

The C major Quartet op. 59 no. 3 is an oddly unsettled piece. It opens with a mysterious slow introduction, paralleling Mozart's 'Dissonance' Quartet K465 in the same key. The following *Allegro vivace*, and the minuet as well, show a retrospective orientation; they breathe the air of the eighteenth century. Perhaps this quality contributed to their contemporary popularity but now somewhat faded appeal. In the *moto perpetuo* finale an enormously extended, rambling theme is treated fugally; the triumphant fury of this conclusion is just a little hollow, quite unlike the masterful C major finale of the

---

[4] *Beethoven's String Quartets*, p. 49.   [5] Thayer-Forbes, pp. 408–9.

Fifth Symphony of 1808. The most impressive movement of op. 59 no. 3 is probably the second, in A minor, marked *Andante con moto quasi Allegretto* (Ex. 34). There is nothing else like it in Beethoven. The strangely static 6/8 rhythm, pedal points, haunting melodic inflections and harmonic dissonances, and use of pizzicato all lend an aura of remote, almost mythical melancholy and bleakness. Is this unique movement Beethoven's attempt to capture a Russian character in music?

Ex. 34 String Quartet op. 59 no. 3/II

*   *   *

A spacious lyrical serenity characterizes several of Beethoven's works from this period, including the Fourth Piano Concerto in G major op. 58. According to a tradition stemming from Liszt and others, the *Andante con moto* is associated with Orpheus taming the Furies; more recently, this interpretation has been extended by Owen Jander and refined by Joseph Kerman.[6] In this movement the classical *topos* juxtaposing stark, unharmonized unisons and pliant,

---

[6] Jander, 'Beethoven's "Orpheus in Hades"'; Kerman, 'Representing a Relationship: Notes on a Beethoven Concerto'.

harmonized lyricism is imposed on the relationship between tutti and soloist, investing the music with a mythic aura. Beethoven bases the movement's general progression on the principle of gradual transformation, so that the bare, harsh orchestral unison on E at the outset is eventually replaced by a soft, sustained, E minor harmony at the conclusion. This, in turn, is superseded by the brighter, more stable sonority of C major that opens the main theme of the ensuing rondo finale. Consequently, the entire slow movement seems to be poised in a dependent relationship with the music to come. Beethoven achieves a similar effect at the end of the B major *Adagio* of the 'Emperor' Concerto, where a pivotal drop of the semitone B–Bb in the orchestra restores the basic tonality of Eb major at the threshold of the finale.

An important dimension of the dialogue between tutti and soloist consists in Beethoven's control of pitch registers. The orchestral passages take on a predominantly descending contour, with the first two phrases closing a fourth and fifth below the initial pitch level of E. In contrast, the piano ascends, *molto cantabile*, closing its phrases in a somewhat lower register in order to connect with the succeeding entries of the tutti. This tug of registers, with the piano gradually gaining primacy, is most vividly illustrated after bar 26, where Beethoven employs his familiar technique of foreshortening to tighten the exchanges between the contenders (Ex. 35). The first of these shortened orchestral phrases descends from E to A, to be answered by an ascending solo phrase whose expressive appoggiatura controls the pitch level of the following tutti phrase, beginning on F and falling to B. The ensuing phrase in the piano now forces a further concession from the orchestra, which is obliged to *ascend* from B to C. The accelerating process of diminution helps to underscore the growing primacy of the soloist; in bars 33–5 the exchanges occur in every bar, with the soloist gaining an increasing monopoly over the texture while the orchestra completes its uncharacteristic ascent to the tonic E. As the tutti is thereby compelled to abandon its uncompromising stance, the solo unfolds for the first time in a more animated motion in continuous eighth-notes, in its characteristic legato articulation.

The following phrases are modelled on the sequences beginning in bar 26, but they sound utterly different in expressive quality. The tutti, while still maintaining its detached articulation, has lost its stolid fortitude; the dynamic level softens to *piano*. Now the soloist can afford to mimic the falling contour of the orchestral phrases, while penetrating still higher in register. Hence the very substance of the tutti phrases is transformed here into the more integrated, harmonized texture of the soloist. The music assumes a human face; the stern, forbidding posture of the orchestral phrases is injected with inner life. As the foreshortening process runs its course, the orchestral dynamic level softens to *pianissimo*, and the incorporation of C# in place of C signals yet another concession in the lost struggle with the

Ex. 35 Fourth Piano Concerto op. 58/II, bars 19–38

soloist—even the hold of the tutti on the minor mode is momentarily put into question.

From this point the dominance of the pianist is absolute, and a new stage in the narrative design of the movement has been reached. Having subdued the antagonists, the soloist exploits them as audience for an unforgettable climactic message. A contrapuntal transition accompanied by subservient pizzicato strokes in the strings leads to a pause on the dominant-seventh chord of E minor (Ex. 36). A chain of trills rises by thirds to reach C, a ninth above the root of the dominant sonority. The C is made to ring through the long, stationary vibration of the trill, played *fortissimo*. Beethoven 'composes out' the diminished-seventh chord supporting the C, with a rapid oscillation across the tritone A–D# below the trill, and an appoggiatura G#–A sounded above it.

The searing intensity of this cadenza is the apex and turning-point of the entire concerto. As the music gradually fades from *fortissimo* to *pianissimo*, the trill unravels into the contour of the figuration played moments before in

Ex. 36 Fourth Piano Concerto op. 58/II, bars 47–62

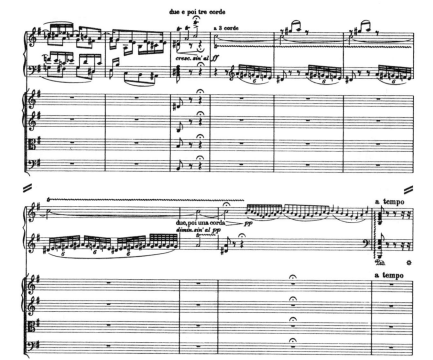

the left hand, and a relaxing process of rhythmic augmentation prepares the
arpeggiated cadential chords that follow. At the cadence in bar 64, the con-
version of the orchestral antagonists is confirmed through the sustained E
octave, marked with a triple *pianissimo*, a rare indication in Beethoven.
Noteworthy too is the stress placed by the orchestral phrases on C; three times
C is sounded below the protracted E, before the music unfolds toward the

final cadence. Now, most significantly, the tutti adopts the harmonic texture and legato articulation from the solo piano. As the movement closes, a complete concordance is established; all traces of conflict have been erased.

The *Andante con moto* of the G major Concerto thus provides a paradigm of musical transformation, whereby the detached, objective idiom of the tutti is gradually infused with human subjectivity, won over by the power of the artistic imagination. It can do no harm to think of the Orpheus myth here, as long as we do not limit the music to this association. For Beethoven's *Andante* is far too subtle to allow a smooth fit between the stages in Orpheus's passage and the musical process we have described. Comparison with the famous setting of Orpheus and the Furies in Gluck's *Orfeo* reminds us of the greater musical integrity of Beethoven's movement. The *Andante con moto* is an intrinsically musical narrative, which urgently invites interpretation without allowing itself to be displaced thereby. The imposition of a definitive verbal interpretation would disrupt the balance in the music between the rational and the sensuous, ignoring the primacy of the *Klangvorstellung*. It is more appropriate to reflect on the impact of Beethoven's climactic, despairing cadenza. Here the soloist's earlier confident tone experiences a crisis. Has his apparent rhetorical triumph masked a hidden weakness? Does the cadenza harbour implications of a Pyrrhic victory? Such questions are raised but not answered by the music. This much is certain: the powerful elaboration of the dominant ninth as a trill on C is not truly resolved here. The sound of the C lingers in the mind after the dissipation of its physical sound; the later emphasis of the strings on the low C picks up traces of these dying resonances. The overall effect is to destabilize the ensuing cadence in E minor, which opens into the C major of the rondo finale. There is an anticipation within the *Andante con moto* of the music to come, making clear that the entire movement is a stage within a larger process.

The first movement of this concerto had already given particular prominence to the dialogue between solo and tutti by beginning with a short piano passage, marked *dolce*. Such an opening was unusual, although Mozart's Concerto in E♭ major K271 provided a precedent. Beethoven sought out novel, experimental openings for each of his later concertos. The Fifth Piano Concerto in E♭ op. 73, for instance, begins with a written-out cadenza for the soloist, and the unfinished D major Piano Concerto of 1815 was also intended to open with a cadenza.[7] At the outset of his beautiful Violin Concerto in D major op. 61, composed during December 1806, he employed an even more striking idea.

The Violin Concerto begins with a bar of soft drum taps, a motif consisting of five repeated notes (Ex. 37). Rhythmic motifs involving repeated notes

---

[7] Cf. Lockwood, 'Beethoven's Unfinished Piano Concerto of 1815'.

Ex. 37 Violin Concerto op. 61/I

often appear in Beethoven's works of these years: the first movements of the *Appassionata* Sonata, Fourth Piano Concerto, and Fifth Symphony each provide examples. In these pieces the repeated notes act as an anacrusis, or upbeat, driving the music forwards. The Violin Concerto, by contrast, opens on a downbeat, anchoring the motif and ensuring its stability. The initial isolation of this motif in the timpani is especially fitting in the Violin Concerto; the device exposes in the most distinct way the tonal substratum and underlying pulse of the musical structure. Its importance is confirmed by the manner in which later themes defer to its rhythm, and no less by Beethoven's imaginative reinterpretation of this elemental gesture. Few pieces by Beethoven achieve such grand effects with such economy of means.

Consider, for instance, Beethoven's treatment of the moment of recapitulation. In many earlier works, as we have seen, he enhances this symmetrical axis of the sonata form by intensifying the dynamic level or by filling out the harmonic texture. The first movements of several of the op. 18 quartets already display his tendency to fortify the point of recapitulation, making clear that this structural point is no mere repetition but a reinterpretation of the earlier music experienced in a qualitatively new way. Other works, such as the *Eroica*, tend to diffuse or enlarge the moment of recapitulation; Beethoven develops this procedure in a variety of ways in later compositions. In the Violin Concerto the moment of recapitulation is glorified through a rhythmic preparation of great breadth, leading to a transformation of the quiet drum beats

into deep, emphatic unison strokes in the full orchestra. This is just one striking example of Beethoven's resourceful manipulation of the seminal rhythmic
motif, which permeates much of the *Allegro ma non troppo*. The luminous
opening phrases in the winds already absorb this rhythm; the entry of the violins on a mysterious, dissonant D♯ employs it as well. An even more conspicuous development of the idea occurs in the memorable lyrical theme
exchanged between the winds and strings, with a shift between major and
minor (Ex. 38). Here, the motif derived from the drum taps is played in the
violins, dovetailed with related rhythmic phrases in the winds in a higher
register. Beethoven's use of such a rhythmic motif with repeated notes to
underpin a broad lyrical subject may have influenced Schubert in the second
theme of the finale of his 'Great' C major Symphony.

The entry of the solo violin exposes another essential dimension of
Beethoven's use of the unaccompanied timpani at the outset. An improvisatory solo passage ascends into the registral stratosphere to the highest D,
four octaves above the repeated drumstrokes that announce the beginning of
the second exposition. Another vast disjunction in register marks a related
pivotal moment near the beginning of the development: here the solo violin
restates its introductory passage, in C major, but Beethoven reinterprets the
high ethereal pitch and its low counterpoint as a harmonically unstable augmented sixth, and the music passes mysteriously into B minor. There is an
affinity between this passage and the uncanny *pianissimo* passage in C♯ in the
middle of the development of the G major Piano Concerto.

One of Beethoven's simplest yet most telling strokes in the Violin Concerto
is his derivation of the sustained dominant pedal that precedes the recapitulation from the elemental drum motif. The hushed sound of timpani and
trumpets underlies and strongly foreshadows the recapitulation itself, where
the drum taps are made gigantic, sounded *fortissimo* in the full orchestra. This
work reminds us of the extent to which Beethoven relies on the reinterpretation of gestures over vast temporal spans, often reserving the most definitive
presentation of his themes or motifs to a late stage in the musical discourse.
Another such example is his decision to delay giving the violin solo the memorable lyrical theme until after the cadenza. Here, at last, the figure of
repeated notes disappears, as the soloist guides the music to its radiant conclusion.

The first movement of the Fourth Symphony in B♭ major op. 60 offers
another example of Beethoven's extraordinary use of the timpani, here in connection with an unorthodox approach to the recapitulation. The general character of the *Allegro vivace* is energetic and even boisterous, but Beethoven
withdraws into a subdued *pianissimo* towards the end of the development.
Mysterious drum rolls are heard on B, and the music lingers for some
moments in the remote key of B major, as hushed, transparent descending

Ex. 38 Violin Concerto op. 61/I, bars 47–58

scales unfold in the strings, while the timpani are silent. Beethoven then returns to the harmony of B♭ major while maintaining the enigmatic *pianissimo*. The drum rolls recur, first intermittently, then as a sustained tonic pedal held for 23 bars until the beginning of the recapitulation. There is no cadence; the approach to the reprise is a protracted crescendo, in which the motivic texture gradually penetrates and then fills the tonal space above the rumbling drum until the recapitulation is affirmed *fortissimo* by the full orchestra.

A fascinating aspect of this passage is that the drum sounds on B can be heard, at least in retrospect, as a subtle foreshadowing of the actual recapitulation, which is ushered in by the long timpani roll on the tonic. The modulation to B major, on the other hand, introduces sufficient contrast to enable Beethoven to relinquish any dominant preparation, or indeed any cadence whatever. This passage may have helped inspire the remarkable approach to the recapitulation in the first movement of Schubert's last Piano Sonata, in B♭ major, in which analogous 'drum rolls' in the form of low trills introduce a foreshadowing of the main theme on (but not in) the tonic, moments before the actual recapitulation is reached.

*   *   *

In March 1807 the first performances of the Fourth Symphony and Fourth Piano Concerto were given at the Lobkowitz palace, together with another orchestral work completed early that year: the *Coriolan* Overture op. 62. Along with the Fifth Symphony, the *Coriolan* Overture is the most intensely dramatic and rhythmically propulsive of the orchestral works in Beethoven's 'C minor mood'. Based not on Shakespeare but on a tragedy by the Austrian dramatist Heinrich von Collin, the story concerns a proud, defiant aristocrat caught in unresolvable inner conflict; seeing no way out of his dilemma, he chooses death. In a perceptive appreciation of the overture, Wagner described Coriolanus as 'the man of untameable force, unsuited for a hypocrite's humility'.[8] A quality of defiant, passionate energy permeates this music. Unlike the Fifth Symphony, the *Coriolan* Overture has no positive resolution; the tragic end of the protagonist is implied in the fragmented, dissolving coda.

Beethoven begins the *Coriolan* Overture with yet another transformation of the *topos* associated with death in the *Joseph* Cantata and in *Fidelio*. As in those works, deep sustained unisons are juxtaposed with harmonized chords employing winds in the upper register (Ex. 39). In the faster tempo of this *Allegro con brio*, Beethoven prescribes tied whole-notes for each of the unisons; the sharp, accented chords that follow are hurled into the void. Sequences of this arresting gesture ensue, with the rising upper voice supported by diminished-seventh chords, before two further chords connect cadentially to the main theme in more rapid eighth-note motion, beginning in bar 15. Michael Broyles suggests that this opening resembles a typical slow introduction notated in the main tempo, but this is wide of the mark.[9] The prescribed metrical structure does apply to these *fortissimo* chords, placed as they are in a context of extraordinary rhythmic tension. In order to sustain the

[8] 'Ouvertüre zu "Koriolan"', *Sämtliche Schriften und Dichtungen*, v, p. 173.
[9] *The Emergence and Evolution of Beethoven's Heroic Style*, pp. 148–51.

Ex. 39 *Coriolan* Overture op. 62

tension, and propel the music forwards, Beethoven foreshortens the metrical pattern just before the cadence, so that the music is pushed ahead of time into the main theme. Characteristically, he compensates for this gain of energy by otherwise relaxing the point of arrival; the new subject begins *piano*, in a relatively simple texture that lends itself to later development. In later sections of the overture he combines the sinuous figuration of the main subject with massive, emphatic sonorities such as were heard at the outset. Thus, like the first movement of the Fifth Symphony, the *Coriolan* Overture shows an interplay between molecular motivic figures and larger harmonic structures.

An important but old-fashioned piano work in this key which reached publication in 1807 is the set of 32 Variations in C minor WoO 80. This piece was seriously underestimated by Beethoven himself, who referred to it disparagingly and failed to assign it an opus number. The C minor Variations are strongly reminiscent of a Baroque chaconne, employing a short, eight-bar

theme with a chromatically descending ground bass. Beethoven often effectively overcomes the terseness of the theme by grouping the variations
together, as in nos. 1–3, 7–8, 10–11, 12–14, 15–16, 19–22, 26–7, and 31–2. These
groupings by no means exhaust the many relationships between individual
variations, which are based on general rhythmic and textural features and on
modal contrast (the *Maggiore* section, Variations 12–16, for example, embraces
two of these groupings, and provides large-scale contrast after the agitated
variation pair nos. 10–11). Variation 31 provides a reprise of the original theme
above an arpeggiated accompaniment, whereas in Variation 32 a rhythmic
elaboration of the theme leads upwards in register to the high C three octaves
above middle C, marking the beginning of the coda. (This high C occurs for
the first time among the sonatas in op. 57, composed in 1804–6, and reflects
the upward expansion of register in the pianos available to Beethoven; in
works up to op. 31, of 1802, the range rarely exceeds high F, a fifth lower.)

   With his first mass, the work in C major eventually published as op. 86,
Beethoven found himself in a particularly direct and taxing comparison with
Haydn. The commission came from Prince Nikolaus Esterházy the younger,
who turned to Beethoven on account of Haydn's advanced age. For Esterházy,
Haydn had written all six of his late masses, four of which were published by
Breitkopf & Härtel during 1802–4. Beethoven's sketches for the C major Mass
contain excerpts from Haydn's *Schöpfungsmesse* (Hob. xxii: 13), and his treatment of the form of the mass largely follows Haydn's models. Nevertheless,
Beethoven's dynamic and richly contrasting musical characterization of the
text departs from Haydn's more restrained, unified approach; this is presumably what displeased the prince, as Jens Peter Larsen has observed.[10] After the
first performance on 13 September 1807 at Eisenstadt, Esterházy is supposed
to have remarked sceptically 'But, dear Beethoven, what is this that you have
done again?'; the composer left in anger, and changed the dedication of the
mass in favour of Prince Kinsky. No more such commissions were forthcoming; twelve years were to pass before Beethoven tackled his second and final
mass, the *Missa solemnis*. On 8 June 1808, in a letter offering the C major Mass
to the reluctant publisher Breitkopf & Härtel, Beethoven proudly emphasized
the very aspect of the piece that must have troubled Esterházy: 'About my
mass . . . I believe that I have handled the text as it has been yet seldom
treated'. In its historical context, this work appears less conservative than
when viewed only in the company of Beethoven's ambitious symphonic compositions of these years.

   The climax of this immensely productive period of Beethoven's career is the
contrasted pair of symphonies that he completed in 1808 and which were first
performed at his musical *Akademie* in the Theater an der Wien on 22

---

[10] 'Beethovens C-dur-Messe und die Spätmessen Joseph Haydns', pp. 12–19.

December of that year. The Fifth and Sixth symphonies are not only sharply profiled individuals but are diametrically opposed to one another in conspicuous features of their structure and expression. Nevertheless, certain kinships between them are revealing: their points of similarity relate to aspects of the narrative design, as well as to style and character. Like the *Waldstein* and *Appassionata* sonatas, the Fifth and Sixth symphonies represent disparate musical worlds that ultimately complement one another. We need not choose between them, but can appreciate each more fully in the light of the opposing perspective embodied in its companion.

Whereas the C minor Symphony is perhaps the most goal-directed or teleological of all Beethoven's works, the *Pastoral* Symphony in F major is remarkably relaxed, even passive. In the first movement of the *Pastoral*, Beethoven not only suppresses dissonance to a remarkable extent, but he nearly banishes the minor triad. The arrival at the recapitulation is treated in a soft, understated manner, through the subdominant. In the development, extended passages are given over to repetitive figures on basic triadic harmonies; mere chords are thereby magnified into tonal regions. If the syntactical discourse of the musical language is flattened, Beethoven compensates the listener through his deliciously sensitive handling of orchestral sonority. The F major Symphony is a transparently sensuous score, in which rhythmic drive is largely suspended, held in reserve for moments of special import.

In its style and expression, the opening *Allegro con brio* of the Fifth Symphony is the opposite: propulsive rhythmic energy and relentless harmonic dissonance sustain it. In place of the broad expansion of sound of the *Pastoral* there is a terse concentration, with strong emphasis on dissonant diminished-seventh chords. Here, more than in his earlier C minor works, Beethoven gives voice to the Schillerian notion of resistance to suffering in a manner that only music can command. In the Fifth Symphony he enlarges this message across all four movements, which are welded into an even tighter and more cohesive narrative design than in the *Eroica*.

In comparing these two symphonies it is tempting to claim that in the *Pastoral* Beethoven precisely inverted the technique of his Fifth Symphony. The idea of a 'Pastoral' Symphony was in no way unprecedented; Beethoven actually adapted his movement titles from those in a symphony by the eighteenth-century composer Justin Heinrich Knecht entitled *Le Portrait musical de la nature*. The realization of the *Pastoral* Symphony, however, is not conventional but unique; it embodies an artistic approach in the mainstream of Beethoven's creative development. Here, as in the C minor Symphony, an overall design is imposed whereby the later movements flow directly into one another. In the Fifth Symphony the scherzo is linked through a transition to the finale and is later recalled before the recapitulation of that movement. Of the five movements of the *Pastoral*, the last three are directly connected: the

'Merry gathering of villagers' is disrupted by the 'Thunderstorm' and resolves into the concluding 'Shepherd's song', expressing 'happy, grateful thanks after the storm'.

In accordance with its less directional or deterministic aesthetic, the *Pastoral* Symphony shows much affinity between the opening movement and the finale, quite unlike the polar opposition embodied in the Fifth. Following the beautifully placid *Allegro*, marked 'Pleasant, cheerful feelings aroused on arriving in the countryside', and the following 'Scene at the brook', with bird-calls in the winds interpolated before the conclusion, Beethoven introduces the symphony's first marked contrast in the central dance movement. The elements of humour and parody that surface here are not unusual for him; F major, the key of this *Allegro*, is the tonality of several of his most comic pieces, ranging from the Piano Sonatas op. 10 no. 2 and op. 54 to the Eighth Symphony and the String Quartet op. 135. One of Beethoven's funniest ideas is his parody of a village bassoonist, in the middle of the first section. The bassoon player is unable to play along with the oboe and strings, since he or she can produce only two notes, which vividly conveys a homely touch of rustic surroundings! Just as humorous, though more subtle, is the following sympathetic imitation by the violas and cellos of the falling pitches produced by the worthy bassoonist.

Beethoven interrupts the merry-making of the peasants with an abrupt deceptive cadence, as the natural elements force their attention on the countryfolk. The effective realism of the 'storm', with its wind, rain, thunder, and lightning, is used here to make a dramatic point that puts the rest of the work into a new perspective. Hector Berlioz saw this clearly when he wrote of the climax of this *Allegro* that 'It is no longer just a wind and rain storm: it is a frightful cataclysm, a universal deluge, the end of the world . . .'.[11] In the peaceful, idyllic environment that has prevailed up to this point, the first impact of the full orchestral forces on the F minor triad early in the 'storm' is already disturbing. The climax that impressed Berlioz, on a vast diminished-seventh sonority enhanced by passing-notes in the basses, is so potent in good performance as to endanger the very premise of a 'programmatic' symphony.

It is perhaps in part for this reason that Beethoven wrote that the work was 'more an expression of feeling than tone painting' ('mehr Ausdruck der Empfindung als Mahlerei'). He does indulge in egregious tone-painting in his 'storm'—his resourceful use of the piccolo to provide streaks of lightning is one example. But unlike many programmatic works, the *Pastoral* Symphony is not at all confined to realistic depiction. At the climax Beethoven gathers together his entire arsenal of instruments, including the trombones, and breaks the syntax of the musical discourse by protracting the great syncopated chord over six bars (Ex. 40). This is a window out of the work into the world,

---

[11] *A travers chants*, p. 45.

Ex. 40 *Pastoral* Symphony op. 68/IV, bars 105–14

a psychic storm that encourages every attentive listener to re-evaluate his or her aesthetic response to the music.

In the Fifth Symphony this reflexive dimension is much more pronounced. In no other work did Beethoven achieve such a concentrated synthesis of successive movements. One aspect of this synthesis is the famous rhythmic motif of repeated notes and a falling third heard at the outset of the whole symphony. In the opening phrases Beethoven dramatizes the figure by pausing on the last notes of the motif, which momentarily holds back the full flood of the musical unfolding. Variants of this so-called 'fate' motif appear in later movements, most obviously in the insistent horn motifs of the scherzo. The motivic integration of the symphony also shapes many aspects of the thematic treatment, orchestration, and form. By combining the scherzo and finale into a composite movement, Beethoven places an elemental polarity at the core of his formal conception. Another complementary relationship holds between the terse C minor idiom of the opening *Allegro con brio*, with its overpowering force and pathos, and the tremendous final *Allegro* in C major, whose *presto* coda accomplishes the seemingly impossible, firmly resolving the formidable tensions of the entire symphony into an elemental substratum of sound and time.

In the narrative design of the symphony, the slow variation movement in Ab major represents both a lyrical diversion after the C minor pathos of the opening *Allegro* and a significant foreshadowing of the triumphant finale. The episodes of this *Andante con moto* turn repeatedly to C major with horns and trumpets, only then to withdraw mysteriously into a twilight of harmonic ambiguity. In his sketches Beethoven tried out a more straightforward anticipation of the C major finale, but settled on a solution that is more precariously balanced, suggesting the distant premonition of a goal that cannot yet be attained. The final cadence of this movement sounds unsettled; it stresses a short, ascending triadic fanfare drawn from the main theme, a figure that also presages the finale. Still another, more obvious link to the final movement is the trio of the scherzo, which employs thematic material in C major with a prominently rising contour. The pervasive ascending tendency of the music is reflected as well in the orchestration of the trio, which begins in the double basses and ends in the flute. The trio is an advance parody of the finale folded into the mocking, grotesque context of the C minor scherzo.

Beethoven originally intended to repeat the entire scherzo and trio, but the published version, without the repetition, is most effective in the overall narrative design. The scherzo thereby yields up some of its formal autonomy in the interest of the unfolding progression between movements. At the reprise of the scherzo its substance is transformed into shadowy accents, with hushed pizzicato strings and mysterious muted sounds in the winds. Then its dark humour fades into deeper obscurity as a cadence is reached in the low register in an extremely soft dynamic range, with the strings marked triple *pianissimo*. At this juncture we have reached a turning-point at the threshold of audibility.

What follows is one of the most celebrated transitions in all music (Ex. 41). The timpani are heard on low C, softly tapping the motivic rhythm, before this figure is gradually transformed into a steady pulsation. This drum sound

Ex. 41 Fifth Symphony op. 67/III, bars 316–end

Ex. 41 *cont.*

is enveloped by the strings; at the structural downbeat in bar 324 the cellos and basses settle onto a long-held A♭, pushing the music into a mysterious deceptive cadence. When the strings now try to pick up the thread of the scherzo, they are stopped in their tracks after three bars and dwell as if hypnotized on the falling intervals from the end of the fragment. Although the thematic fragment is drawn from the scherzo, its earlier temporal and formal context is completely suspended; opposing forces have come into play. The motivic scrap from the scherzo is quietly repeated over and over, and drifts higher and higher until it converges into the dominant-seventh chord for full orchestra that resolves to the emphatic beginning of the ensuing *Allegro*, marked by the first appearance of trombones in the symphony. The impact of the dominant seventh is enhanced by the mysteriously understated, yet logical and even inevitable quality of the transitional passage. The finale of the Fifth Symphony emerges suddenly, like a mirage in the desert. As it appears, however, the apparent mirage takes on the glaring force of reality, and exposes the desert as the illusion.

The finale of the Fifth absorbs something of the character of an *éclat triomphal*, with ties to French revolutionary music,[12] and this accounts in part for the dismissive reaction of some of the older critics. Alexander Ulibischeff saw the coda of the finale as 'filled up with commonplaces of military music';[13] Hermann Kretzschmar found the themes 'simple to the point of triviality'.[14] The first movement already shows a striking parallel with Cherubini's *Hymne du Panthéon*, as Arnold Schmitz observed.[15] The rich connotations of this music owe much less to such conventions, however, than to the gigantic, overreaching polarity of minor and major that embraces the whole symphony. Lawrence Kramer has rightly emphasized the relationship between the end of the first movement, with its vehement effect of minor conquering major, and the inverse process at the end of the finale, the positing of C major in a form *'that cannot be followed'*.[16] Beethoven reminds us of the conditional, and perhaps provisional, status of his triumphant final movement by recalling the scherzo in C minor in place of the development. The moment of recapitulation thus represents not merely a return of the exposition in the tonic key, but a reinterpretation of the entire intermovement transition. As the scherzo is recalled, the presence of the oboe harks back to the short expressive oboe cadenza at the recapitulation of the first movement, a moment of brief respite in the furious temporal drive of the *Allegro con brio*.

The *presto* coda leaves all doubts about a further relapse into the minor far behind by delivering the C major 'that cannot be followed'. Here, as in certain passages of the first movement of the *Eroica*, the rhythmic tension becomes so great as to flatten and almost obliterate the harmonic syntax; the movement ends with no fewer than 29 bars reiterating the tonic triad of C major, with no harmonic change whatsoever. Earlier in the coda Beethoven

---

[12] Cf. Gülke, *Zur Neuausgabe der Sinfonie Nr. 5*, esp. pp. 56–7.

[13] *Beethoven—ses critiques et ses glossateurs*, p. 205.

[14] *Führer durch den Konzertsaal*, i, p. 97.

[15] *Das romantische Beethovenbild*, p. 167; see also Rolland, *Beethoven: Les grandes époques créatrices*, who draws attention to the influence of Gluck.

[16] *Music and Poetry: the Nineteenth Century and After*, p. 235.

introduces extravagant touches in orchestration, including a high trill in the piccolo. Climax builds on climax, as the rising triadic theme of the *Allegro* is compressed into at least double time, generating an exciting linear ascent of an octave and a half from C to the highest G. This is the peak; the final phrases strive to repeat the ascent, but succeed only in reaching E, a third lower. The final chords are positioned with the mathematical precision of a gothic cathedral (Ex. 42). There are three groups of three contained in the last 13 bars: the three chords of the example, separated by rests and containing the descent of the tenth from E to C; the next three chords, at the beginnings of bars 438–40; and the overlapping closing group of three chords, each set two bars apart. But superimposed on these groupings is a bigger pattern of rhythmic impulses four bars apart, so that the closing beats of each of the basic configurations, in bars 436, 440, and 444, resonate as a larger embodiment of the same rhythm. This is the final, unsurpassable transformation and glorification of the motif that began the entire symphony.

The Fifth Symphony, like the *Andante* of the Fourth Concerto, embodies a process of symbolic transformation, which is projected with remarkable coherence over the work as a whole. Unifying motifs are almost inevitable in any such intermovement narrative design, but no less essential is the directional tension culminating in the finale—a feature that resurfaces in later masterpieces such as the Ninth Symphony and the C♯ minor Quartet. A shifting of weight to the finale occurs in certain eighteenth-century pieces—notably in Mozart's 'Jupiter' Symphony—but in Beethoven this tendency assumes such prominence as to realign the aesthetic foundations of music. In the Fifth Symphony Beethoven departs from the more static, successive classical formal models by explicitly connecting the movements, undermining their individual autonomy. A mythic pattern seems to be imposed on the overall artistic sequence, guiding the processive chain of interconnected musical forms. In its embrace of the dichotomous and its evocation of the ineffable or even the demonic, the Fifth Symphony opens the door to Romanticism, yet the profound lucidity of its musical shape defies unequivocal programmatic interpretation. In this respect, as in many others, Beethoven's importance lies in his synthesis of the old and new, of the universality of the classical harmonic framework with the quest for particularity of expression characteristic of the nineteenth century.

*   *   *

When the two new symphonies were first performed, in the Theater an der Wien on 22 December 1808, they were joined in the programme by several other pieces, including the aria 'Ah perfido!' and the G major Concerto, with the composer at the piano. The concert had some severe shortcomings, due to lack of rehearsal and the fact that the hall remained unheated in the cold

Ex. 42 Fifth Symphony op. 67/IV, bars 428–end

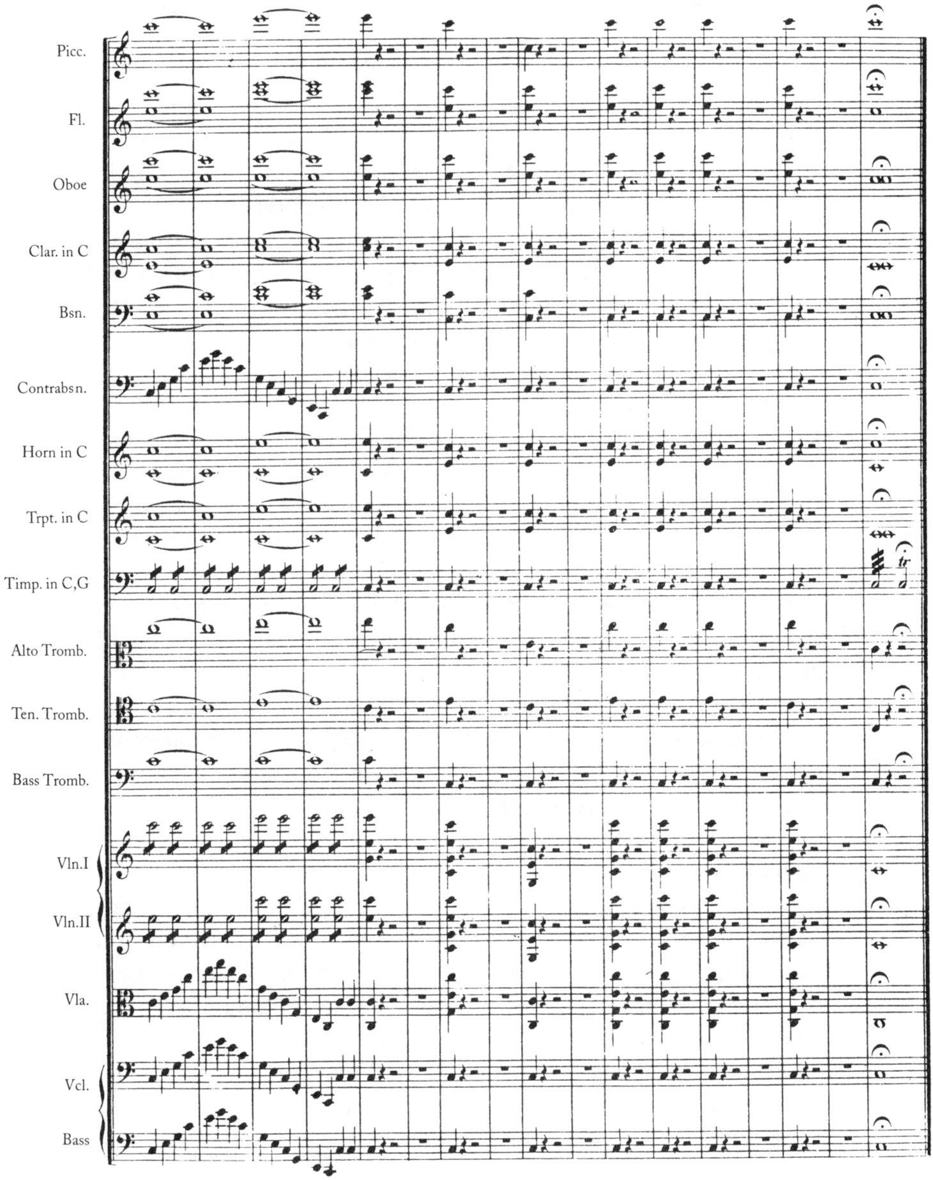

weather. Johann Friedrich Reichardt reported that 'I accepted with hearty thanks the kind offer of Prince Lobkowitz to let me sit in his box. There we continued, in the bitterest cold, too, from 6:30 until 10:30, and experienced the truth that one can easily have too much of a good thing . . .'.[17] Despite the large amount of music to be performed, Beethoven directed his energies to completing yet another work to serve as the crowning final piece of his *Akademie*: the Choral Fantasy in C major for piano, orchestra, and chorus op. 80. Its performance did not run smoothly: at one point in the middle Beethoven was obliged to stop the orchestra and begin again.

The Choral Fantasy begins with an improvisatory piano introduction, leading to a set of variations on the theme Beethoven had used in his song *Gegenliebe* WoO 118 of 1794 or 1795. Czerny reported that the poet Kuffner was engaged at the last minute to write new words for the Choral Fantasy, following hints given by the composer.[18] Beethoven probably conceived much of the music before the text was completed, since the words are missing from his sketches. The text took the form of an idealistic 'Ode to Music', reminding us of Beethoven's fascination with other poems of this general type, such as Tiedge's 'Ode to Hope' and Schiller's 'Ode to Joy'. In fact, many aspects of the Choral Fantasy anticipate Beethoven's later setting of Schiller's text in the choral finale of the Ninth Symphony, as the composer himself recognized. In a letter from March 1824 Beethoven described the choral finale of the Ninth as 'a setting of the words of Schiller's immortal "Lied an die Freude" in the same way as my pianoforte fantasia with chorus, but on a far grander scale'.[19]

Yet another work from this period captures Beethoven's abilities in keyboard improvisation: the Fantasy for piano solo op. 77. Although not finished until October 1809, this piece may represent a revised version of the improvised solo fantasy Beethoven played at the *Akademie*. The op. 77 Fantasy also culminates in a set of variations, in B major, following a strikingly free opening section abounding in thematic contrasts and sudden modulations, in a style reminiscent of C. P. E. Bach. The initial gesture of this work is a rapid descending scale, which seems torn, as it were, from the celestial ether; rather than support its key, G minor, Beethoven proceeds to the remote D♭ major, the key of the contrasting lyrical theme. The op. 77 Fantasy and op. 80 Choral Fantasy both offer insight into Beethoven's considerable powers of invention outside the formal demands of the classical sonata style.

1809 was a year of upheaval in Vienna, bringing events that had much impact on the composer. The high inflation and unstable economic condi-

---

[17] Thayer-Forbes, p. 448.

[18] Thayer-Forbes, pp. 448, 451. Nottebohm questioned Czerny's attribution of the text to Kuffner and speculated that the author might have been Georg Friedrich Treitschke, who revised the libretto of *Fidelio* in 1814.

[19] Anderson, iii, L. 1269.

tions wrought by the Napoleonic wars worried Beethoven, who considered leaving the city. The circumstances are tangled and hard to evaluate; once again, Beethoven's ambivalent attitude to Napoleon lies at the heart of the matter. Shortly before, Beethoven had received a tempting offer of employment at Cassel from Napoleon's brother Jerôme, who had been installed there as King of Westphalia one year earlier. On 1 November 1808 Beethoven wrote to Count Oppersdorf that 'I have been asked to become Kapellmeister to the King of Westphalia, and it could be that I will accept this offer'.[20] In a letter dated 7 January 1809 to Breitkopf & Härtel Beethoven indicated that he had decided to move, and Ries asserted that around February the contract for the position at Cassel was ready and 'lacked only the signature'.[21]

In response to Beethoven's imminent departure, a counter-offer and annuity contract were drawn up by three of Beethoven's loyal patrons, the Archduke Rudolph, Prince Lobkowitz, and Prince Ferdinand Kinsky. All three were younger than Beethoven: the archduke only 21, Lobkowitz 35, and Kinsky 27. The agreement, dated 1 March 1809, guaranteed Beethoven a substantial income for life in return for the continuation of his artistic contributions in Vienna. The later history of the annuity payments was complicated not only by steep inflation and currency reform but by the premature death in 1812 of Kinsky and the virtual bankruptcy of Lobkowitz, whose excessive expenditures on art had drained his resources. Beethoven struggled with considerable determination and occasional legal interventions to assure the continuance of the stipend to the end of his life.

Three of Beethoven's major works of chamber music were dedicated to the persons who helped negotiate the annuity agreement: the Cello Sonata in A major op. 69 was dedicated to Ignaz Gleichenstein, and the two Piano Trios op. 70 to Countess Erdődy. In the op. 69 Sonata the cello begins unaccompanied, *dolce* and legato, with motifs that permeate the entire first movement. After the main theme has been heard in both instruments it is suddenly dramatically altered, and cast into A minor. This contrast between the quiet atmosphere of the lyrical opening and a turbulent, rhythmically charged continuation is characteristic of the *Allegro, ma non tanto*. The second movement is a scherzo, whose main theme takes on a strong rhythmic tension through syncopation. Like the cello sonatas of op. 5, this work has no independent slow movement, but the finale is introduced by an expressive *Adagio cantabile* in E major, whose thematic material bears a subtle relationship to the finale.

At the beginning of his D major Trio op. 70 no. 1 Beethoven reshapes the basic thematic outline from his earlier piano sonata in this key, op. 10 no. 3, to endow the music with an intense forward drive. Instead of an upbeat figure descending a fourth followed by a sequential rise in pitch, as in the sonata,

---

[20] Anderson, i, L. 178.   [21] Thayer-Forbes, pp. 453–4, 458.

Beethoven compresses the *initial* four-note motif, starting on the downbeat, *fortissimo*. This foreshortening generates a kind of metrical dissonance within the triple metre that infuses much energy into the succeeding motivic figures based on fourths. He thereby reverses his normal procedure, whereby rhythmic diminution follows the basic motivic presentation, and he heightens the outcome of this arresting unison phrase through a shocking turn into the minor mode, as F is substituted for F♯ in bar 5. Beethoven packs an extraordinary density of ideas into the concentrated unison opening of this work.

No less remarkable is the slow movement of op. 70 no. 1, on account of which the work has become known as the 'Ghost' Trio. Czerny wrote about this *Largo assai ed espressivo* in D minor that it 'resembles an appearance from the underworld. One could think not inappropriately of the first appearance of the ghost in *Hamlet*'.[22] Beethoven's sketches do imply a Shakespearean connection here, though to a different play, *Macbeth*. During 1808 Heinrich von Collin offered Beethoven part of an opera libretto based on Shakespeare's *Macbeth*; the drama, like Shakespeare's, was to have begun with the witches' scene. In leaves originally belonging to Beethoven's Pastoral Symphony Sketchbook, entries for the projected opera on *Macbeth* are juxtaposed with work on the slow movement of the trio. An uncanny atmosphere invests Beethoven's *Largo*, with its mysterious tremolos, chromatic textures, and powerful dynamic contrasts. Lockwood has shown how intensively Beethoven laboured on the final cadence, painstakingly devising a solution that does not resolve but sustains the tension until the beginning of the ensuing *presto* finale.[23]

During 1808–9 Beethoven showed a marked tendency to compose works in E♭ major; the Trio op. 70 no. 2, Piano Concerto op. 73, String Quartet op. 74, and Piano Sonata op. 81*a* are all in this key. The E♭ Trio looks back to Mozart and especially Haydn, while at the same time anticipating Schubert in its gracious third movement, marked *Allegretto ma non troppo*. In the first movement, the relationship of the *poco sostenuto* slow introduction to the *Allegro ma non troppo* shows parallels with Haydn's 'Drumroll' Symphony (no. 103) in the same key, as Anthony Burton has observed; an affinity with Haydn's work can also be felt in the slow movement, a set of variations on two alternating themes.[24] Tovey wrote of an 'integration of Mozart's and Haydn's resources' in op. 70 no. 2;[25] the subtle stylistic play at work in this trio transcends the classicizing impulse in some of Beethoven's earlier compositions, such as the C major Mass of 1807, with its more obvious debt to Haydn. The most

---

[22] *On the Proper Performance of All Beethoven's Works for the Piano*, p. [87] 97.

[23] 'Beethoven and the Problem of Closure', *Beiträge zu Beethovens Kammermusik*, pp. 267–70; *Beethoven: Studies in the Creative Process*, pp. 191–7.

[24] Anthony Burton, notes to the recording by Wilhelm Kempff, Henryk Szering, and Pierre Fournier (Deutsche Grammophon), p. 17.

[25] *Beethoven*, p. 88.

stylistically progressive movement of the E♭ Trio is the gentle, scherzo-like third movement. Beethoven breaks with convention by placing this *Allegretto* not in the tonic but in the subdominant key, A♭ major, and he introduces enharmonic shifts of Schubertian delicacy in the trio, with the piano penetrating the highest register in a transparent, *pianissimo* texture.

The Fifth Piano Concerto, from the beginning of 1809, is cast in a more brilliant, heroic mould. Its outer movements assume a majestic character, with rhythmic figures evocative of military style and a formal breadth reminiscent of the *Eroica* Symphony. Yet the important dramatic events often depend on the withdrawal of the music into a mysterious stillness. In the solo exposition of the opening *Allegro* the pianist presents a transparent, *pianissimo* subject in B minor and C♭ major, thereby presaging the *Adagio un poco mosso* in B major, the enharmonic equivalent of C♭. The last section of the development almost recedes into inaudibility, as the music is reduced to its seminal rhythmic motif before increasingly intense repetitions of this figure open the door to the recapitulation. Beethoven had employed such a quiet withdrawal preceding the recapitulation in the first movement of his Fourth Symphony, as we have seen. By no means do Beethoven's development sections in his sonata designs always require a steady increase in tension leading up to the recapitulation. As early as 1800, in the first movement of the Piano Sonata in B♭ op. 22, Beethoven had experimented with a development that unfolds into a vast *descrescendo*, to be followed by a fresh start at the beginning of the ensuing reprise. Another example from the period in question is the first movement development of the Quartet in E♭ op. 74, which gradually fades into *pianissimo* before the use of pizzicato brings an even softer dynamic level; only in the last three bars does Beethoven prescribe a *crescendo* leading to the reprise in *forte*.

In the overall design of the E♭ major Concerto the serene slow movement in B major acts as an immense parenthesis; its mood of dream-like reflection is dissipated with wonderful sensitivity at the transition to the finale. The cadential figure of the *Adagio* theme, with its repeated motif B–A♯–B, is reinterpreted in a long *diminuendo* passage, beginning at the point where the leading-note A♯ falls to A♮ instead of rising to B. The cadence is thereby interrupted, and the piano descends out of the high pitch registers to alight eventually on a soft B in the bass. The pivotal moment is reached when this B octave is sustained through a bar in the bassoons. For the next downward shift of a semitone is not merely motivic but signals a structural modulation: A♯ becomes B♭, the dominant of E♭ major. When the resolution to B♭ is sounded and then prolonged in the horns, the slow movement is finished, but Beethoven preserves its tempo and dynamic level in his ensuing anticipation in the piano of the finale's rondo theme. Schumann imitated this passage at the transition to the finale of his Piano Concerto in A minor op. 54.

By the spring of 1809 political events in Austria had reached a crisis. On

9 April Austria declared war on France; Tyson has noted that Beethoven's sketches for Collin's *Östreich über Alles* and for a *Jubelgesang* may be connected with the patriotic fervour engendered by these conditions.[26] By the end of April the French armies had invaded Austria. On the night of 11–12 May the French bombarded Vienna; Beethoven took refuge in the cellar of his brother Carl's house, and, according to Ries, 'covered his head with pillows so as not to hear the cannons'.[27] Vienna capitulated the next day. During the ensuing occupation Beethoven is supposed to have displayed contempt for the French military, but he did not avoid friendly contact with individual Frenchmen. He repeatedly met the Baron de Trémont, a French officer and music lover who vividly described Beethoven's improvisations and commented on the composer's fascination with Napoleon.

In the wake of the war with France and occupation of Vienna, many of Beethoven's friends and patrons left the city, including the Archduke Rudolph, who departed on 4 May 1809, not to return until 30 January 1810. Shortly thereafter, on 4 February, Beethoven offered Breitkopf & Härtel three new piano sonatas for publication: the two-movement Sonata in F♯ dedicated to the Countess Therese Brunswick and eventually issued as op. 78, the 'Sonatina' in G op. 79, and the Sonata in E♭ major op. 81a. Notwithstanding its compact dimensions and motivic similarities to Beethoven's *Ritterballett* of 1791, op. 79 is a highly polished work. The rhythmic élan of its outer movements is reflected in the unusual direction 'Presto alla tedesca' for the first movement: the relaxed pace more typical of a German dance is supplanted here by vivacious energy. The second movement, in G minor, marked *Andante*, displays metrical ambiguity and a remote, archaic quality suggesting the influence of Eastern folklore; one is reminded at least distantly of the *Allegretto* of the C major Quartet op. 59 no. 3.

An unusual feature of the F♯ major Sonata op. 78 is the introductory motto encapsulated in the four opening bars, marked *Adagio cantabile*. Euphonious chords enhanced with expressive appoggiaturas rise above a deep pedal point in the bass; the gesture is declamatory, yet tender and heartfelt. This quality of *Innigkeit* is found often in Beethoven, yet nowhere more prominently than in some of the solo piano sonatas, from the gracious finale of the E♭ Sonata op. 7 to the glowing lyricism of the opening *Allegretto* of op. 101. Several such works were dedicated to Beethoven's female piano pupils: Countess 'Babette' Keglevics (later Countess Odescalchi) received the dedications of op. 7 and other works, while the distinguished pianist Baroness Ertmann, whom Beethoven once addressed as his 'dear, valued Dorothea-Cäcilia', received the dedication of op. 101. Therese Brunswick was presumably a less accomplished player than Keglevics or Ertmann, but Beethoven devoted long hours to

---

[26] *The Beethoven Sketchbooks*, p. 188.   [27] Wegeler-Ries, *Biographische Notizen*, p. 121.

teaching her and her sister Josephine as early as 1799, when, as she later recalled, he 'never tired' of 'holding and bending my fingers'. Uhde has suggested that the choice of key for the F♯ major sonata may have had a pedagogical purpose, and that the intimately lyrical character of the music was influenced by Bach's works in this key in *The Well-Tempered Clavier*.[28] A tight network of motivic relationships takes shape in op. 78 as the ascending contour and harmonic colour of the fervent opening motto are reinterpreted in ensuing passages of the *Allegro, ma non troppo*. In turn, the second group of the exposition introduces a motif of three emphatic chords, the last marked *sforzando*, which are juxtaposed with more gentle figures marked *piano*. A variant of this motif is employed in the principal theme of the finale.

The most weighty of the three sonatas is the 'Lebewohl' in E♭ major op. 81*a*, a piece which, like op. 78, uses a motto technique in its opening movement. In this instance Beethoven entered the dates of the archduke's departure and return into the score and allowed the emotional progression of 'farewell–absence–reunion' to determine the basic character of the three movements. He was irritated by the use, in the first edition, of French instead of German titles, probably not only because of the difference in meaning between 'Les adieux' and 'Das Lebewohl', but also because of the relationship between the falling horn motif (G–F–E♭, with E♭–B♭–G in the lower voice) at the outset of the slow introduction and the syllables 'Le-be-wohl', which are written above these chords.

The initial harmonization of this 'Lebewohl' motif in the slow introduction of the first movement does not affirm the tonic, E♭ major, but leads first deceptively to the submediant, C minor, and then, in the eighth bar, to a sustained harmony on the more remote flat sixth, C♭ major. The first strong cadential arrival at the tonic triad of E♭ is thus delayed until five bars into the following *Allegro*. The tonal ambiguity of the slow introduction contributes to its suspended, searching character, qualities that reappear in the second movement, 'Abwesenheit' ('Absence'). At the same time, the 'Lebewohl' motto of a stepwise descending third assumes much importance throughout the *Allegro* of the first movement, which begins with an energetic reinterpretation of the progression G–F–E♭ above a chromatically falling bass. In the development Beethoven further exploits the association of this motto with ambiguous harmonies, leading the music into remote key areas; but the harmonic boldness characteristic of this sonata is most of all evident in the coda, where the tonic and dominant are repeatedly sounded together (Ex. 43). Here the imitations of the original motto seem to recede into the distance, implying that the departure has taken place. (In many passages of this *Allegro*, the 'Lebewohl' motif is written in whole-notes, so that its actual duration in

Ex. 43 Piano Sonata op. 81a/I, coda

performance approximates its initial appearances in the *Adagio*, where it is notated in quarter-notes.)

The 'Absence' has a slow processional character and (like the *Introduzione* of the *Waldstein* Sonata) leads directly into the finale. Though the principal key is C minor, the opening dwells not on the tonic triad but on a diminished-seventh chord; indeed, in a later restatement of the initial motif at the same pitch level (bar 11), the harmony is intensified through the use of a dissonant chord of the eleventh. Immediately afterwards the motif is foreshortened and stressed by accents above a descending bass; this poignant and expressive passage leads through a brief transition to a consoling, cantabile subject in the dominant key. The entire period embracing these two themes is then repeated, beginning in Bb minor; and we are given the sense that this cyclic repetition of grief and consolation could continue indefinitely.

After six bars of a third period, in which the music ascends to the dominant-seventh chord of Eb, the long-awaited event occurs in the form of a decisive and jubilant elaboration of this chord in a ten-bar transition to the finale. This is, of course, the moment of reunion. A dancing *Vivacissimamente* in sonata form now transforms the 'Lebewohl' motif from the first movement into scintillating figuration. Beethoven recalls the symbolic progression from the 'Absence' to 'Reunion' by transforming hard, bleak, unharmonized octaves into delicate turns with grace-notes in the swinging 6/8 metre. This finale embodies not only an outcome of the overall narrative progression of movements, as in the *Pathétique* Sonata, but acts as dramatic culmination of the entire work. Beethoven apparently delayed the completion of this exuberant finale until the actual return of the archduke gave him cause for celebration and a reason to immortalize their friendship through a work of art.

6

Consolidation

1810–1812

ACCORDING to Czerny, Beethoven once said that 'Schiller's poems are extremely difficult for the musician. The composer must know how to lift himself far above the poet; who can do that with a Schiller text? In that respect Goethe is much easier!'[1] Schiller himself had grappled with this difference in his treatise *Über naive und sentimentale Dichtung* ('On Naive and Sentimental Poetry') of 1795–6, where he postulated two basic mental attitudes, the 'naive' and the 'sentimental', with the latter understood in the sense of 'reflective'. Goethe, like Shakespeare and the greatest Greek poets, was regarded as 'naive' because his work mirrors the external world directly and unreflectingly; Schiller saw his own poetry and much literature of his time as 'sentimental', in that it reconstructs, reflects, and modifies the world through an active intrusion of the imagination. Beethoven's art straddles both sides of the distinction; the 'sentimental' aspect is perhaps most succinctly captured by Nietzsche's comment that Beethoven 'writes music about music'.[2] The less idealistic, more realistic cast of Goethe's poetry made it more accessible to the musician, in Beethoven's view. Nevertheless, Beethoven experienced difficulty in setting Goethe's poetry in earlier years. Of the eight songs to texts by Goethe that Beethoven attempted between 1800 and 1804, six remained incomplete. And in 1808, when Beethoven tackled 'Nur wer die Sehnsucht kennt' from *Wilhelm Meister*, he produced no one definitive setting. On his autograph score Beethoven wrote, perhaps ironically, that 'I

---

[1] *On the Proper Performance of All Beethoven's Works for the Piano*, p. 19; translation amended.
[2] 'Der Wanderer und sein Schatten', no. 152 in *Menschliches, Allzumenschliches I and II*, p. 616.

lacked time to produce a *good* setting, therefore several tries'. He left four settings of this text.[3]

The climax of Beethoven's engagement with Goethe's writings came in
1810. His main project during the first half of the year was the incidental music
to Goethe's tragedy *Egmont* op. 84, which was first performed on 15 or 18 June.
During the following months he also completed three songs to Goethe texts
that were published as op. 83 nos. 1–3: *Wonne der Wehmut*, *Sehnsucht*, and *Mit
einem gemalten Band* (see Plate 9). *Wonne der Wehmut* might be translated as
'Bliss in Sorrow'; we shall examine this song in detail in order to illustrate
some characteristic features of Beethoven's text-setting (Ex. 44). Beethoven's
best lieder have not received the attention they deserve; the songs have always
been overshadowed by his much larger production of instrumental music.

The key of *Wonne der Wehmut*, E major, was associated by Beethoven with
a reflective, elevated, and often ethereal or religious character. Examples
among the songs include the first of the Gellert Lieder, *Bitten* (op. 48 no. 1),
the *Opferlied*, and the *Abendlied unterm gestirnten Himmel* of 1820. Similar
qualities surface in some of Beethoven's instrumental works in this key. As we
have seen, he is said to have conceived the E major slow movement of the second 'Razumovsky' quartet while 'contemplating the starry heavens and thinking of the music of the spheres'. His piano music in this key and general
character ranges from the main theme of the *Adagio* of the Piano Sonata op.
2 no. 3 to the slow movement of the Third Concerto and the variation finale
of the Sonata op. 109.

A comparison of the song with Goethe's original poem reveals how freely
Beethoven has altered the text by repeating and interpolating certain words.
'Trocknet nicht!' is inserted between the third and fourth lines of Goethe's
poem. Subsequently, Beethoven reiterates the last two lines of the text, and he
closes the song by changing the order of words, with a last repetition of
'unglücklicher Liebe!', followed by a final, resolving statement of 'Trocknet
nicht!'. He has reshaped the text in accordance with his musical interpretation.

Beethoven's means are simple but telling; like Schubert's six Heine settings
of 1828, *Wonne der Wehmut* displays a miraculous artistic economy whereby the
most basic elements of harmony and melody are endowed with a pregnant
significance. The song begins without introduction. The twofold statement of
'Trocknet nicht!' is supported by a harmonic progression from the tonic triad
in root position through a dominant-seventh chord to another tonic in first
inversion in the middle of bar 2; the bass ascends by step, with the subdominant reached in bar 3 and the tonic in second inversion in bar 4. The resolution to the dominant in this bar marks the end of the first larger phrase.

[3] Cf. the facsimile edition with commentary by Helga Lühning, *Nur wer die Sehnsucht kennt*
(Bonn, 1986).

Ex. 44 *Wonne der Wehmut* op. 83 no. 1

Ex. 44 *cont.*

Dry not, dry not, tears of eternal love! Ah, it is only to the half-dried eye that the world seems bleak and dead!
Dry not, dry not, tears of unhappy love!

Beethoven's basic voice-leading in this opening passage involves an ascending stepwise progression from the third degree, G♯, in the voice and right hand of the piano, supported by a parallel ascent in the bass beginning a third lower on the tonic note E and reaching B at the half-cadence on the dominant. It is in relation to this firm structure that Beethoven introduces telling expressive nuances. Especially striking are the vocal appoggiaturas on 'nicht', stressing the negative import of 'Dry not!' as a means of heightening the poignant, almost masochistic conflict within the protagonist. These vocal appoggiaturas embellish and resolve to the pitches A and B heard in the piano; their dissonance imparts forward impulse to the music by twice emphasizing a weak beat, the second eighth of the duple metre.

In a stronger metrical position on the second quarter of each of these bars, the pianist plays a falling scale with slightly detached articulation, beginning exactly an octave above the voice, sounding the same note, A, in the higher register. Rhythmically, moreover, the initial A in the piano corresponds to what has just been sung a moment before; this A, too, serves as a vocal appoggiatura in its character and structure. The entire descending scale in the piano is thus set into motion by the sigh figure derived from the vocal setting of 'nicht'.[4] The first appearance of the falling scale sounds parenthetical, as a linear unfolding of the dominant-seventh chords heard immediately before and after. This important motif is strictly derived from the voice part, and its presence greatly heightens the impact of the vocal delivery of 'Trocknet nicht!'.

Some commentators have described this descending scale figure in the piano as a 'veil of tears', but it is more than a pictorial device. In fact, Beethoven uses the evocative descending scale in a much more generalized relationship with the text; the last two times the word 'Thränen' ('tears') is sung, the scale is not heard in the immediate context. This is not to deny that the falling scale is associated with tears: the link is indeed unmistakable near the beginning of the second larger musical phrase, when the voice declaims 'Trocknet nicht!' while the motif reappears in the piano. The point is that Beethoven's sensitive development of the vocal appoggiatura into the descending motif in the piano is part of a larger process whereby the expressive affect derived from the poem is transformed into the musical structure. He does not simply depict particular words by means of musical motifs; the words enter into a dialogue with the music, which is not subordinated to the text but, on the contrary, creates a new formal context for it.

By imitating the initial vocal phrases in the piano in bars 5 and 6, and incorporating the words 'Trocknet nicht!', Beethoven introduces the subsequent lines of the poem in a manner that parallels the beginning. This procedure departs from the structure of Goethe's poem; but it allows Beethoven to set up expectations of a paired phrase beginning in bar 5, implying a pattern that would normally lead to a cadence in the tonic key in bar 8. There is no such continuation, however, since the words 'Ah, it is only to the half-dried eye that the world seems bleak and dead!' motivate a change in character. In place of the rising melodic motion in E major from the opening Beethoven now employs a vocal descent laden with chromaticism. The word 'öde' ('bleak') is stressed by a dissonant appoggiatura against a dynamically emphasized seventh chord in the piano. But most striking is the treatment of the words 'wie todt die Welt ihm erscheint!', with its accented chords and descent in octaves in the bass of the piano.

The voice reiterates a single pitch to these words: G♮, a dark point of sound a semitone below the bright G♯ of the opening. One reason for Beethoven's stubborn emphasis on this note is that he is to return to the G in later sections of the song, recapturing the same bleak sound in relation to different words. The continuation in bar 11 provides yet another variant of the opening motif, with the rising figure in the piano twice juxtaposed with 'Trocknet nicht' in

---

[4] Cf. Boettcher, *Beethoven als Liederkomponist*, p. 115.

the voice. What is touching here is the very absence of the descending scale figure that was previously heard. The tears no longer flow; the cheeks dry. The current of sustaining inner life threatens to expire.

The second interjection of 'Trocknet nicht' (bar 12) leads directly into the following phrase, a double setting of 'Thränen unglücklicher Liebe'. By repeating these words Beethoven underscores their importance in the piece as a whole. The inner drama of this paradoxical poem resides in the tension between 'tears of eternal love' and 'tears of unhappy love'; at stake here is the human capacity to experience happiness despite the pain of loss. In the language of the poem, Goethe only juxtaposes these sentiments, although his striking title *Wonne der Wehmut* does conjoin them. A remarkable feature of Beethoven's setting of 'Thränen unglücklicher Liebe' is that he combines aspects of two earlier passages, 'tears of eternal love' and 'how dead the world seems'. The rhythm and melodic ascent to E remind us of the beginning of the song, but the dark tell-tale G at 'Liebe' harks back to the end of the preceding phrase, alluding to the loss of feeling signalled by the drying of the tears.

In this context Beethoven cannot end his song where Goethe concluded his text. The musical sentiment spills over, forcing extensive re-use of the preceding words. Such a practice is by no means confined to Beethoven's lieder but is characteristic of his text-setting in his most massive vocal works. The final sections of the choral finale of the Ninth Symphony, for instance, are based entirely on the repetition of earlier parts of the text, and the great fugue and coda of the Credo in the *Missa solemnis* elaborates no more than the last five words, 'Et vitam venturi saeculi Amen'. Something of the same process is at work in miniature in this astonishing song from 1810.

In the final eight bars Beethoven brings together the conflicting sentiments and at last succeeds in truly integrating them, absorbing melancholy into bliss in the unconsummated symbol of musical expression. 'Trocknet nicht' is recalled as a reprise of the beginning of the song, complete with the descending scale; but Beethoven now carries the voice part into the upper register to find its peak at 'Thränen', on high G♮. This pitch is held over the barline; the very full harmonic support in the piano recalls the earlier setting of 'wie todt die Welt ihm erscheint!'. Here, finally, the music strives toward that cadence in E major that had already been implied in the second of the paired phrases near the beginning. Beethoven imposes a formal symmetry on the song as a whole by employing paired phrases again at the conclusion. The first of these reaches a deceptive cadence in bar 19; the second supplies the authentic E major cadence two bars before the end.

But we have not yet touched the heart of Beethoven's conception, that moment when the emphasis on G♮ and the descending motif converge in the vocal part. This occurs fittingly at the word 'Thränen' ('tears'); the rhythm of an eighth and two sixteenths in bar 18 corresponds to the falling motif in the piano. The consequent phrase recaptures the climactic sonority in the piano and retraces the descending contour of the preceding bars. The overall drop in register spans the interval of a tenth, from G to E.

One of the most fascinating aspects of Beethoven's song is that this descent represents an elaboration, or 'composing out', of the descending scale motif. Even between the two phrases there is a remarkable sense of organic growth. The second phrase supplies the neighbour-note A above the G♮ in bar 20 and a stepwise descent from C♯ to B in bars 20–1. The original descending linear progression from A through a seventh to B is thus embedded in the voice and piano part of these bars. Conspicuous as well is the linear discontinuity after the dominant note B is reached at 'Liebe'; here both voice and piano drop by the interval of a sixth; the last segment of the linear path is left open.

The compelling logic of this melodic gap is revealed in the last two bars. With a last, framing assertion of 'Trocknet nicht!' the voice appropriates the falling motif, fills the linear gap, and carries the progression firmly into the E major cadence. This gesture provides both a linear and rhythmic resolution of the motif. But it remains for the piano to restate its version of the descent, which for the first and only time is now extended to reach the same stable tonic resolution as was affirmed in the voice. The consolation of 'bliss in sorrow' is conveyed through Beethoven's ingenious techniques of musical transformation and resolution.

*　　　*　　　*

The small scale of *Wonne der Wehmut* allows for a more comprehensive analysis in a short space, illustrating aspects of Beethoven's musical language that surface in many of his larger instrumental compositions. Among his lieder this setting particularly stands out; here Beethoven did 'lift himself above the poet', revealing new perspectives on the poetry that Goethe probably did not fully understand. As is well known, Goethe preferred settings of his poetry that kept the text in the forefront to those in which the music assumes pre-eminence. But *Wonne der Wehmut* also invites consideration in relation to the biographical context of this period. The theme of the 'distant beloved' surfaces repeatedly in Beethoven's songs from *An den fernen Geliebten* of 1809 to the cycle *An die ferne Geliebte* of 1816. One is also reminded in this connection of *An die Geliebte*, a copy of which Beethoven gave to Antonie Brentano in March 1812, as Solomon has shown.[5] *Wonne der Wehmut*, with its touching meditation on 'tears of eternal love' and 'tears of unhappy love', gives compelling artistic expression to issues that were of surpassing personal importance to Beethoven during these years.

[5] *Beethoven*, p. 175.

Early in 1810 Beethoven proposed marriage to the young Therese Malfatti, who rejected him. His famous piano piece *Für Elise* WoO 59 is connected to this episode of his life. As Max Unger first pointed out, Ludwig Nohl's reading of the inscription as 'For Elise' is probably an error, since the manuscript was found among the possessions of Therese von Malfatti and was apparently entitled 'For Therese'.[6] Still more significant than his relationship to Therese Malfatti was Beethoven's association with the Brentano family, and especially with Antonie Brentano and her sister-in-law Bettina Brentano. Antonie (see Plate 10) was the daughter of the distinguished diplomat, art collector, and scholar Johann Melchior von Birkenstock; Beethoven was a welcome guest in the Birkenstock mansion. Bettina vividly described the house in a letter to her friend Goethe:

Here I live in the house of the deceased Birkenstock, surrounded by two thousand copperplate engravings, as many marble vases, antique fragments of hands and feet, paintings, Chinese garments, coins, geological collections, sea insects, telescopes and countless maps, plans of ancient buried empires and cities, skillfully carved walking-sticks, precious documents, and finally, the sword of the Emperor Carolus.[7]

After her father's death in October 1809 Antonie returned to her home town with her husband Franz Brentano; she was to stay until 1812, when the couple permanently left Vienna to return to Frankfurt, where his business was located. Thus it was that this cultured family came into close contact with Beethoven at precisely that time when his interest in Goethe's poetry and drama was most intense. The Brentano family figured very significantly in the literature of German Romanticism. Bettina's brother Clemens was author of the important novel *Godwi*, published in 1801; she married the distinguished scholar and writer Ludwig Achim von Arnim. She was closely acquainted with Goethe and took it upon herself to encourage an exchange between Beethoven and the great poet at Weimar. The accounts she left of her experiences with Beethoven are not free from literary exaggeration and even occasional deception, but they assume special interest because of their bearing on Beethoven's aesthetic attitudes and ideas. Meanwhile, the heavily revised manuscript of Beethoven's early version of *Wonne der Wehmut* (Hess 142) came into Goethe's hands, probably through Friedrich Rochlitz. A decade later, in October 1821, Goethe placed this treasure before the young Felix Mendelssohn, who delighted the ageing poet with his performance and with his clean transcription of the song, which is housed, together with Beethoven's autograph, in Weimar.

When Beethoven first met Bettina in May 1810, he sang and played for her two of his Goethe songs: *Kennst du das Land?* from *Wilhelm Meister* (op. 75 no. 1) and *Trocknet nicht, Thränen der ewigen Liebe*. Immediately after this

---

[6] Thayer-Forbes, p. 502.   [7] Cited in Solomon, *Beethoven Essays*, p. 166.

encounter Bettina wrote enthusiastically to Goethe about Beethoven; in his reply Goethe suggested that Beethoven meet him in the summer at Karlsbad. That the two great artists actually did meet at the Bohemian spas two years later, in July 1812, surely owed much to the initiative of Bettina Brentano.

In Bettina's letters to Goethe about Beethoven she repeatedly emphasizes the notion of a synthesis between rational and sensuous faculties—an idea that particularly captivated her and which she attributes to the composer. Thus she writes on 28 May that 'Beethoven feels himself to be the founder of a new sensuous basis in the intellectual life'. Later in the same letter she describes Beethoven as having said that 'Music, verily, is the mediator between the life of the mind and the senses'. The later elaborations in her letter about music as 'the one incorporeal entrance into the higher world of knowledge' and of music as 'the electrical soil in which the mind thinks, lives, feels' similarly imply a bond between the mind and sensibility that is potentially achieved through music. In yet another passage Bettina attributes to Beethoven the statement that 'Music gives to the mind the relationship to harmony. An isolated thought still has the feeling of the whole, of relatedness in the mind'.[8]

Many of these statements are variations on a theme, and it is not necessary to have full confidence in the details of Bettina Brentano's report in order to evaluate the general import of her testimony. At bottom, what we confront here is a sometimes fanciful embellishment of Schiller's basic conviction about the merging of the rational and sensuous in the work of art. By 1810 the time was ripe for such speculations, and an urgent need was felt to augment the critical vocabulary in order to better describe the artwork as a tensional synthesis of conflicting elements. A landmark in this development appeared less than two months after Bettina's letter to Goethe: E. T. A. Hoffmann's famous review of the Fifth Symphony, with its appropriation from Jean Paul Richter of the idiosyncratic term *Besonnenheit*, or 'self-possession', to describe Beethoven's combination of structural control and expressive vehemence.

At the time Bettina Brentano met Beethoven he was hard at work on the incidental music to *Egmont* op. 84. In Goethe's play, the Flemish Count Egmont faces execution by the Spaniards, against whom he has led an uprising. He accepts his fate proudly, predicting the liberation of his country. In the *Egmont* Overture, Beethoven seizes upon the conflict between the personal tragedy of Count Egmont and the larger ideal of freedom for which Egmont sacrifices himself. The pause at the end of the reprise of this stern, concentrated overture is of symbolic import—in his sketches Beethoven wrote that 'the death could be expressed through a rest'. Unlike the *Coriolan* Overture, however, a tragic end is avoided here: the piece is capped by the

---

[8] These letters are reproduced with commentary in Thayer-Forbes, pp. 494–8.

'Victory' Symphony in F major, with its gripping apotheosis of the fallen hero and his just cause.

The *Egmont* Overture opens with a slow introduction that juxtaposes massive orchestral unisons and low, accented motifs in the strings with plaintive, transparent phrases in the winds in the higher registers. These contrasting ideas reappear in the ensuing *Allegro*, where they are paired together and developed extensively. The expressive associations of these motifs—the relentless, *fortissimo* gestures on the one hand, and a more yielding, lyrical expression on the other—are clarified at the end of the F minor *Allegro*. First, the ominous knocking rhythms are given to the horns and trumpets; then the dismal fanfare is heard *fortissimo* from most of the orchestra. The following lyrical response of the strings is abruptly cut off, and a short pause follows; this is the moment symbolizing Egmont's death. Significantly, the following quiet transition is accomplished in the woodwinds. In the *Egmont* Overture the winds are used consistently to hint at an alternative to the tragic outcome, which is now to be manifested in the F major *Allegro con brio* of the 'Victory' Symphony. The triumphant close of the overture thus extracts a moral thread from the F minor pathos of the preceding *Allegro*, and asserts this alternative strain with a grandeur and power that subvert the tragedy.

Beethoven's other major work of 1810 is also in the key of F minor: the String Quartet op. 95, which was dedicated to Zmeskall. This piece was withheld from publication until 1816. Beethoven titled it 'Quartetto serioso', which befits its dark, introspective, and vehement character. Its idiom is concise if not laconic, with many of the conventional transitional and cadential passages of the Viennese Classical style curtailed or eliminated altogether; also drastically compressed is the recapitulation in the first movement. As in Beethoven's last quartets, there is a special emphasis here on counterpoint and fugue. The slow movement in D major, marked *Allegretto ma non troppo*, contains extended fugal passages based on a chromatic subject, whereas the following march-like *Allegro assai vivace ma serioso* in F minor makes much use of contrapuntal imitation of its basic dotted-rhythm motif.

As in the *Appassionata* Sonata in the same key, Beethoven makes the Neapolitan scale degree of G♭—a semitone above the tonic—serve as a crux for powerful dramatic tensions. Already near the beginning of the *Allegro con brio* the terse opening motif is heard on G♭; an analogous rising semitone relationship is embodied in prominent and disruptive rising scales, while an emphatic D♭ chord—the analogous semitone above the dominant—opens the coda. The mysterious descending cello scale beginning on D♮ that opens the slow movement is related to this harmonic complex in the opening *Allegro con brio*, and particularly to the gesture of rising scales, which in the first movement have twice been heard on D. At the end of the slow movement the crucial pitch D is harmonized with a soft diminished-seventh chord, before a sudden, forceful reinterpretation of that sonority launches the third movement, in F minor.

The finale, marked *Allegretto agitato*, stresses some of the same harmonic relationships, particularly the dissonant semitone D♭–C of the first movement, but its astonishing coda, in F major, leaves the brooding character of the work as a whole far behind. There is a curious parallel here with the *Egmont* Overture: in the coda of the quartet the dramatic tensions are not resolved but are forgotten and seemingly transcended in a brilliant, exhilarating conclusion. Randall Thompson wrote of the passage, as cited by Daniel Gregory Mason, that 'no bottle of champagne was ever uncorked at a better time'.[9]

*   *   *

Between the summer of 1810 and the end of 1812 Beethoven concentrated on four major compositions, the *Archduke* Trio in B♭ major op. 97; the Seventh Symphony in A major op. 92; the Eighth Symphony in F major op. 93; and the Violin Sonata in G major op. 96. During 1811 he also wrote incidental music for stage works by August von Kotzebue, *Die Ruinen von Athen* ('The Ruins of Athens') op. 113 and *König Stephan* ('King Stephen') op. 117. Much of this stage music is hackwork far beneath the level of his other compositions. In 1811 a trend emerges that was to assume more importance in the immediately following years: around this time Beethoven made a clear distinction between serious compositions and works written for public or ceremonial use but not fashioned to the highest artistic standards. The gap in quality widens between pieces that may have been written almost concurrently but with a fundamentally different aim. The fact that Beethoven titled a bold, advanced work like the F minor Quartet 'Quartetto serioso' is interesting in this regard, since the title may be understood to allude not merely to the work's dark emotional tone but also to its challenging stylistic demands. Op. 95 is one of the pieces of these years that is most prophetic of the style of Beethoven's later music.

Whereas the quartet is terse and concentrated, the *Archduke* Trio is broad and expansive, the largest and most outstanding of all Beethoven's pieces in this genre. This Piano Trio in B♭ major stands dead-centre in Beethoven's creative development. In some ways it looks back to the spacious, lyrical style of the masterpieces from around 1806, like the Fourth Piano Concerto. But it also prefigures important features of Beethoven's later works. As he was to do in the *Hammerklavier* Sonata and the Ninth Symphony, Beethoven inverts the traditional order of the middle movements, placing the scherzo before a meditative set of variations, which itself foreshadows the final movements of two of the last piano sonatas, op. 109 and op. 111.

[9] Cited in Radcliffe, *Beethoven's String Quartets*, p. 97.

Ex. 45 *Archduke* Trio op. 97/I

The beginning of the *Allegro moderato* is of the utmost breadth (Ex. 45). The effect derives in part from the poise and inner strength of the theme itself. Built into the opening thematic statement is a subtle treatment of linear relationships and rhythmic foreshortening. The rhythmic stress falls on the second bar of each of the initial two-bar phrases, emphasizing the melodic progression from F in bar 2 to G in bar 4. The rising stepwise motion through the fourth F–Bb in the third bar is elaborated on a much larger scale across the first eight bars. Beethoven's fifth bar compresses the content of the preceding two bars; a further sequence in the next bar substitutes A for G, extending the linear ascent. At this point Beethoven varies the ascending figure from bar 3, which carries the melody upwards more rapidly to a firm half-cadence on the dominant in the eighth bar; at the same time, the long tonic pedal in the bass is succeeded by a stepwise descent in the left hand. The linear ascent of the theme thus extends through an entire octave, with a strong effect of intensification arising from a rich combination of structural factors. The crescendo and trills in the piano are generated by the inner growth of the theme itself.

At this point of articulation Beethoven avoids an immediate restatement of the opening phrases and, instead, expands the music from within. The cello and violin seem to meditate on possible continuations, before finally taking up the counterstatement as the piano re-enters with the pedal figuration, now in both hands. As the music reaches the half-cadence, however, it takes a new turn. In place of the stable dominant of the earlier passage, Beethoven substitutes an ambiguous diminished-seventh chord, and the music withdraws mysteriously into *pianissimo*. Only after a brief excursion through sequences stressing diminished and minor harmonies does the continuation pass through the subdominant to the cadential phrases of this immense theme. The opening subject of the *Archduke* Trio is no less than 33 bars in length, one of the broadest in the entire Classical repertory.

The second half of the development again withdraws into *pianissimo*, employing pizzicato strings with soft, ethereal trills in the piano. The texture is veiled and muted, yet dynamically shaped; a single pizzicato line in the cello gradually builds into more rapid, contrapuntal voices. All of this serves to throw the recapitulation into relief. Trills lead to an unfolding of the main theme, and Beethoven now deepens its *cantabile, dolce* character by adding expressive appoggiaturas in the piano.

The scherzo is invested with jaunty humour and lively counterpoint rich in contrary motion. Emil Platen has compared its exhaustive permutations of a basic motivic cell to those in Beethoven's aforementioned letter from the 1790s addressed to Zmeskall as 'Baron Dreckfahrer', where he writes 'Adieu Baron Ba ron ron/nor/orn/rno/onr', mixing up the order of letters in all possible ways; Platen is also reminded of the passage near the end of the *Alla danza tedesca* in the op. 130 quartet, with its juggling of the expected sequence of bars in the main theme.[10] The formal scale of the scherzo, like the other movements of op. 97, is large, and Beethoven uses an abbreviated return of the trio to serve as a coda. This is especially appropriate on account of the complementary relationship between scherzo and trio. Riezler has compared the trio to 'an abyss into whose gloomy depths a ray from the triumphant sun suddenly strikes'.[11] He refers here to the contrast between the uncanny chromatic canon in B♭ minor at the outset of the trio and the radiant waltz which suddenly emerges in D♭ major. This duality within the trio is clarified in turn by a thematic relationship linking the scherzo and trio. The scherzo begins with a rising scale through the octave in the cello alone. The trio also opens with an ascent from B♭ in the cello, but its theme does not show the same carefree spirit (Ex. 46*a* and *b*). Instead, the music explores those spaces between steps of the diatonic major scale that were passed over lightly by the scherzo. The reflective chromaticism greatly slows the rising motion and deepens it, revealing an unsuspected seriousness lurking behind the gaiety of the scherzo subject. The canonic entries form part of Beethoven's transformation of the scherzo theme. Since each entry of the canon rises only a fourth, it requires two such entries, in the cello and left hand of the piano, to retrace the same ascent through the octave. In the coda, by contrast, Beethoven reduces the trio to its basic semitonal shape, especially C♭–B♭, before resolving it into the gaiety of the rising scale in the major.

[10] '"Voila Quelque Chose aus dem alten Versatzamt". Zum Scherzo des Klaviertrios B-Dur opus 97', pp. 168–84.
[11] *Beethoven*, p. 177.

Ex. 46 *Archduke* Trio op. 97/II

(*a*) Scherzo

(*b*) Trio, bars 122–45

The theme of the *Andante cantabile ma pero con moto* in D major is of hymn-like serenity. Rhythmically it resembles a sarabande, with frequent stress on the second beat of the triple metre. The stately, chorale-like character of the theme is decorated through rhythmic subdivisions in each variation: the triplet eighth-notes of Variation 1 are succeeded by textures of sixteenths, triplet sixteenths, and thirty-second-notes with syncopations. A reprise of the

original theme follows, varied in many details of harmony and instrumentation. But the movement is far from over: a surprising modulation to the bright
key of E major ushers in a coda that dwells on the falling melodic step and
dotted rhythm from the cadential phrases of the theme. At the ensuing transition this rhythm and motivic step are inverted to launch the main theme of
the rondo, which begins with yet another transformation of the rising linear
pattern familiar from the first two movements. The humour and high spirits
of this *Allegro moderato* carry everything before them. The rondo finale is a
fitting culmination to the work, and shows the same bold spaciousness that
characterized the earlier movements. At the beginning of the *presto* coda,
Beethoven even incorporates an unusual modulatory excursion to the key of
the leading-note, A major, distantly foreshadowing his more radical use of
this tonal relationship in the finale of the Piano Sonata in A♭ op. 110.

During the months after March 1811, when he finished the *Archduke* Trio,
Beethoven's compositional output was modest. That summer he journeyed to
the Bohemian spas at Teplitz, where he met a group of writers and intellectu-
als including Christoph August Tiedge, and Karl August Varnhagen von
Ense and his wife Rahel Levin. It was at about this time that Beethoven
worked on the revision of his oratorio *Christus am Oelberge* ('Christ on the
Mount of Olives') for publication, and that his Mass in C major of 1807 was
at last successfully performed, to be published the following year. Beethoven's
first sketches for the Seventh Symphony in the Petter Sketchbook appear to
date from the time at Teplitz. This work and its companion, the Eighth
Symphony, were Beethoven's main projects during the following year. When
he returned to Teplitz in the summer of 1812 he made sketches for the Eighth
Symphony in later parts of the same sketchbook.

In 1827 a reviewer of the Seventh Symphony and professed admirer of
Beethoven's earlier works asked 'what had become of the good man in his later
period? Did he not succumb to a kind of insanity?' The tone of the review
echoes that of other dismissive contemporary assessments of Beethoven; it is
the length, strong contrasts, and expressive vehemence of the music that provoked rejection: '. . . the whole thing lasts at least three-quarters of an hour,
and is a true mixture of tragic, comic, serious, and trivial ideas, which spring
from one level to another without any connection, repeat themselves to excess,
and are almost wrecked by the immoderate noise of the timpani'.[12] A similar
judgment was attributed, probably falsely, to Carl Maria von Weber by the
untrustworthy Anton Schindler, Beethoven's self-appointed secretary and
biographer: according to Schindler, Weber is supposed to have declared that
the Seventh Symphony showed Beethoven 'ripe for the madhouse'.[13]

[12] Cited in Kunze, ed., *Beethoven: Die Werke im Spiegel seiner Zeit*, pp. 288–9.
[13] See the discussion of this famous attribution by Robin Wallace in *Beethoven's Critics*, pp.
102–3.

Despite such reactions, the A major Symphony, and particularly its *Allegretto*, rapidly became one of Beethoven's most popular works. Perhaps no other work by Beethoven is so intensely animated and driven by the power of rhythm. In response to this quality Wagner dubbed the symphony 'the apotheosis of the dance', and imaginative commentators have produced various programmatic interpretations. Solomon has sought a common denominator for these opinions in the notion of a 'festive Paradise, outside of time and history, untouched by mortality'.[14] For the Seventh Symphony, unlike the Fifth, does not involve struggle against adversity, even if a darker, contrasting range of character emerges in the A minor *Allegretto*. It is an accident of history that the first performances of this radiant symphony in 1813 and 1814 exactly coincided with the celebration of the victory over Napoleon.

The slow introduction is the most weighty in all Beethoven's symphonies, and it generates out of the most fundamental relationships of sound and time a propulsive rhythmic energy that is to infuse the entire work. Especially important is the series of four short but emphatic chords with a descending bass heard at the outset. These sonorities are placed two bars apart in the 4/4 metre; they outline the harmonic progression I–V–I⁷–IV. Connecting these majestic chords are motifs of legato half-notes, heard first in the oboes and then in the other wind instruments. Beethoven soon reinterprets this opening gesture in compelling fashion. Beginning in bar 15, the harmonic progression over a descending bass is restated, but the chords are sustained in the winds and trumpets and played *fortissimo* (Ex. 47). The oboe line in half-notes is assigned to the violins. At this moment Beethoven introduces a third rhythmic level—a texture of rising scales in detached sixteenth-notes that spans and connects the various pitch registers outlined by the chords. The power of this music derives in part from its synthesis of three rhythmic levels, which subdivide the basic slow pulse of the chords according to precise proportions. Thus the larger, controlling impulses at the beginning of each two-bar group are divided into four, in half-notes, and these impulses in turn are divided into eight, yielding 32 sixteenth-notes in each two-bar unit (see Fig. 1). The tension generated by these relationships depends on the fact that Beethoven's second rhythmic division doubles the proportions of the first. At the same time, the rising scales 'compose out' the sound of the chords through the tonal space. They are derived from the chords, yet they introduce an energy that later serves to prepare the rhythmic transition into the *Vivace*.

The *fortissimo* passage combining the three rhythmic levels changes the harmonic progression from the outset of the movement. The descent of the bass is now chromatic, tracing the pitches A–G♯–G♮–F♯–F–E, and Beethoven alters the harmonies to effect a modulation to C major, the key of

[14] *Beethoven*, p. 213.

Ex. 47 Seventh Symphony op. 92/I, bars 10–19

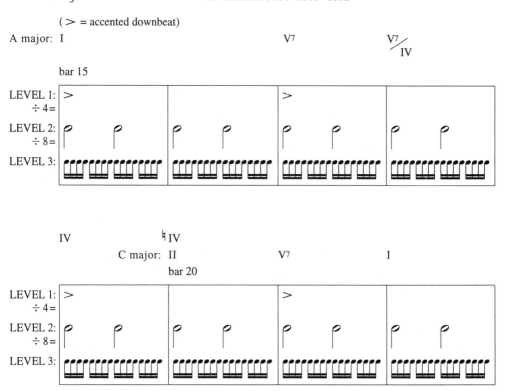

Fig. 1   Rhythmic structure of the slow introduction to the first movement of the Seventh Symphony, bars 15–22

the ensuing *dolce* subject, played first in the winds and then in the strings. This theme reappears later in the slow introduction in F major, which, like C, is a significant key in the main body of the movement. But Beethoven's use of these mediant and submediant tonalities in the introduction is not merely a foreshadowing of later events. Above all, it enables him to set the gracious *dolce* melody into marked tonal contrast with the rest of the introduction, before integrating both in the passage that leads into the beginning of the *Vivace*.

The *dolce* passages are not just episodes in the introduction. They are more like musical samples, excerpts of a pleasant, charming style that could not puzzle or offend Beethoven's listeners. His treatment of these passages in the slow introduction of the Seventh illustrates Nietzsche's comment about Beethoven's writing 'music about music'. For in the second episode a transformation takes place. Beethoven repeats the rhythm of the tune in the strings, while a rhythmic and dynamic intensification leads to the structural downbeat on the dominant in bar 53 (Ex. 48). Twice the winds attempt to

Ex. 48 Seventh Symphony op. 92/I, bars 47–60

carry on a musical discourse whose harmonic texture and dotted rhythm is unmistakably related to the earlier *dolce* episodes. But these interjections are not taken up; the stronger rhythmic impulses and their reverberations are reasserted and then seemingly distilled to their essence. Beethoven restructures his framework of rhythmic levels to *absorb* the dotted rhythm drawn from the *dolce* theme. The crucial turning-point at the end of the introduction occurs as the dotted rhythm is infused with this intense energy, creating thereby the ostinato figure of a dotted rhythm in 6/8 metre that dominates large sections of the first movement.

Other passages in Beethoven most comparable to this generative process in the Seventh Symphony include not only the slow introductions in the Second and Fourth symphonies but also the slow introductions to some of his instrumental finales. One is reminded, very distantly, of the *Introduzione* of the *Waldstein* Sonata and, much more concretely, of the introduction to the finale of the *Hammerklavier* Sonata. Quite unlike the symphony, however, these movements begin in a quiet, almost motionless state of calm. The opening of the Seventh Symphony, by contrast, harbours virtually inexhaustible reserves of rhythmic energy that spill over into every one of the four movements.

The famous *Allegretto* in A minor also features a prominent rhythmic ostinato, which endows this movement with a processional aura, imposing a strong unifying character that is felt throughout the variations of the theme and even the contrasting episodes in the major. Here is one of the sources of inspiration for Schubert's many processional pieces associated with the Romantic theme of the wanderer. The following, propulsive scherzo in F major emphasizes iambic rhythms, whereas the closing *Allegro con brio* displays a considerable diversity of rhythmic figures and patterns. The trio of the scherzo, on the other hand, represents the still centre of the symphony. Its majestic, yet almost static character is conveyed in part by impressive pedal points on A that resound through extended passages, played *fortissimo* in the trumpets and drum. Yet even here, a suggestion of processional movement is retained; according to a report from Abbé Stadler, the theme of the trio was drawn from an Austrian pilgrimage hymn.[15]

In the *Allegro con brio* finale Beethoven's main theme itself becomes an ostinato, a kind of revolving cam whose driving momentum is reflected in insistent syncopation in the winds and low strings. The primary motif is like a coiled spring, whose tension permeates the broader thematic idea that circles in quarter-notes around C♯, the third degree of A major (Ex. 49). This is hardly the idea of a madman. What is involved is a sudden *fourfold* rhythmic augmentation of the basic motif, so that the rapid motivic contour that had occupied less than one bar of music is suddenly enlarged over several bars,

---

[15] Thayer-Forbes, p. 527.

Ex. 49 Seventh Symphony op. 92/IV, bars 36–45

while the structural accent on E is reflected in the prolonged notes of the winds and horns. Here, as elsewhere in the Seventh Symphony, Beethoven does indeed 'spring from one level to another', but the connections are real and tangible. The music is dependent on these relationships and it only truly comes alive when they are felt and conveyed in performance.

Ernest Newman once wrote that the Eighth Symphony 'takes the overspill of the mighty Seventh'.[16] Despite the strong differences between these works, the extraordinary rhythmic intensity of the preceding symphony reappears in certain passages of the Eighth, particularly in the development of the first movement and in the finale. In its character the Eighth Symphony is somewhat reminiscent of the sublime comedy of the Second Symphony. Beethoven often associated the key of F major with humour, and this work is no exception. One of the humorous anecdotes often related about the symphony must be disallowed, however. Schindler wrote that the *Allegretto scherzando* of the Eighth was based on a canon that Beethoven improvised in the spring of 1812 at a farewell dinner for Johann Nepomuk Mälzel. Mälzel was an inventor best known for his devices to measure musical tempo. His first such device was the 'chronometer', which he was anxious to publicize at precisely this time (it was only several years later, in 1815, that he invented the metronome), and Beethoven's interest in him was connected in part to Mälzel's efforts to fash-

[16] Notes to the Klemperer recording, p. 21, cited by Solomon, *Beethoven*, p. 213.

ion ear-trumpets for the deaf composer. According to Schindler, Beethoven's party canon on 'ta ta ta'—representing the beat of the chronometer—supplied the principal motif for the second movement of the symphony. Research since the 1970s has indicated that the Mälzel canon is almost certainly a forgery.[17] Schindler forged many entries in the conversation notebooks that came into his possession. He had no scruples about fabricating history and did not hesitate to falsify sources to support the account published in his Beethoven biography. There is no manuscript for the alleged Mälzel canon, and the historical facts and sketch sources contradict Schindler's account of the genesis of the *Allegretto scherzando*. Thus this colourful story must be laid to rest, despite its illustrious career in Beethoven biography.

Another recent finding is Sieghard Brandenburg's discovery from manuscript sources that Beethoven sketched the opening *Allegro* of the Eighth Symphony as a piano concerto.[18] Much of the symphonic exposition, up to the passage in dotted rhythm, was to have served as the introductory orchestral ritornello in the tonic key; at this point the solo piano was to enter with a cadenza. The transformation of the nascent concerto into a symphony required no changes in the basic progression of themes. But something of the genesis of the work can be felt in the contrast between the lighter, more transparent textures of the exposition and the forceful motivic repetitions and sustained syncopations of the development, which would not have found a home in a concerto. The recapitulation marks the climax of this progression, and Beethoven writes a triple *fortissimo* in all the parts, creating problems of balance between the thematic return in the low register and the rest of the orchestra. In this instance Beethoven enlarges the process of thematic return, diffusing the moment of recapitulation, which might also be placed at the more harmonically stable, *dolce* return of the theme in the winds.

The concluding *Allegro vivace* of the Eighth Symphony has been regarded as a sonata form with a coda almost as long as the rest of the movement, or, more convincingly, as a combination of sonata form and rondo, with two developments and two recapitulations. Haydn had often resourcefully merged rondo and sonata form in the finales of his symphonies, but he had never attempted anything resembling this finale. Beethoven's sublime humour is reflected above all in his treatment of the intrusive 'false note', the C♯ that is played between the paired statements making up the principal theme. In the main body of the movement this striking dissonance is juxtaposed with the theme, but it exerts no further influence upon it. Near the end of the movement, however, the C♯ asserts itself, shifting the entire perspective of the

---

[17] See especially the symposium of essays by Standley Howell, Kathryn John, and Harry Goldschmidt in *Zu Beethoven*, ed. Goldschmidt, ii, pp. 163–204.

[18] 'Ein Skizzenbuch Beethovens aus dem Jahre 1812', *Zu Beethoven*, ed. Goldschmidt, i, pp. 135–9.

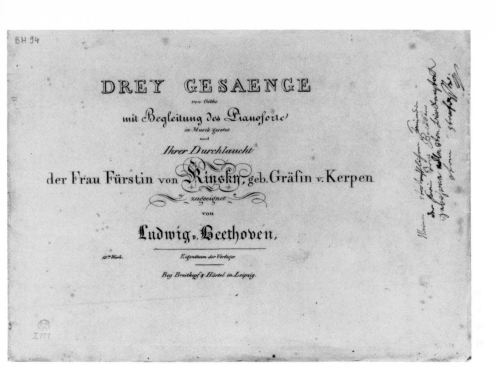

9 Title page of the first edition of the three Goethe songs op. 83 (Leipzig: Breitkopf & Härtel, 1811), dedicated to Princess Caroline Kinsky. Beethoven inscribed this copy to Antonie Brentano.

10 Miniature on ivory, presumably of Antonie Brentano, previously believed to be of Marie Erdödy.

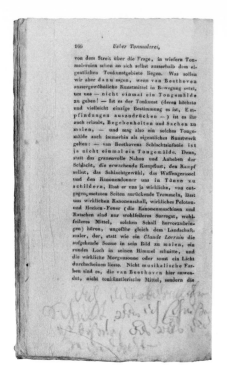

11 Bronze bust of Beethoven, aged 42, by Franz Klein, 1812, based on a plaster cast of the composer's face.

13 Beethoven's response to a negative critique of *Wellingtons Sieg* by Gottfried Weber in his copy of the music journal *Cäcilia* of August 1825: 'ach du erbärmlicher Schuft, was ich scheisse, ist besser, als wie du je|gedacht' ('ah you pitiful scoundrel, my shit is better than [anything] you have ever thought').

12 Title page of the piano arrangement of *Wellingtons Sieg* prepared by Beethoven (Vienna: Steiner & Co., 1816).

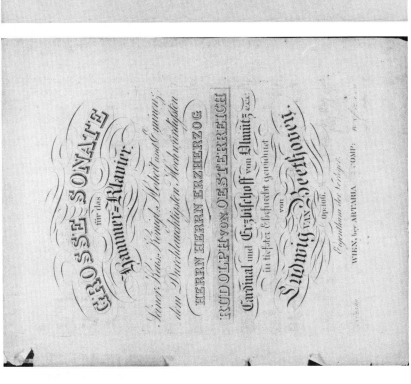

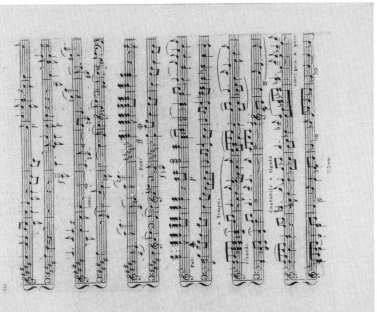

14–15 The first edition of Beethoven's *Hammerklavier* Sonata op. 106, issued in September 1819: title page and p. 10, showing the start of the recapitulation of the first movement.

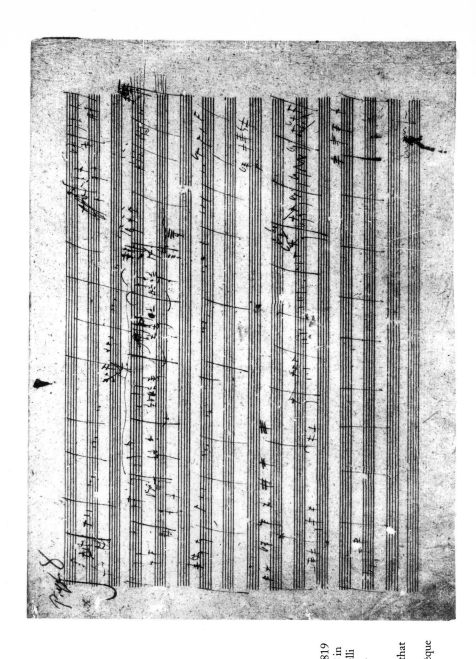

16 Beethoven's draft of 1819 for Variation 10 (no. 8 in the draft) of the Diabelli Variations. Beethoven first entered the turn figure from Diabelli's waltz before rejecting that embellishment of the upbeat. (Paris, Bibliotèque Nationale, MS 77A, fol. 2v).

music. The theme is subverted, and even the tonal equilibrium is thrown into question, as the music turns into F♯ minor, with the effect of an overturning of restraints. Riezler described the passage as one of 'those sudden and surprising contrasts, which seem to tear open a gaping chasm beneath the hearer's feet, but which illumine the whole movement—the whole symphony—and are prepared with the greatest mastery and form part of the living organism'.[19]

*　　　*　　　*

During his stay in Bohemia in July 1812 Beethoven experienced the emotional crisis that is documented in his famous letter to the 'Immortal Beloved'. Maynard Solomon has demonstrated that Antonie Brentano fulfils the external criteria to qualify as Beethoven's beloved. She was in sustained contact with Beethoven from May 1810 and visited Prague and Karlsbad at times compatible with the information in Beethoven's letter. The scepticism that still exists about Solomon's identification is most often connected with doubts that Antonie Brentano fulfils the internal criteria. That she was so long overlooked as a candidate was surely due to her status as a married woman and mother; indeed, the last of her children was born at Frankfurt in March 1813, approximately nine months after Beethoven's letter was written. Proof of the identity of the 'Immortal Beloved' may never be forthcoming, but the circumstantial evidence pointing to Antonie Brentano is substantial, and she is the only known candidate who remains in serious contention on the basis of documentary evidence from the period in question.[20] Antonie's marital status would have inhibited Beethoven from committing himself to her, since that act would have involved a betrayal of his friend Franz Brentano. Solomon offers plausible reasons for Antonie Brentano's having been drawn to Beethoven: she was probably not emotionally fulfilled in her marriage; she intensely wished to remain in Vienna; and she idolized Beethoven.

Solomon interprets the letter as an expression of Beethoven's inner conflict between acceptance and renunciation, as his 'gratitude toward and love for Antonie . . . struggled against the ingrained patterns and habits of a

---

[19] *Beethoven*, p. 159.

[20] Arguments continue to be advanced occasionally for Josephine Brunsvik Deym, to whom Beethoven was strongly attracted during 1804–5, as we have seen. In his *Um die Unsterbliche Geliebte: Eine Bestandsaufnahme* of 1977, Harry Goldschmidt analysed the candidacy of both Josephine Brunsvik Deym and Antonie Brentano, without resolving the issue one way or the other. In identifying Josephine as the 'Immortal Beloved' in her book *Beethoven und seine 'Unsterbliche Geliebte' Josephine Brunswick* of 1983, Marie-Elisabeth Tellenbach rejects the case for Antonie Brentano hastily and seemingly on principle, while compensating for the lack of supporting evidence for Josephine from the period around 1812 by a leap of faith, asserting that 'Since the letter . . . can only have been written to Josephine, she must have been in Bohemia in the summer of 1812' (p. 113).

lifetime'.[21] It is ironic but fitting that one of the songs Beethoven sang and gave to Antonie was *Trocknet nicht* (see Plate 9). For the very language of his love letter shows a sublimated, distancing tendency. The name 'Immortal Beloved' itself serves to emphasize an exalted devotion but not a passionate realization. Beethoven writes in the second postscript, 'Be calm, only by a calm consideration of our existence can we achieve our purpose to live together—Be calm—'. The suffering of Beethoven's beloved may have arisen in part from a realization that his capacity to transform 'unhappy love' into 'eternal love' was itself a barrier to commitment in a relationship.

In the autumn of 1812 Franz and Antonie Brentano left Vienna for Frankfurt. There is evidence that Beethoven was under emotional stress around this time; the aftermath of the 'Immortal Beloved' affair was one of the most troubled and least creative episodes in his life, quite unlike the artistically productive period of crisis in 1802. Before the end of the year, however, he did complete one more major work: the Violin Sonata in G major op. 96, which was performed by Pierre Rode and the Archduke Rudolph on 29 December. Like the *Archduke* Trio, the final violin sonata stands in the mainstream of Beethoven's compositional development. These two pieces are the most advanced works that Beethoven had produced in their respective genres. His efforts to surpass his previous achievements in various musical forms were to continue in later years in works like the *Hammerklavier* Sonata, but this tendency is visible at least as early as the *Archduke* Trio.

The op. 96 Violin Sonata is an intimate work, rich in lyricism and subtle in its motivic relationships. The delicate opening for violin alone—a trill connected to an expressive appoggiatura a third higher—bears a family resemblance to various other motifs in the first movement using appoggiaturas or neighbour-note figures. At the beginning of the coda Beethoven introduces a mysterious dialogue based on the trill figure in the lower registers of both instruments. Beethoven's manuscript shows that this section was an afterthought; the change was evidently made in 1815, when he prepared the sonata for publication.[22] The incorporation of this passage is linked to the final reinterpretation of the first theme of the movement at the end of Beethoven's coda, where the open continuation characteristic of earlier appearances of the theme is replaced, for the first time, by a progression to an emphatic tonic cadence. Beethoven's revision thus expands the role of the coda in probing and eventually resolving the opening theme, whose motivic potential had been explored throughout.

The inner movements of the sonata—an *Adagio* in E♭ major and scherzo in

---

[21] *Beethoven*, p. 184; Solomon devotes an entire chapter to the riddle of the 'Immortal Beloved', pp. 158–89.

[22] Cf. the facsimile edition with an introduction by Martin Staehelin (Munich, 1977), and Brandenburg's 'Bemerkungen zu Beethovens Opus 96', pp. 22–5.

G minor—form a striking contrast but are directly connected to one another. The melodic interval of a descending tone or semitone assumes importance in these movements as well. In the *Adagio* the hymn-like principal theme in the piano is followed by a melodic continuation in the violin stressing the falling tone B♭–A♭, which initiates a change in key to A♭ major, the subdominant. A modulating, developmental passage then leads to the dominant of E♭ and eventually to the recapitulation of the opening theme in the violin. At the *attacca* transition to the ensuing scherzo, the pivotal falling tone—spelt enharmonically as E♭–C♯ in the violin—represents a variant, in rhythmic augmentation, of the B♭–A interval stressed earlier in the movement. Now, surprisingly, the descending second leads through an augmented-sixth chord into G minor, the key of the scherzo. Beethoven reinterprets the dissonant augmented sixth as the first upbeat of the scherzo, setting into motion the insistent syncopations so characteristic of that movement. This passage illustrates Beethoven's concern to establish subtle transitions in sonority between successive movements, even when these involve a strong contrast in character. Another such example is found at the end of the coda of the scherzo, where the turn to the major mode and broadening in register create a sonorous transition to the finale.

The theme of the closing variation movement predates the rest of the work, since it appears on a sketchleaf from 1807–8, among sketches for the Cello Sonata in A op. 69, for which it may originally have been intended. The finale comprises a set of six variations on this dance-like melody of seemingly naive character (Ex. 50), which reminded Nottebohm of a tune from J. A. Hiller's

Ex. 50   Violin Sonata op. 96/IV

operetta 'The Happy Cobbler'.[23] The variations are anything but naive, however, and thoroughly transform the surface of the theme while developing its
motivic substance. In the first few variations Beethoven follows the familiar
practice of introducing a progressive foreshortening of rhythm, with one
strong beat per bar in Variation 1, followed by two accented beats in Variation
2 and four in Variation 3, where the persistent syncopations in the melody and
faster motion in sixteenth-notes in the accompaniment reflect the increasing
rhythmic energy. Variation 4 shows an intensification of the internal phrase
structure of the theme, as emphatic ascending chords in the first two bars of
each phrase are juxtaposed with the descending linear motion of the remaining bars.

The movement's centre of gravity rests in the fifth variation, where the thematic model is greatly expanded through a slowing in tempo to *Adagio espressivo* and a change in metre to 6/8 (Ex. 51). This aria-like variation freely
elaborates the basic melodic structure of the theme in intricate chromatic
diminutions. Twice the figuration crystallizes into sustained trills in the piano

Ex. 51 Violin Sonata op. 96/IV, Variation 5, bars 1–6

[23] *Beethoveniana*, p. 30.

followed by soft, cadenza-like interpolations of falling chromatic scales that seem to suspend the forward progress of the music (bar 4). The piano trill arises out of the appoggiatura B–A; the threefold chromatic run from C to F♯ and the following extension to F♯ in the lower octave serve to compose out the dominant seventh of G, leading in the next bar to the arrival in the tonic of the melody in the violin. These gestures hold back the unfolding of the theme, exploring its structure from within.

Such florid, decorative textures are normal in the penultimate slow variation in a Classical variation set, but the depth of expression touched on here retains a lingering influence over the rest of the movement. A tension arises between the contemplative transformation of the theme in Variation 5 and the return of the naive folk-like tune as the basis for the conclusion. One is reminded in this connection of the Diabelli Variations op. 120, whose richly decorated slow variation in the minor, Variation 31, seems to leave Diabelli's commonplace waltz so far behind. In the Diabelli set, of course, there is no closing da capo of the original theme; the final variation and coda seem to transcend Diabelli's waltz once and for all.

In the sonata Beethoven follows established precedent in placing an *Allegro* variation and return to the original theme after the slow, decorated penultimate variation. Remarkable, however, is the way in which he evokes a more serious, contemplative atmosphere in his coda. After the abrupt return of the original theme, initially in the 'wrong' key, E♭ major, and the boisterous final variation, Beethoven introduces a dark-hued fugal passage in the minor, written in longer note values. A return to the major mode and the original theme follows, in a somewhat faster tempo, leading to rushing scale passages played *fortissimo* in both piano and violin. The final cadence is near. But Beethoven now again interrupts the musical discourse with a reminiscence of the tempo and harmonic inflections of the slow fifth variation (Ex. 52).

Although Beethoven does not literally quote the *Adagio espressivo*, a sensitive performance can unmistakably recall its character. As in the E major transformation of the rondo theme in the finale of the Piano Concerto in C minor op. 37, with its evocation of the *Largo* movement in that key, the slow variation is delicately recaptured here, glimpsed through the veil of the original theme. Then, in the last bars before the *Presto*, Beethoven dwells on the closing motifs of the theme, before suddenly accelerating the tempo as the pattern of rising thirds and fourths drives to the cadence, played *fortissimo* in the upper register. The brilliant closing flourish seems to complete the earlier *Allegro* passage, whose cadences had been first avoided in the higher register, five bars before the *Poco Adagio*, and then interrupted deceptively at the *Poco Adagio* itself, with its withdrawal into thoughtful reminiscence. Thus, at the end of the sonata, two levels of experience are juxtaposed: the inward world of the slow variation and the outward world of the dance. The ending of

Ex. 52 Violin Sonata op. 96/IV, bars 259–end

Beethoven's last violin sonata deepens the registral contrast of the first-movement coda into a tensional play of tempos and character that embraces both of Schiller's poetic categories.

7

The Congress of Vienna Period

1813–1815

T HE aftermath of the 'Immortal Beloved' affair of 1812 opens the most contradictory chapter in Beethoven's life. At no other time did he enjoy so much public veneration or receive such generous monetary rewards. Half of the public concerts held for Beethoven's benefit in his lifetime took place in the single year 1814. Never before nor since has a musician received such recognition from assembled monarchs and heads of state. Beethoven basked in the limelight and exploited the opportunity financially for all it was worth, although benefits also accrued to public causes. His enhanced popularity helped bring about the revival of his opera *Fidelio*. In 1815 he was awarded the 'freedom of the city' in recognition of his efforts to raise money for charity through performances of his works in Vienna. As far as his fame and public recognition were concerned, this was the climax, 'The Glorious Moment', to cite the title of his ceremonial cantata for the Congress of Vienna.

What is remarkable is that this success rested on some of the weakest music Beethoven ever wrote. The issues raised thereby are not only aesthetic but historical, sociological, and even psychological in nature. For despite the outward brilliance of his success, this was a time of deep inner conflict for Beethoven. In 1813 he experienced a creative impasse that was undoubtedly linked to his personal life. He produced virtually nothing of artistic importance during that year. There is evidence, moreover, that his life was in disarray during the aftermath of the 'Immortal Beloved' affair. At about this time he began a *Tagebuch*, or personal diary, that he kept for six years, until 1818.[1] An excerpt from the very first entry reads as follows:

[1] The following quotations are taken from Solomon's edition of the *Tagebuch*, first published in 1982 in *Beethoven Studies*, iii, pp. 193–285, and subsequently in *Beethoven Essays* and as *Beethovens Tagebuch* (Bonn, 1990).

You may not be a *human being, not for yourself, but only for others*, for you there is no more happiness except within yourself, in your art. O God! give me strength to conquer myself, nothing at all must fetter me to life.—Thus everything connected with A will go to destruction.

'A' may refer to Antonie Brentano, from whom Beethoven was presumably attempting to disengage himself. Several other entries in his diary document Beethoven's intention to embrace art while rejecting 'life', reflecting a disposition akin to Arthur Schopenhauer's 'negation of the will to life' in his book *Die Welt als Wille und Vorstellung* ('The World as Will and Idea'), published a few years later, in 1819. Beethoven writes in an 1814 entry in the *Tagebuch* that 'Everything that is called life should be sacrificed to the sublime and be a sanctuary of art'. Another, later, inscription reads, 'Live only in your art, for you are so limited by your senses. This is therefore the *only existence* for you'.

If Beethoven meant to compensate for shortcomings in his life through creative activity, he failed, at least during 1813. His creativity may have been paralysed by depression. His resignation to the prospect of a permanent solitary existence was accompanied by a marked withdrawal from society. Other factors also played a role. Financial worries plagued him, since his annuity income had been reduced at the very time that his ailing brother Caspar Carl required assistance. The illness and near death of Caspar Carl from consumption in the first months of 1813 also took its toll on the composer. Solomon has speculated that Beethoven attempted suicide during the spring or summer of 1813; reports of a suicide attempt were made by Schindler and Joseph August Röckel, although the date has always remained uncertain.[2] Descriptions of Beethoven's social isolation stem from Nanette and Andreas Streicher, who commented on his despondent state of mind and on the 'deplorable condition' of his clothes and personal and domestic affairs. According to the painter Blasius Höfel, Beethoven neglected his appearance and cleanliness to the extent that his dining-table at a favourite inn, although large, 'was avoided by the other guests due to the very uninviting habits into which he had fallen'.[3] Solomon and others have suggested that Beethoven visited prostitutes around this time, in the company of his old friend Zmeskall. Beethoven's notes to Zmeskall contain puns using code names, whereby 'fortresses' stands for prostitutes and 'assaults' for sexual acts.[4] That Beethoven would have felt guilt about such encounters may be surmised from entries in his *Tagebuch* like the following (no. 122): 'Sensual gratification without a spiritual union is and remains bestial, afterwards one has no trace of noble feeling but rather remorse'.

If Beethoven had strayed from higher ethical ideals in his personal life, a deviating trend can also be discerned in his music. He was now exploring

    [2] *Beethoven*, p. 220.   [3] Thayer-Forbes, p. 590.   [4] *Beethoven*, p. 220.

another 'new path', a path leading to a steep decline in artistic quality. More than at any other time in his career, economic and political factors exerted a dominating influence. Little scholarly attention has been given to Beethoven's patriotic compositions from 1813 and 1814, which have often been dismissed as uncharacteristic aberrations or altogether disregarded. The neglect is unjustified, however, since fascinating aesthetic issues are raised by such pieces as *Wellingtons Sieg*, *Germania*, *Ihr weisen Gründer*, and *Der glorreiche Augenblick*.

In these works Beethoven appears as a pioneer of kitsch at the dawn of the age of mass production and modern commercial propaganda. This is a surprising role, perhaps, for a cultural hero of Beethoven's stature, but one nonetheless supported by the historical evidence. Beethoven's patriotic potboilers offer the spectacle of a great composer lowering his art to gain economic reward and court political favour. This episode in his career raises fundamental aesthetic and ethical questions. In order to evaluate these matters, it is helpful to review some of the critical literature devoted to art and kitsch.

In two classic essays from 1933 and 1950 Hermann Broch defined kitsch as 'evil in the value system of art'.[5] According to Broch, kitsch involves a false association between fundamental principles. Whereas the true work of art shows qualities of openness, originality, and irrationality, kitsch displays a closed and rational system of imitation. Broch compares kitsch to an anti-Christ, who looks like Christ, and 'acts and speaks like Christ and is nevertheless Lucifer'. He asks,

Wherein is the difference ultimately noticed? An open system . . . is an ethical one, that is, it offers the individual a guiding framework, within which he or she can act. A closed system, on the other hand, cannot go beyond fixed rules—even if these are given an ethical coloring—and it thus transforms those parts of human life that it touches into a game that is no longer ethical, but only aesthetic in nature.[6]

Broch admits, even for himself, 'that one is not infrequently very well disposed to kitsch', but he insists at the same time that 'the goddess of beauty in art' is 'the goddess of kitsch'.[7] He argues, in other words, that beauty alone is an insufficient basis for art. Rather, beauty needs to be integrated with other dimensions of the work in order that it does not become an end in itself, or a simple play of effects. For in that case we would be dealing not with art, but with kitsch.

Other leading thinkers on aesthetics have shared the opinion that art is concerned with more than mere beauty. Consider, for instance, Susanne

[5] 'Das Böse im Wertsystem der Kunst', p. 123; 'Einige Bemerkungen zum Problem des Kitsches', p. 170. For an abridged version of this work in English, see Broch's 'Notes on the Problem of Kitsch'.

[6] 'Einige Bemerkungen', p. 169.   [7] Ibid.', pp. 171, 167.

Langer's concept of a successful artwork as an 'unconsummated symbol', or even Adorno's paradoxical description of a true performance as 'a copy of a nonexistent original'. What is essential is that the symbolic artistic content be recognized without it being diminished or reduced, as in some programmatic interpretations in which the integrity of the work threatens to vanish behind an unequivocal verbal interpretation. The danger that arises thereby is of art being degraded into kitsch—a common enough tendency in the reception history of art.

Broch's insights can be refined on the basis of recent studies by Wolfgang Welsch, who employs the pair of concepts 'aesthetic' and 'anaesthetic'. Welsch writes that

Whereas aesthetic experience increases our sensibility, the anaesthetic stands for a loss of sensibility . . . the anaesthetic is the converse of the aesthetic . . . Through anaesthesia we block out feeling—and the loss of a higher perceptive capacity is the direct result. The anaesthetic realm thus deals with the most elementary level of the aesthetic, and furnishes its condition and boundary.[8]

This pair of concepts applies to the phenomenon of kitsch, and offers us a means of critically testing Broch's thesis. We can discern two opposing processes at work. In the Viennese Classical style, and in Beethoven's music generally, we observe tendencies to widen the boundaries of art. Thus material can be absorbed from the commonplace, taken from the anaesthetic into the aesthetic realm. With kitsch we evidently encounter the opposite—what is offered as art demands no higher perceptive capacity and brings a regression; material from the aesthetic sphere returns to the realm of the anaesthetic. It would be misleading, however, to regard art only as the expansion and kitsch as the surrender of aesthetic substance. For, according to Broch, kitsch tends to wallow in beauty—its shortcoming is not aesthetic, but ethical. Thus the boundary between aesthetic and anaesthetic experience is not to be understood merely negatively. As Welsch remarks, 'one anaesthetizes, in order to avoid aesthetic pain'; and not a few artists, stoics, or mystics, for instance, 'strive toward a transcendence of the senses in the attainment of "another condition"'—which can presumably be understood as a type of anaesthetic state.[9] These possibilities are contained in Broch's somewhat questionable attack on beauty as the 'goddess of kitsch'. Broch is undoubtedly right, however, that kitsch, if regarded as a system of imitation, can imply an ethical failure, inasmuch as it embodies a false pretence.

Let us consider in this light Beethoven's 'Battle Symphony' *Wellingtons Sieg* ('Wellington's Victory'), which was composed in late 1813, well before the beginning of the Congress of Vienna (see Plate 12). After Wellington's military victory in Spain on 21 June 1813, Johann Mälzel spotted an excellent

---

[8] *Ästhetisches Denken*, p. 10.   [9] Ibid., p. 11.

business opportunity in the form of a commemorative piece to be performed on his elaborate mechanical instrument, the Panharmonicon. Mälzel approached Beethoven, who agreed to take up the task. From the beginning the work was tailored for popular success, particularly in England. Moscheles maintained that the entire plan of the work, with its flourishes, marches, use of the hymns *Rule, Brittania* and *God Save the King*, and even the fugue based on the latter, came from Mälzel, but Küthen has suggested on the basis of the manuscript sources that Mälzel's input was mainly confined to the battle signals and fanfares.[10] In the end, the 'battle symphony' was first given not by Mälzel's Panharmonicon but in a version for augmented orchestra at two gala charity performances on 8 and 12 December 1813. Its enthusiastic reception led to further performances for Beethoven's own benefit. At the first of those, on 2 January 1814, Beethoven dropped all reference to Mälzel from the programme, substituting pieces from *The Ruins of Athens* music for Mälzel's Mechanical Trumpeter, which had been featured in the charity performances. Beethoven's action contributed to a serious break in his relationship with Mälzel that was not repaired until 1817.

Thayer cites Tomaschek's comments on *Wellington's Victory* that he was

very painfully affected to see a Beethoven, whom Providence had probably assigned to the highest throne in the realm of music, among the rudest materialists. I was told, it is true, that he himself had declared the work to be folly, and that he liked it only because with it he had thoroughly thrashed the Viennese.

Thayer comments that

There is no doubt that this was so; nor that they, who engaged in its performance, viewed it as a stupendous musical joke, and engaged in it *con amore* as in a gigantic professional frolic.[11]

Among the musicians who took part were the famous double bass player Dragonetti, the cellist Bernhard Romberg, the composer and violinist Ludwig Spohr, and the future master of French Grand Opera Giacomo Meyerbeer, whose timid drum playing reportedly met with Beethoven's scorn.

Some critics have viewed this 'professional frolic' kindly; Ludwig Misch deemed it a masterpiece of its own genre.[12] Is *Wellington's Victory* shielded from critique if it is regarded as practical 'Gebrauchsmusik' with no higher pretensions? We should resist the temptation simply to collapse the work into its historical context. In its style *Wellington's Victory* departs radically from Beethoven's aesthetic norms, quite unlike other 'characteristic' pieces such as the *Pastoral* Symphony or the *Lebewohl* Sonata. The crude realism of *Wellington's Victory* is well illustrated in its first main section, which is devoted

---

[10] 'Wellingtons Sieg oder die Schlacht bei Vittoria', pp. 262–3.
[11] Thayer-Forbes, p. 565.   [12] *Beethoven Studies*, pp. 153–62.

to the battle. After the preliminary fanfares and national marches heard from the opposing ensembles representing the French and British forces, the engagement begins with an *Allegro*, sporting syncopations and motivic figures of descending scales. Initially, Beethoven favours these syncopated beats for his placement of the cannon shots, which are meticulously specified in the score with dark circles for the British and open circles for the French artillery. A well-known aspect of the historical battle was the British capture of the French guns; this is clearly reflected in Beethoven's distribution of the 188 cannon shots. As the tide turns against the French, their cannons are heard less and less frequently and are then silenced altogether.

Characteristic of *Wellington's Victory* are insistent repetitions of a few basic figures on a broad but flat musical canvas. As the British launch their assault in the 'Storm-March', the music consists largely of 24 almost undifferentiated repetitions of the single note A♭, followed by 16 strokes on A and 16 more on B♭, leading to still more repetitions on B (Ex. 53). Beethoven pushes up the music notch by notch, a familiar device in popular music. This is symptomatic of the almost complete absence, in the Battle Symphony, of a unifying tonal and formal perspective such as we normally find in Beethoven. Wellington's soldiers have no need of subtlety; they force their way heavily and brutally into the French defences.

There are nevertheless a few finer points to Beethoven's musical depiction of the collapse of the French resistance. He employs a motif with a triplet figure and falling semitone to serve as a tag for the French forces—this turn of phrase is clearly derived from the 'Marlborough' French marching-song heard at the outset. As the British gain the upper hand, the motif is deprived of its downbeat, suggesting an effect of breathless panic.[13] While the British cannons pound relentlessly, Beethoven even dismembers what is left of the French motif. In the bars following the 'double hits' of the cannoneers—as designated by two dark circles on successive beats—the 'Marlborough' figure is reduced to a single note (Ex. 54). The subsequent rout of the French army is conveyed not only by the long descending lines and *decrescendo* but by a limping and forlorn F♯ minor version of the 'Marlborough' tune. This dismal departure of the French army makes room for the triumphant 'Victory Symphony' that makes up the remainder of the work.

The occasional subtle touches do little to relieve the impression of pastiche and bombast. Some of the same rhetorical figures appear here as in Beethoven's important compositions, but an integrating aesthetic context is absent or undeveloped. The Battle Symphony is a fascinating historical artefact, but a dubious work of art; it is a 'consummated', not an 'unconsummated', symbol. As Solomon has claimed, elements of Beethoven's heroic

---

[13] Cf. Küthen, 'Wellingtons Sieg', p. 267.

style are recalled here, but only as parody or farce.[14] In this instance, identifiable aspects of Beethoven's aesthetic enterprise dissipate into the realm of the anaesthetic. The narrative design of the music is mainly extrinsic rather than intrinsic.

It was in response to these aspects that Alfred Einstein once described *Wellington's Victory* as 'the lowest point in Beethoven's work.[15] But a better candidate for that distinction might be *Der glorreiche Augenblick* ('The Glorious Moment'), the cantata for chorus, orchestra, and soloists that

Ex. 53 *Wellington's Victory* op. 91, 'Storm-March'

14 *Beethoven*, p. 222.　　　15 'Beethoven's Military Style', p. 244.

Ex. 53 *cont.*

Beethoven wrote during the autumn of 1814 in fawning tribute to the assembled dignitaries at the Congress of Vienna. *The Glorious Moment* was performed on 29 November and 2 December 1814 in a programme containing *Wellington's Victory* and (as the reviewer in the *Wiener Zeitung* put it) 'a symphony composed to accompany' these works—the Seventh Symphony!

Ex. 54 *Wellington's Victory* op. 91, 'Storm-March', bars 331–49

The text, written by the deaf surgeon Alois Weissenbach, is an exercise in bathos. One recurrent motif is a hymn of praise to 'the queen of cities', Vienna, or 'Vindobona', the archaic name for the town, used in the fugal setting of the closing chorus. 'I am Europe, give way, proud Rome', is the message in the aria in which the soprano becomes the voice of Vienna herself.

Ex. 54 *cont.*

The Glorious Moment is mostly sweetness and light, with a correspondingly
'triumphant' musical setting. The moments of pathos are exaggerated. 'Oh
kneel down, people, and worship those who have rescued you!' are the words
of the recitative praising the 'gleaming crowned heads' of Europe. To be thus
'worshipped' are the same monarchs who were already consolidating their

restoration of political power. Only a few years later Austria was to suffer the oppressive police state of Metternich. In historical retrospect, at least, the ideological content of this work is blatant and cynical.

Beethoven's music closely follows the rhetorical overemphases of Weissenbach's text. Thus, at the end of the recitative and quartet (no. 5), Beethoven brings about a great climax at the mention of Emperor Franz (Ex. 55). The commotion in the orchestra matches the effect of overstated pathos in the poem, with its dubious rhymed pairing of 'Glanz' ('splendour') and 'Franz': 'And God has drawn this splendour, this glorious arch, through the world, in our Franz'. The majestic rhythms and rising string arpeggios contribute to the stirring *fortissimo* climax on a D major chord in the full orchestra. This is an example of the manner in which words and music in this work have been subordinated to the political adoration of authority.

More than the Battle Symphony, *The Glorious Moment* offers an example of kitsch in Broch's sense, whereby beauty and harmony reign supreme and unchallenged. There is no trace of critique in the cantata, although Beethoven surely could have chosen a somewhat more differentiated approach without interference from the censors. His own attitude towards the piece was by no means dismissive. He offered it for performance or publication to contacts in London and urged his new publisher Steiner to issue it. Beethoven considered writing an overture to preface the cantata, and even five months before his death the cantata is mentioned in one of his conversation notebooks. When it was eventually published in 1837, with a different text, it received the opus number 136, one higher than the last of the great string quartets.

In its style *The Glorious Moment* is not without parallels in Beethoven's greater works. Certain passages in the aria with violin solo (no. 3) vaguely foreshadow aspects of the Benedictus of the *Missa solemnis*, and the choral fugue on 'Vindobona' faintly echoes, in its rhythm and texture, the Handelian flavour of the fugue in the Gloria of Beethoven's Mass in D. *The Glorious Moment* is more smooth and refined than *Wellington's Victory*, but it consistently lacks those qualities of expressive tension and formal integrity that we normally expect from Beethoven. Especially after his experience with *Wellington's Victory*, Beethoven may have felt it appropriate to dilute much of the strength of his musical style in order to please and flatter his listeners without really demanding their attention.

It is hard to know just how seriously Beethoven took *The Glorious Moment* and some of his other pieces for the Congress of Vienna, such as the choral-orchestral works *Germania* WoO 94 and *Ihr weisen Gründer glücklicher Staaten* ('You Wise Founders of Happy Countries') WoO 95, whose title alone betrays the same mindless obsequiousness as *The Glorious Moment*. His angrily dismissive response to a negative critique of *Wellington's Victory*, however, shows a streak of defensiveness: he wrote 'nichts als Gelegenheitsstück' ('nothing but

Ex. 55 *Der glorreiche Augenblick* op. 136, Quartet (no. 5), bars 172–90

Ex. 55 *cont.*

an occasional work') and then added '. . . pitiful scoundrel, my shit is better than [anything] you have ever thought' (see Plate 13). But intentionally or not, Beethoven held up a very unflattering mirror to this grand party of the restoration. In giving his audience what they wanted, his Congress of Vienna pieces exposed the superficial veneer that concealed the far less glorious realities of post-Napoleonic politics.

The hollow splendour of *The Glorious Moment* represents an overextended pretence in artistic guise, and the glaring contrast with Beethoven's other music implies a conscious decision on his part to adjust priorities. To be sure, his occasional patriotic works indulge far less in hedonism than in aggressive nationalist sentiments. Even in *The Glorious Moment*, a seductive wallowing in beauty remains a secondary rather than a primary characteristic. It is not dreamy sentimentality but the underlying criterion of a false pretence that betrays the affinity of Beethoven's Congress of Vienna works with Broch's categories.

*   *   *

During 1814 Beethoven returned to serious composition with two major projects, the revision of *Fidelio* with the librettist Georg Friedrich Treitschke, and the Piano Sonata in E minor op. 90. Important revisions were made throughout the opera and in aspects of its staging. As we have seen, some crucial additions were made, such as the F major concluding section of Florestan's aria, and Beethoven finally resolved the problem of the overture by writing a new one in E major. One aspect of his revision that has received little attention is his compression of numerous passages in various numbers of the opera. A more concise, terse concentration is characteristic of his later style in general, and the revision of his opera helped initiate this new approach. A work like the F minor Quartet op. 95, which was revised for publication in 1815, already displays this heightened density, as does the first movement of the op. 90 sonata. Beginning with the two Cello Sonatas of op. 102, from 1815, such concentration becomes an abiding feature of Beethoven's music. After his patriotic pot-boilers of 1813–14, with their thin, vapid character, Beethoven turned about-face in his important works, significantly raising the specific gravity of their artistic content.

The first movement of the E minor Sonata op. 90 tends to elide the formal divisions between the exposition and development and between the development and recapitulation. As in the next sonata, op. 101 (as well as in opp. 57 and 110), the exposition is not repeated. The development begins quietly, in bar 82, on the pitch B, drawn from the preceding dominant chords that close the exposition, and it is based almost entirely on the first theme, though the accompaniment in repeated notes and chords is drawn from the second group. The entire second half of the development (bars 113 ff.) employs a different accompanimental texture outlining broken chords in the right hand, while a figure drawn from the opening theme is intensified with *sforzandi* in the left hand (Ex. 56).

Ex. 56 Piano Sonata op. 90/I, Development, bars 109–23

Especially fascinating is how the musical content of bar 130—where Beethoven changes the key signature to one sharp, indicating E minor—is treated in the ensuing canonic passage to allow the recapitulation to emerge. This bar already contains the essence of the recapitulation in its second and third beats, in particular in the descent of the third G–E in the high register. After three repetitions (bar 131) this figure is isolated and stressed dynamically in the next bar, with an imitation an octave lower. Then a series of canonic mutations elongates the figure in three successive rhythmic augmentations, and its relationship with the principal theme gradually becomes clear. The close stretto at the unison (bars 138–41) stresses the pitch level of the imminent recapitulation; in performance, these bars are difficult to bring out effectively, on account of their dense texture, as the motif continues to turn onto itself. Finally, the stretto expands across other registers and yields to the recapitulation (bar 144). As in the first movement of the Fourth Symphony, there is no cadence; harmonically, this entire static passage has remained on the tonic. The rapid sixteenth-note figuration of the development (beginning in Ex. 56) has proven against all expectations to belong to the head of the principal theme. Instead of defining a single structural moment, the recapitulation represents a process that extends over the 18 bars that precede the literal point of recapitulation. As in the first movements of two of the last quartets, opp. 130 and 132, the tonal and thematic recapitulations do not coincide.

The second and final movement, in E major, is the most Schubertian movement in Beethoven, a luxurious rondo dominated by many, almost unvaried, appearances of a spacious cantabile theme. This is the last big lyrical rondo finale in the Beethoven sonatas, the successor to the closing movements in op. 2 no. 2, op. 7, op. 22, op. 31 no. 1, and the *Waldstein*. In this rondo, and in the A major Sonata op. 101, Beethoven comes closest to the emerging Romantic style, yet there are elements here that point unmistakably towards the unique synthesis embodied in many compositions of his last decade. The op. 90 Sonata is a reminder that even during the Congress of Vienna period Beethoven's basic compositional integrity remained intact and continued to grow, work by work, as he forged the elements of a new style. Continuity from the past is especially felt in some songs of these years. Apart from his occasional folk-song settings, Beethoven returned, in his second setting of *An die Hoffnung* and in his later song *Sehnsucht* ('Yearning') WoO 146, based on the poem by Reissig, to abiding preoccupations—he had already written five songs entitled *Sehnsucht* based on two poems by Goethe (the four settings of WoO 134; op. 83 no. 2). Another significant piece from this time is his sensitive setting of two Goethe poems for chorus and orchestra *Meeresstille und glückliche Fahrt* ('Calm Seas and Prosperous Voyage'), which was composed in 1814–15 but published only in 1822, as op. 112, with a dedication to the poet.

The two Cello Sonatas in C major and D major of op. 102 are Beethoven's only other important works of 1815. Though shorter than his earlier cello sonatas, they are more concentrated and richly polyphonic. The C major Sonata opens with an unaccompanied *dolce cantabile* phrase in the cello, as did the op. 69 Sonata in A major. The effect there is broader, but his treatment of the opening phrase in the C major Sonata goes perhaps still deeper, since the thematic material is immediately worked out contrapuntally with the entry of the piano. Much happens here in a small space. The form of the whole also takes on some unprecedented features: for this pregnant, lyrical opening of the first movement is recalled, in slightly varied form, shortly before the beginning of the finale; its thematic substance seems to be plumbed, and the fourth G–C—the main motif and point of departure of the finale—is discovered as an outcome of contemplative reminiscence.

Beethoven's last cello sonata, in D major, begins with a contrast-laden and yet superbly coherent theme: the opening fanfares in the piano preface a reflective, *dolce* phrase in the cello, before the robust character of the theme is restored (Ex. 57). This theme well illustrates the enhanced density of Beethoven's evolving musical language and its implications for analysis and performance. The succinct four-bar opening in the piano is a configuration of durational time, in which disruptive and unifying forces are held in balance. The syncopated upward leaps of an octave to D and a tenth to G outline precisely the tonal space that is traversed in continuous motion in the descend-

Ex. 57 Cello Sonata op. 102 no. 2/I

ing gesture of the third bar. The inversion of the linear motion leads to the register of the beginning in bar 4, making clear that the second half of the phrase closes the first half. This closure is not merely conventional symmetry, however: the second half of the phrase seems to turn back, or even reverse, the driving upward sallies of the first half, producing a kind of contrapuntal mirroring effect.

After its initial rising arpeggios the cello reaches its *dolce* melody in bar 5, stressing in two registers the dominant note, A—a pitch prepared in turn by the contour of the ascending fourth D–G in the opening piano fanfares. The cello melody then elaborates that intervallic relation as G–D in the descending contour of bars 6–7. Beethoven absorbs here the rhythm in sixteenths from the piano fanfares into the cello line, while displacing the notes of the turn-figure by one sixteenth. The ensuing phrases also develop the fourth D–G. In bars 8–9 the cello and piano both play a linear configuration outlining D–G–D, which is treated in a descending sequence in the following bar. But even this motif has been foreshadowed in an inner voice of the piano at the beginning of the *dolce* theme. In both cases the voices rise from D to D♯ before continuing to ascend. That chromatic inflection, in turn, is developed in the E♯ of bar 10, and further in the G♯ of bar 12, which opens up the energetic drive into the dominant. The ascending syncopated octaves in piano and cello in bars 13–14 transform the initial fanfares and at the same time balance the opening phrase of four tonic bars with a varied concluding phrase over a dominant pedal.

The overall structure of this sixteen-bar theme is almost parenthetical: an eight-bar *dolce* melody in the cello is nested into two four-bar units of more assertive character, with the piano in the dominating role. Beethoven has cast many connecting threads over these contrasting components and woven the sections tightly together to form a complex composite theme. Essentially, he has experimented here with a variant of the openings of his two earlier cello sonatas, opp. 69 and 102 no. 1, in which the cello begins with a lyrical *dolce* gesture. The corresponding gesture here in the D major Sonata is the *dolce* theme beginning in bar 5, which even shows a rhythmic resemblance to the beginning of op. 69. Most extraordinary is the way Beethoven devises the continuation of this theme. The music unfolds in dialogue with what had preceded and what is to follow, gradually building an organic transition from the reflective, *dolce* character into the brilliant, extroverted passage leading to the cadence in the dominant. It is a tall order to convey these qualities clearly in performance, a challenge rarely met.

The rich network of motivic and formal relationships carries implications for the temporality of the music. A piece such as the *Allegro con brio* of op. 102 no. 2 seems to arise out of a sustained tension between an anticipation of the future and memory of the past. Inasmuch as this is perceived and adequately conveyed in performance, it is no longer appropriate to attend to the artistic content as if it were simply a succession of events in measured, quantitative time. This phenomenon is undoubtedly connected to the confusion or grief that Beethoven's most advanced works have sometimes caused listeners. The very first reviewer of op. 102 in the *Allgemeine musikalische Zeitung* in 1818 wrote:

These two sonatas certainly belong to the most strange and unusual . . . that have ever been written for piano. Everything is different, completely different from what could be expected, even from this composer. He should not take it badly if we add that not a few things . . . are shaped *in order that* they should appear very strange.[16]

---

[16] Cited in Kunze, ed., *Beethoven: Die Werke im Spiegel seiner Zeit*, pp. 341–2.

Op. 102 no. 2 is the only one of Beethoven's cello sonatas to incorporate a fully independent slow movement. This is an *Adagio con molto sentimento d'affetto* in D minor, reminiscent in its mysterious character of the *Largo* of the 'Ghost' Trio, in the same key. Also analogous to the 'Ghost' Trio is Beethoven's combination of a slow, almost static theme with more intricate textures employing dotted rhythms. A more distant but equally fascinating kinship may be felt with one of the last and greatest of all Beethoven's slow movements: the 'Heiliger Dankgesang' of the Quartet in A minor op. 132. For the *Adagio* of the cello sonata begins with solemn strains of a chorale-like subject, which are subsequently blended with more elaborate, expressive textures. The austerity of the chorale is deepened by Beethoven's use of the low register of the piano, by modal inflections, and by the ritual pauses after every second bar. The setting exudes a remote, archaic, and even oppressive atmosphere, which is suddenly, even miraculously, relieved by the shift into D major in the middle section of the movement, marked *dolce*. Beethoven emphasizes the affective contrast of the middle section in several ways. The dragging pace of the chorale is supplanted by gentle pulsation of the accompanimental figuration, the sombre heaviness of texture by transparent, lyrical gestures reaching into the upper registers.

In the 'Heiliger Dankgesang' movement, by contrast, Beethoven chooses a lydian modality for his hymn, and he pits against this chorale a luxurious, dance-like subject in the major, marked 'feeling new strength'. The roots of this extraordinary conception can be recognized in the impressive slow movement of op. 102 no. 2. Quite unlike the quartet, however, is the conclusion of the *Adagio con molto sentimento d'affetto*. At the threshold of the final cadence in D minor he introduces a mysterious, deceptive shift to a sonority of C♯ minor, leading into the transition to the final movement, the *Allegro fugato* (Ex. 58). This transition supplies a good example of Beethoven's increasing propensity for isolating the basic motivic material in advance. The cello and piano each play a rising scale, which soon becomes the point of departure for the culmination of the sonata in the fugal finale.

This fugue has often proved a stumbling-block for critics. One early review of 1824, probably by Adolf Bernhard Marx, includes the following comments:

The theme is too merry for such serious treatment, and it therefore makes too shrill a contrast to the other movements. How much we would rather have heard another movement—a Beethovenian finale!—in place of this fugue. It would be therefore desirable that Beethoven not exploit fugue in such a wilful manner, since his great genius is naturally lifted above every form.[17]

The reviewer's dismissal of the finale seems motivated by his conviction that the very traditional form of the fugue has obstructed Beethoven's artistic

[17] Ibid., p. 344.

Ex. 58 Cello Sonata op. 102 no. 2/II, bars 79–85; III, bars 1–14

expression; despite its originality and skill, this fugue is not beautiful and 'will not please anyone, neither the connoisseur nor—and even less—the amateur'.

This contention touches central aesthetic issues in Beethoven's later music. For the fugal finale of the D major Cello Sonata is not an isolated experiment. This is the first of a series of important fugal finales which Beethoven was to set forth in the piano sonatas opp. 106 and 110 and in the huge finale of the original version of the Quartet in B♭ major op. 130, the *Grosse Fuge*. In this respect, as in many others, op. 102 no. 2 is a prophetic composition.

There are motivic parallels linking this fugue with the fugal finale of the *Hammerklavier* Sonata. The main subject of the *Hammerklavier* fugue also uses scalar segments, which at first descend, instead of ascending, as they do in the cello sonata. Both fugues make much use of inversion, as well as rhythmic augmentation. In a sense, the fugal subject of the *Hammerklavier* might be regarded as combining motivic elements from the first movement of that work—the rising tenth and chain of falling thirds—with the stepwise, scalar contour of op. 102 no. 2. Other motivic parallels of this kind link the cello sonata fugue with the fugal development in the middle of the finale of Beethoven's next sonata, op. 101.

As in these works, there is a grainy, even harsh quality to some of the contrapuntal developments in the D major Cello Sonata. Quite unlike the *Hammerklavier* is the humorous character of the original subject, the quality that irritated Marx in 1824. Beethoven's choice of character is undoubtedly linked to the slow movement, with its despairing mood, which is resolved or superseded in the unhampered gaiety of the beginning of the fugue. The intensity of the contrapuntal operations lends weight to the finale, thereby anchoring the sonata as a whole. Beethoven's fugal subject undergoes a kind of passage from innocence to experience, a progression guided by the cold logic of the contrapuntal combinations and culminating in an almost violent chain of strettos—one of those passages that must have most shocked the reviewer from the *Allgemeine musikalische Zeitung* (Ex. 59).

Ex. 59 Cello Sonata op. 102 no. 2/III, bars 129–49

Immediately following this *fortissimo* climax, the music pauses on F♯ as it fades into *pianissimo*. A new fugal subject enters in long notes and flat legato articulation. Unlike the rest of the *Allegro fugato*, this subject has a feeling of motionlessness. It resists the swift, unfettered movement of the finale in favour of the static world of the *Adagio*. Hence a pivotal moment in the narrative design of the fugue, and of the entire sonata, comes as each of the three contrapuntal voices in turn breaks out of this detached stillness to re-emerge into the dynamic, propulsive experience of the movement proper. The process occurs first in the cello; but the crescendo to *fortissimo* marks the precise passage in which this emancipation takes place in the piano, clearing the way for the exuberant closing section, with its textures of contrary motion and trills.

Beethoven's resource of the fugal finale in his last cello sonata can be seen in part as an outgrowth of his practice, begun in works like the fantasy sonatas op. 27, of reserving the fastest and most continuous rhythmic motion for the finale. The lively, dance-like gait of the *Allegro fugato* is well calculated to supersede the contrast-laden first movement and the sombre, chorale-like *Adagio con molto sentimento d'affetto*. What the fugal texture adds is the necessary density to allow the finale to stand up successfully against the other movements, and indeed to act as culmination of the whole.

By 1815 Beethoven had accomplished a further deepening in his art, fulfilling the intention expressed in the first *Tagebuch* entry three years earlier. His unproductive spell at the close of the 'Immortal Beloved' affair had been left behind; the extravagant artistic misadventures of the Congress period were a closed chapter. His public popularity was now on the wane; the composer of the hour was Rossini. As complete deafness closed in on Beethoven, he approached his greatest artistic challenges. Slowly and deliberately he assembled the elements of an unprecedented stylistic synthesis, whereby nothing was lost and yet everything changed.

8

The Hammerklavier *Sonata*

1816–1818

I N the summer of 1816 Fanny Giannatasio recorded notes in her diary about Beethoven's visit to her family at Baden, outside Vienna, which included the following:

My father thought that B. could rescue himself from his unfortunate domestic conditions only by marriage, did he know anybody, etc. Now our long foreboding was confirmed: he was unhappy in love! Five years ago he had made the acquaintance of a person, a union with whom he would have considered the greatest happiness of his life. It was not to be thought of, almost an impossibility, a chimera—nevertheless it is now as on the first day.[1]

Shortly before, on 8 May, Beethoven had written to Ries:

Unfortunately I have no wife. I found *only one*, whom I shall no doubt never possess.[2]

As Solomon has observed, the *Tagebuch* contains two entries from 1816 implying the possible identity of the woman as Antonie, or 'Toni', Brentano:

Regarding T. nothing is left but to trust in God; never to go where weakness might lead to do wrong; to Him alone, the omniscient God, leave all this.

But toward T. [be] as good as possible; her devotion deserves never to be forgotten—though, unfortunately, advantageous consequences for you could never result therefrom.[3]

In the spring of 1816, after Beethoven's 'Immortal Beloved' had remained a 'distant beloved' for several years, he gave definitive artistic expression to this abiding and universal human theme in the song cycle *An die ferne Geliebte* op.

---

[1] Thayer-Forbes, p. 646.   [2] Ibid., p. 639.   [3] *Beethoven*, p. 173.

98. Thayer wrote about these songs that 'no one can hear them adequately sung without feeling that there is something more in that music than the mere inspiration of the poetry'.[4] Yet, as Kerman has claimed, it seems likely that this music helped Beethoven to bring his emotional conflicts to rest; 'by bringing his feelings into the open, Beethoven was renouncing or abandoning them'.[5] *An die ferne Geliebte* relates to the 'Immortal Beloved' crisis in a manner analogous to the role of the *Eroica* Symphony in the *Heiligenstadt* crisis more than a decade earlier. But there was another factor that ameliorated Beethoven's loneliness and isolation at this time. He had formed a close attachment to his nephew Karl, son of his brother Caspar Carl, who had died in 1815. Beethoven's relationship to Karl undoubtedly helped fill the emotional void in the bachelor existence to which he was now permanently resigned. (We shall return later to the problems surrounding Beethoven's guardianship of his nephew.)

The text of *An die ferne Geliebte* stems from the Moravian medical student Alois Jeitteles, who presumably gave Beethoven the poems in manuscript— they were never published separately from the music. Beethoven made musical sketches for the cycle in the Scheide Sketchbook, immediately preceding work on the A major Piano Sonata op. 101. As Christopher Reynolds has pointed out, Beethoven sketched the first song of the cycle most intensively; the music of the following five songs often varies or transforms elements from the first.[6] The songs are directly interconnected by transitions in sonority; they outline a cyclical key scheme passing from E♭ major to G (no. 2), A♭ (nos. 3 and 4), and C (no. 5), returning to the tonic for the sixth song. But the primacy of the opening song 'Auf dem Hügel sitz' ich spähend' is reflected most vividly by Beethoven's decision to link its text and music with the conclusion of the cycle.

Kerman has convincingly suggested that Beethoven added the last stanza to the opening strophic song in order to promote this cyclic connection.[7] The fifth stanza of 'Auf dem Hügel' contains a closing couplet identical to the end of the last song, preceded by two lines that may stem from Beethoven himself:

> Denn vor Liedesklang entweichet
> jeder Raum und jede Zeit,
> und ein liebend Herz erreichet,
> was ein liebend Herz geweiht.

> For the sound of song transcends
> all space and time,
> that a loving heart receive
> what a loving heart has consecrated.

---

[4] Thayer-Forbes, p. 647.   [5] 'An die ferne Geliebte', p. 131.

[6] 'The Representational Impulse in Late Beethoven, I: *An die ferne Geliebte*'.

[7] 'An die ferne Geliebte', pp. 126–7, 129.

The import of these lines resists literal translation; what is involved is a communication from one soul to another, overcoming spatial and temporal constraints. Much the same message is conveyed in the dedication Beethoven was to write over the Kyrie of his *Missa solemnis*: '*Von Herzen—möge es zu Herzen gehen!*' ('From the heart, may it go to the heart!').

The beginning of the final song, 'Nimm sie hin denn, diese Lieder, die ich dir, Geliebte, sang' ('Take to your heart these songs that I sang to you, beloved') is quoted with moving effect by Robert Schumann at the end of the first movement of his C major Fantasy op. 17[8] (Ex. 60*a* and *b*). Schumann's quotation is at once a homage to Beethoven and an allusion to his own 'distant beloved' at the time, Clara Wieck. It is noteworthy that Schumann originally intended to repeat the quotation at the end of the final movement of the fantasy, a gesture that would have echoed Beethoven's procedure in *An die ferne Geliebte*, where the last song brings a return of the music and words of the first. This device is the most striking single idea in Beethoven's song cycle, an inspiration with broader ties to his instrumental music from these years.

It is for the last stanza of this closing song that Beethoven recalls the music from 'Denn vor Liedesklang entweichet' in the first song:

> Denn vor diesen Liedern weichet,
> was geschieden uns so weit,
> und ein liebend Herz erreichet
> was ein liebend Herz geweiht!

> Then the distance that so divides us
> dissolves through these songs,
> that a loving heart receive
> what a loving heart has consecrated!

A short piano introduction and a longer postlude frame the stanza, setting the recall of the music from the fifth stanza of the opening song on a pedestal. As Kerman observes, this device also marks an important moment in the gradually increasing prominence of the piano throughout the cycle.[9] The beginning of the cycle had not strayed far from the *Volksweise* ideal, in which the words and vocal line remain dominant; only the end of the cycle could have elicited Goethe's disapproval by giving the music sway over the text.

The two-bar piano introduction was probably an afterthought that Beethoven inserted into the autograph score.[10] As a result of this interpolation, the vocal line takes its cue from the piano; and now Beethoven uses every

---

[8] Cf. Rosen, *The Classical Style*, pp. 451–3. Recent research has failed to discover any documented references to Schumann's Beethoven allusion before the twentieth century, but that does not invalidate the tangible artistic kinship between these works.

[9] 'An die ferne Geliebte', pp. 154–5.   [10] Ibid.

Ex. 60 (*a*) *An die ferne Geliebte* op. 98 no. 6

(*b*) Schumann, Fantasy in C op. 17/I

rhetorical and formal device at his disposal to highlight the message of the final stanza (Ex. 61). The words are repeated over and over, as motivic elements from the postlude of the first song, such as the decorated inflection on high B♭ in the piano, are developed in a new context. Beethoven reserves the peak of the vocal tessitura on high G for the passionate closing repetitions of 'was ein liebend, liebend Herz geweiht!' The piano echoes the final inflection of the voice and brings the music to a close with an emphatic reiteration of the phrase that had begun the cycle.

Beethoven's cadence is left open, with the final accented E♭ major chord

Ex. 61 *An die ferne Geliebte* op. 98 no. 6, bars 38–end

Ex. 61 *cont.*

placed on a weak beat of the triple metre. The cycle turns back on itself, forcing the listener to reflect on the meaning of the circular design of the whole,
with its symbolic embodiment of the perennial, unending theme of human
communication and separation. It is the possibility of a true intimacy that is
at stake here: 'From the heart, may it go to the heart!', as Beethoven wrote into

his score of the *Missa solemnis*. This is the first of a series of open-ended conclusions of works that Beethoven was to compose in following years, including the last three piano sonatas and the Diabelli Variations.

*   *   *

As Alfred Brendel has suggested, Beethoven's late music involves a general expansion and synthesis of the means of expression, whereby opposites are often juxtaposed, with every new complexity of style seeming to parallel, as its antithesis, a childlike simplicity. Normal modes of analysis are inadequate to grasp the tremendous richness of this idiom, which 'embraces equally the past, present, and future, the sublime and the profane'.[11] This expansion in expressive range is often associated with new departures in large-scale formal organization, and especially with a tendency to replace symmetrical forms with a central climax by a progression leading to a final, culminating experience. Not only does Beethoven avoid the enclosure of literal recapitulation within movements; he also tends to arrange successive movements into a directional sequence leading towards the finale, now usually the most weighty movement of the sonata cycle.

Beethoven now devises new, unique means of linking the movements of his works. In the C major Cello Sonata op. 102 no. 1 and in *An die ferne Geliebte*, as we have seen, his later recall of the opening lyrical music assumes unusual importance, going well beyond the most analogous earlier example—his reminiscence of the slow movement in the finale of the first of the fantasy sonatas op. 27 no. 1, of 1801. But Beethoven's most subtle use of this device is found in his next composition, the Piano Sonata in A major op. 101, from 1816. The crux of this sonata is contained not in the opening *Allegretto, ma non troppo*, despite its quiet, lyrical beginning *in medias res* on the dominant. The suspended quality of the music is enhanced by Beethoven's seamless lyricism, his placement of the exposition in the dominant key, and by his avoidance throughout of strong tonic cadences. Following this short movement of yearning character, and the brusque, angular, contrapuntal march in F major forming the second movement, a more fundamental level of feeling or state of being is uncovered in the slow introduction to the finale, marked *Langsam und sehnsuchtsvoll*. Here the music is drawn progressively lower in pitch, falling through a series of diminished-seventh chords, before it drops still further in register, collapsing onto a soft sustained chord that is to serve as a turning-point and a new beginning (Ex. 62). This passage anticipates in striking fashion the *Praeludium* to the Benedictus of the *Missa solemnis*, where a low chord reached through a similar descending progression is transposed upwards several octaves to the solo violin and flutes, to symbolize, with astonishing effect, the divine presence.

---

[11] *Music Sounded Out*, p. 63.

Ex. 62 Piano Sonata op. 101, slow introduction to Finale

In the case of the sonata, this soft chord, which represents the end of the descending progression and the termination of the *Adagio*, also embodies the *a priori* condition for the first movement, since it presents the exact sonority, in the precise register, out of which the opening of that movement has sprung. In view of this, the opening of the sonata *in medias res* assumes a new and deeper significance. The importance of this original sound—an E major sonority marked by a fermata—is confirmed by its transformation, after a short cadenza-like passage, into the actual beginning of the opening movement. This reminiscence lasts a few bars before it dissolves into the emphatic beginning of the finale, marked by the first strong tonic cadence (in A major) that has yet been heard in the sonata.

The finale is in sonata form, with its development assigned to a fugato. Contrapuntal devices have already been prominent in the march, particularly in its transparent canonic trio; but the fugal textures in the finale unfold with an uncompromising determination and virtuosity comparable only with the fugal finale of Beethoven's next sonata, the *Hammerklavier*. Op. 101 is among the most difficult of the sonatas, and Beethoven himself once described it as 'hard to play'. The characteristically ironic context of this remark—which relates to a critique of performance difficulties in the Seventh Symphony—in no way invalidates the comment.

The challenge of this work lies not only in the complex polyphony of the march and finale but in the delicate narrative sequence of the whole. Twice we pass from spheres of dream-like reflection into the vigorous musical landscapes of the march and finale. A complex network of tonal and thematic relationships makes clear that these are not merely ruptures in the musical form but moments of transformation. Especially characteristic is Beethoven's abiding memory, at the end of op. 101, of earlier stages in the artistic process. It is almost uncanny how this enhanced vision or enlarged perspective nourishes the humorous wit of the conclusion. Thus, the *dolce* passage beginning the coda is subtly reminiscent of the slow introduction to the finale; and the continuation not only alludes to the earlier fugal development but recalls harmonic features of the first two movements. Near the end, Beethoven brings back as a pedal point the low contra E previously used in the climactic cadence to the recapitulation of the finale, and adds above it a long, dissonant trill, both of which are emphatically resolved into the final triadic fanfare—a fanfare that itself ultimately derives from the climactic cadence to the recapitulation. The depth of synthesis and richness of allusion in passages such as this make special demands on listener and interpreter alike.

Few of Beethoven's pieces exerted such a strong spell on the Romantic composers as this A major Sonata. Mendelssohn imitated it in his op. 6 Sonata; Wagner found in its opening movement the ideal of his 'infinite melody'; Schumann was captivated by its march-like second movement. Along with the cello sonatas op. 102 and the song cycle *An die ferne Geliebte*, the A major Sonata marks a major transition in Beethoven's style, pointing unmistakably to the unique synthesis achieved in works of his last decade.

*　　*　　*

Let us pause at this point to reconsider the traditional periodization of Beethoven's career. The conception of three main periods—a classicizing or 'imitative' style in the 1790s, followed by a more expansive, 'heroic' idiom forged in the *Eroica* Symphony, and finally a concentrated 'late' style inaugurated in pieces like op. 101 and op. 102—has a venerable history reaching back at least to Wilhelm von Lenz in the nineteenth century. The tripartite division is not unjustified, and its transitional points correspond roughly to events in Beethoven's life: his crisis over his incurable loss of hearing, and the onset of nearly total deafness more than a decade later. Nevertheless, such a periodization easily risks obscuring the strong lines of continuity in Beethoven's artistic development, as well as other significant demarcations in his career. As we have seen, certain early works, notably the *Joseph* Cantata, foreshadow aspects of his later music, without yet demonstrating the structural mastery and sustained intensity of his mature style. Beethoven's achievement in the various musical genres did not proceed at an even pace; his piano sonatas of the 1790s, for instance, can hardly be regarded as products of an 'imitative' style. On the other hand, after 1809 we can discern a change in his approach to composition that may be related in part to his income from the princes Kinsky and Lobkowitz and the Archduke Rudolph. Beginning around 1810, Beethoven concentrated on a smaller number of pieces, some of which display an enhanced scope in their respective genres: the *Archduke* Trio, Seventh Symphony, and Violin Sonata in G major. By 1815, major works like the cello sonatas op. 102 show even more conspicuous experimental features. For the composer of the *Eroica*, such an innovative tendency was in no way new; it is the striking consistency of this progressive trend from work to work that eventually signals another important stylistic shift. *An die ferne Geliebte* is one product of this impulse toward a richer artistic integration, with a group of individual songs merged into a larger unity. Diametrically opposed to this integrating tendency are the patriotic potboilers such as *Wellington's Victory* and *The Glorious Moment*, pieces that fall out of the main line of Beethoven's artistic development and demand therefore a different critical approach.

The three 'periods' are a convenient simplification, which reflects some of Beethoven's abiding stylistic changes but fails to apply to a number of his works. Ultimately, a convincing periodization needs to take biographical and historical factors into account while nevertheless giving priority to the musical works. To that end, we may discern four main periods, which are reflected in the chapter organization of this book. The first and most heterogeneous period embraces Beethoven's apprenticeship, as well as his path to mastery, and extends from the Bonn years up to 1802. The second or 'heroic' period begins in 1803 with the composition of the *Eroica* Symphony and extends to the end of 1812. Characteristic of the music of this highly productive decade is

a heightened symbolic or mythic dimension that is embodied in an intrinsically musical narrative; examples include the *Appassionata* Sonata, the
Andante con moto of the Fourth Concerto, the Fifth Symphony, and the
Egmont Overture, among many others. The onset of a third period can be
placed for biographical and historical reasons in 1813, although the emergence
of Beethoven's 'late' style was a gradual process in which the pivotal work, the
Hammerklavier Sonata—a primary focus of the present chapter—was completed only in 1818. The culmination of the third period comes in May 1824,
with the performance of the pair of choral-orchestral masterpieces, the *Missa
solemnis* and the Ninth Symphony.

The fourth period is fragmentary, extending from 1824 to Beethoven's death
in March 1827. During these years Beethoven's creative energies were devoted
almost entirely to his last five string quartets. The late quartets are deeply
grounded in his earlier music, but they open up new artistic territory in ways
comparable with the *Eroica* or the *Hammerklavier*; for this reason it is possible
to regard these works—or at least opp. 132, 130 with the *Grosse Fuge* as finale,
and 131—as marking the onset of a new period rather than serving as a subset
of the third period. Were it not for the collapse of Beethoven's health in
December 1826, he might have continued these explorations in some of the
pieces that he talked about or had just begun to sketch: a String Quintet, a
Tenth Symphony, an Overture on B–A–C–H, a Requiem Mass. As it was,
the task of building on the legacy of the last quartets was left to the future: to
Schoenberg, Bartók, and others.

*   *   *

Beethoven composed little music during 1817. His preoccupation with the
education and well-being of his nephew Karl and health problems both con-
spired to hinder the completion of new compositions. Among his few works
from this year is the melancholy song *Resignation* WoO 149, which Beethoven
completed only in a solo version but sketched as well for vocal quartet, a setting reminiscent of his mournful *Elegischer Gesang* op. 118 for four voices and
string quartet of 1814. One of Beethoven's main projects of 1817 was actually
his arrangement of the C minor Piano Trio op. 1 no. 3 as the String Quintet
op. 104. This transcription was motivated by an unsatisfactory attempt by a
certain Herr Kaufmann, in response to which Beethoven undertook the task
himself. With characteristic humour, Beethoven described the finished
arrangement in an inscription as having been 'raised from the most abject
misery to some degree of respectability'; the original quintet arrangement was
'ceremonially sacrificed as a burnt offering to the gods of the underworld'. As
Tyson has shown, however, Beethoven's completion of the arrangement was
actually somewhat uncritical and careless; in this case, he evidently lacked the

patience to redeem the arrangement in all respects from the faulty standard of 'Mr. Goodwill', as Beethoven dubbed Kaufmann.[12]

If Beethoven undertook few such transcriptions, he did make numerous arrangements of Scottish, Irish, English, Welsh, and Continental songs that were commissioned by George Thomson between 1809 and 1820. In 1816 another British publisher, Robert Birchall, requested variations on folk-songs, and Thomson subsequently commissioned variations on 16 melodies, pieces Beethoven completed by early 1819. Thomson published only nine of these sets; the variations on all 16 folk-songs first appeared as opp. 105 and 107 in the editions of Artaria and Simrock. In addition to 11 Scottish, Welsh, and Irish songs, these collections include variations on two Russian and three Tyrolean tunes.

As the publisher specified, the folk-song variations are of modest difficulty and provide an optional flute or violin part in the manner of the old-fashioned accompanied keyboard sonata. In essence, however, they are piano music of considerable subtlety that easily dispenses with the accompaniment. They deserve to be better known, and represent a not insignificant stage in Beethoven's evolving treatment of variation technique, which assumes sur- passing importance in his later works. In his fine study of these variations, Uhde points out an impressive richness of detail, as well as cyclic connections between the pieces, and concludes that 'they demonstrate convincingly . . . that nothing is too slight to serve as the point of departure for great music . . . The most humble things can be illuminated to reveal a deeper meaning'.[13]

Beethoven's blending of the exalted and the commonplace also surfaces in one of his numerous letters from 1818 to Nanette Streicher, who showed an almost maternal concern at this time for the well-being of the deaf master. As we have seen, Beethoven's attraction to puns was an abiding character trait; Czerny reported that 'he always knew how to devise a pun. While listening to an overture by Weber ['weaver'] he said: "Hm! It's woven!" [gewebt]'.[14] As Küthen has observed,[15] a subtle allusion to the Catholic Mass is incorporated into the following note to Nanette Streicher:

Ich bitte in Eile mit Eile und durch Eile, dass Sie Streicher bitten, dass wir heute gegen 12 Uhr allein sind.

　　In eiligster Eile ihr Freund Beethoven

---

[12] See 'The Authors of the Op. 104 String Quintet', pp. 158–73; the quotations are from 159–61, 173.

[13] *Beethovens Klaviermusik*, i, p. 456. For a detailed study of the folk-song settings, see Barry Cooper, *Beethoven's Folksong Settings: Chronology, Sources, Style*.

[14] *Über den richtigen Vortrag*, p. 13. *On the Proper Performance*, p. 7; translation amended.

[15] Personal communication.

I ask in haste with haste and through haste, that you ask of Streicher, that we are alone around 12 o'clock today.

In the most hasty haste your friend Beethoven[16]

There is a double parody at work here. Beethoven's other communications to Nanette Streicher often contain the close 'In Eil' ('in haste'). This time he comically amplifies that formulation as 'eiligster Eile' ('the most hasty haste'). But that is not all. The words 'in Eile mit Eile und durch Eile' are a parody of the *Ordo Missae*, part of the divine service preceding the consecration: 'Durch Ihn und mit Ihm und in Ihm wird Dir, Gott allmächtiger Vater, in der Einheit des Heiligen Geistes, alle Ehre und Verherrlichung' (in Latin, 'Per ipsum et cum ipso, et in ipso, est tibi Deo patri omnipotenti . . .'). Beethoven unexpectedly twists this solemn exhortation to dramatize the urgency of his wish for a noonday meeting with Frau Streicher. He delivers his message from the high altar, so to speak.

*   *   *

As we have seen, the almost feverish pace of Beethoven's earlier productivity had by now slowed considerably. To a substantial extent this more deliberate approach was motivated by the changing nature of his artistic enterprise. He lavished more and more attention on each of his major new compositions, which were usually sketched at great length. As he began work on the largest of his piano sonatas, the mammoth work in B♭, op. 106, Beethoven was virtually stone deaf; the first of his conversation notebooks, in which visitors and friends wrote down their comments to him, date from this period. Yet Beethoven's inward powers of imagination now gained new strength, as the great sonata abundantly reveals. The name 'Hammerklavier' reflects Beethoven's concern at this time to use German terms in music in place of Italian ones; the word was originally also associated with op. 101 but came to be linked specifically with op. 106. The *Hammerklavier* Sonata is but the first of a series of works that includes Beethoven's most monumental achievements in several other important musical genres: the Diabelli Variations, the *Missa solemnis*, and the Ninth Symphony. The sonata became his major compositional preoccupation in late 1817 and throughout 1818. Beethoven himself claimed that op. 106 was 'a sonata that will give pianists something to do' and that it would 'be played 50 years hence'—a fairly accurate prediction since, apart from Liszt and von Bülow, few pianists tackled the immense challenges of this great sonata before the last decades of the nineteenth century.

The op. 106 Sonata offers unusual challenges not only to pianists but to all listeners. It was this work in particular that provoked a crisis in the reception of his music. The notion of Beethoven's later music as inaccessible, too

[16] Kastner and Kapp, eds., *Ludwig van Beethovens sämtliche Briefe*, L. 859; my translation.

difficult, or even incomprehensible arose particularly in reaction to pieces like the fugal finales of op. 106 and of the quartet op. 130 in its original version—the *Grosse Fuge*. Beethoven was fully aware that he had broken new ground with the *Hammerklavier* and succeeding works, and he expressed resentment about what he saw as undeserved enthusiasm for certain of his earlier pieces, such as the popular Septet op. 20. The significance of the *Hammerklavier* was not lost on some of Beethoven's friends; a conversation-book entry from late 1819 records that Zmeskall 'listens to no music apart from op. 106'.[17] Not surprisingly, other listeners took a contrary view. One reviewer wrote about the septet in 1826, for instance, that 'It is strange, that Beethoven declared precisely this work to be one of his least successful. For even if the dimensions are somewhat broad, it is infinitely richer in true beauty than many of his later works, for instance the big sonata, op. 106'.[18]

The *Hammerklavier* Sonata is concerned with much more than mere beauty; it is profoundly shaped by forces of conflict and tension. An extraordinary role is assumed in each movement by B minor—a tonality Beethoven once described as a 'black key'. B minor functions in the *Hammerklavier* like a focus of negative energy pitted against the B♭ major tonic, creating a dramatic opposition with far-reaching consequences. In the first movement this generates an important climax after the beginning of the recapitulation, an event deeply anchored in the musical structure. The melodic detail and the harmonic and tonal progressions of op. 106 mirror one another with uncanny precision, often elaborating chains of falling thirds, as Charles Rosen has pointed out.[19] The opening chordal fanfares triumphantly spell out the descending thirds D–B♭ and F–D; the G major theme beginning the second subject-group brings graceful falling thirds in a smooth legato figuration; and the powerful fugal development elaborates the descending thirds relentlessly, periodically substituting rising sixths (their inversion) in order to maintain a stability of register within the extended chains of thirds.

On the larger, architectural level of the tonal structure, Beethoven develops the same relationships based on descending thirds. Beginning at the abbreviated restatement of the opening fanfare, he modulates from B♭ major to G major, whereas the fugal development begins with another conspicuous tonal drop of a third, to E♭. Then, instead of preparing the recapitulation with the usual dominant key, F major, he continues the series of descending thirds by modulating to B major (enharmonically equivalent to C♭ major) for the last section of the development. The shift to B♭ major at the recapitulation is abrupt, undermining the reassertion of the tonic, and he soon makes yet

[17] *Ludwig van Beethovens Konversationshefte*, i, p. 92.
[18] Cited in Kunze, ed., *Ludwig van Beethoven: Die Werke im Spiegel seiner Zeit*, p. 21.
[19] *The Classical Style*, pp. 404–34; also Ratz, *Einführung*, pp. 201–41.

another change of key down a third, to G♭. He now seizes upon the enharmonic equivalence of G♭ to F♯ to expose the opening fanfare of the movement
in the remote, yet rigorously prepared key of B *minor*, climactically destabi-
lizing the B♭ major tonic while opening a rift into the 'black key' (Ex. 63).

Ex. 63 *Hammerklavier* Sonata op. 106/I, bars 262–73

Never before had Beethoven achieved such close coordination between
motivic and harmonic detail, tonal structure, and formal shape. We have
noted various passages in earlier works in which he turns a melodic inflection
into a pivotal structural gesture; the shift from B to B♭ at the end of the slow
movement of the *Emperor* Concerto is one such example. In the
Hammerklavier Sonata this practice is taken to a new stage. The difference is
perhaps best illustrated through a comparison with Beethoven's previous
compositions that exploit the same motivic relationships that are so prominent in the *Hammerklavier*: the semitone from the Neapolitan B to the tonic
B♭ and the related semitone above the dominant, G♭–F, in the key of B♭
major.

As we have seen, it is especially characteristic for Beethoven to emphasize
dramatically the semitones above the tonic and dominant in his F minor
works: the Quartet op. 95 and the *Appassionata* Sonata spring to mind. The
Appassionata goes furthest towards 'composing out' this relationship on the
various possible levels of structure: Beethoven distils the D♭–C tension as a
motto within the main theme, places the lyrical second theme in the key of
D♭ major in the development, and has the entire slow movement in this key
as well. These interlocking levels of structure contribute to the quality of
gigantic simplicity in the *Appassionata*, as well as to its expressive force.

In the *Hammerklavier* Sonata the semitone tension is more deeply and per-
vasively lodged in the musical substance. Beethoven does not employ a
motivic tag or motto here, as he does in the *Appassionata* Sonata. Instead, as
Rosen observes, he allows the same relationships that are highlighted in the

large-scale tonal structure to invest the harmonic texture of individual themes. The Gb–F semitone is emphasized in the bass line of the polyphonic continuation to the opening theme, after the majestic opening fanfares. A striking phrase in the second subject-group in G stresses the corresponding relationship Eb–D and each time supplies the alternative, E♮–D, in a higher register (Ex. 64). In the next few bars Beethoven transfers this tension between Eb and

Ex. 64 *Hammerklavier* Sonata op. 106/I, bars 74–83

E♮ into the bass progression B–E–C#–D–Eb and develops it in turn in a series of sequences. The theme that follows, marked *cantabile dolce ed espressivo*, is similarly poised between the major and minor. Beethoven repeatedly supplies both the minor (Bb) and major (B♮) thirds in its melodic structure, and, although the major tonic triad retains primacy, the balancing presence of the minor is reflected in his very consistent use of the lowered sixth degree, Eb instead of E♮.

In this context Beethoven's stroke of substituting Bb for B in the first-time bar leading back from the end of the exposition to its repetition carries special conviction. When the exposition is repeated, in the second-time bar, the Bb is superseded by B♮, which carries the music into the development. Elements of the minor are structurally assimilated into the basic tonality of the *Hammerklavier* Sonata, as part of the pervasive emphasis on third relationships. Nowhere in the opening *Allegro* is this modal tension involving a rising semitone more conspicuous than in the final section of the development leading to the recapitulation. The long fugal passage in Eb shows a gradual broadening in harmonic rhythm, until the music dwells on repeated Ds in both hands. Here, the energy of the descending third chain shifts from a harmonic to a tonal level, as Beethoven recalls the cantabile theme in B, a key enharmonically a third below Eb and Neapolitan to Bb, the tonic (Ex. 65).

At this transitional moment the melodic semitone tension is between D and D#, the minor and major third degrees of B; in the fifth bar of the

Ex. 65 *Hammerklavier* Sonata op. 106/I, bars 197–202

cantabile, marked *espressivo*, and again two bars later, Beethoven restates this
semitone, whereas the following decorated variant in eighth-notes expresses
the tension as D♯ against C𝄪. The rising linear motion is developed by
Beethoven in the passage leading to the recapitulation. The bars immediately
before the reprise are a foreshortening of the preceding music and incorporate
the chromatic ascending motion derived from the cantabile theme. This relationship supports a reading of A instead of A♯ at the famous disputed passage
beginning at the upbeat, two bars before the recapitulation. The first edition
(Plates 14 and 15) contained no natural signs here to cancel the A♯, but that
was presumably an error (there are numerous other mistakes and omissions on
the same page). The autograph score is not extant, but a sketch implies the
accuracy of A♮, as Nottebohm pointed out.[20] If the passage is played as originally printed, the shift from G♯ to A♯ as the lowest notes in these sequences
causes the music to avoid the dominant triad altogether, not only weakening
the harmonic preparation for the reprise but breaking the ascent by semitone
to the tonic note B♭, a progression implied by the intrinsic logic of the musical structure.

Beethoven underscores the importance of the cantabile theme by recalling
it once more at the beginning of his coda. Here, a slow trill on the semitone
C♭–B♭, enharmonically equivalent to B–B♭, is at first combined with the
theme; moments later, this new reflection of the work's central harmonic tension is resolved by a double trill in the inner voices on C♮–B♭. Still, the corresponding semitone tension on the dominant, G♭–F, darkens most of the
remainder of the coda. These tensions prove too powerful to be resolved in the
first movement; they spill over into every movement of this enormous work.

The following scherzo is a humorous yet dark parody of the opening
Allegro, transforming the motivic material based on thirds. A sardonic dimension surfaces here in the *presto* passage connecting the B♭ minor trio to the
repetition of the scherzo, and again, more tellingly, in the closing moments of
this *Assai vivace*. Characteristic of the scherzo is a tendency for its phrases to
close softly on the tell-tale B♮. The drift towards B undercuts the tonic B♭
octaves that closed the first scherzo section and might otherwise have closed

[20] A thorough discussion of this sketch and other issues bearing on the disputed passage is
in Badura-Skoda, 'Noch einmal zur Frage Ais oder A in der Hammerklaviersonate Opus 106
von Beethoven', pp. 53–81.

the entire movement. What follows is an eerie disruption of the tonal equilibrium, as the music lingers in the 'wrong' tonality of B minor, even ventur-
ing a 'distorted' version of the opening motif in that key (Ex. 66). Only
through a tremendous exercise of will does Beethoven bring these subversive
forces under control, as 18 repeated double octaves build in a furious crescendo
to a brief closing restoration of the tonic B♭ major.

Ex. 66 *Hammerklavier* Sonata op. 106/II, bars 153–end

The two mysterious octaves on A and C♯ that open the following slow
movement were an afterthought by Beethoven, added just before the sonata
was printed. The added bar acts like a pedestal, setting the ensuing music into
relief. But the A also captures the descending linear energy from the end of
the scherzo, carrying the B–B♭ progression one step further, to A, before a
change of key casts this pitch into a new perspective.

The great *Adagio sostenuto* that follows is the longest slow movement in
Beethoven, an immense sonata form, described by von Lenz as 'a mausoleum

of collective suffering of the world'.[21] Its key, F♯ minor, is enharmonically a third below B♭, poised between the overall tonic of the work and the focus of contrary forces in B minor. The opening section in F♯ minor contains two themes, the first of which is played with the left pedal (*una corda*) throughout, its sombre restraint brightened intermittently by fleeting lyrical glimpses of the Neapolitan G major in the higher pitch registers. In the second theme the left pedal is lifted, yielding a more direct sound quality, as a passionately inward expression is rendered in intricate melodic decoration of the melody. Only now, after 40 bars, does the music change key to D major (a third lower), opening up new, more hopeful regions of feeling in a theme whose phrases are first sounded in the cavernous bass register before being echoed four octaves higher in the treble. A return to muffled *una corda* inflections eventually leads to the cadence of the exposition in a passage of vast contemplative stillness.

In the development Beethoven dwells on the opening theme and the juxtaposition of *una corda* and *tutte le corde*, while a long series of harmonic sequences based on descending thirds eventually converges onto the recapitulation. The music seems at once suspended and in flux. The recapitulation is no mere symmetrical return, but a profound reinterpretation of the opening theme, which is 'composed out' into moving thirty-second-note figuration in the right hand, balanced against deep chordal pedal points in the bass. But if the recapitulation brings the inner climax of the *Adagio sostenuto*, the outward, dramatic climax is reserved for the coda. Here the theme characterized by vast registral echoes returns in G major, and Beethoven incorporates a rising bass progression bringing the music for once a third *higher*, to B minor. A series of high, climactic repeated F♯s follows; after this dramatic outbreak, the return of a curtailed form of the opening *una corda* theme has the effect of deep resignation. Yet here, for the first time, the theme is conclusively resolved into F♯ *major*, with the major third, A♯ (enharmonically equivalent to B♭), prominently doubled in the inner voices in the final bars.

The ensuing slow introduction to the finale begins with the drop of a semitone, as F is sounded across all the pitch registers. Beethoven now distils the intervallic basis of the whole sonata, reducing the music to a fundamental, underlying level of content consisting solely of the chain of falling thirds in the bass, accompanied by soft, hesitant chords in the treble. This chain of thirds is interrupted three times by brief glimpses of other music, and the last of these evocations is obviously Bachian in character. As in the transition to the choral finale in the Ninth Symphony there is thus a search towards new compositional possibilities, with the clear implication here that Baroque counterpoint is transcended by the creation of a new contrapuntal idiom embodied in the revolutionary fugal finale of the sonata.

---

[21] *Kritischer Katalog sämtlicher Werke Ludwig van Beethovens mit Analysen derselben*, iv, p. 41.

No less fascinating is the manner in which Beethoven seems to derive elements of the fugal finale from this *Largo* introduction. Following the Bachian 'quotation', he repeats the searching unison octaves across all the pitch registers, now on A instead of F; the head of the fugue subject employs precisely these pitches, F and A, to span a rising tenth—an interval reminiscent at the same time of the initial upbeat in the first movement. Another, more obvious foreshadowing of the finale is rhythmic in nature. After the strangely still and expressively blank chain of falling thirds, Beethoven introduces an astonishing rhythmic intensification and acceleration to *fortissimo* and *prestissimo* in the final moments of the introduction, before a *ritardando* and harmonic pivot from A to F lead into the *Allegro risoluto*.

Beethoven described the fugue as 'con alcune licenze', but it is exhaustive in its contrapuntal resources. Most of the seven main sections of the finale unfold like fugal variations on the main subject, which is worked out in rhythmic augmentation (section 2), retrograde motion (section 3), and inversion (section 4). The subject bears an audible resemblance to the beginning of the first movement. Its striking opening leap of a tenth to a sustained trill and its sharp profile of sequences outlining falling thirds lend themselves particularly well to contrapuntal processes. Even the most abstract thematic transformation—the retrograde version, played in reverse, or *Krebsgang*—can be readily recognized through the rhythm and placement of repeated notes (Ex. 67*a* and *b*).

This section in retrograde with its implied negation of the theme, as well as the sublime interlude heard later in D major, raise fundamental aesthetic issues. The smooth, somewhat faceless cantabile of the retrograde section and its tonality (B minor!) set it apart from the remainder of the movement. By reversing the pattern of thematic unfolding Beethoven seems almost to annul time, opening a dimension apart from the main action. The role of B minor as a focus of negative energy receives its ultimate embodiment in this passage, though one, to be sure, that depends vitally on an understanding of the structural operations in the music and not merely on a response to the outward expressive effect.

By contrast, the D major episode, played *una corda*, is wholly positive in character and akin to Beethoven's setting of 'in nomine Domini' in the Benedictus of the *Missa solemnis*, as Uhde observed.[22] As a still oasis amid the harsh brilliance and rhythmic fury that generally characterize the finale, the D major interlude creates an even greater contrast than the B minor episode in retrograde. Yet both contrasting modalities are but stages within a larger process, and exert little lasting influence on the final sections of the movement.

---

[22] *Beethovens Klaviermusik*, iii, p. 457.

Ex. 67 *Hammerklavier* Sonata op. 106/IV

(*a*) fugue, bars 1–7

(*b*) fugue, bars 141–9; the retrograde version of the theme is in the left hand in bars 144–9

The fugue of the *Hammerklavier* seems not to affirm a higher, more perfect or serene world of eternal harmonies, as in Bach's works, but to confront an open universe. Beethoven utilizes an initially abstract, retrograde rhythm ♪♪♪♪ ♪ to generate a vigorous, propulsive forward momentum in the transition to the fourth section, when this figure is juxtaposed with the original subject in inversion. And the wonderful transition from the sublime D major interlude to the penultimate section is like an awakening from a dream. As Uhde pointed out, there is no *deus ex machina* in the *Hammerklavier* finale. '"Man thinks", but whether "God guides" is left open, not denied, but also not affirmed here'.[23]

A relevant mythic analogy to the *Hammerklavier* Sonata may be *Prometheus*, the legend that gripped Beethoven more than any other and

[23] Ibid., p. 464.

became an inspiring force for the *Eroica* Symphony, as we have seen. Of possible significance are certain motivic parallels between op. 106 and the *Eroica*—the trio of the scherzo in the sonata sounds much like a minor-mode variant of the opening of the symphony. Prometheus was, of course, condemned to suffering in reprisal for his gift to humankind of knowledge and art. Like the *Eroica*, yet even more profoundly, the *Hammerklavier* Sonata implies an analogous narrative progression of heroic struggle and suffering, leading to a rebirth of creative possibilities. After the purgatorial *Adagio sostenuto*, the return of vital forces in the slow introduction to the finale, and the fiery defiance of expression in the fugue itself, embody one of Beethoven's most radical artistic statements, a piece of 'new music' among the most uncompromising ever written.

9

Struggle

1819–1822

UNTIL recently, 1819 seemed to have been one of Beethoven's least productive periods, with only a few canons and the 11 Dances for Seven Instruments WoO 17 attributed to that year. This impression has been substantially revised through the scrutiny of manuscripts unknown to earlier scholars, particularly the Wittgenstein Sketchbook in the Bodmer Collection held at the Beethoven-Archiv in Bonn and related documents in other collections. The chief discovery is that by the summer of 1819 Beethoven had already conceived much of his next gigantic undertaking after the *Hammerklavier* Sonata: the 33 Variations on a Waltz by Diabelli op. 120, a work that was finished and published only four years later, in 1823.

The Diabelli Variations is the most paradoxical work that Beethoven ever wrote, an enormous musical edifice built on a trivial waltz that he originally dismissed as a 'cobbler's patch' on account of its mechanical sequences. The publisher Anton Diabelli circulated this waltz of his own invention to 50 composers, each of whom was requested to contribute a variation to the collective endeavour; the project was tailored to generate publicity for Diabelli's firm. It is astonishing and yet characteristic of Beethoven in his last decade that such a commonplace stimulus could trigger a major creative brainstorm. Instead of the requested single variation, Beethoven conceived a microcosm of his art embodied in a vast collection of transformations, or 'Veränderungen'. In the end, the Variations became one of his longest and most intellectually demanding pieces; Brendel has described it as 'the greatest of all piano works'.[1] The unique formal design and psychological complexity of this

---

[1] *Musical Thoughts and Afterthoughts*, p. 14.

composition have inspired literary responses from writers such as Michel Butor and, most recently, Irene Dische, whose novel *Sad Strains of a Gay Waltz* imitates the form of a 'theme' and 33 changes or transformations in a 'German'—in this case, variations not on a waltz ('Deutscher') but on her main character, Benedikt August Anton Cecil August, Count Waller von Wallerstein.

The revelation of the genesis of the Diabelli Variations sheds new light on this monumental work. Like many of Beethoven's sketchbooks, the Wittgenstein Sketchbook has not survived intact, as Beethoven originally used it. Among the papers he used in the Wittgenstein Sketchbook are four pages of sketches for the Diabelli Variations now held in Paris; these two bifolia belong with the 14 pages of sketches for the Variations found near the beginning of the book. Even more important is a draft on loose papers that can be conceptually reconstructed from sources now dispersed in various locations (see Plate 16; Beethoven originally kept this page together with other manuscripts, which are now in collections in Berlin and in Montauban, France, as well as in Paris). The content of the draft corresponds intimately to the entries in the Wittgenstein Sketchbook, preserving a remarkably coherent record of the genesis of the Variations in their early draft version.[2]

This source reconstruction shows that in 1819 Beethoven composed no fewer than 23 variations, ten fewer than the final number. Then, by the summer of that year, he set the work aside to attend to the *Missa solemnis* op. 123. When he returned to the Variations several years later, in late 1822 and early 1823, he expanded his draft from within, retaining the pre-established order while inserting new variations at strategic points and greatly elaborating the conclusion. The added variations from 1823 include nos. 1–2, 15, 23–6, 28–9, and 31, as well as the present form of the final Minuet variation and coda. We shall assess the special role of these variations and the unique formal design of the work in the following chapter, which considers the period when the Diabelli Variations was completed.

The impetus behind the Diabelli Variations is basically comic in nature, touching issues that are by no means confined to Beethoven's art but which surface in his biography as well. No other work by him is so rich in allusion, humour, and parody. We might almost regard the Variations as an enormously extended chain of puns; in each transformation, motivic aspects of the waltz are developed with far more determination than is evident in Diabelli's ditty. Beethoven treats the waltz as a reservoir of unrealized possibilities, out of which the variations generate an almost encyclopaedic range of contexts. The psychological complexity of the Diabelli Variations arises above all from this

---

[2] A discussion and full transcription of the 1819 draft is offered in my book *Beethoven's Diabelli Variations*.

tension between the commonplace theme as point of departure and the almost unlimited horizon of the variations.

Beethoven's most striking joke is his reference, in the unison octaves of Variation 22 (no. 19 in the draft), to 'Notte e giorno faticar' from the beginning of Mozart's *Don Giovanni* (Ex. 68). In devising this variation Beethoven is reputed to have been grumbling at all his hard work in composing the Variations, but, even if true, this story touches only one dimension of the parody.[3] The allusion is brilliant, not only through the musical affinity of the themes—which share, for example, the descending fourth and fifth—but through the reference to Mozart's Leporello. For Leporello shares a psychological trait usually developed to a considerable degree by great artists—a capacity for ironic detachment. A quotation from Leporello fits the work, whereas a quotation from Don Giovanni or from virtually any other character in the opera would not: Beethoven's relationship to his theme, like Leporello's to his master, is critical but faithful, inasmuch as he thoroughly exploits its motivic components. Moreover, like Leporello, the variations after this point gain the capacity for disguise, as if they were not what they seem to be. With uncanny wit, this variation expands the scope of the set beyond the formalistic limits of art.

Ex. 68 Diabelli Variations op. 120, Variation 22

It is relevant here to recall Beethoven's passion for verbal puns, which is especially well documented in the letters and sketchbooks of his later years. He found it absolutely irresistible to pun on words such as *gelehrt* ('learned') and *geleert* ('emptied'), or *Verleger* ('publisher') and *verlegen* ('embarrassed'), and on names like 'Steiner', 'Gebauer', 'Hoffmann', and others in which double or multiple meanings occurred to him. In the case of the choir director and

---

[3] This story appears, for example, in Martin Cooper, *Beethoven: The Last Decade*, p. 208.

concert organizer Franz Xaver Gebauer, Beethoven reinterpreted the name as 'Geh! Bauer' ('Go! peasant'), and in one note he requested 'toilet tickets' (*Abtrittskarten* instead of *Eintrittskarten*) to attend Gebauer's 'music in the corner' (*Winkelmusik*).[4] This, of course, exemplifies Beethoven's use not of a high, but of a low comic style.

Beethoven's verbal wit rarely approaches the level of the best of his comic music. As early as 1795, in the scherzo of the C major Piano Sonata op. 2 no. 3, for example, he produced a resourceful play of paradox comparable to the most brilliant literary devices in Laurence Sterne's comic masterpiece *Tristram Shandy*. In this scherzo a motivic turn-figure serves as the pivot between two drastically opposing moods: light, humorous music in the major pitted against mock bluster in the minor in the developmental middle section. Subsequently, in the coda, the two hands of the pianist even agree to disagree about the mode of the piece, with droll minor accents in low ostinato figures sounded against major harmonies in the upper registers.[5] This delightfully humorous yet highly rational strain of Beethoven's art resurfaces time and again in different ways, in pieces like the sonatas of opp. 10 and 31, the bagatelles op. 33, and the *scherzando* of the first 'Razumovsky' Quartet.

In Beethoven's verbal puns and accompanying music, on the other hand, the comedy can fall short. Martin Cooper has described Beethoven's verbal humour as 'the kind that friends tolerate, and even come to enjoy, not because it is in fact amusing but because they associate it with the good humour and the happy moods of a man they love and admire'.[6] The blunt or even crude side of Beethoven's sense of humour is illustrated in his vocal piece *Lob auf den Dicken* ('Praise to the fat one'), written at the expense of the stout violinist Schuppanzigh; more amusing is his canon *Bester Herr Graf, Sie sind ein Schaf* ('Dear Mr Count, you are a sheep', i.e. a gullible fool) directed at Count Moritz Lichnowsky. These pieces are not works of art but spontaneous effusions of mood within a social context. By contrast, Beethoven's important works of comic music contain a deeper symbolic dimension; Cooper cites in this connection Goethe's shrewd comment about the poet Lichtenberg: 'Whenever [he] makes a joke you will find some problem hidden'.[7] Even in a masterpiece like the Diabelli Variations, however, with its multitude of hidden 'problems', Beethoven makes room for a direct and even provocatively aggressive vein of humour.

This sharp edge of his wit is felt above all in his reinterpretation of trivial or repetitious features of the waltz. The C major chords repeated tenfold in

[4] Thayer-Forbes, p. 771, where *Winkelmusik* is mistranslated as 'musical obscurity'. In this context, *Winkelmusik* must refer to 'music in the corner', or 'music in the outhouse', i.e. sounds emanating from the place where the 'Abtrittskarten' were to be used.

[5] For a more detailed discussion, see my essay 'Beethoven's High Comic Style in Piano Sonatas of the 1790s' or 'Beethoven, Uncle Toby, and the Muck-Cart Driver'.

[6] *Beethoven: The Last Decade*, p. 103.   [7] Ibid., p. 210, note.

the right hand in its opening bars, for instance, are mercilessly exaggerated in Variation 21 (Ex. 69*a* and *b*). The first four bars of the variation form a grotesque exaggeration of the primitive chord repetitions in the waltz and of its conventional turn at the head of the melody: the chords repeat each harmony 16 times, the turns multiply themselves down three octaves. The juxtaposition of this passage with the following *Meno allegro* in 3/4 is one of those instances in Beethoven's late music in which the notes speak with rhetorical significance. It is as if he meant to say, after the *Schreckensfanfare* of the first four bars, 'nicht diese Töne'.

Ex. 69 Diabelli Variations op. 120

(*a*) Theme

(*b*) Variation 21

In another parody variation, no. 13, the harmonically static bars of Diabelli's theme are suppressed altogether, obliterated into the silence behind rhythmically charged chords (Ex. 70). Here the sheer strength of Beethoven's rhythmic conception makes a mockery of Diabelli's theme and the inconsequential complacency of its opening bars. The humour of the variation consists in its expressive use of silence: our expectations are alternately strained by the forceful gesture of the chords and then dissipated into nothing. At the same time Beethoven resourcefully exploits contrasts in register and dynamics. In this variation the humour of expressive silences that characterizes the bass theme of the *Eroica* Variations op. 35 (see chapter 3) is carried to a higher level, while absorbing Beethoven's implied critique of the waltz.

Beethoven also assimilates into this comic masterpiece variations embodying his most serious, exalted, or transcendental styles. Some of these pieces seem to allude to Handel and, especially, to Johann Sebastian Bach, the great artistic predecessors noted by Beethoven in his aforementioned letter to the

Ex. 70 Diabelli Variations op. 120, Variation 13

Archduke Rudolph of 29 July 1819—the letter containing his evocative expression *Kunstvereinigung*. In the same document Beethoven mentions his researches in the archduke's music library, work presumably connected with his labours on the *Missa solemnis*.

The Mass is the great watershed composition of Beethoven's later years, the piece that consumed him more than any other. Early in June 1819 he wrote to the archduke that 'The day on which a High Mass composed by me will be performed during the ceremonies solemnized for Your Imperial Highness will be the most glorious day of my life', and by August he wrote to him again: 'But I hope to complete the Mass and in good time too, so that, if the arrangement still stands, it can be performed on the 19th'.[8] The elevation of the archduke to archbishop of Olmütz in March 1820 provided the occasion for Beethoven's composition of the *Missa solemnis*, but, like the Diabelli Variations, this project assumed unprecedented dimensions and its completion took years longer than expected. Only in 1822 was the Mass finished in its basic substance, while Beethoven continued to make revisions in the autograph long after that date.

Beethoven's struggle with the *Missa solemnis* involved the achievement of a balance between tradition and innovation in this most conservative of musical genres. The work shows the evidence of his studies of much sacred composition from the sixteenth and seventeenth centuries and his assimilation of the traditional rhetoric of Mass composition.[9] The greatest historical strokes in the Mass, however, rely not on assimilation of tradition but on the bold juxtaposition of different idioms. For his setting of the 'Incarnatus est' Beethoven revived the Dorian mode, yet moments later, at the words 'et homo factus est', the music shifts into D major and the warmth of tonality. This passage derives

[8] Anderson, L. 963.
[9] Cf. Kirkendale, 'New Roads to Old Ideas in Beethoven's *Missa solemnis*'.

power not only from the remote ethos of the distant past but from our sense that the later idiom is actually an advance, that the birth of tonality is itself capable of dramatizing the birth (or rebirth) of humankind. In other archaizing passages in the Mass, and in the G major section of the Ninth Symphony finale, there is often no sense that these historical references are superseded, as in the Credo of the Mass. But it is significant that the conclusions of both works stress an immediacy of experience that leaves all such references behind. The end of the Mass, in particular, in its 'depiction of inner and outer peace',[10] is highly subjective, though without a trace of sentimentality.

Because of the close affinity between the musical symbolism of the *Missa solemnis* and the choral finale of the Ninth, we shall reserve detailed discussion of the Mass until the next chapter. The Diabelli Variations, *Missa solemnis*, and Ninth Symphony offer ever more striking instances of a trend reaching back to the *Hammerklavier* Sonata, or even to the *Archduke* Trio or the *Eroica*—Beethoven's tendency to produce pieces of special ambition and enhanced scope that surpass his previous achievements in particular genres. This process is reflected in his sketching procedure. For the *Missa solemnis* he made more than 600 pages of sketches, filling generous portions of four large-format sketchbooks as well as numerous pocket sketchbooks and loose gatherings of sketchleaves. A comparable amount of preliminary labour was invested in other late works, with the number of sketches for the C♯ minor Quartet op. 131 exceeding even that for the Mass.

In view of this pattern one must question the claim advanced recently by Julia Moore that financial considerations motivated Beethoven to undertake more ambitious artistic plans. Moore writes that 'He set very high prices for his works at an early stage of composition and then had to justify these fees by producing works large in scope and original in style'.[11] If financial concerns were as dominant as Moore maintains, Beethoven would hardly have delayed the completion of projects like the Variations and the Mass for such a long time. On the contrary, it was the unique artistic demands of these projects that apparently compelled him to prolong the process of composition. Moore argues that Beethoven aimed at deliberate inaccessibility in his later music, since 'his public no longer much cared whether they understood his works . . . and they were moved to inordinate admiration of works by the great Beethoven, works they could not understand'.[12] This statement is hard to reconcile with either the artistic or historical evidence. Notwithstanding his financial anxieties and his sharp business practice in connection with the *Missa solemnis*, Beethoven's greater musical masterpieces can scarcely be regarded as works written 'for money'; such a view loses sight of the priority

---

[10] Beethoven's original inscription in the autograph score used the word 'Darstellung' ('depiction'); he subsequently changed it to 'prayer for inner and outer peace'.

[11] 'Beethoven and Inflation', p. 217.

[12] Ibid.

of his artistic enterprise, which is more evident during these years than ever before. We do not need to seek special economic motives for his *Missa solemnis*, or for his later sonatas and quartets: he quite justifiably demanded higher fees in view of the enhanced scale and content of such works. The relatively small number of pieces completed lent urgency to his concern to be fairly compensated.

Beethoven's creative struggle from 1819 to 1822 resulted not from any loss of inspiration but from the formidable compositional challenges he set himself, in conjunction with the distractions of custody battles over his nephew Karl and bouts of ill-health. The climax of the custody hearings came in 1820. In February Beethoven prepared a massive document presenting his side of the case, brimming with accusations against Karl's mother, his sister-in-law Johanna, whom elsewhere he dubbed 'the Queen of the Night'. In July the case was finally decided in Beethoven's favour, and Karl remained in his guardianship. Meanwhile, the Berlin publisher Adolf Schlesinger had approached Beethoven about piano sonatas, an impulse that led to the final sonata trilogy, opp. 109–11, works that we shall examine in some detail. These three sonatas represented interruptions in Beethoven's protracted ongoing labours on the *Missa solemnis*, but their completion was in turn held up by severe illness during the first half of 1821, which brought Beethoven's compositional activity to a virtual standstill for several months. Only in 1822 and 1823 was he able to finish a number of major projects that had occupied him for years.

*   *   *

The compositional origins of the Sonata in E major op. 109 can be traced to the first months of 1820 and actually preceded Beethoven's negotiations with Schlesinger. Recent research suggests that it was another request, from the musician and editor Friedrich Starke, that motivated Beethoven by April of that year to break off work on the *Missa solemnis* to write what soon became the first movement of op. 109. Starke asked Beethoven for a contribution to his piano anthology, the *Wiener Pianoforteschule*, in response to which the composer eventually offered the Bagatelles op. 119 nos. 7 to 11 inclusive. But it appears that 'the new little piece'—as described in Beethoven's conversation book in late April—was originally identical with what became the opening *Vivace, ma non troppo* of the sonata.[13] Its unusual design suggests a bagatelle interrupted by two fantasy-like episodes, and in his draft in the Grasnick 20*b* manuscript Beethoven even labelled the slow continuation in triple metre, marked *Adagio espressivo* in the completed work, as a 'Fantasie'.[14]

[13] Cf. Meredith, 'The Origins of Beethoven's op. 109'.
[14] A facsimile and transcription of this draft is contained in my article 'Thematic Contrast and Parenthetical Enclosure in Beethoven's Piano Sonatas, Opp. 109 and 111'.

Brandenburg has proposed on the basis of sketches (Grasnick 20*b*, fol. 1ᵛ) that Beethoven may have at first contemplated a new two-movement E minor Sonata, without the independently conceived first movement.[15] Some of the prominent motivic links connecting the *Vivace* with the following *Prestissimo* movement and the closing set of variations were evidently created or developed only after Beethoven's decision to weld the three movements together as one work.

The first movement of op. 109 reflects Beethoven's intense interest at this time with parenthetical structures that enclose musical passages within contrasting sections. His use of such procedures assumes more and more importance in the last sonatas and seems to have increased as a result of his labours on the Credo of the *Missa solemnis* during the first half of 1820, when he devised an immense parenthetical structure separating the musical setting of the events on earth (from the 'et incarnatus est' to the 'Resurrexit') from the remainder of the movement; here, an abrupt interruption of the cadence at 'descendit de coelis' prepares a later resumption of the music at 'ascendit in coelum'.[16] The opening movement of the sonata was composed at about the same time, and its unique formal design is evidently the product of similar techniques of parenthetical enclosure. The opening *Vivace* material is interrupted after only eight bars, as it reaches the threshold of a cadence in the dominant of E major (Ex. 71). The cadence is not granted but evaded in the

Ex. 71 Piano Sonata op. 109/I

[15] 'Die Skizzen zur Neunten Symphonie', p. 105, note 35.
[16] See chapter 10, pp. 241–4.

ensuing fantasy-like *Adagio* passage, whose elaborate arpeggiations make a striking contrast with the initial *Vivace* material, with its uniformity of rhythm and texture. Yet, when the music finally arrives firmly on a dominant cadence (bar 15), this is timed to coincide with the resumption of the *Vivace* music in the very same register as before. The entire *Adagio* section is thus positioned at the moment of the interrupted cadence, and the resulting parenthetical structure gives the effect of a suspension of time in the contrasting section, or the enclosure of one time within another.

Awareness of this parenthetical structure is essential to a proper understanding of the formal design of the movement, which has resisted the schematic categorization so often advanced by analysts. Charles Rosen and others have suggested that the 'second subject' is found already in bar 9, at the beginning of the *Adagio*, but that explanation is partial and not entirely satisfactory.[17] In fact, the firm arrival of a cadence in the dominant, which typically marks the beginning of a second subject-group, is delayed here until the beginning of the development section based on the *Vivace* material. The central idea of the exposition consists precisely in the interdependence of the two contrasting thematic complexes, in which the parenthetical structure plays an essential role. The bold and unpredictable quality of this design is sustained by Beethoven's avoidance of literal recapitulation in later stages of the movement, such as at the point of recapitulation (bar 48), where the music penetrates the highest register, or the return of the *Adagio* (bars 58 ff.), which is no mere transposition of the exposition but a reinterpretation of it, carrying the music emphatically and climactically into the remote key of C major. It remains for the coda to synthesize the contrasting themes and bring them into a new and closer relationship. These elements of continuing development and reinterpretation represent a paradoxical assertion of Beethoven's fidelity to Classical principles: since the initial material had involved an astonishing and abrupt contrast, a predictability of design involving literal transpositions in the recapitulation would be out of keeping with the unpredictable, exploratory character established at the outset.

Beethoven's coda actually does more than synthesize aspects of the two contrasting themes, since it simultaneously prepares the movements to come (Ex. 72). Its melodic crux lies in the falling tone C♯–B, which occurs twice in the chordal legato passage and then repeatedly in both the minor (with C♮) and major in the following bars, where the original texture of the *Vivace* is restored. This melodic emphasis on the descent from C♯ provides a direct link to the second half of the theme of the finale. Later, in the penultimate bar of the coda, a sudden dislocation in register and rhythm emphasizes the closing E major chord and sets up the surprising plunge into the ensuing *Prestissimo*

---

[17] *Sonata Forms*, pp. 283–4.

Ex. 72 Piano Sonata op. 109/I, bars 73–88

in E minor. As in opp. 110 and 111 Beethoven builds a bridge to the following music into the conclusion of the opening movement, which seems in its yearning incompleteness to hint at more than it can encompass. A similar narrative thread, whereby the coda of a first movement acts simultaneously as a reminiscence and a foreshadowing, can be observed in both the following sonatas.

The *Prestissimo* is in 6/8 metre and takes on much of the character of a scherzo, though it is in sonata form and lacks a trio. Like the first movement it employs a stepwise falling bass, and the motivic relationship C–B, or C♯–B, from the end of the *Vivace* again assumes considerable importance. The second subject begins on the supertonic, F♯, by replacing the motivic step C–B by C♯–B, whereas in the development a prominent bass pedal rises from B to C. The driven, agitated character of the music relents at the end of the brief contrapuntal development, leading to an *una corda* passage so devised as to slow and then virtually suspend all sense of forward motion after the fermata nine bars before the recapitulation (Ex. 73). Beethoven accomplishes this effect by introducing a melodic and rhythmic retrograde of the basic thematic cell, whose treble line E–F♯–G–E–F♯ and rhythmic pattern long–long–short–short–long is turned back on itself in the following bars, with their melodic pattern E–G–F♯ and rhythmic pattern short–short–long. At the centre of this mirroring retrograde effect is a renewed stress on the supertonic F♯; thus it is the dominant not of the tonic E minor but of the dominant B minor—the 'wrong' key—that leads into the reprise. The remote quality of this retrograde gesture arises not only through tonal means but also through the spareness of texture and the extremely soft dynamic level, *pianissimo* and *una corda*, in contrast with *fortissimo* and *tutte le corde* at the recapitulation. Consequently, the music is wrenched violently into the recapitulation, overthrowing harmonic conventions. Yet the stroke seems fully convincing in context, after the still moment of introspection that ends the

Ex. 73 Piano Sonata op. 109/II, bars 81–111

development. Here again, as in the coda of the first movement, the music transcends itself and seems to look beyond its immediate context as in an act of clairvoyance, distantly foreshadowing the serene inwardness of the finale before the reassertion of the agitated character of the movement as a whole.

Some parallels with these special procedures are found in the faster movements of both opp. 110 and 111. In the scherzo-like *Allegro molto* of op. 110 the music slows in tempo just before a brusque reassertion of the basic character leads to the cadence of the main section in F minor. The thematic contour of this prominent repeated gesture is later developed in the 'coda' of the movement, which acts as a bridge to the weighty finale. In op. 111, on the other hand, the contrasting lyrical theme in A♭ major in the exposition of the turbulent *Allegro con brio ed appassionato* is presented parenthetically, slowing the tempo and transforming the prevailing character. And although this theme is cut off abruptly in the exposition by a resumption of the tempestuous music of the *Allegro*, its return in the recapitulation is developed at greater length in C major, preparing the remarkable transition in the coda to the ensuing Arietta movement. In each of the last three sonatas, thematic contrast in the faster movements thus serves the larger function of foreshadowing the spiritualized final movements; the narrative significance of this procedure is subtle but unmistakable.

Like the slow variation theme of the *Archduke* Trio op. 97, the theme of the variations that close op. 109 resembles a sarabande, a dignified Baroque dance type whose rhythm stresses the second beat of each bar of triple metre. Its reflective character results in part from a meditative dwelling on the tonic note

E, which is approached at first from the third above and then from more expressive, distant intervals above and below. The pervasive descending bass motion familiar from the earlier movements is reversed here: the bass ascends one and a half octaves in the first two bars, forming an effective counterpoint to the melody in the treble, whose falling thirds similarly invert the texture of rising thirds from the beginning of the sonata. Beethoven's indication *Gesangvoll, mit innigster Empfindung* underscores the sublime lyricism that characterizes the whole, culminating in the extraordinary sixth variation and the following, closing da capo of the original theme.

As with the op. III Arietta movement, Beethoven's manuscripts for these variations reveal a rigorous process of selection, with many sketched variations left unused and a number of early ideas combined in some of the finished variations. In the completed work the first variation maintains the tempo of the theme, while expanding its register in an unfolding of passionate melody of an almost operatic character (see Plates 17 and 18). The more flowing second variation has a tripartite structure in each half with varied structural repetitions: while the first and last sections somewhat resemble the texture of the *Vivace* in the first movement, the beginning of the second section elaborates the lower pitch of each falling third in expressive trills. The other variations bring metrical changes and an increased density of counterpoint: Variation 3 suggests a two-voice Bachian invention in invertible counterpoint; Variation 4 introduces four imitative voices; and Variation 5 develops a complex fugal web infused with intense rhythmic energy. The climactic quality of this fifth variation even motivated Beethoven to include an extra, more subdued repetition of the second half of the thematic structure; this passage acts as a transition to the final variation, with its initial restoration of the tempo and basic character of the original theme.

Several of the variations are directly connected by subtle transitions in sonority, thus enhancing the unity of the whole. The strong contrast between the swift *Allegro vivace* in 2/4 time and the more gentle, contrapuntal fourth variation, with its spacious bars of 9/8 metre in a tempo slower than the theme, is bridged through a common tied note, for instance. A direct harmonic transition links the fugal *Allegro, ma non troppo* of Variation 5 with the last variation, since the last chord of the former is left on the dominant and resolves to the tonic only at the outset of the ensuing reprise of the head of the original theme. An even more telling cadential overlap later connects the end of the ethereal sixth variation with the closing da capo of the entire theme.

After the striking contrasts of the preceding variations, the sixth at first seems to bring us full circle, with a return of the sarabande in its original register; but Beethoven now explores the theme by developing the dominant pedal from the beginning of each half. This pedal is prolonged and soon elaborated as a slow trill; after a total of five progressive rhythmic diminutions, it grows into an unmeasured pulsation of fast trills sounded in both hands. At this point Beethoven continues the process of rhythmic intensification by increasing the motion of the melodic voices first to triplet-eighths and then to thirty-second-notes, as the trill on the dominant drops into the lowest register. Yet another stage of transformation is reached at the repetition of the second half of the thematic structure, where the original contour of the theme appears in syncopation in the highest register, above the trill in the middle register and rapid thirty-second-note figuration in the left hand (Ex. 74). Thus, through a rigorous process of rhythmic acceleration and registral expansion, the slow cantabile theme virtually explodes from within, yielding, through a kind of radioactive break-up, a fantastically elaborate texture of shimmering, vibrating sounds.

Ex. 74 Piano Sonata op. 109/III, bars 177–80

This ecstatic moment in the final variation reaffirms in the celestial upper register the progression leading to the melodic peak on C♯ that derives from the theme itself, three bars from the conclusion of the sarabande. It is this gesture that was foreshadowed in the coda of the first movement and stressed at the *fortissimo* climax of the fourth variation, among other passages; but perhaps nowhere else is the expressive impact of the dissonant major ninth chord supporting C♯ so striking as here. After this climax a gradual diminuendo on the protracted dominant eventually resolves to the slightly varied da capo of the theme, which now seems transfigured by the experience we have undergone in re-approaching it.

In a sense, then, the variations concluding op. 109 embody two cycles of transformation: the first five variations recast the theme and develop its structure and character in a variety of expressive contexts, while the sixth initiates a new series of changes compressed into a single continuous process that is guided by the logical unfolding of rhythmic development. In the final variation an urgent will to overcome the inevitable passing of time and sound

17–18 The first edition (November 1821) of the Piano Sonata in E major op. 109, dedicated to Maximiliane Brentano, daughter of Franz and Antonie Brentano: title page and p. 12, showing the theme and first variation of the finale.

19–20 Autograph score of the Agnus Dei of the *Missa solemnis*, showing
Beethoven's substantial revisions (Staatsbibliothek Preussischer Kulturbesitz,
Berlin, Artaria 202, pp. 220-21 = fol. 18ᵛ and 19ʳ).

21 Oil portrait on canvas of Beethoven by Ferdinand Georg Waldmüller, April 1823 (66 × 57 cm). This picture formed the basis for the famous portrait that Waldmüller prepared for Breitkopf & Härtel which was destroyed in Leipzig in 1943. This little-known study was done from a single sitting; it differs in its expression and some detail from the later painting.

22 Autograph score of the choral finale of the Ninth Symphony, showing the combination of the 'Joy' theme with 'Seid umschlungen Millionen' in a double fugue for chorus and orchestra (Staatsbibliothek Preussischer Kulturbesitz, Berlin, Artaria 204, p. 77).

23–24 Two pages from a sketchbook used by Beethoven in 1824, showing the theme and first variation of the slow movement of the String Quartet in E♭ op. 127. His attempts at revision can be seen in his verbal entries and connective devices. Both pages were cancelled and superseded by new sketches and drafts. (Staatsbibliothek Preussischer Kulturbesitz, Berlin, Mus. ms. autogr. Beethoven 11/2, fols. 11ᵛ–12ʳ).

seems to fill up the spaces of the slow theme with a virtually unprecedented density of material, challenging the physical limits of execution and hearing. This idea, in turn, was to be greatly expanded by Beethoven into the controlling framework of the variations on the Arietta that conclude op. 111, the last movement of his last sonata.

*   *   *

On 6 December 1821 Beethoven wrote a moving dedication of the E major Sonata to Maximiliane Brentano, daughter of Antonie Brentano, who was to receive the dedication of the Diabelli Variations. In the dedication Beethoven describes his spiritual bond to the Brentano family as something that 'can *never* be destroyed by *time*', and he recaptures his own fond memories of the experiences of a decade earlier. He was now living in the Landstrasse, in the vicinity of the former Birkenstock mansion, a circumstance that must have helped draw his thoughts to the past, although his financial indebtedness to Franz Brentano may also have played a role in these dedications.

The first half of 1821 had been a dismal time for Beethoven. The scant documentation of his activities, his letters attesting sickness, and the sketch sources all point to a significant drop in productivity. He must have been too sick to compose at all during some of this period. After a rheumatic attack in the winter, he suffered in the spring from an outbreak of jaundice, an ominous symptom of the liver disease that eventually claimed his life. After this onset of long-term hepatitis, Beethoven's basic physical condition was especially vulnerable, and even his moderate intake of wine would have had a damaging impact. In a recent study, Horst Scherf divides the composer's life into two clinical phases separated by the appearance of incurable illness in 1821.[18] Still, five extremely productive years remained to Beethoven before the ultimate breakdown of his health in December 1826. These years may be regarded as his last 'creative period' if the emphasis is placed on biographical criteria. The works of 1821–4, however, show deep affinities with his earlier music and were begun in part well before 1821, even if some of their conspicuous symbolic features were devised only later in the compositional process, after his convalescence in September 1821. Beethoven's recovery sparked his sense of humour and his creative forces, resulting in the genesis of the Piano Sonata in Ab major op. 110, the composition of which overlapped somewhat with that of the final Sonata in C minor op. 111, from 1822.

Humour is abundantly evident in Beethoven's canon *O Tobias Dominus Haslinger O! O!* from September 1821, one of his numerous joking communications to Haslinger, a partner in Steiner's publishing firm. Beethoven explained the origin of the canon as entwined with a twofold journey: a trip

---

[18] 'Die Legende vom Trinker Beethoven', esp. pp. 242–6.

by carriage from Baden to Vienna, during which he fell asleep; and an ensuing dream-journey to Syria, India, Arabia, and finally Jerusalem. 'The Holy
City made my thoughts turn to the sacred books. So it is no wonder that I
then began to think of that fellow Tobias', Beethoven wrote in the letter
accompanying the canon he sent to Haslinger. According to Beethoven, he
forgot the canon upon awakening. Another journey in the same vehicle the
next day allowed him 'in accordance with the law of the association of ideas'
to recall the piece and commit it to paper.[19] This story well illustrates
Beethoven's delight in the paradoxical joining of the exalted and the commonplace, the sacred and the profane.

A somewhat analogous contrast is embedded in the A♭ major Sonata op.
110. Its second movement serves as a scherzo in form and character, although
it bears only the tempo designation *Allegro molto*, in 2/4 metre. This movement shows the humorous temper characteristic of Beethoven's scherzos, even
though the tonic is minor. As others have observed, Beethoven alludes to two
popular songs, *Unsa Kätz häd Katzln ghabt* ('Our cat has had kittens') and *Ich
bin lüderlich, du bist lüderlich* ('I'm a slob, you're a slob'), in the main section of
this movement.[20] The opening phrase, with its use of *Unsa Kätz häd Katzln
ghabt*, is stated *piano* before being answered, in Martin Cooper's words, by a
'C major shout', and the *sforzandi* at cadences contradict the rounded phrase
endings normal in Beethoven, and sound comic and parodistic.

One key to the expressive associations of the *Allegro molto* rests in the text
'I'm a slob, you're a slob' (the source of Beethoven's quotation and the passage
in the *Allegro molto* are compared in Ex. 75a and b). The word 'lüderlich' refers
to a bedraggled or slovenly individual not fit for polite society. Beethoven
himself was once taken for such around this time when, miserably clothed
and having lost his way in Wiener Neustadt, he was seen peering in at the

Ex. 75 (*a*) Piano Sonata op. 110/II, bars 17–21

(*b*) Song, *Ich bin lüderlich*

Ich   bin   lü- der- lich,   du   bist   lü- der- lich

---

[19] The letter and canon appear in Anderson, ii, L. 1056.
[20] Cooper, *Beethoven: The Last Decade*, pp. 190–1; A. B. Marx, *Ludwig van Beethoven: Leben
und Schaffen*, ii, p. 416.

windows of the houses, whereupon the police were summoned. When arrested, he protested, 'I am Beethoven', to which the policeman replied, 'Well, why not? You're a bum: Beethoven doesn't look like that' ('Warum nit gar? A Lump sind Sie; so sieht der Beethoven nit aus').[21] But even if there is an autobiographical resonance in this passage, its main artistic significance lies in Beethoven's assimilation of the lowly, droll, and commonplace into the work, where such material proves complementary to the most elevated of sentiments. Some musicians, such as von Bülow and Martin Cooper, have looked askance at the unsophisticated humour of *Ich bin lüderlich*; Cooper comments on 'that Dutch vein of humour which reminds us that the composer's forebears may well have been among the peasants whose gross amusements we know from the pictures of the Breughels'.[22] Yet here, once more, 'a problem may lie hidden', in Goethe's sense. Important in this connection is Beethoven's apparent allusion to *Ich bin lüderlich* in a passage much later in the sonata, to be discussed below.

Transcendental and even religious characteristics surface in the unique finale of op. 110, with its pairing of *Arioso dolente* and fugue. As in the *Hammerklavier* Sonata and in the Ninth Symphony Beethoven incorporates a transition before reaching the finale proper; the music is notated partly without bar lines and with a profusion of tempo and expressive directions. An explicit recitative emerges in the fourth bar and carries us to A♭ minor, tonic minor of the sonata as a whole. For some moments the music dwells contemplatively on a high A♮; the recitative then falls in pitch, briefly affirming E major before returning to A♭ minor in the bars immediately preceding the beginning of the great lament. In a sense, the ensuing *Arioso dolente* is operatic in character, with a broadly extended but asymmetrical melody supported by poignant harmonies in the repeated chords of the left hand. The recitative already foreshadows the tragic passion of the lament and prefigures some of its motivic relationships. There is even a framing cadential gesture at the conclusion of the *Arioso dolente* that harks back to the end of the passage in recitative (cf. bars 6–7 and 25–6).

The pairing of the *Arioso dolente* with the fugue in A♭ major has no precedent in Beethoven's earlier instrumental music; its closest affinity is with the Agnus Dei and 'Dona nobis pacem' of the *Missa solemnis*, the movements of the Mass that occupied him contemporaneously with the sonata. The Agnus Dei, in B minor, is burdened by an overwhelming awareness of the sins of humanity and the fallen state of earthly existence; by contrast, the 'Dona nobis pacem' represents the promise of liberation from this endless cycle of

---

[21] Thayer-Forbes, p. 778, polishes the language of the Austrian policeman; the colloquialisms are retained in Frimmel, 'Beethovens Spaziergang nach Wiener Neustadt', *Beethoven-Forschung: Lose Blätter* 9 (1923), p. 7.

[22] *Beethoven: The Last Decade*, p. 191.

suffering and injustice, symbolized by the recurring and ominous approach of bellicose music. Significantly, Beethoven's setting of the 'Dona nobis pacem', in D major, employs a prominent motif outlining ascending perfect fourths, which are filled in by conjunct motion. The fugue subject of op. 110 consists similarly of three ascending perfect fourths, the last of them filled in by stepwise descending motion, while smooth conjunct motion also characterizes the countersubjects (Ex. 76a and b). The closest stylistic parallels to this exalted fugal idiom in Beethoven's piano music are the D major cantabile fugal episode in the finale of the *Hammerklavier* Sonata and the superb Fughetta from the Diabelli Variations, written soon thereafter, in early 1823. Each of these recalls the polyphony of J. S. Bach, assimilating that idiom into the rich context of Beethoven's *Kunstvereinigung*.

Ex. 76 (*a*) *Missa solemnis* op. 123, Agnus Dei, bars 107–10

(*b*) Piano Sonata op. 110/III, bars 27–35

The importance of the fugue subject in op. 110 is underscored by Beethoven's foreshadowing of this theme in the first movement. Its intervallic structure, with three successive rising fourths (Ab–Db, Bb–Eb, C–F) is already latent in the opening four bars. This initial phrase is set apart from the continuation through its polyphonic texture, fermata, and trill, and functions almost like a motto for the entire sonata. The later fugal subject represents a kind of intervallic crystallization or even purification of the motto. The vocal character and harmonic consonance of the fugal subject in op. 110 bear comparison with the 'Dona nobis pacem' of the *Missa solemnis*, and, in its function within the whole sonata, the fugal subject acts like a symbolic counterpart to the 'Joy' theme of the Ninth Symphony.

Beethoven's later fugues make extensive, sometimes exhaustive use of the devices of inversion, stretto, diminution, and augmentation. These devices tend to be used not for their own sake but as a means of expressive intensification, especially in the later stages of a work; in op. 110 they are concentrated in the second part of the fugue, beginning in the remote key of G major. The central idea of this finale consists in the relationship between the earthly pain of the lament and the consolation and inward strength of the fugue. Initially, however, the fugue cannot be sustained; it is suddenly broken off on a dominant-seventh chord of Ab major, which is interpreted as a German augmented-sixth chord, resolving to a triad of G minor, and this dark sonority is treated as tonic for the return of the *Arioso dolente*. The tonal relationship involved is bold and virtually unprecedented in Beethoven: the entire lament is restated, in intensified and varied form, in G minor; and the framing cadential gesture brings a shift to the major, which assumes the character of a miraculous discovery. Nine increasingly intense repetitions of this G major sonority follow, and a gradual arpeggiation of that sound leads upwards to the inversion of the fugue subject, which now enters, quietly and *una corda*, in G major.

The concluding fugue thus begins in the key of the leading-note, to re-emerge only later into the tonic, Ab major, in the triumphant final passages. This unusual tonal relationship enhances the power of the conclusion; equally striking is Beethoven's treatment of contrapuntal permutations in the transition from G major to Ab major. Not only does the subject appear against itself in diminution and augmentation, but it appears in double diminution at the *Meno allegro*, comprising a decorating motivic cell that soon surrounds the sustained notes of the inverted subject (Ex. 77*b*).

Tovey claimed that in this closing fugue Beethoven eschewed an 'organ-like climax' with its ascetic connotations as a 'negation of the world': 'Like all Beethoven's visions this fugue absorbs and transcends the world'.[23] It is significant in this regard that the transitional double-diminution passage seems to recall the earlier comic allusion in the *Allegro molto*. The rhythmic and registral correspondence renders the beginning of the *Meno allegro* transparent to *Ich bin lüderlich*, reinforcing Tovey's sense of an absorption of the 'world'; a similarity is clearly audible, in part because Beethoven compresses the fugal subject in diminution, deleting the second of its three rising fourths (Ex. 77*a, b*). Both motifs stress the fourths spanning Ab–Eb and C–G, which are inverted in the fugue, and there is a parallel placement of faster note values.

The import of Beethoven's inscription for the entire transitional passage, 'nach u. nach sich neu belebend' ('gradually coming anew to life'), is embodied in this musical progression. The abstract contrapuntal matrix beginning with the inverted subject is gradually infused with a new energy, which arises not naturally through traditional fugal procedures but only through an exertion of will that strains those processes to their limits.

The rhythmic developments that point the way out of Beethoven's fugal

[23] *A Companion to Beethoven's Piano Sonatas*, pp. 270, 285–6; see also Mellers, *Beethoven and the Voice of God*, pp. 238–9.

Ex. 77 (*a*) Piano Sonata op. 110/II, bars 17–21

(*b*) Piano Sonata op. 110/III, bars 165–75

labyrinth thus distort the subject, compressing it almost beyond recognition, while simultaneously opening a means of connection with the earlier movements through what Carl Dahlhaus calls 'subthematic figuration'.[24] The entry of the original subject in bar 174 is accompanied by sixteenth-note figuration continuing the texture of double diminution, giving the effect of the theme being glorified by its own substance; at the same time this rapid figuration recalls the ethereal passagework from the first movement of the sonata. The transition from the darkness and pessimism of the *Arioso dolente* to the light and ecstasy of the fugue is now fully accomplished; and in the final moments Beethoven extends the fugal subject melodically into the high register before it is emphatically resolved, once and for all, into A♭ major sonority five bars before the end. This structural downbeat represents a goal towards which the

[24] *Ludwig van Beethoven*, pp. 261–2.

whole work seems to have aspired. Yet the true conclusion lies beyond this chord in a rapport with silence, as (in Brendel's words) the work throws off even 'the chains of music itself'.[25]

Like op. 110 the design of Beethoven's final sonata op. 111 shows a powerful directional progression towards its finale, consisting, as in op. 109, of a weighty series of variations on a contemplative, hymn-like theme. The variations on the Arietta in C major that form the second movement of op. 111 are more tightly integrated than those that close op. 109 and unfold according to the venerable device whereby each transformation of the theme brings increasing subdivisions in rhythm. Beethoven carries this process so far in op. 111 that the series of rhythmic diminutions first transforms the original character without altering the basic tempo, and then re-approaches the sublime quality of the choral-like theme, as the most rapid rhythmic textures, culminating in sustained trills, are reached in the closing stages. Something of the same plan underlies the final variation in the finale of op. 109, but in his final sonata Beethoven developed this procedure to serve as the structural basis for the entire closing movement. The variations on the Arietta became a suitable culmination and resolution for the work, which dispenses with any further movements and leaves the tempestuous C minor idiom of the opening *Allegro* far behind. Moritz Schlesinger's naive query whether a concluding third movement had been omitted from the manuscript was received disdainfully by Beethoven, who is supposed to have responded to a similar question from Schindler with the ironic, and perhaps even contemptuous remark that he had 'no time to write a finale, and so had therefore somewhat extended the second movement'.[26] Thomas Mann (in consultation with Theodor W. Adorno) devoted a chapter of his famous novel *Doktor Faustus* to the piece, and had the fictional character Wendell Kretzschmar describe the climactic and yet open quality of the end of the Arietta movement as an 'end without any return', comprising a farewell to the art form of the sonata in general.

The first movement of op. 111 represents the last example of Beethoven's celebrated 'C minor mood', evidenced in a long line of works from the String Trio op. 9 no. 3 and *Pathétique* Sonata to the *Coriolan* Overture and Fifth Symphony. As in these works great stress is placed on diminished-seventh chords in a turbulent, dissonant idiom. As in the *Pathétique* there is a slow introduction, but the greater musical tension of the later sonata is evident at once in the tonal ambiguity of the octaves outlining the diminished-seventh interval E♭–F♯, and in the use of the three possible diminished-seventh chords in the opening sequences, emphasized by majestic double-dotted rhythms and trills. The closest relative to this passage is Beethoven's setting of the Crucifixus in the *Missa solemnis*, as Mellers has pointed out.[27] The

[25] 'Beethoven's New Style', *Music Sounded Out*, p. 70.   [26] Thayer-Forbes, p. 786.
[27] *Beethoven and the Voice of God*, p. 325.

tension of the slow introduction is sustained in the *pianissimo* continuation, leading first to a convergence onto a dominant pedal expressed as a bass trill, and then to a transition to the new tempo, *Allegro con brio ed appassionato*, and the long-delayed resolution of the trill to C minor that marks the beginning of the sonata exposition. The interval of the diminished seventh is incorporated prominently into the principal subject, which is first presented in unison octaves and is developed only gradually, after several hesitating closes on the tonic. A major portion of the sonata exposition (bars 35–50) consists of a fugal exposition on a variant of this subject, combined with a countersubject in octaves. This material is coordinated to create a large-scale ascending progression, beginning on C and rising through an octave, before the bass brings the music climactically to Db, D♮, and finally Eb (bars 48–50; Ex. 78). This extraordinary climax is underscored by the registral disparities of the sustained pitches played in the right hand, F–Db–D♮–Cb, which represent a variant, in rhythmic augmentation, of the principal fugal motif. The shift from this low D to the high Cb traverses an ascent of almost five octaves, so that the motif appears enlarged, or gapped, over an immense tonal space. Then, suddenly, with the arrival of the bass at Eb in bar 50, a lyrical voice is heard in the contrasting key of Ab major. A three-bar phrase with expressive appoggiaturas fills bars 50–2, a fleeting lyrical moment that is extended by a decorated restatement in the following bars and by a gradual slowing in tempo to *Adagio*.

Ex. 78 Piano Sonata op. iii/I, bars 48–58

The formal isolation of this lyrical second subject is an example of Beethoven's important technique of parenthetical enclosure, a device that also surfaces prominently in two of his immediately preceding works—the first movement of op. 109 (as we have seen) and the Credo of the *Missa solemnis*. In op. 111 this technique assumes special significance as a means of linking the two movements, which are so antithetical in character. An effect of parenthetical enclosure is created not only through the sudden thematic and tonal contrast and slowing in tempo but also through the sudden return of the original tempo and agitated musical character at the upbeat to bar 56, where Beethoven brings back the same diminished-seventh sonority heard earlier, when the climactic progression had been broken off (also shown in Ex. 78). Here the high C♭ is stressed as the clear link back to the earlier passage, and the diminished seventh is elaborated by descending sequences through those pitch registers that had been spanned in the earlier gesture. Consequently, the intervening lyrical utterance in A♭ major is isolated, like 'a soft glimpse of sunlight illuminating the dark, stormy heavens', in the imagery of Mann's character Kretzschmar in *Doktor Faustus*.

In the recapitulation this lyrical material is not so easily swept aside; rather, Beethoven extends the passage and, beginning in bar 128, reshapes it to lead us back into the tempest. The lyrical passage has now reached C major, the key of the second movement; when it slows to *adagio* in bars 120–1, it seems to foreshadow the sublime atmosphere of the Arietta finale. A direct transition to the ensuing Arietta is built into the coda, when threefold phrases resolving plagally to the tonic major seem to resolve the tension and strife of those threefold phrases that had opened the slow introduction. The rhythm and register of the last bars of the coda allude unmistakably to the forceful diminished-seventh chords that interrupted the lyrical episode in the exposition (bars 55–6). Here, however, the diminished seventh is resolved, once and for all, into the C major triad, whose high register and wide spacing foreshadow aspects of the Arietta and variations, marked *Adagio molto semplice e cantabile*.

The Arietta movement is perhaps the most extraordinary example of a new type of variation set characteristic of Beethoven's later years. Formerly, variations were most often used in inner movements of the sonata cycle; but here, and in op. 109, they assume such weight and finality as to render any further movements superfluous. As we have said, the op. 111 variations are based structurally on the model provided by the final variation of op. 109: there, a reprise of the slow rhythmic values of the original theme is followed by a series of rhythmic diminutions culminating in sustained trills. Now, in the op. 111 Arietta movement, each variation brings diminutions in the rhythmic texture without affecting the slow basic tempo: consequently, the theme seems to evolve from within through a rigorously controlled process. By the third variation, there is a resulting transformation in character, due to the agitation and complexity of the rhythm, which Beethoven notates in the metre 12/32. Thereafter, in the fourth variation, the tremolos and arabesques of thirty-second-note triplets, together with the syncopated chords in the right hand and the striking registral contrasts, create an ethereal atmosphere, as if the music has entered a transfigured realm.

The outcome of this gradual process of rhythmic diminution is reached in the cadenza that precedes the recapitulatory fifth variation. This cadenza and the following transition represent an extended parenthesis in the formal plan, for the cadence in C major is fully prepared before the cadenza is reached but is delayed by a protracted trill on the supertonic. Moments later this trill becomes part of a sustained triple trill above a Bb pedal point, and the tonality shifts for the first time, to Eb major. Beethoven contemplates the theme from within, as an ascent into the highest register unfolds, expressed entirely through trills. Here a phrase from near the end of the first half of the theme is heard in Eb major, with a vast registral gap between treble and bass, a feature that fascinated Thomas Mann's Kretzschmar. As Charles Rosen has observed, this episode seems to suspend the flow of time;[28] it involves an intensely contemplative vision embedded within the context of a variation series which is itself highly introspective. The contemplative vision is not untouched by darker shadows, however: immediately after the climax in Eb, we hear a modulating *espressivo* passage that meditates on the head of the Arietta theme in rhythmic diminution, with a striking drop in register. This poignant transition absorbs diminished-seventh harmonies which are subtly reminiscent of the first movement, and suggests thereby a moment of regression in the developmental unfolding of the whole.

The ensuing fifth variation then restores the C major tonality and brings a synthesis and superimposition of the various rhythmic levels: the triplet thirty-second-notes in the bass derive from the ethereal fourth variation, while the sixteenths in the inner part derive from the transition and the first two variations. Here Beethoven recapitulates the original Arietta theme in a formal gesture of considerable weight and significance. This movement is the first important example of the ageing Beethoven's preference for decorated recapitulatory variations preceded by episodes in foreign keys, a procedure at work in the slow variation movements of two of the late quartets, opp. 127 and 131, as well as in the third movement of the Ninth Symphony. In the coda of the op. 111 Arietta, however, we move beyond this recapitulatory gesture, entering a second and more ethereal synthesis of rhythmic levels. The theme is now heard in the high register, accompanied by the triplet sixteenths in the left hand, and the sustained trill, now on high G.

[28] *The Classical Style*, p. 446.

In retrospect, the climactic progression of the variations can be seen to involve not only a system of progressive rhythmic diminutions but also a gradual registral ascent in which the dominant, G, assumes a central role. This pitch is already emphasized at the close of the theme and the first two variations, where it is approached through a long crescendo and underscored by a *sforzando*. In the fourth variation the arrival at G in the high register marks the moment of departure from the structural framework of the theme, leading into the cadenza-like passage with its multiple trills. In the recapitulatory fifth variation the climax falls on the widely spaced dominant chord of a major ninth, with the pitch of melodic resolution, G, then sustained through much of the following coda. The tonal and textural weight of this gesture on the dominant resonates beyond the closing tonic resolution, contributing thereby to the sense of openness of the final cadence and to the directional quality of the whole.

In the performance of the variations, it is essential to sustain continuity between the still, contemplative aura of the theme and the gradual transformation in character effected by the intensification of rhythm and expansion of register and contrapuntal texture in the first three variations. The highly agitated character of Variation 3 leaves room, in the *piano* phrases at the beginning of its second half, for a subtle anticipation of the ethereal quality of later passages; the extroverted energy expressed in the jagged, accented rhythms of this variation is then reshaped in Variation 4 to become an even faster yet now suspended, inward pulsation. Important as well is an identity in tempo between the original theme and the recapitulatory fifth variation and coda. As the theme is recaptured, so too are various developmental stages recalled from the intervening variations.

The Arietta theme itself is one of the most sublime examples among Beethoven's piano works of that hymn-like character that often inspired reflective slow movements surrounded by contrasting outer ones. Here, however, the inward vision is more sustained and far more affirmative and ecstatic than in earlier slow movements; yet, this variation framework is not incompatible with dynamic processes, such as the system of rhythmic diminutions and the modulating cadenza preceding the recapitulatory fifth variation. Being and Becoming are merged here into a unified structure. The uplifting and visionary quality of the second half of the Arietta derives not only from the transformation of the theme and from the culminating effect of synthesis and recapitulation, but also from the role of this movement as a transcendence of the turbulent *Allegro* movement and all it implies. In many respects, the Arietta strives toward perfection, whereas the *Allegro* is obviously imperfect; even the progression from the duple metre of the opening movement to the triple metre of the Arietta movement, with its many subdivisions in groups of three, is significant in this connection.

Various commentators have rightly perceived a philosophical and even religious dimension in this great work. As Alfred Brendel has pointed out, the dichotomy embodied in the two movements of op. III has been variously described in terms of 'Samsara and Nirwana' (von Bülow), the 'Here and Beyond' (Edwin Fischer), and 'Resistance and Submission' (Lenz); Brendel also mentions the dichotomy of 'Male and Female Principles' (of which Beethoven sometimes spoke) and that of the real and the mystical world.[29] It is revealing in this connection to compare op. III with some of Beethoven's other works from the 1820s. In the Ninth Symphony, by contrast, the contemplative, inwardly absorbed slow variation movement leads to a reconfrontation with the 'external world' in the form of the dissonant *Schreckensfanfare* and the ensuing setting of Schiller's *Ode to Joy* in the choral finale. In op. III, of course, the reflective modality governs the conclusion; there are few hints here of a strife-ridden 'world background', such as the music of war that haunts the Agnus Dei of the *Missa solemnis*.

The conclusion of the preceding sonata, op. 110, for all its transcendental characteristics, projects a greater sense of an 'absorption of the world' through its distortion of the fugal subject in the double-diminution passage and its ensuing emergence out of the fugal labyrinth in the closing passages of apotheosis. But any convincing assessment of op. III has to stress more than the remarkable power and coherence of Beethoven's transformations of the Arietta, with their cumulative sense that the contemplative vision has become more real than the 'external' world symbolized in the *Allegro*; crucial as well is the complementary relationship of the two movements. As we have seen, Beethoven's use of parenthetical enclosure places a foreshadowing of the Arietta into the midst of the first movement; in the recapitulation and coda this tentative foreshadowing grows into a transition to the Arietta itself. At the same time, in his coda Beethoven balances and transforms important passages heard earlier in the movement, such as the beginning of the slow introduction and the assertion of diminished sevenths that had cut off the lyrical second subject in the exposition. The symbolism projected in op. III thus has two principal moments: the acceptance and resolution of conflict embodied in the *Allegro* and transition to the Arietta; and the rich, dynamic synthesis of experience projected in the ensuing variations.

Beethoven's last piano sonata is a monument to his conviction that solutions to the problems facing humanity lie ever within our grasp if they can be recognized for what they are and be confronted by models of human transformation. Maynard Solomon has argued that 'Masterpieces of art are instilled with a surplus of constantly renewable energy—an energy that provides a motive force for changes in the relations between human beings—

---

[29] 'Beethoven's New Style', *Music Sounded Out*, p. 71.

because they contain projections of human desires and goals which have not yet been achieved (which indeed may be unrealizable)'.[30] Among Beethoven's instrumental works op. III assumes a special position as an 'effigy of [the] ideal', in Schiller's formulation; and every adequate performance must re-enact something of this process, reaching as it does beyond the merely aesthetic dimension to touch the domain of the moral and ethical.

[30] *Beethoven*, pp. 315–16.

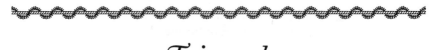

Triumph

1822–1824

'das Moralische Gesetz in uns, u. der gestirnte Hiṁel über uns' Kant!!![1]

THIS is an entry made by Beethoven in a conversation book at the beginning of February 1820: 'The moral law within us, and the starry heavens above us'. Beethoven's citation, with its enthusiastic attribution, has been often re-cited and commented on. The conversation-book entry takes on new significance, however, when considered in relation to the genesis of the composition that was occupying—or, rather, consuming—him at the time: the *Missa solemnis*. The issues raised are crucial to the structure and expression of the Mass, especially in its later movements, the Credo, Benedictus, and Agnus Dei. The symbolic ideas that surface here are not confined to the Mass, moreover, but re-emerge in other major compositions that he wrote between 1823 and 1825. These matters are so central to our investigation as to require more detailed scrutiny than we have given to much of Beethoven's earlier music. The works he wrote from 1820 to 1826 are not large in number but they pose formidable aesthetic challenges. A richer context for discussion of the *Missa solemnis* can be gained if we consider not only the existing score, which was virtually complete by 1822, but also the compositional genesis of this great work.

The sketchbooks show that when Beethoven copied down this quotation from Kant he had already worked intensely on the Mass for most of a year but was far from finished. At this point in the compositional process he had not

---

[1] *Ludwig van Beethovens Konversationshefte*, i, p. 235. According to the editors, this entry was copied not directly from the conclusion of Kant's *Critique of Practical Reason* but from the article 'Kosmologische Betrachtungen' by the astronomer Joseph Littrow, printed in the *Wiener Zeitung* on 20 January and 1 February 1820.

yet devised one of the most impressive symbolic and structural musical elements of the Mass: the use of specific related sonorities to serve as a focal point of the musical setting in the Credo and Benedictus. Subsequently, after completing the Mass, he absorbed and implanted this network of referential sonorities into his next great choral orchestral composition, the choral finale of the Ninth Symphony, in the treatment of a text strikingly similar to the dictum from Kant cited above.

A distinctive harmonic feature of the finished Credo is its use of the subdominant E♭ triad in place of the tonic B♭ as the first vertical sonority of the movement (Ex. 79). An upward leap of an octave reaches to this high, sustained E♭ chord, which resolves to the dominant of B♭ in the second bar. The position of the E♭ chord, with the third, G, uppermost, is noteworthy, as is its orchestration, employing the oboes and flutes in the high register. Particularly arresting is the rhythm of the passage: the chord is prolonged for six beats, resolving to the F major triad only in the middle of the second bar. As a result, the introduction acts as a metrical unit of two bars anticipating in rhythmic augmentation the dotted rhythm of the 'Credo' motif heard in bar 3. This rhythmic relationship, as well as the distinctive spacing of the initial chord and its unusual harmonic basis on the subdominant, all serve to bring the introductory gesture strongly into relief.

Ex. 79 *Missa solemnis* op. 123, Credo

Beethoven's decision to place this introduction at the beginning of the Credo raises issues that concern the musical organization of the entire movement. For a closer examination of the Credo reveals that the initial E♭ chord, in its original register and spacing, is treated not only as a ritornello but as an important thematic element throughout the movement. It assumes special

prominence at the climax of the 'Et vitam venturi' fugue and in the closing
'amen' section. Sketches from the spring and early summer of 1820 record
Beethoven's first use of this high, protracted E♭ sonority as part of the concluding plagal cadence to 'amen', as well as his employment of a closely related
progression at the earlier cadence to 'amen' that immediately precedes the
fugue.[2] In sketches for the opening section of the Credo in the same sources
the high sustained E♭ chord is conspicuously absent, however. The evidence
from the sketchbooks implies that in this instance Beethoven worked backwards, by making this crucial sonority associated with the end of the movement serve also as an introduction and ritornello in the first half of the Credo.
The full musical significance of the opening gesture of the Credo can be
assessed, then, only in the context of the whole movement.

    We are dealing here with an outstanding example of Beethoven's charac-
teristic device of anticipation—the foreshadowing, early in the work, of
important musical events to come. Another familiar example is the opening
section of the finale of the Ninth Symphony, where the *Schreckensfanfare*, the
orchestral recitative passages, and the citation and rejection of the earlier
movements are fully intelligible only in light of the following choral sections
of the movement. In the Credo, by contrast, the anticipation of events to
come is concentrated in the orchestral ritornello beginning with the opening
E♭ chord. Analysis of the broader role of this E♭ sonority brings us into the
midst of the musical architecture that embraces the entire movement, a formal symphonic organization quite unusual in settings of the Credo, with its
lengthy doctrinal text.

    The form of the Credo falls into four main parts: the opening *Allegro ma
non troppo* up to 'descendit de coelis', in B♭; the section in slow tempo from
the Incarnatus up to the Resurrexit, with a basic tonality of D; the *Allegro
molto* beginning at 'et ascendit in coelum' and leading into the recapitulation
of the Credo in F major; and finally the fugue and coda on 'et vitam venturi
saeculi, amen', in B♭. Within this framework the second section in slow tempo
makes the strongest possible contrast to the rest of the movement, a contrast
made even more startling by the use of modality—the Dorian mode in the
Incarnatus and the Mixolydian (briefly) in the Resurrexit, which is heard as
unaccompanied vocal polyphony. Overlapping cadences and unity of key-
centre link the internal episodes: the D Dorian of the Incarnatus is followed
by D major at 'homo factus est' and D minor in the Crucifixus. Set apart by
its archaic modality, by the entry of the vocal soloists, by the secondary key-
centre of D, and by the absence of thematic material associated with the rest
of the movement, this section represents an interpolation within the larger
framework of the whole Credo.

    [2] For detailed citations of the sketch sources, see my article 'Beethoven's Symbol for the
Deity in the *Missa solemnis* and the Ninth Symphony'.

Surprisingly, the symbolic aspect of this musical setting has been over-looked by critics, who have confined their attention to the conventional tone painting in the setting of the words 'descendit' and 'ascendit'.[3] The more pro-found symbolism is expressed through the utter contrast—in texture, the-matic material, register, and key—between all the music from the Incarnatus to the Resurrexit on the one hand, and the rest of the Credo on the other. The large interpolation in the musical form assumes a rhetorical or symbolic func-tion, for it reflects musically the descent of Christ from heaven to earth, with his subsequent ascent after the crucifixion and burial being embodied in the return and continuation of music heard earlier in the movement. This feature is of special interest in view of Beethoven's enthusiasm for the dictum from Kant cited above, since it involves the association of a specific high sonority with heaven or the heavens which imparts a symbolic association to the larger musical context.

In order to establish an audible musical relationship between descent and ascent, Beethoven employs a device prominent in other works from his later years—a grandiose interrupted cadence. The musical setting of the words 'descendit de coelis' is a powerful seven-bar phrase, closing with an emphatic cadence in Bb in the highest register on the word 'coelis'. The orchestra repeats the phrase, reaching the dominant of Bb in the last bar before the *Adagio* (Ex. 80). This time, however, the highest pitch, A, of the F major triad does not resolve upwards to Bb; instead, the cadence is cut off and the F major sonority altered to become the dominant of D. Here the full orchestral forces drop out, with a precipitous plunge in register for the Incarnatus, which is scored at first only for low strings. The descent from heaven is thereby reflected in a sudden transformation of the musical texture.

Then, throughout the ensuing slow movement, higher pitch registers are used sparingly; where they do appear in the solo flute in the Incarnatus it is with special symbolic intent, to evoke the hovering of the dove. The orches-tration is also lighter here than in the rest of the movement, due in part to the absence of brass and timpani. Only at 'et ascendit in coelum' do the full orchestral forces return with the arrival at the F major chord that serves as the goal of the long series of rising scales (Ex. 81). This sonority is emphasized dynamically and sustained for four bars, but its importance extends well beyond the immediate musical context. To begin with, it is the same sonority, in an identical register and very similar orchestration, that served as the point of transition at the interrupted cadence in the 'descendit' passage (cf. Ex. 80). The use of a matching sonority is symbolically fitting, for this high F major chord with A at the top was there used for the word 'coelis', and on its return here, at the end of the rising scales, it is used for the same word, 'coelum'.

[3] See, for example, Kirkendale, 'New Roads to Old Ideas in Beethoven's *Missa solemnis*', pp. 665–701.

Ex. 80 *Missa solemnis* op. 123, Credo, bars 112–26

The ascent into heaven coincides with the resumption of the musical texture from the opening *Allegro* section of the Credo, with the F major chord
serving as a point of reference back to the suspended, unresolved sonority at
the end of 'descendit de coelis'. But at this point the sonority assumes yet
another function: it forms the beginning of an extended thematic unit, which
is later repeated sequentially—with a parallel sonority—as the music for 'cujus
regni non erit finis', the passage leading up to the recapitulation (cf. bars
202–21 and 240–63). This passage is decidedly developmental in character,
owing to its modulations and persistent syncopations, a hallmark of
Beethoven's later development procedure. The F major sonority used for the
word 'heaven' is thus a cornerstone in the formal architecture of the Credo,
linking its first and third sections and initiating the development, while at the
same time creating a symbolic role for the music that transcends any details of
tone painting.

Ex. 81 *Missa solemnis* op. 123, Credo, bars 197–202

In view of the formal importance of this F major chord, it is interesting to note that in Beethoven's early drafts for the Credo the orchestral repetition of the phrase 'et descendit de coelis' and the interrupted cadence are absent; other, unused attempts at a transition appear. It was later in the compositional process that Beethoven strengthened the link between the first and third sections of the Credo—a link centred on a single, crucial sonority rooted in the broad formal structure of the music which at the same time served the symbolic function of relating the music more closely to the Mass text.

Much the same procedure seems to have been at work in Beethoven's decision, again late in the process of composition, to employ the Eb sonority as a unifying element for the entire movement. We are now in a position to examine the formal and symbolic implications of this chord, which occurs for the first time in the introductory orchestral gesture at the very beginning of the Credo and recurs subsequently no fewer than 11 times.

As we have said, this opening orchestral gesture is treated as a ritornello, preceding the 'Credo' motif. As such, it appears three times in the movement, reflecting the threefold affirmation of belief in the Trinity (as is well known, Beethoven emphasized this by adding two extra statements of 'Credo' to the Mass text, before the words 'in unum Dominum Jesum Christum' and 'in Spiritum Sanctum'). At the beginning of the movement the orchestral ritornello and imitative statements of the 'Credo' motif occupy ten bars, to the text 'Credo in unum Deum'. On its second appearance (bar 34) the initial Eb chord is sustained for only two beats instead of six, so that the entire passage occupies nine bars, to the text 'Credo in unum Dominum Jesum Christum'.

The next appearance of the Eb chord occurs not as part of the ritornello but in the powerful seven-bar repeated phrase to 'descendit de coelis' discussed above (see Ex. 80). It is this sonority, in fact, that resolves to the tonic of B♭ three bars before the interrupted cadence. The E♭ chord is thus directly linked here with the music of descent/ascent, with its unmistakably symbolic implications.

On their third appearance, later in the movement, the ritornello and statements of the 'Credo' motif assume the role of a recapitulation and are expanded to about 30 bars. Here the return and development of the 'Credo' motif carries the music through the most doctrinal parts of the Mass text, where the words are rattled off syllabically, rendered inconspicuous by the many imitative entries of the 'Credo' motif. The selective emphasis given the Mass text is indeed striking; beginning with the words 'Credo in Spiritum Sanctum', the last third of the text is covered in only 42 bars of music, whereas the five closing words, 'et vitam venturi saeculi, amen' ('and the life to come, world without end, amen'), occupy 166 bars, comprising the fugue and the coda.

Since the recapitulation has been in the dominant, F major, this third appearance of the orchestral ritornello is not at the original pitch level. The motif from the ritornello returns, however, as part of the emphatic cadence on the word 'amen' that closes the section (bars 300–2), just before the 'Et vitam venturi' fugue, and here it relates clearly to the E♭ chord at the beginning of the movement. The rhythmic context is the same, with the chord sustained for six beats, as previously; once again, G is uppermost, and the chord appears in the same high register in similar orchestration. The correspondence in sonority is thus unmistakable, in spite of the new harmonization of the high G within the dominant seventh of F. Subsequently, yet another harmonization of this motif is heard as cadence to the first part of the fugue.

Only at the climax of the fugue and in the coda, however, is the full significance of the E♭ chord revealed. It is important at this point to consider the thematic material of the Credo, especially in the latter parts of the movement. For in the fugue and coda it becomes evident that the E♭ chord is not merely a recurring harmony heard from the beginning but a sonority closely related to the thematic material on which much of the music is based.

Like the *Hammerklavier* Sonata, the Credo of the Mass relies heavily on the interval of a descending third. This is nowhere more evident than in the fugue subject, which is based on a chain of seven descending thirds (the fourth inverted to form a rising sixth) outlining the tonic, subdominant, and dominant triads (see Fig. 2). The 'Credo' motif is related to this configuration of thirds. Most striking, however, is the parallel between the series of descending thirds passing through the subdominant on the one hand, and emphasis on an analogous harmonic progression through the subdominant on the other, which allows Beethoven to combine the harmonic progression from the orchestral ritornello with the motivic descending thirds of the fugue. This

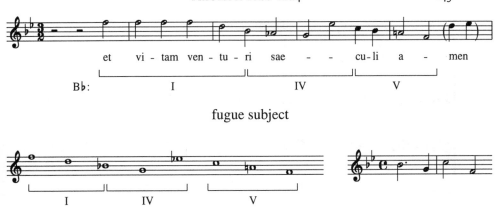

fugue subject

intervallic basis of fugue subject   'Credo' motif

Fig. 2   Descending thirds in the fugue subject of the Credo of the *Missa solemnis*

synthesis occurs as early as the crucial 'et descendit de coelis' passage and later becomes the basis for the climax of the fugue.

The fugue has an unusual two-part structure, with the second part undergoing a process of rhythmic intensification created from diminution of the original subject, a procedure Beethoven used again, with some modification, in the fugue of the Diabelli Variations. The climax occurs in the second part, where the longer note values of the original subject are superimposed on the complex texture of other voices treating a diminution of the subject, all over a sustained dominant pedal. Here the series of descending thirds is extended and rearranged as a rising sequence, leading to a climactic subdominant sonority, repeated four times, to the words 'saeculi amen' (Ex. 82). This sonority, which may be regarded as the climax of the entire movement, is identical with the striking E♭ chord of the orchestral introduction (cf. Ex. 79). The rhythmic context is also similar, since the chord is protracted for a bar and a half on each of its four appearances. In the fugue, however, it is glorified by the presence of motivic elements from the fugue subject, both in the original note values and in diminution.

Just as this sonority serves as the goal and climax of the fugal development, its arrival also signals the dissolution of the fugue. The motif formed from the E♭ chord and its harmonic resolution, treated sequentially, serves as transition to the coda, marked *Grave*, which immediately brings a return of the same E♭ chord. It is now approached in the lower instruments by the upward leap of an octave derived from the opening orchestral ritornello. This motivic reminiscence of the beginning of the Credo is most prominent in the organ part,

Ex. 82 *Missa solemnis* op. 123, Credo, bars 402–7

where it may have been added late in the compositional process, since it is absent from the autograph score.

As in the analogous passage towards the end of the finale of the Ninth Symphony, there follows an extended cadenza for the soloists, who sing a series of rising scales to the word 'amen'. The scales pass into the lowest register of the orchestral texture in the strings, gradually rising to the highest register in the flute. An emphatic, fourfold repetition of the tonic triad of B♭ to the choral 'amen' then generates a second, more elaborate series of rising and descending scales (see Ex. 83). The descending scale pattern passes through two fifths, from F to B♭, which is twice repeated, and from B♭ to E♭, repeated once. This descending scale thus corresponds to the structure of the fugue subject; the descending thirds are here filled in with stepwise movement. Just as this descending scale reaches the subdominant E♭ in the bass, the ascending scales in the winds come to rest on the high E♭ chord that has played such an important role throughout the Credo. As the soprano and alto enter on G and E♭, four bars before the end, the ascending scales are heard again, in the orchestra, in rhythmic diminution, quietly rushing upwards to the resolution of the plagal cadence on 'amen' in the highest register. With this high B♭ major chord, and a final reminiscence of the head of the fugue subject in the lower strings and timpani, the movement ends.

We may now schematize the formal organization of the Credo, showing the appearances of the E♭ sonority, as well as the F major chord associated with 'coelis' (see Fig. 3 on page 248).

Ex. 83 *Missa solemnis* op. 123, Credo, bars 463–end

Formal outline of the Credo in the *Missa solemnis*

	Allegro ma non troppo		Adagio	Andante	Adagio	Allegro	Allegro molto	Allegro ma non troppo	FUGUE — Allegretto ma non troppo	Allegro con moto	CODA — Grave
Tempo	Allegro ma non troppo		Adagio	Andante	Adagio	Allegro	Allegro molto	Allegro ma non troppo	Allegretto ma non troppo	Allegro con moto	Grave
Metre	e		e	3/4	3/4	e	¢	e	3/2	3/2	
Sonority	X	X	X X Y				Y	X (varied; in F)	X (varied; in D)	XX XX	X X
Text	Credo in unum Deum ...	Credo in unum Dominum ...	descendit de cœlis...	et incarnatus est...	et homo factus est...	Cruci-fixus...	et resur-rexit...	et ascendit in cœlum...	Credo in Spiritum Sanctum... Amen.	Et vitam venturi saeculi amen.	
Key	B♭	B♭ → (F)		d Dorian	D	d	G Mixolydian	F D → F *modulates*	F	B♭	B♭	B♭
Structure			*interpolation*					*developmental*	*recapitulatory*		*climax*

Appearances of

X = E♭ sonority from opening ritornello

Y = F major sonority from interrupted cadence at 'descendit'

Fig. 3   Formal outline of the Credo in the *Missa solemnis*

Let us now consider the symbolism inherent in the musical architecture of Beethoven's Credo. Tovey once described the extreme contrasts of the Mass as 'Beethoven enraptured at the thought of the Divine Glory, but immediately prostrated by the sudden consciousness of the nothingness of man'.[4] This dichotomy applies particularly to the first *Allegro* section of the Credo, which motivates abrupt contrasts that have posed difficulties for many listeners and critics. Subsequently, through the interpolation of the composite slow movement within a larger formal context, Beethoven achieves the musical equivalent of the disjunction between heaven and earth. A symmetry of form is created through the subsumption of the most doctrinal parts of the text into the recapitulation and through the development of the 'Credo' motif. After the dominant recapitulation, the movement is crowned by the great fugue in B♭, the climax of which had been foreshadowed by the very first chord of the Credo. In the coda, finally, this crucial sonority becomes the penultimate chord of the plagal cadence, arising out of the same thematic material that had generated the fugue. Those parts of the music associated with the godhead and eternal life—the references to the Trinity, the descent from and ascent into heaven, and the setting of the closing words 'et vitam venturi saeculi, amen'—present a remarkably coherent formal structure spanning the entire movement.

One moment in the creation of this formal structure has been documented by reference to the sketchbooks—Beethoven's decision to employ, as an opening orchestral ritornello, the same high E♭ sonority that was later to serve as the climax and plagal close of the movement. What is noteworthy is the manner in which Beethoven isolates and develops this particular sonority, treating it as a unifying element throughout the movement. Its role in the Mass also has symbolic implications, which are clarified by the close musical affinity between the Credo and another of the Mass movements, the Benedictus. The high chord that opens the Benedictus appears like a ray of light, breaking the darkness of the long descending progression of the Praeludium. Mellers has drawn attention to the similarity between the penultimate E♭ chord of the Credo and this initial sonority of the Benedictus—a high G major chord in first inversion (see Ex. 84, where it appears just before the *Andante molto cantabile e non troppo mosso*).[5] The parallel is convincing, and is supported by features of the music not cited by Mellers, particularly the presence of the thematic material based on descending thirds. The beginning of the celebrated *dolce cantabile* theme in the solo violin, with its descending third and rising sixth, the thirds filled in by stepwise movement, is almost identical in structure to the fugue subject of the Credo. The G major chord, on the other hand,

[4] *Essays in Musical Analysis: Vocal Music,* p. 167.
[5] *Beethoven and the Voice of God,* pp. 334, 342.

Ex. 84 *Missa solemnis* op. 123, Benedictus, bars 106–21

is treated analogously with the E♭ chord of the Credo as a referential sonority—it begins and closes the movement and appears repeatedly, always with the solo violin on high G. The highest pitch of the E♭ chord from the Credo is retained in the Benedictus to become tonic in the new sonority, signalling the arrival of the divine messenger. From this sonority the violin solo emerges; thus the network of referential sonorities becomes closely identified with this very unusual feature of the orchestration in the Mass—the assignment of the single most prominent solo part not to one of the vocalists but rather to the violin. The violin solo of the Benedictus effectively symbolizes the absolute, ideal quality of the divine presence, using the high G major chord as a point of departure and return.

In his sketches for this passage Beethoven contemplated an earlier entry of the solo violin in a lower register, followed by a gradual ascent in pitch. By eliminating this transition he highlighted the initial chord of the Benedictus by means of an astonishing disjunction in pitch. In a sense, this sudden upward shift in register is analogous to the sudden downward shift at the Incarnatus in the Credo, where Beethoven also contemplated, and rejected, a transition in sonority. At the end of the Credo, on the other hand, Beethoven emphasizes the high E♭ chord in a different manner from the Benedictus, making it the goal of the long series of ascending scales beginning in the lowest register. In each case these high sonorities evoke celestial regions that transcend earthly existence; their symbolic importance is unmistakable.

As we have seen, Beethoven's interest in the 'starry heavens above' is already reflected in a piece like the slow movement of the String Quartet in E minor op. 59 no. 2, from 1806. Another such example, from the period when the *Missa solemnis* was being composed, is his song *Abendlied unterm gestirnten Himmel* WoO 150, whose autograph score is dated 4 March 1820; here a high E major sonority in the piano begins and ends the piece, acting as a symbolic framing gesture. In the *Missa solemnis* this significant image-content is merged with the thematic and formal structure to shape an unconsummated symbol; there is no contradiction here between structure and expression, but rather an interdependence of the syntactic and semantic aspects of artistic meaning. The Agnus Dei of the Mass displays symbolism of a much less affirmative nature. Beethoven sets the Agnus Dei in the 'black' tonality of B minor, and underscores his setting of the 'miserere nobis' with poignant chromaticism, syncopation, and dark orchestral textures. The shift to the 6/8 D major *Allegretto vivace* for the 'Dona nobis pacem' brings a drastic contrast, as a prayer for peace is juxtaposed with the awareness of worldly strife. The series of themes employed in the 'Dona' culminates in a moving phrase sung by the voices *a cappella*. In its contour and rhythm this intimate melody is reminiscent of his setting of 'Nimm sie hin denn, diese Lieder' ('Take these songs to your heart then') in the last song of *An die ferne Geliebte*.

Beethoven exposes this fragile prayer to threats, initially in the form of the music of war embodied in the *Allegro assai*. The approach of the military procession in B♭ motivates the return of the text 'Agnus Dei, miserere nobis' which is sung 'fearfully' (*ängstlich*) in recitative. This passage underscores the unfulfilled nature of our hopes for peace. Even after the D major music of the 'Dona nobis pacem' is restored, the threats to peace never entirely recede from the horizon of the work. The agitated, hurly-burly *presto* orchestral episode at the heart of the movement may represent a threat to 'inner peace'; this passage eventually leads into a powerful resumption of the bellicose trumpet-and-drum fanfares. (Plates 19–20 show Beethoven's substantial revisions in the passage that first juxtaposes the 'Dona nobis pacem' in D major with approaching sounds of war in B♭ major: the drum taps on F are written on the eighth stave from the top of each page. After making numerous preliminary sketches for this transition on other papers, Beethoven wrote out and revised fol. 18ᵛ of the score; on stave 12 his erasures wore a hole in the thick paper. Then he cancelled fol. 18ᵛ altogether, and replaced the original fol. 19 by the second leaf shown (p. 221). Two extra bars of music were written on each side of this leaf, so that the 12 bars of music originally contained on three pages could be compressed onto two.)

While sketching the Agnus Dei Beethoven contemplated a symphonically conceived coda, only to reject that option at an advanced stage in composition.[6] His decision was surely bound up with the open conclusion to the Mass, which is strangely shadowed by hints of the music of war in the form of distant drum-rolls. In an inscription to one of his sketches Beethoven referred to the withdrawal of the sounds of war as a 'sign of peace'; still, it is striking how close to the end of the movement the disquieting drum-rolls appear. There is an almost epigrammatic quality to the end of the *Missa solemnis*. The chorus concludes with a concise statement of the lyrical phrase originally heard *a cappella*, but now heard with the support of the strings and winds. An orchestral echo of the vocal phrase 'pacem, pacem' leads to the terse, four-bar conclusion in the full orchestra, played *fortissimo*. The end of the Mass is left ambiguous, since a prayer for peace is far from being its fulfilment. In the *Missa solemnis* the ultimate goal for human aspiration is located in a transcendental quest, as is reflected symbolically above all in the lofty referential sonorities of the Credo and the Benedictus.

*   *   *

After the virtual completion of the *Missa solemnis* in the summer of 1822 Beethoven turned his energies in the autumn to the last of his dramatic overtures, *Die Weihe des Hauses* ('The Consecration of the House') op. 124. Parts of the *Missa solemnis*, and especially the Gloria, reflect his professed admiration of Handel in their choral textures and rhetoric, but no other work displays this influence more clearly than *Die Weihe des Hauses*, in its lucid counterpoint, formal breadth, and festive solemnity. Beethoven's lifelong admiration for Handel is amply documented; his extensive acquaintance with Handel's music dates back at least to the 1790s, when he attended the musical gatherings at Baron van Swieten's home and wrote his 12 Variations for Violoncello and Piano on a theme from Handel's *Judas Maccabaeus* WoO 45. When asked by a visitor in 1817 to name the greatest of past composers Beethoven is supposed to have placed Handel above all others. According to Schindler, whose testimony for once we can accept, Beethoven entertained a 'long cherished idea of writing an overture specifically in the style of Handel',[7] an ambition finally realized in 1822 in *Die Weihe des Hauses*. Beethoven contemplated

---

[6] Cf. Drabkin, 'The Agnus Dei of Beethoven's *Missa solemnis*', pp. 154, 156–7.
[7] *Beethoven As I Knew Him*, p. 324.

another overture, on B–A–C–H, in homage to the other great Baroque master, but that project did not advance beyond the stage of sketching.

It is tempting to associate a conversation-book entry from 1820 concerning Beethoven's intention to write variations on the 'Dead March' from Handel's *Saul* with the stately, majestic march in C major near the beginning of the *Weihe des Hauses* overture.[8] The affinity with Handel does not involve direct quotation but suggests a more generalized stylistic kinship. Beethoven's piece opens with a slow section suggestive of French-overture style that leads without break into an imposing double fugue. Fugues that begin with such paired entries of subject and countersubject are characteristic of Handel but uncommon in Beethoven; a rare example is the fugue forming the penultimate variation in the Diabelli Variations. One of the quintessentially Beethovenian passages in op. 124 is the transition from the slow introduction to the double fugue, where a long ascent featuring a motivic rising fourth leads to a pivotal reversal of direction at the outset of the fugal *Allegro*, as the fourths are integrated into a stepwise descent in two voices. Beethoven's control of the dynamics and orchestration, as well as the *stringendo* or acceleration in tempo, all act to heighten the dramatic impact of the emergence of the double fugue, whose insistent syncopations endow the theme with an exciting metrical tension.

A few weeks after completing the overture in early October 1822 Beethoven's thoughts turned to an unfinished major project that had been put aside about three and a half years earlier: the Diabelli Variations. In November the composer wrote to Anton Diabelli that 'The fee for the variations would be 40 ducats at most, provided they are worked out on as large a scale as is planned. But if this does not materialize, then I would quote a smaller fee'.[9] (In Beethoven's own words, '. . . im Falle sie so gross ausgeführt werden als die Anlage davon ist; sollte dies aber nicht statthaben . . .'.) As Beethoven himself implies in this letter, the 'Anlage', or plan for the variations, was large; it included the 23 variations of Beethoven's early draft. During the first months of 1823 the piece was worked out on an *even larger* scale than Beethoven had planned, becoming in the process the biggest of all his compositions for piano.

One of Beethoven's guiding inspirations when he expanded the early draft of the Diabelli Variations shows a curious parallel with a formal device he used in the large-scale design of the Credo of the *Missa solemnis*: the occasional recapitulation of the work's initial sonority in later passages. This is given a comic twist in the Variations. In the Mass, as we have seen, the high, protracted E♭ chord assumes both formal and symbolic importance; its

[8] Cf. Göllner, 'Beethovens Ouvertüre "Die Weihe des Hauses und Händels Trauermarsch aus "Saul"'; Bruner, ' The Genesis and Structure of Beethoven's Overture *Die Weihe des Hauses*, Op. 124', pp. 33, 121–4.

[9] Anderson, L. 1105.

recurrences in the Credo are associated with a sublime vision of the celestial. Diabelli's waltz, by contrast, is firmly rooted in the everyday world of the commonplace. Accordingly, in his early draft Beethoven was much concerned with the transformation and aesthetic improvement of the waltz, and he was attracted as well by the possibilities of caricature offered by Diabelli's 'cobbler's patch'.

In his late work on the Variations Beethoven introduced another kind of travesty as distinct from the examples we have discussed in Variations 13 and 21 (see chapter 9). Here he harps on the actual substance of the waltz itself—specifically those features of it that are particularly trite—and reproduces them in comically exaggerated form so that they become insufferable. It is this form of parody that is most important for the overall progression of the Variations, because Beethoven's criterion for criticism is precisely the melodic outline of Diabelli's theme. Most of the other variations thoroughly reshape the surface of the theme, and, though motivic materials from the waltz are exploited exhaustively, its affective model is left far behind. In these late parody variations, however, the waltz's melodic outline and supporting context are restored—recapitulated, in a sense—and they stand out because of Beethoven's consistent suppression of them in the other variations. Only in these added variations, furthermore, does the melodic outline reappear in its original register, which strengthens the thematic reference. Diabelli returns, as it were—the material is not Beethoven's—but he returns in a different *Stimmung*, a kind of Lisztian transformation.

When Beethoven returned to the Variations in 1822–3 he confronted a unique formal dilemma. He normally strove to endow the opening of any major work with a pregnant tension and significance; the op. 120 Variations are the great exception, an outstanding example of a major work with origins in the commonplace. But these variations are not confined to the possibilities of Diabelli's theme *per se*. The nature of the theme in no way anticipates the scope and immensity of the Variations. How then was Beethoven to establish a relationship between the theme and variations such that the waltz was not rendered superfluous, a mere prologue to the whole? This implicit contradiction may have had something to do with Beethoven's uncharacteristic decision to lay the work aside for several years. But in any case the apparent absurdity of building a monumental edifice on such slight foundations had, by 1823, supplied an unexpected stimulus to his own imagination.

By parodying the waltz theme directly, with its melodic contours intact, Beethoven made it into an indispensable foundation for the overall musical progression. In fact, in the work's final form, the supporting pillars of the total structure depend on the recapitulation of the melodic shape of Diabelli's theme. Thus the listener's first impression of the theme is utilized in a manner not unlike that in Beethoven's other variation sets, such as the C minor

Variations WoO 80, in which a series of recapitulatory references to the theme embraces the work as a whole. In the Diabelli Variations, moreover, the last of these references presents an ideal point of departure for an evolutionary progression towards a final, culminating experience. The project was, therefore, in a peculiar way, tailor-made to fit the revolutionary aesthetic of Beethoven's third period.

A conspicuous characteristic of the waltz recalled in these added variations of 1823 is the repeated tonic chord with G at the top that opens the dance (Ex. 85); this G, repeated ten times in the first four bars, continues as the highest note of the dominant-seventh chords in the next four-bar phrase. With their persistent emphasis on G, these repeated chords serve to underscore the waltz's static harmonic scheme. It is not surprising that in most of his variations Beethoven should wish to depart from this aspect of the waltz. What is remarkable, however, is that in the variations added later he adopts and exaggerates precisely these features.

Ex. 85 Diabelli Variations op. 120, Theme

We are now in a position to judge why Beethoven inserted a vigorous, majestic variation *Alla marcia maestoso* immediately after Diabelli's waltz. The refined third variation, originally planned as the first, did nothing to smooth over the discrepancy between theme and variations, since it already transforms the theme so thoroughly. But in his singular solution of adding the march variation Beethoven achieved a sense of gesture, of grand anticipation—albeit tinged with irony, since the melodic contours of Diabelli's theme are so clearly preserved (Ex. 86). This pointed reference to the waltz is unmistakable: Beethoven would not otherwise have allowed himself nine consecutive repetitions of the tonic triad in root position in the right hand, while the left solemnly spells out the descending fourth of the waltz, creating accented harmonic clashes with the treble. The grand gesture is simultaneously a parody of the theme.

Ex. 86 Diabelli Variations op. 120, Variation 1

It is only after this opening march variation that the melodic outlines of Diabelli's theme—with its falling fourth and fifth and persistent emphasis on the dominant note G—are avoided. In some variations, such as the third and the eighth, the melodic line is reshaped as a descent from the third, E, of the tonic triad. In others, manifold changes in texture, harmony, and rhythm leave only a tenuous link between the melody and its successive transformations. It is therefore a significant event when Beethoven finally recapitulates the melodic contour of the theme in Variation 15, the *Presto scherzando*, and then again in the paired variations that follow it. Variation 15, unlike the paired variations, also brings a return of the original register. Variations 16 and 17 were present in the draft of 1819, as we have seen; but Variation 15, like Variation 1, was an afterthought, added as the piece was nearing completion.

If the opening march variation is a mock-heroic gesture bearing the seeds of irony, this *Presto scherzando* (Ex. 87) is an even more obvious caricature. Its role as a miniature juxtaposed with two of the most massive variations (no. 14 and the pair nos. 16–17) reinforces its parodistic quality, as does its unusually static harmonic plan: the first half actually closes on the tonic! Furthermore, its harmonic rhythm is rather peculiar in alternating the tonic triad with an augmented triad on the dominant. In its overall linear-harmonic structure it mimics the simple C(I)–D(V)–E(I)–D(V)–C(I) progression of Diabelli's theme, and this is underscored by a capricious increase in spacing in the second half, which has provoked attempts at 'correction' by solemn editors.

This reference to the theme is broadened into a more general allusion in the pair of march variations, nos. 16 and 17, that immediately follows. The sequence of nos. 15–17 is counterpoised to the sequence of the theme and Variation 1, which is also a march (though admittedly of a rather different,

Ex. 87 Diabelli Variations op. 120, Variation 15

more stilted character); and in a curious, elusive way this long-range
correspondence draws Diabelli's theme more closely into the fabric of the
work.

The waltz finds its final reincarnation in Variation 25, in the guise of a
German dance, with the rhythm of Diabelli's bass shifted to the treble.
Beethoven's tongue-in-cheek attitude is perhaps even more obvious here than
in no. 15: monotony of rhythm, dissonant clashes between treble and bass, and
aimlessness in the voice-leading confirm his humorous intentions. At the end
of the first half he goes so far as to omit a bar before the cadence, causing the
music to stumble prematurely back to the beginning (Ex. 88).

This lumbering caricature of Diabelli's theme is actually the first of an
unbroken succession of variations (nos. 25–33) leading to the coda and culmination of the work. In fact, a thread of continuity, tracing the path from banal-
ity to sublimity—from the world of Diabelli's ditty to the world of the Arietta
of op. 111—sounds through all these last nine variations. By extraordinary
means, Beethoven first obliterates his distorted image of the theme and then
gradually reconstitutes its essence in a series of variations that culminates in
the last of the slow minor variations, the penultimate fugue, and the concluding minuet and coda.

Through the three parody variations 1, 15, and 25 Beethoven has established
a series of periodic references to the waltz that draw it more closely into the
inner workings of the set, and the last of these gives rise to a progression that
transcends the theme once and for all. This is the central idea of the Diabelli
Variations. The artistic journey embodied in the great chain of variations is
enormously wide-ranging, however, and Beethoven fully exploits the potential of the form to incorporate allusions to various musical styles. After the
witty reference to Mozart's *Don Giovanni* in Variation 22 (see chapter 9), the
following variations, like Leporello, gain the capacity for disguise. No. 23 is an

Ex. 88 Diabelli Variations op. 120, Variation 25

étude-like parody of pianistic virtuosity alluding to the *Pianoforte-Method* by J. B. Cramer, whereas no. 24, the Fughetta, shows in its intensely sublimated atmosphere an affinity not only with the fugue of op. 110 but also with some organ pieces from the third part of J. S. Bach's *Clavierübung*. In no. 25, as we have seen, the waltz is reincarnated as a humorous German dance, but this image is gradually dispersed in the series of interconnecting fast variations culminating in no. 28, in which harsh dissonances dominate every strong beat.

The process of rhythmic intensification from no. 25 to no. 28 merits detailed attention. Beethoven spreads the sixteenth-note motion drawn from the bass of the waltz parody (no. 25) over all the pitch registers in the ensuing variation (no. 26). The legato phrasing embraces paired groups of three sixteenths each, suggesting a metre of 6/16, but Beethoven retains the 3/8 metre (as well as the basic tempo) of no. 25. The rhythmic impulses of the triple metre thus fall on the second and fourth sixteenths of each group of six notes, with the phrasing extended over the bar-lines throughout. This shifting pattern of metrical impulses imparts dynamic tension to the figuration, enhancing the upbeat character of the first half of each phrase. Then, in no. 27, Diabelli's 'cobbler's patch' sequences of a rising semitone and a third become the basis for the figuration in rhythmic diminution, expressed in rapid triplet sixteenth-notes. Diabelli's motif is written in steady quarter-notes, but Beethoven compresses his motivic variant so radically that it appears no fewer than 24 times in the opening eight bars of the variation! The dissonant semitone relation derived from the theme infuses the music with an intense energy, generating a frenzied chain of imitative motivic entries driving into the highest register in the second half of the variation. This climactic passage is Beethoven's ultimate parody of the 'cobbler's patch' sequences from the waltz. Variation 28 then carries Beethoven's rhythmic development to yet another stage, as the process of foreshortening motivates a compression of the metre to shorter bars of 2/4 time, while reducing the basic content of the music to the dissonant semitone—now expressed in the multiple contrapuntal voices embodied in the accented diminished-seventh and augmented-sixth chords.

After Variation 28 we enter a transfigured realm in which Diabelli's waltz and the world it represents seem to be left behind. A group of three slow variations in the minor culminates in no. 31, an elaborate aria reminiscent of the decorated minor variation of Bach's *Goldberg* set but also foreshadowing Chopin. The following energetic fugue in E♭ is initially Handelian in character; its second part builds to a tremendous climax with three subjects combined simultaneously, before the fugue dissipates into a powerful dissonant chord. An impressive transition leads to C major and to the final, most subtle variation of all: a Mozartian minuet, whose elaboration through rhythmic means leads in the coda to an ethereal texture that unmistakably recalls the fourth variation of the Arietta of op. 111, Beethoven's last sonata, composed in 1822. The parallels between op. 111 and the final Diabelli variation are structural in nature: they extend to the thematic proportions and to the use of an analogous series of rhythmic diminutions leading, in each case, to a suspended, ethereal texture. But the most obvious similarity surfaces in the concluding passages, outlining the descending fourth C–G that is so crucial to each work (Ex. 89a and b). Herein lies the final surprise: the Arietta

Ex. 89 (a) Diabelli Variations op. 120, Variation 33, bars 42–4

(b) Piano Sonata op. 111/II, coda

movement, itself influenced by the Diabelli project, served in turn as Beethoven's model for the last of the Diabelli Variations. The final allusion thus became a self-reference, a final point of orientation within an artwork whose vast scope ranges from ironic caricature to sublime transformation of a commonplace waltz.

Like the close of the *Missa solemnis*, that of the Diabelli Variations is ambiguous, and pregnant with implications. It ends, essentially, in the middle of the thematic structure, poised before an open door, which leads, if it leads anywhere, into the midst of the Arietta of op. 111. At the same time in these closing moments Beethoven looks back and across the entire vast cycle of variations and delicately recaptures the repeated stress on G in the waltz that had earlier provoked his scorn and stimulated his imagination. As Brendel observed, the following sentence from Kleist's essay 'On the Marionette Theater' suits the conclusion of the Diabelli Variations: 'When perception has passed through infinity, gracefulness reappears'.[10]

*   *   *

Beethoven produced only one important work for piano after the Diabelli Variations: the 'Cycle of Bagatelles' op. 126, in 1824. He had long been interested in the genre of the bagatelle, a short, intimate piano piece making modest technical demands on the performer. The popular *Für Elise* WoO 59 is an example, and in his op. 33 from 1802 Beethoven had already published a group of seven bagatelles. Several other unpublished bagatelles from earlier years were revised and included in the 11 bagatelles of op. 119 that appeared in 1823, together with newly composed pieces, two of which were actually byproducts of the Diabelli Variations. As we have seen, even the first movement of the Sonata op. 109 may originally have been conceived as a bagatelle.

While opp. 33 and 119 are collections of individual pieces, op. 126 suggests an integrated cycle, as the sketches reveal; Beethoven took special pains in ordering this group of six pieces. Lyrical pieces in slow or moderate tempos alternate with more rapid, agitated ones, up to no. 6, in which a short, furious *Presto* frames a reflective *Andante amabile e con moto*. The bagatelles are characterized by directness of expression and use of three-part song form, yet the apparent simplicity is deceptive: almost all the reprise sections, for instance, vary the initial passages and offer significant reinterpretations. In the middle section of no. 1, where the metre changes from 3/4 to 2/4 (bar 21) the music seems to turn inwards, arresting the forward momentum through meditation on the motif from the preceding bar, now rhythmically elaborated to lead into a cadenza. In the ensuing recapitulation Beethoven places the head of the opening theme in octaves in the bass against a new chordal texture in the treble, which leads to an imitation of the theme in the highest register. The

[10] *Music Sounded Out*, p. 53.

opening material of the bagatelle is compressed, and a cadential phrase with close motivic links to the theme appears in imitation in the final bars. Beethoven thus conspicuously avoids a literal restatement: in the reprise the transformation in texture, broadening in register, and many other changes produce an effect of the theme being explored from a new, heightened perspective. This is not unlike the enhanced recapitulatory techniques used in the variation movements of Beethoven's later years.

The fifth bagatelle, a *quasi Allegretto* in G major, evokes an atmosphere of childlike naïveté, especially in its middle section, beginning in C major. Here, as elsewhere, the effect of simplicity results from the utmost purity of the musical language: the parallel thirds in the treble (bars 17 ff.) derive from the bass of the first section, while the return to the C major sonority in bar 20 is enhanced by means of the C♯ in the tenor voice and the asymmetrical phrasing. The pedal on C contributes to the static, idyllic quality of the passage and sets off the more active continuation in bars 20–30, with its crescendo, modulation to G major, and expansion in register. The yearning character of the ascent into the high register carries over into the ensuing reprise of the opening, now stated in the upper octave.

The framing device of the *Presto* in the final bagatelle seems to draw attention to the boundary separating inward, subjective feeling from external reality—or art from life. The relation of his art to society was of course an important theme for Beethoven, one he addressed most explicitly in *Fidelio*, the *Missa solemnis*, and the Ninth Symphony. His aesthetic convictions were far removed from the doctrine of *l'art pour l'art*. In the case of op. 126 no. 6 we are reminded of Czerny's account of Beethoven's practice, after moving his listeners to tears through his improvisations, of bursting into loud laughter and mocking his hearers' emotion, saying 'You are fools!'[11] The easy sentimentality that Beethoven scorned is indeed alien to his musical style, but depth of emotion is essential to it. And although the framing gesture of the *Presto* in the last bagatelle effects a bold contrast that is almost ominously like a kick downstairs, the music so enclosed in the *Andante amabile e con moto* assumes an intensely meditative character while transforming the material from the *Presto*.

The beginning of the *Andante amabile e con moto* clearly derives from the opening gesture: the bass pedal on E♭ and B♭ comes from the sustained tremolos of the *Presto*, while the register of the treble line and the harmonic texture in thirds are outlined in its rapid eighth-note figures (Ex. 90). But in contrast to the *Presto*, the music of the *Andante* has taken on a contemplative quality, and in the course of the piece it undergoes a further evolution. Beethoven places the reprise section in the subdominant, A♭ major, and

11 Thayer-Forbes, p. 185.

Ex. 90 Bagatelle op. 126 no. 6

arranges the pedal figure into a pattern of sixteenth-note triplets reminiscent of the Arietta movement of op. 111. The initial six-bar phrase now reappears in varied form, so that its disjunct intervals are filled in by conjunct motion, bringing the thematic profile closer still to the initial *Presto*. Then, after the repetition of the second section of the form, the music reaches a climax on high C (bars 55–6), the registral ceiling of the bagatelle.

The descent from this climax embraces three levels of experience as the adornments of art are progressively stripped away. In bar 64 the elaborate texture in sixteenths and sixteenth-note triplets is suddenly broken off to reveal the music from the beginning of the *Andante*, corresponding to bars 10–12 but with the pedal now placed initially on the dominant instead of on the tonic (Ex. 91). A varied sequence of these bars carries the progression into the low register, leading to an exact restatement of the framing gesture in *presto* tempo. Whereas previously the *Presto* had offered raw material out of which the *Andante* had been shaped, Beethoven now reverses the process: the *Andante* is dissipated into the frenetic activity of the *Presto*, whose fanfare of chords on the E♭ tonic concludes the bagatelle. A humorous or ironic quality arises here through Beethoven's juxtaposition of highly introspective music with a ges-

Ex. 91 Bagatelle op. 126 no. 6, bars 61–end

ture more evocative of the common daylight of outward events. And, inasmuch as this passage implies humble or low origins for the work of art, like the use of Diabelli's waltz in op. 120, it also embodies a universal breadth of experience that is typical of Beethoven.

*   *   *

Beethoven's main compositional preoccupation during 1823 was his Ninth Symphony in D minor op. 125, the grandest of his symphonies and most influential of all his works. The Ninth Symphony has become an unsurpassable model of affirmative culture, embodying as it does a mythic narrative that depicts inescapable problems of modern life and envisages a potential solution. Broadly considered, the symphony seems to respond to the dualistic world picture that emerged from the collapse of older certainties. The process was double-edged. As the human mind came to construe the universe as impersonal, mechanistic, and soulless, expropriating higher consciousness to itself, it participated in the ultimate anthropomorphic projection. The mechanization of the world picture greatly aided the goals of natural science, but it also contributed to an increasing sense of existential isolation. For if, as Kant argued, we have access only to appearances, not to things-in-themselves, then the ultimate ground of the world lies beyond us, mysterious and unknowable.[12] It is hardly coincidental that the early nineteenth century brought new sensitivity to the polarity between impersonal nature and the introspective individual human being. In Kant's famous formulation this polarity was viewed positively, as a sublime contrast between 'the starry heavens above us and the moral law within us'. The familiar Romantic image of the wanderer confronting the elements, as in Caspar David Friedrich's paintings, for instance, is less comforting and more mysterious, wrapped in an aura of opaque impressionistic landscape and archaic ruins. The closest musical counterpart to Friedrich is probably Beethoven's Viennese contemporary Franz Schubert.

In a work like Schubert's *Winterreise* of 1827 the existential tension concentrated in the wanderer archetype absorbs tragic qualities, since the epistemological gap between the self and the external world seems absolute and unbridgeable. As Peter Gülke points out in his recent book on Schubert, the protagonist of Schubert's earlier song cycle *Die schöne Müllerin* is rooted in concrete poetic images, which are largely withdrawn in the *Winterreise*.[13] The wanderer figure of 'The Winter's Journey' is not 'poetized' in descriptive terms but himself becomes the poet. His identity and background remain shadowy. Attention focuses on points of correspondence between his inward sensibility

---

[12] A recent analysis of the dualistic world picture is offered by Richard Tarnas in the epilogue of his book *The Passion of the Western Mind*.

[13] *Franz Schubert und seine Zeit*, pp. 236–9.

and outward natural objects such as the frozen stream, cold wind, circling crow, or howling dogs. As in Friedrich's paintings this wanderer does not face us but peers into the unknown and unfathomable. The ultimate destination of the journey in *Winterreise* is identified with 'the path from which no-one has ever returned', that is, death.

Beethoven's Ninth Symphony points to a way out of this dualistic dilemma, avoiding a tragic or solipsistic posture while safeguarding itself against the gravest risk of affirmative art—the danger of a lapse into ideology, or even kitsch. As we have seen in connection with Beethoven's Congress of Vienna works, the characteristic mark of kitsch is the presence of a false or over-extended artistic pretence. Miraculously, this pitfall is avoided in Beethoven's Ninth Symphony. The very frequent use of the 'Joy' theme in television commercials for beer or food introduces such an overextended pretence, since the supposed excellence of the proffered commodity is too facilely associated with an artistic exaltation taken out of context; as so often in advertisement, simplification or even deception is the very point of the message. The same failure invests certain pieces by Beethoven himself, as we have seen in the case of *Der glorreiche Augenblick*, but the Ninth Symphony and its companion works of Beethoven's last years earn our trust by paying dearly for their sustaining visions of perfection and aspiration. The narrative design of Beethoven's Ninth Symphony unfolds as a tensional balance containing powerful regressive elements that resist the utopian import of the choral finale and against which the meaning of the finale must be gauged. As Solomon has stressed, the vision of brotherhood in Schiller's text is conditional; 'alle Menschen werden Brüder' ('all men become brothers') is expressed neither in the present, past, nor even the future tense, but in a process tense, implying what will happen 'if'.[14] The choral finale is placed as it were in the subjunctive, on the horizon of possible realization, not yet quite within our grasp.

Beethoven's Ninth Symphony is a great work of synthesis, at once retrospective and futuristic in orientation. Beethoven's lifelong interest in Schiller's famous poem began at Bonn; it probably predated by several years Fischenich's letter of January 1793 reporting the young composer's intention to set *An die Freude*, whose designation as an ode stems from Beethoven rather than from Schiller. Beethoven returned repeatedly to the poem, first around 1798, and later during the initial labours on his opera *Fidelio*—two lines from Schiller's *An die Freude* found their way into the text of the opera's finale (see Plate 7). In the Petter Sketchbook of 1811–12 Beethoven made the following entries: 'Freude schöner Götterfunken to be worked out as an overture'; 'selected lines like Fürsten sind Bettler [princes are beggars] etc. not the whole'; 'selected lines from Schiller's Joy brought together into a whole'. As

[14] 'Beethoven's Ninth Symphony: A Search for Order', p. 30.

Otto Baensch suggested, these entries probably imply not a choral overture but rather a larger work, or 'whole' ('Ganzen') that would need to be preceded by an 'overture'.[15] By 1812 Beethoven apparently recognized the need to realize his long-desired setting of Schiller's ode not as a song but as a major choral-symphonic work.

At about this time Beethoven also contemplated a symphony 'in D minor' as a possible companion to the Seventh and Eighth Symphonies, but it is not clear that the anticipated symphony was to have incorporated a setting of Schiller's text. In 1815, while at work on the Cello Sonata op. 102 no. 2, he sketched the theme later used in the scherzo of the Ninth Symphony, and by 1817 he entertained thoughts of two new symphonies to be written for London. His most detailed notation of these plans is as follows:

Adagio Cantique—Frommer Gesang in einer Sinfonie in den alten Tonarten—Herr Gott dich loben wir—alleluja—entweder für sich allein oder als Einleitung in eine Fuge. Vielleicht auf diese Weise die ganze 2te Sinfonie charakterisirt, wo alsdenn im letzten Stück oder schon im Adagio die Singstimmen eintreten. Die Orchester Violinen etc. werden im letzten Stück verzehnfacht. Oder das Adagio wird auf gewisse Weise im letzten Stücke wiederholt, wobei alsdenn erst die Singstimmen nach und nach eintreten—im Adagio Text griechischer Mithos Cantique Ecclesiastique—im Allegro Feier des Bachus.

Adagio Cantique—devout song in a symphony in the old modes—our Lord we praise you—alleluja—either by itself or as introduction to a fugue. The whole second symphony could perhaps be characterized this way, whereby the voices enter in the last movement or already in the Adagio. The orchestral violins, etc., will be multiplied tenfold in the last movement. Or the Adagio will be in this way repeated in the last movement, whereby only then the voices enter gradually—in the Adagio a text of a Greek myth Cantique Ecclesiastique—in the Allegro the celebration of Bachus.[16]

Many special qualities of the Ninth Symphony are alluded to in this remarkable inscription. The notion of an 'Adagio Cantique . . . in the old modes' relates to the slow sections of the choral finale as we know it, namely the *Andante maestoso* and especially the *Adagio ma non troppo, ma divoto*. In the end this section did serve as 'introduction' to a fugue—it leads to the double choral fugue (see Plate 22) in which the 'Joy' theme is combined with the main subject of the *Andante*, set to the words 'Seid umschlungen Millionen' ('Be embraced, millions'). At this early stage Beethoven had not yet envisaged how a series of such interrelated symphonic and choral movements could be brought together into a whole. It was surely in response to this basic problem that he eventually resorted to the effective solution embodied in the completed work: the entry of the voices is delayed until the finale, or last main stage in the narrative progression between movements, with this finale in turn

---

[15] *Aufbau und Sinn des Chorfinales in Beethovens neunter Symphonie*, pp. 44-5.
[16] Thayer-Forbes, p. 888.

devised as a composite form embracing its own progression of four basic movements.

The allusion in Beethoven's inscription to 'the celebration of Bac[c]hus' recalls his rudimentary sketches for a pastoral opera on Bacchus in the Scheide Sketchbook of 1815, as well as those verses of Schiller's *An die Freude* that express Dionysian sentiments. However, Beethoven eventually excluded from the text such overtly Dionysian images as 'the brimming cup [whose] foam to heaven mounts up'. Nor did he follow up the provocative remark contained in his sketches for the 'Bacchus' opera:

Dissonances perhaps [to be left] unresolved in the entire opera or [treated] entirely differently since in these uncultivated times our refined music is unthinkable.[17]

The 'uncultivated times' of mythic antiquity held no such musical consequences for the choral finale. Instead, Beethoven fused archaic and visionary aspects into a depiction of humanity and nature in the spirit of Rousseau and Goethe, affirming the compatibility of civilized refinement with mythic universality.

Recent studies of the Artaria 201 Sketchbook by Robert Winter and Sieghard Brandenburg have indicated that Beethoven devised a melody for the *Ode to Joy* and a basic outline of the layout of the symphony by about October 1822.[18] Nevertheless, he wavered in his intention to crown the work with the choral finale, and alternative sketches for an 'instrumental finale' appear even at an advanced stage; the unused theme was eventually incorporated into the finale of his String Quartet in A minor op. 132, composed in 1825.

Beethoven's evolving plans for the intermovement narrative progression are clarified by those entries in the Landsberg 8 Manuscript from 1823 that contain his sketches for the recitatives and quotations from earlier movements at the threshold of the choral finale. These entries make clear the reasons for the rejection of each of the preceding movements. The first, for instance, is rejected because 'it reminds us of our despair', whereas the second 'is not better, but only somewhat more cheerful', and the third 'is too tender', too far removed from action. In the finished work Beethoven left this first group of recitatives in a purely instrumental form, without text. As we have seen, this process of anticipating the later appearance of the human voice through accents and inflections of instruments alone had an exact counterpart in the Choral Fantasy op. 80, where Beethoven devised an introductory horn call to precede the main theme set to the text 'Hört Ihr wohl' ('Hear ye well'), words that were subsequently suppressed while the musical motif remained. In a for-

---

[17] Nottebohm, *Zweite Beethoveniana*, p. 329.

[18] Winter, 'The Sketches for the "Ode to Joy"'; Brandenburg, 'Die Skizzen zur Neunten Symphonie'.

mal sense the treatment of the citations and the eventual discovery of the 'Joy' theme in the Ninth Symphony are also reminiscent of several earlier works from the period 1815–18, including *An die ferne Geliebte*, the Cello Sonata op. 102 no. 1, the Piano Sonata op. 101, and most of all the *Hammerklavier* Sonata. In each of these the finale is reached as the outcome of a quest for new possibilities, a process that is underscored by a cyclic relationship to earlier parts of the work, often involving explicit quotation of foregoing passages at the threshold to the finale. In the *Hammerklavier* explicit quotation is not involved, but the three parenthetical glimpses of 'other musics' in its transition are close, in their formal and symbolic function, to the threefold citations of preceding movements in the transition to the choral finale of the Ninth.

Each of the four movements of the Ninth Symphony is conceived on a vast scale, and each expands the forms and textures of Beethoven's earlier symphonic works. The closest counterpart to the opening *Allegro, ma non troppo, un poco maestoso* of the Ninth is the first movement of the *Eroica*. As in the *Eroica*, the development and coda are unusually extended and closely interrelated, with the latter acting in part as a recapitulation of the former. The opening of the Ninth Symphony, however, has no parallel in Beethoven's earlier symphonies: it is the outstanding example of a work that takes its origin from a rapport with silence. Beethoven showed a truly modernistic concern with the boundaries of art—the manner in which the artwork confronts the world. We have noted instances of this sensitivity in connection with the A major Piano Sonata op. 101, with its opening *in medias res*, and the last bagatelle of op. 126, with its startling transformation of the anaesthetic into the aesthetic.

In the Ninth, the arrival of the main theme in D minor is delayed until the upbeat to bar 17. The opening passage presents a trajectory towards this event, disclosing an ongoing process rather than a fixed and determined entity (Ex. 92). The hushed beginning, with its ambiguity of key, mode, and even rhythm, shows the impress of the journey out of the sphere of the inaudible into that of the audible. The seminal upbeat rhythm is first heard *sotto voce* at the upbeat to bar 3; this rhythmic motif spreads itself over falling open fourths and fifths on the dominant of D minor, while the wind instruments simultaneously build up the same harmonic sonority in the upper pitch registers. Only at bar 11 does Beethoven prescribe a crescendo, as a process of rhythmic diminution and motivic intensification shapes the transition to the outbreak of the powerful principal theme, played *fortissimo* and in unison by the full orchestra.

This vehement theme thus emerges as the dramatic outcome of the opening passage, and its musical continuation retains in turn a memory of the quiet, mysterious accents whence it arose. Not only does Beethoven soon restate the *pianissimo* opening before presenting a varied return of the theme, modulating to B♭, but in addition the second subject-group is characterized

Ex. 92 Ninth Symphony op. 125/I

by an unusually subtle interplay of dramatic and lyrical phrases. In the entire
Classical repertory, as William Caplin has observed, there is no more complex
formal structure within the second subject-area of a sonata design.[19] In part,
this richness of hierarchical relationships is bound up with Beethoven's far-
reaching narrative design, which involves thematic forecasts and reminiscences in all four movements. The *dolce* theme in the first movement, immediately before the change in key signature to B♭ in bar 80, is the first subtle
foreshadowing of the 'Joy' theme, and later episodes in D major, particularly
the horn passage in the coda, may also be heard as anticipating the choral
finale.

---

[19] 'Structural Expansion in Beethoven's Symphonic Forms', p. 53.

Ex. 92 *cont.*

The thrust from D minor into D major is a conspicuous feature of the symphony as a whole, and this modal tension is given unforgettable expression in
the first movement. At least as early as the op. 18 quartets Beethoven showed
a marked tendency to enhance the moment of recapitulation; in some later
pieces, such as the first movement of the Eighth Symphony, he tended to

diffuse or broaden its impact. The first movement of the Ninth Symphony provides one of the most compelling instances of a recapitulation conceived as a dramatic reinterpretation of the opening of a work. The structural downbeat marking the recapitulation occurs at a return not of the main theme but of the opening passage, which is now utterly transformed through the impact of the powerful rhythmic arrival. Instead of the faint, barely audible sonic vibrations heard at the outset, we hear a blazing *fortissimo* in the full orchestra on the sonority of D *major*, but with the third, F♯, in the bass. As Heinrich Schenker pointed out, this D major tonality is not real but only apparent;[20] the unstable position of the chord allows it to be heard in retrospect as dominant of G minor. Beethoven has intensified here the effect of tragic irony evident in a passage from the recapitulation of the first movement of the *Appassionata* Sonata, in which a single emphatic fanfare of chords is heard unexpectedly in the tonic major in place of the tonic minor. Instead of securing a breakthrough into the major, the music is now drawn with renewed strength into the darkness of the minor, with unmistakable expressive overtones of 'Verzweiflung', or despair.

Unlike the corresponding passages in the Fifth Symphony, the recapitulation remains rooted in the tonic minor; as in the exposition, however, much harmonic stress is laid on the Neapolitan degree, a semitone above the tonic. Beethoven reserves the major mode of D for the *dolce* passage for horn and other winds beginning in bar 469 of the coda, with its remarkable development of bars 3–4 of the main theme, but the music soon reverts to the minor, reapproaching, with a prominent slowing in tempo, that great pivotal cadence that had initiated the fugato passage of the development (cf. bars 218 and 513). There is an abysmal, almost funereal character to this impressive passage, in which the chromatic bass gradually comes to dominate the entire orchestral texture, leading to the emphatic reassertion of the main theme at the close.

As in the *Hammerklavier* Sonata, Beethoven places the scherzo before the slow movement, and he gives it a somewhat parodistic role in relation to the opening *Allegro*. The falling fourths and fifths from the outset of the first movement are mimicked in the opening fanfare of the scherzo, and Beethoven at once highlights the timpani in F, which are to assume a marked prominence. The tuning of the timpani on F is linked to the modulatory plan, with its move from the tonic D minor to C major in the exposition and to F major in the development. This scherzo is in a fully developed sonata form, like that of the Piano Sonata op. 31 no. 3, and it also incorporates an important trio in D major, the key of the choral finale. Beethoven adds weight to the opening section of the scherzo by treating it as a fugal exposition, with thematic entries spaced four bars apart. The basic four-bar theme is virtually

---

[20] *Beethoven's Neunte Sinfonie*, pp. 96–7.

identical to Beethoven's 1815 sketch; but by 1823 he had discovered extraordinary rhythmic and metrical means of developing his idea.

The heart of the scherzo lies in its development, in the passages marked 'Ritmo di tre battute' ('rhythm of three bars')—Beethoven's acknowledgment of what some recent theorists have termed 'hypermetre'. He first shortens the four-bar phrases beginning with the characteristic dotted rhythm to groups of three bars, which he then skilfully manipulates. The music passes from E minor into A minor, with the motivic tag sporting the dotted rhythm placed on E. At this moment the timpani vividly interject the head motif on F, pulling the music into the key of F major. This driving, galloping movement is one of Beethoven's most fascinating essays in metrical manipulation and rhythmic intensification, not the least in the *stringendo il tempo* passage that pushes the music over the threshold into the *alla breve* duple metre of the trio.

Beethoven would not have intended the designation 'Presto' at the climax of the *stringendo il tempo* to apply strictly to the trio, which assumes a relaxed, pastoral character while repeating over and over the same configuration of notes that coalesces into the 'Joy' theme in the finale. The closing passage of the trio, in which tonic and dominant are incessantly reiterated over a pedal in the bass, sounds reminiscent of the first movement of the *Pastoral* Symphony. Beethoven's decision not to repeat the entire trio and scherzo, as in the Seventh Symphony, was probably dictated by considerations of overall length, but he does bring back the *stringendo il tempo* passage leading to a brief recall of the trio, which is framed by abrupt reaffirmation of the climactic *Presto* gesture.

The contemplative *Adagio molto e cantabile* is in B♭ major, a conspicuous secondary tonality in the outer movements. In the *Adagio*, as so often in Beethoven, the flat sixth serves as a key of inward reflection whose contemplative mood is eventually to be shattered at the later emergence into 'action', when the tonic minor is reasserted. B♭ major shares two pitches with D minor—D and F; the crucial semitone that joins these triads is B♭–A—precisely the initial pitches of the introduction played in the bassoons and immediately imitated in the clarinets. This opening gesture foreshadows the second theme of this double-variation movement, marked *Andante moderato*, whose vocal aura, linear contour, and initial key of D major all presage in turn the 'Joy' theme of the finale.

Slow variation movements employing two themes are characteristic of Haydn but uncommon in Beethoven. The most analogous earlier example is the *Andante* of the Fifth Symphony, which not only displays a similar shift in key to the overall tonic at the secondary theme but also assigns to it a similar narrative function—that of prefiguring the principal subject of the finale, just as in the Ninth Symphony. In both slow movements we glimpse the finale from afar, as it were, as the thematic foreshadowing combines with an anticipation of the key that is to be triumphantly attained in the final stages.

The main theme of the *Adagio* has a serene, hymn-like character; its lyric breadth is enhanced by exquisitely scored echoing of the string phrases by the woodwinds. As in the *Archduke* Trio and the Arietta movement of op. III, successive returns of the theme are enhanced by figurative elaboration; at the same time the recapitulatory effect of these variations is set off by excursions to D major and G major at the appearances of the secondary theme. Beethoven even interpolates a further modulatory development after the G major episode, which culminates in a transparent texture for horn and winds and finally a solo for horn in C♭ major, Neapolitan to the B♭ major tonic of the ensuing recapitulatory variation of the main subject. Here the theme unfolds in a broad 12/8 metre, as sixteenth-notes yield to triplet-sixteenths and ultimately to trills in the violins, while the winds sound the sustained original version of the theme against this embroidered texture.

Beethoven does not grant his theme closure in the tonic B♭ but twice interrupts the imminent cadence by disruptive fanfares with trumpets and drums. These seem to evoke a call to action and contribute to a strangely disquieting atmosphere in the coda. The inflections of the minor mode and the low tremolos in triplets beginning seven bars from the conclusion disturb the serenity; even the final cadence is undermined by being completed in a weak rhythmic position, in the second half of a bar. The stage has thus been set for a pivotal event of potentially catastrophic impact.

*   *   *

That event, of course, is the 'terror fanfare', or *Schreckensfanfare*, the frenzied *presto* passage that arises out of the dissonant combination of the tonic triads of the slow movement and the symphony as a whole—B♭ major and D minor. The *Presto* should follow the *Adagio* without much pause (certainly not after an interruption to bring out the chorus and soloists!). For the impact of this shocking passage is to destroy the peaceful contemplation of the *Adagio*, precipitating a crisis in the inner workings of the artwork itself. How is it to continue? The ensuing review of the earlier movements implies not only their insufficiency but also in some sense their continued valid presence at the threshold of the finale: these stages in the narrative design have not been forgotten, but what can succeed them?

As in the last piano sonatas, the artistic quest leads to the discovery of a seemingly simple, eminently lyrical tune, which supports an unsuspected wealth of development. But no other work, not even *Fidelio* or the *Missa solemnis*, carries such important social and political connotations as the finale of the Ninth Symphony. As we have seen, the work as a whole embraces numerous transformations in character and embodies a narrative pattern unusually rich in its foreshadowings and reminiscences of themes. These qualities are, of course, typical of Beethoven's music in general; a work such as the Piano Sonata in A♭ op. 110 displays a somewhat analogous narrative design compressed into much smaller dimensions. What is unusual in the choral finale is Beethoven's incorporation of a more radical type of transformation, from instrumental into vocal music. Only in the Choral Fantasy had he attempted anything similar. A guiding principle of both pieces is the adoption of a concerto-like plan exploiting the capacity of instruments to evoke vocal expression. Thus, in the Choral Fantasy, the horn motif implying 'Hear ye well?' prefaces the main theme in the solo piano, setting up the later vocal presentation of the theme. In the Ninth Symphony it is the recitative in the low strings that evokes vocal expression without yet requiring words. Here, as in the Choral Fantasy, Beethoven decided to remove the text he originally contemplated for the initial recitatives.

The vocal recitative is thus confined to 'O friends, not these sounds! let us create more pleasant and happier ones!' ('O Freunde, nicht diese Töne! sondern lasst uns angenehmere anstimmen, und freudenvollere'). Which 'sounds' are meant? In the most immediate sense, it is the preceding *Presto*, or 'terror fanfare', that the baritone seeks to negate. In the broader context, a continuation to the sequence of movements has been sought and discovered; yet this progression had reached a crisis in the passage leading up to the *Schreckensfanfare*. The initial series of instrumental variations lacks the strength to sustain the musical development of the 'Joy' theme and eventually breaks down, as does the first fugue in op. 110.

At this juncture, as in the disquieting passage near the end of the slow movement, Beethoven alludes or reverts to musical textures drawn from earlier passages. Thus the triplet sixteenth-figures of the *Adagio* recall the more rapid vibrating string textures from the outset of the opening *Allegro*. Now, just before the return of the *Schreckensfanfare*, he makes subtle reference to the succession of movements. First he stresses in bars 201–2 in the full orchestra the falling fourth interval A–E, the pitches around which the music of the first movement had come into focus. This strident gesture is given an inward, lyrical response in the ensuing passage, marked *poco ritenente* and slowing to *poco adagio*. The orchestration, featuring flutes and oboes, the expressive appoggiaturas, and the *ritardando* all relate to the earlier focus of inward lyricism in the symphony as a whole, the *Adagio molto e cantabile*. The intervallic contour, however, with its fall through a fifth and stepwise ascent to the third degree, relates audibly to the 'Joy' theme (Ex. 93*a* and *b*). This is one of those gripping narrative moments in Beethoven's music that looks backwards and forwards at one and the same moment, creating a connective bond between the reflective contemplation of the *Adagio* and the archetypal symbol of the 'Joy' theme. But only when Beethoven gathers together his full orchestral

Ex. 93 Ninth Symphony op. 125/IV

(*a*) bars 203–7

forces in the main tempo of *Allegro assai* is the imminent turning-point
sufficiently prepared. The extreme collision of lyrical, idealistic music with the
dissonant fanfare motivates the emergence of the human voice to render
explicit what had up to this point remained implicit.

We should now reassess the implications of Beethoven's narrative succes-

(*b*) bars 237–44

sion of movements. After the tragic and parodistic modalities of the first two movements, the *Adagio* turned inwards, to a contemplative mood. Such subjectivity is by its very nature private and ultimately passive; it does not intrude into the public sphere of social activity, which can be engaged artistically only through the seemingly universal archetypes of shared human experience. It is the function of Beethoven's choral finale to depict such symbolic archetypes, and in so doing to provide a potential model for the transformation of society. There is evidence that Beethoven himself may have regarded the project in these terms. In 1820 Beethoven's acquaintance Friedrich Wähner made the following entry in a conversation notebook: 'Philosophie und Musik sollen leben! Den Plato müssen Sie in der deutschen Übersetzung von Schleiermacher lesen. Sie müssen, ich bringe ihn Ihnen. Er und der Schelling sind die Grössten!' ('Long live philosophy and music! You have to read Plato in the German translation by Schleiermacher. You must, I'll bring it to you. He and Schelling are the greatest!').[21] We have already seen the relevance of Schelling's thought to Beethoven's artistic enterprise, but have yet to consider the role of Plato, whose *Republic* may well have influenced the choral finale, as Baensch has suggested.

One of Plato's fundamental points in *The Republic* concerns the need for common human experience as the basis for common action, based on agreement about ends and means. In Book 5 Socrates asks 'Is there any worse ill for a state than to be divided or a greater good than being united?', whereas in Book 9 he claims that '. . . the best is for everyone to be ruled by a wise and godlike power, if possible seated in his own heart; if not, let it act upon him from without; in order that we may all be, as far as possible, like one another and friends, being all guided by the same pilot'. Plato is, however, extremely guarded about the conditions under which such harmony can be achieved. The centrepiece of the entire dialogue is Socrates' paradoxical solution to the political dilemma:

> Till philosophers become kings, or those now named kings and rulers give themselves to philosophy truly and rightly, and these two things—political power and philosophic thought—come together, and the commoner minds, which at present seek only the one or the other, are kept out by force, states will have not rest from their troubles, dear Glaucon, and if I am right, man will have none. Only then will this our republic see the light of day.[22]

We need not accept all of Baensch's analogies between Plato's philosophers and guardians and Beethoven's shaping of specific sections in his choral finale, but the general relevance of *The Republic* seems almost inescapable, even if it was merged in Beethoven's conception with a variety of other influences. As Baensch reminds us, the ageing Beethoven who arranged his text from Schiller's early poem was a seasoned artist who contemplated the material from a retrospective and elevated point of view, with the benefit of critical insight presumably derived in part from Schiller's own later writings, such as

---

[21] *Ludwig van Beethovens Konversationshefte*, i, p. 350. Earlier editors and commentators attributed this entry to Beethoven's erudite friend August Friedrich Kanne.
[22] *Plato's Republic*, ed. and trans. I. A. Richards, p. 97.

the *Aesthetic Letters*.[23] The need for a 'selection of lines' from Schiller's ode was already specified in Beethoven's sketch inscription from around 1812. In the end he removed all the most obvious references that mark the *Ode to Joy* as a glorified drinking-song, while preserving a series of powerful and direct images with universal social connotations.

In a letter to Johann Kanka from the period of the Congress of Vienna, Beethoven once compared his artistic enterprise to the political sphere by indulging in one of his characteristic puns. He wrote, 'I shall not say anything to you about our monarchs . . . I much prefer the empire of the mind, and I regard it as the highest of all spiritual and worldly monarchies'.[24] His experience with political art at that time seemed to confirm this implied dissociation between politics and art. Yet in the Ninth Symphony, completed a decade later, Beethoven produced a work that fills the gap, bridging the apparently impassable gulf between artistic truth and political relevance. According to the Schillerian concept embraced by Beethoven, as we have seen, freedom is manifested in a resistance to despair or suffering, modalities associated in this case with the first movement or with the *Schreckensfanfare*. The message of the Ninth Symphony is positioned between the 'negative' and 'positive' concepts of freedom associated, for instance, with John Locke and John Stuart Mill on the one hand and with Karl Marx on the other. The former tradition has regarded liberty as a matter of individual rights based particularly on the right to property; the latter replaced the emphasis on isolated individuals and their abstract rights by a collectivist view, whose basic insight into 'man as an ensemble of social relations' retains a core of validity, despite the disastrous authoritarian misapplications of the principle in this century. Some recent commentators have recognized the shortcomings of both concepts of liberty, and seen 'the formation of the common will in a rational discussion' as the basis of social freedom, a proposal not easily realized in a contemporary consumer society that encourages the pursuit of security rather than social responsibility.[25] The relevance of Beethoven's Ninth Symphony to calls for a revitalized ethical consciousness in politics (such as Michael Harrington's 'visionary gradualism') has a double aspect, since it is rooted not merely in the social accessibility of the work but also in the challenge of an 'unconsummated symbol' that resists facile appropriation. As Herbert Marcuse argued in his book *Eros and Civilisation*, the Schillerian 'aesthetic education of mankind' involves a rejection of the tyranny of reason over sensibility; the sway of a merciless rationalization of means is thereby held in check. In his Schiller setting in the Ninth, Beethoven achieved an interpenetration of the rational and

---

[23] *Aufbau und Sinn*.   [24] Anderson, L. 502.
[25] See Árnason, 'The Discourse of Freedom', *Rechtstheorie*, xix (1988), pp. 491–501 (the quotation is from p. 499); a classic study of related issues is Isaiah Berlin's *Four Essays on Liberty* from 1969.

sensuous in a composite design with universal social implications, a work whose adequate performance contributes to the formation of a common will through an integrated process of artistic symbolization.

Robert Winter has shown how painstakingly Beethoven laboured to devise the 'Joy' theme itself; the memorable shape of this famous tune, with its conjunct vocal motion and circular pattern, was the product of sustained reflection.[26] The heritage of 'popular' style stemming from some of Haydn's symphonic finales or Mozart's *Magic Flute*, as well as Beethoven's extensive experience with folk-song, may have helped prepare him for the task, but most important, as Richard Kramer has noted, is the emblematic or symbolic role of the theme 'as a purge to the troubled music of earlier movements'.[27] The emblematic character of the tune invites figurative decoration more than thoroughgoing transformation, and Beethoven's initial choral variations, like the preceding three instrumental variations, remain close to the original theme. Only at the section in B♭ major and 6/8 metre does he transform the hymn-like theme into a parodied version, whose displaced accents confirm their humorous effect at the hasty cadences. The unforgettable vividness of this scherzo section owes much to the Shakespearean juxtaposition of a comic military march with the solemnity of the grand pause on the words 'und der Cherub steht vor Gott' that immediately precedes it (the juxtaposition of key contributes substantially to this, too). Following the incomplete orchestral variation and choral variation with tenor solo in B♭ is an exciting double fugue for orchestra, which leads to the most emphatic presentation yet of the 'Joy' theme: a recapitulatory variation for full chorus and orchestra in the tonic D major. Beethoven then incorporates the slow *Andante–Adagio* section, whose archaic, modal qualities and religious text suggest the 'Cantique Ecclesiastique' of his early plan. What remains is the brilliant combination in a double choral fugue of the 'Joy' theme with the 'Seid umschlungen Millionen' subject from the slow section (see Plate 22), as well as the weighty final sections that reiterate earlier parts of the text.

The overall form of the choral finale combines aspects of concerto and sonata form with the basic chain of variations and the suggestion of a four-movement design encapsulated in a single movement. Concerto-like features include the 'double exposition' of instrumental followed by choral variations, as well as the cadenza in B major for the vocal soloists near the conclusion. The analogy with sonata form lies in the developmental character of the vari-

[26] 'The Sketches for the "Ode to Joy"'.

[27] Review of *Beethoven, Performers, and Critics*, in *Journal of Music Theory*, xxvii (1983), p. 301. Küthen attempts to explore the emblematic ramifications of the 'Joy' theme in two recent articles, which deserve consideration, even if his proposal of a Mozartian model for the theme is not accepted: 'Schöpferische Rezeption im Finale der 9. Symphonie von Beethoven' and 'Mozart—Schiller—Beethoven: Mozarts Modell für die Freudenhymne und die Fusion der Embleme im Finale der Neunten Symphonie'.

ations in Bb and of the ensuing orchestral fugue, in relation to which the following choral variation acts like a decorated recapitulation; the later double choral fugue also serves a recapitulatory function by restoring the tonic key of D major while synthesizing the two main themes. At the same time, the following overall sequence may be seen as outlining a 'multi-movement' plan: (1) the theme and initial variations in D major; (2) the 6/8 scherzo section with 'Turkish' orchestration; (3) the archaic *Andante–Adagio* passages featuring trombones and modal tendencies; (4) the final sections beginning with the choral double fugue. The choral finale is the most celebrated single example in Beethoven of a composite form that successfully blends the possibilities of different genres. It was an important progenitor of later efforts along these lines, ranging from Liszt's symphonic poems to Bruckner's grandiose symphonic finales. The enhanced orchestral and vocal forces and the formal grandeur of Beethoven's Ninth helped point the way to Wagner's later works, as well as to the monumental compositions by Mahler and Schoenberg from the beginning of this century.

For Beethoven himself, the single most decisive compositional model for the choral finale was his own *Missa solemnis*. Its influence is felt particularly in those parts of the choral finale that have a religious text, such as the pivotal phrase 'und der Cherub steht vor Gott', the setting of which forms the first great climax of the movement. Beethoven's treatment here of the modulation from D to Bb and the ensuing military processional music recall the Agnus Dei of the Mass, despite the different expressive connotations of the *Alla marcia* section in 6/8 in the symphony. At the same time, the setting of 'Gott' as a long-protracted sonority, with A at the top, corresponds with the climax on the dominant of Bb in the Credo. In orchestration and register the two sonorities are nearly identical, with the rise to high A motivated by the word 'God' in the symphony and 'heaven' in the Mass. But their placement within the larger formal context of each work is also closely parallel. We have already seen that in the Credo this chord occurs at an interrupted cadence, involving a drastic downward shift in register for the earthbound music of the Incarnatus. In the symphony the corresponding cadence, to Bb, is completed, but there is a very similar disjunction in register, at the appearance of the 'Turkish' music in Bb and its parodied version of the hymn-like 'Joy' theme. Beethoven thus concentrates aspects of both these passages from the Mass into his setting of 'vor Gott' in the symphony (Ex. 94; cf. Ex. 80).

A similar process of concentration based on the network of referential sonorities from the Mass can be observed in Beethoven's setting of the very last line of his text in the *Adagio ma non troppo, ma divoto*, 'Über Sternen muss er wohnen' ('Above the stars he must dwell'), often regarded as the climax of the entire symphony. The first section of the *Adagio* has brought a drop in register, a shift motivated by the text 'Ihr stürzt nieder, Millionen?' ('Do you

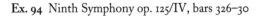

Ex. 94 Ninth Symphony op. 125/IV, bars 326–30

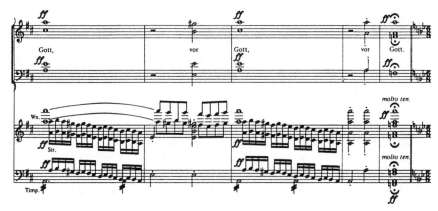

fall on your knees, millions?'). In its rhythm, texture, orchestration, and thematic material this passage bears comparison to the Preludium of the Benedictus in the Mass. There follows a long, gradual ascent in the music which sets the last three lines of text:

> Ahnest du den Schöpfer, Welt?
> Such' ihn über'm Sternenzelt
> Über Sternen muss er wohnen.

> Do you sense the Creator, world?
> Seek him above the canopy of stars
> Above the stars he must dwell.

The rise in pitch is accomplished only gradually, the music twice falling back earthwards before its long, melodic ascent continues chromatically to reach F♯, the leading-note of the tonic G minor, at 'über'm Sternenzelt'.

At this point the long ascending progression reaches its goal, arriving at the *very same* E♭ sonority that had played so crucial a role in the Credo (Ex. 95; cf. Exx. 79, 82, 83). As in the Credo, this chord assumes a symbolic importance in relation to the idea of a divine presence above the stars. The sonority is repeated eight times, to accompany each syllable of the text. It seems static and immutable, becoming in effect an audible monolithic symbol; even when it is transmuted to a diminished seventh in the orchestra and moments later to a minor ninth chord, the high G is retained. In its controlling idea the entire passage is thus remarkably close to that in the *Missa solemnis*, using the same symbolic contrast in register and even an identical referential sonority. One measure of the significance of this passage is the continuing sway of its high register over some following sections of the choral finale, where Beethoven re-uses parts of his earlier text. He seems to have fixed the monolithic setting of 'Über Sternen muss er wohnen' only late in the compositional

Ex. 95 Ninth Symphony op. 125/IV, bars 643–50

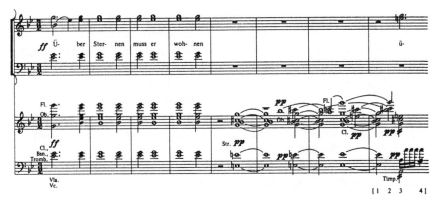

process; a sketch for the passage is found in a conversation book from early April 1824, just a few weeks before the first performances.[28] As Solomon has pointed out, Beethoven himself alluded to the symbolic character of this passage in an inscription on an earlier sketch, where he wrote: 'The height of the stars [can be pictured] more by way of the instruments'.[29] The symbolism is therefore literal and explicit, but it nevertheless retains an idealistic character since it depicts boundlessness and infinitude, concepts that by their very nature are incapable of direct representation.

An affinity with Kant can be felt here in the consistent use of a musical symbol associated with the naturalistic realm of phenomena to stand for the Deity. Kant argued that we cannot have knowledge of God, even when his existence is posited as the guiding moral ideal of the *summum bonum* (the highest good). 'The starry heavens above me, and the moral law within me': this dictum from Kant, embraced by Beethoven, gives expression, in terms not of speculative or received doctrine but of concrete experience, to the relationship between eternal, infinite nature on the one hand and man's subjective inwardness on the other. This polarity resonates throughout the Mass, and especially in its later movements. The passages we have discussed from the Credo and the Benedictus allude emphatically to the heavens as a symbol of perfection and a goal for spiritual aspiration. Other passages of restless, questioning character, such as the fragile prayer for peace juxtaposed with threats of war in the Agnus Dei, may be associated with the Kantian notion of the moral law and its inevitable conflict with earthly realities. In these instances the Mass text is not simply affirmed in its literal content but is interpreted

---

[28] *Ludwig van Beethovens Konversationshefte*, vi, pp. 19–20.
[29] 'Beethoven's Ninth Symphony: A Search for Order', *Beethoven Essays*, p. 25. The inscription is transcribed in Nottebohm, *Zweite Beethoveniana*, p. 186. Also see Ludwig Nohl, *Beethovens Leben*, iii, p. 395.

by means of universal images, thereby imposing a broader humanistic perspective on the received doctrines.

The Kantian vision of the heavens is thus absorbed, in the Mass, into a transcendental musical symbol, secular in its naturalism yet sacred in its role as a focus for the awe and devotion of humankind. In the choral finale of the Ninth Symphony this symbolic musical gesture reappears, and its universality and independence of religious dogma are affirmed through its association with Schiller's text. It provides a climax to the choral finale, and to the entire symphony, through its effective depiction of a fundamental aspect of human experience: our confrontation with the infinitude and mystery of creation. At the same time the idea retains close links with Beethoven's instrumental idioms in works such as the last piano sonatas and the great variation movement of his next major composition, the String Quartet in E♭ op. 127. These connections remind us of the central position of the choral finale in Beethoven's art in general, as well as of the presence in his instrumental music of layers of symbolic and associative meaning beyond the reach of a merely formalistic aesthetic.

The triumph of the Ninth Symphony took time. Although the work received enthusiastic accolades when first performed in Vienna on 7 May 1824, together with the Kyrie, Credo, and Agnus Dei of the Mass and the Overture to *Die Weihe des Hauses*, the quality of the performance cannot have been very satisfactory, and Beethoven was disappointed and even embittered about the financial return. A second performance that month was poorly attended. As Karl-Heinz Köhler has written, 'the shining hour of music history in which the Ninth Symphony began its victorious march around the globe came amid summer lightning storms of hypersensitivity, misunderstandings, and pettiness'.[30]

One of the recent 'shining hours' commemorated by Beethoven's Ninth was the fall of the Berlin Wall in 1989, when Leonard Bernstein conducted the work with a crucial change of text, changing 'Freude' ('joy') to 'Freiheit' ('freedom'). It has sometimes been speculated that this was the text that the young Schiller originally intended and that he was discouraged by censorship from publishing the poem in this form in 1785, four years before the outbreak of the French Revolution. The known use of the poem as a revolutionary or masonic ode supports this interpretation, but no documentary evidence for a change in text has been uncovered. Beethoven's own convictions, like Plato's, or Schiller's at a more advanced age, were better represented by 'Freude', with all due acknowledgment of the liberating effects of the 'effigy of [the] ideal'. For one protection against the possible ideological misuse of 'brotherhood' in the Ninth Symphony is its explicit precondition of a state of 'Freude', the charac-

---

[30] 'The Conversation Books: Aspects of a New Picture of Beethoven', p. 154.

ter of which is inextricably interwoven into the narrative design of the symphony as a whole. Beethoven, like Plato, was no advocate of unbridled freedom without responsibility, but he despised tyranny, and he would presumably have approved of Bernstein's decision. The Ninth Symphony is a magnificent refutation of Plato's scepticism about the social and political value of art, and an enduring monument to the compatibility of beauty and truth.

II

The 'Galitzin' Quartets

1824–1825

The composition of Beethoven's last important group of works, the five final quartets, is bound up with a commission from the Russian prince and amateur cellist Nikolaus Galitzin in St Petersburg. Beethoven had already been thinking of composing quartets (and had received an enquiry from Carl Friedrich Peters about one) prior to Galitzin's request, but the prince seems to have acted as the major catalyst. In November 1822 Galitzin wrote to Beethoven requesting the composition of as many as three new quartets. Beethoven accepted the proposal in January 1823; but the actual composition of the first of these new quartets was delayed for more than a year by other projects, notably the Ninth Symphony. On 29 November 1823 the prince wrote to Beethoven:

I am really impatient to have a new quartet of yours, nevertheless, I beg you not to mind and to be guided in this only by your inspiration and the disposition of your mind, for no one knows better than I that you cannot command genius, rather that it should be left alone, and we know moreover that in your private life you are not the kind of person to sacrifice artistic for personal interest and that music done to order is not your business at all.[1]

In the end Galitzin's patience was richly rewarded. He had meanwhile subscribed to Beethoven's *Missa solemnis* and organized its first complete performance, which was given in St Petersburg on 7 April 1824. A few weeks later, after the first performance of the Ninth Symphony in Vienna in May, Beethoven was finally able to begin sustained work on the Quartet in E♭ major op. 127. It became his chief preoccupation between June 1824 and

---

[1] Thayer-Forbes, p. 924.

February 1825; as the sketches show, his most concentrated work took place in the late summer and autumn of 1824. Like so many of his pieces of these years, op. 127 was to assume large dimensions and display original, even unprecedented features. It is a pivotal composition among the masterpieces of his last creative period, one in which structural and symbolic aspects from his two great choral-orchestral works are absorbed into the sphere of chamber music.

New light on the genesis of this quartet has been shed by Brandenburg, who reassessed the sketch sources first examined by Nottebohm more than a century ago.[2] Nottebohm was especially impressed by the immense quantity of sketches for the second movement—a great set of variations on a slow theme of sublime character. The overall design of the finished quartet still adheres to the traditional four-movement plan, but Brandenburg has pointed out that Beethoven considered including two additional, alternative movements—a character piece in C major entitled 'La gaieté' that was evidently planned at one point as the second movement, and a slow introduction to the finale in the key of the Neapolitan, E major. These preliminary plans show how Beethoven's attempts to shape the work as a cyclic whole were already anticipating elements akin to those of his later C♯ minor Quartet op. 131, which has seven interconnected movements.

The quartet opens with a thematic statement suggestive of a motto: a six-bar *Maestoso* segment featuring rising melodic fourths leads to a sustained trill. Only then, at the *Allegro*, does Beethoven strike a more intimate tone: *teneramente, sempre piano e dolce* (Ex. 96). This thematic juxtaposition embodies a shift from a receptive, distanced gesture in the *Maestoso* to the more direct and spontaneous character of the *Allegro*. The massive, chorale-like setting of the *Maestoso* contributes to its solemn intensity, as does the unusual rhythmic structure. Beethoven sustains the tonic throughout the first and third bars, changing the harmony only at the accented syncopated chords in bars 2 and 4. Consequently, the rhythmic structure of the two-bar groups falls into a pattern of 5 + 3 eighth-notes; the metric pulse, however, unfolds in quarter-notes. A challenge in performance is to avoid making the syncopated changes in harmony sound like downbeats, while realizing the six-bar motto as a single unified gesture. In voicing the chords it is necessary to convey the imposing linear ascent that is shared between the voices: the cello rises from E♭ to F in bar 2, whereas the next step, to G in bar 3, is given to the violins, and the following one, to A♭ in bar 4, to the cello. Each of the six bars stresses a rising step, until C, the sixth degree above the tonic, is attained and elaborated as a trill at the end of the motto.

The rhythmic pattern of short and long notes in each second bar of the

<hr/>

[2] Brandenburg, 'Die Quellen zur Entstehungsgeschichte von Beethovens Streichquartett Es-Dur Op. 127', pp. 221–76; Nottebohm, 'Skizzen zum zweiten Satz des Quartetts Op. 127', *Zweite Beethoveniana*, pp. 210–20.

Ex. 96 String Quartet op. 127/I

motto may be a subtle foreshadowing, in augmentation, of the relentless iambic rhythm of the second movement, the scherzo (Fig. 4). Beethoven adjusts this pattern in the penultimate bar of the *Maestoso* to emphasize the subdominant—the first non-tonic chord to be heard on a downbeat. The rhythmic and harmonic context of this A♭ chord enhances its impact as both culmination of the *Maestoso* and point of transition into the lyric continuation. The significance of the opening motto is far-reaching and extends well beyond its twofold return in the development. The monolithic gesture of the *Maestoso* serves not merely as introduction to the first movement but as preface to the work as a whole.

Beethoven reverses the rising linear progression of the *Maestoso* in the ensuing *Allegro*, which is based on a stepwise descent starting on C in the first

Maestoso

Scherzo

Fig. 4   Rhythmic patterns in the String Quartet op. 127

violin and A♭ in the cello, two octaves lower; this relaxes the tension of the motto. The basic character of the *Allegro* is intimate, despite the occasional eruption of vigorous passages, notably in the middle of the development. The texture is contrapuntal, above all in the first half of the development, where an impressive chain of canons probes the thematic substance from within before an agitated, *fortissimo*—and still canonic—continuation leads dramatically to the last, curtailed appearance of the *Maestoso*, in C major. Kerman described these passages as 'one of Beethoven's most extraordinary conceptions for a development section, comparable only to the first-movement development in the Quartet in B♭, op. 130'.[3]

The climactic canonic passage leading to the *Maestoso* in C major opens a dimension with symbolic implications, one that is deepened further in the following variation movement, the *Adagio, ma non troppo e molto cantabile* (see Plates 23 and 24). Before we examine this relationship in detail, however, it is important to assess the formal analogy between the slow movement of the quartet and the choral finale of the Ninth Symphony, the work Beethoven completed immediately before op. 127.

The *Adagio* movement in the quartet, in A♭ major, contains five variations on its broadly lyrical theme, with an episode in D♭ major/C♯ minor and a coda. Both of the last two variations have a recapitulatory character and follow passages in foreign keys. After the hymn-like third variation in the flat submediant, E major, the fourth variation brings a return to the tonic and the original version of the theme, which is animated rhythmically by the substitution of sixteenth-notes for eighth-notes in the melody and by trills in the accompaniment. This variation also restores the 12/8 metre of the theme, after changes in metre in the second and third variations. The recapitulatory variation is then followed by the mysterious episode in the subdominant, a passage Beethoven sketched and revised more than almost any other, entering changes even into the autograph score. A final half-variation in the tonic and a coda of the same length complete the design. The half-variation, while not strictly recapitulatory in function, remains audibly close to the original melodic shape of the theme, which is decorated in flowing sixteenth-notes in the violin, in a texture reminiscent of the second variation of the principal theme in the slow movement of the Ninth Symphony.

In the choral finale of the Ninth, as we have seen, the basic framework of ten variations on the 'Freude' theme encloses two main episodes: the double fugue for orchestra in B♭ (the flat submediant); and the slow section in G (the subdominant), set to the last two stanzas of the text, beginning 'Seid umschlungen Millionen'. Each of these passages is followed by a variation of recapitulatory character in the tonic, D major. After the orchestral fugue,

[3] *The Beethoven Quartets*, p. 206.

Variation 9 brings an emphatic return to the original melodic shape of the 'Freude' theme, heard in the full chorus and orchestra. Subsequently, after the slow section in G, a double fugue for chorus and orchestra combines the head of the 'Freude' theme with the setting of 'Seid umschlungen Millionen'. In both quartet and symphony, therefore, the penultimate variation recapitulates the theme after a contrasting section in the submediant, while the final variation again restores the tonic key and the basic thematic material after an episode in the subdominant.

The relationship between these works is by no means confined to their tonal plan, however, and bears on the actual character and thematic substance of the E major variation in the quartet, which Kerman has described as the 'spiritual crown' of the entire work.[4] Martin Cooper suggested in this regard that the rising third C♯–E at the beginning of the variation acts like a pedestal, lifting the ensuing passage above the preceding music in a manner similar to the rising third at the beginning of the slow movement of the *Hammerklavier* Sonata.[5] The image of the pedestal is especially apt in this case, in view of the aspirational character of the music. There is a parallel here with a specific passage in the choral finale of the Ninth Symphony, as well as with a related movement in the *Missa solemnis*. The corresponding passage in the symphony is the second part of the slow section in G, set to the last stanza of the text, from 'Ihr stürzt nieder' to 'Über Sternen muss er wohnen'; this is the passage that is itself so strongly reminiscent of parts of the *Missa solemnis* and which exploits a vivid contrast in register between the earthbound music of 'Ihr stürzt nieder' on the one hand and, on the other, a gradual but inevitable rise in pitch to symbolize the divine presence above the stars. The climax at the words 'Über Sternen muss er wohnen' reaches the high, mono-lithic E♭ major chord with G at the top, the same sonority that Beethoven used, with similar symbolic implications, in the Credo of the Mass.

In his chamber works Beethoven tends to employ the key of E major in music associated with the heavens, as in the slow movement of the second 'Razumovsky' quartet and the song *Abendlied unterm gestirnten Himmel*. As we have seen, he is supposed to have conceived the slow movement of the 'Razumovsky' quartet 'while contemplating the starry heavens and thinking of the music of the spheres'. In fact, as Warren Kirkendale has pointed out,[6] there is a musical kinship between that movement and the Benedictus of the *Missa solemnis*, in which the descent of the solo violin from high G sym-bolizes the arrival of the divine messenger. Yet another related piece is the *Adagio* of the op. 127 quartet. The theme of the *Adagio*, like that of the Benedictus, is characterized by iambic rhythm in 12/8 metre, and the similar-ities of the two themes extend to their melodic profiles and even to their

---

[4] *The Beethoven Quartets*, p. 216.   [5] *Beethoven: The Last Decade*, pp. 428–9.
[6] 'New Roads to Old Ideas in Beethoven's *Missa Solemnis*', pp. 690–1.

instrumentation, in view of the role of the solo violin in the Benedictus. In the light of the character and probable associations of the *Adagio* theme, then, it is not surprising that Beethoven should have included a variation evoking the contemplation of the heavens as a centrepiece, set apart by the sudden modulation to E major.

In the Ninth Symphony the rise in pitch from 'Ihr stürzt nieder' to 'Über Sternen muss er wohnen' is from the E above middle C to the G two octaves higher. This is exactly the compass of the melodic ascent in the E major variation in the quartet, regardless of the difference in key (Ex. 97). Whereas in the symphony the final part of this ascent into the highest register is abrupt and reserved for the orchestra, in the quartet the first violin gradually rises to the high G, which is the goal and endpoint of the progression. The E is still part of the pedestal that introduces the variation. From it the first violin ascends, and, as in the passage in the symphony, the melody falls earthwards momentarily before rising again. In the fifth bar of the variation (bar 63) the repetition of the first phrase in the cello substitutes G♮ for G♯, foreshadowing the turn to the flat sixth two bars later.

Ex. 97 String Quartet op. 127/II, bars 57–72

The climax itself involves an emphatic shift to a C major chord in root position with the first violin on high G in the eighth bar of the variation (bar 66). This is the moment corresponding in the symphony with the arrival on the E♭ major chord at 'Über Sternen muss er wohnen', where the same high G♮ is reached through a similar turn to the flat sixth in the larger tonal context of G minor. Since this ascending melodic progression to the climax is built directly into the structure of the variation in the quartet, it is restated, with some modification and intensification, in the second half of the variation. The treatment of high G as the goal and endpoint for each half is reminiscent of the Benedictus of the Mass, where the same pitch provides a consistent point of return for the solo violin. It is indicative of the scope of Beethoven's variation procedure in his final years that even the symbolic 'Blick nach oben' is assimilated here into the variation form.

We are now in a position to return to the first movement to reconsider the third and last appearance of the opening *Maestoso* motto, which appears in C major (bars 135–40). Beethoven sets apart this presentation of the *Maestoso* by intensifying the dynamics to *fortissimo* and by harmonic means, avoiding the turn to the subdominant that characterized its earlier appearances. As a consequence the sonority of C major is stressed three times, in a chorale-like configuration with the broadest possible spacing, in which the first violin ascends to high G for the last statement. What is striking here is the parallel with the threefold articulation of C major in Variation 3 of the ensuing *Adagio*. There are no further appearances of the motto, which has puzzled some commentators. But the significance of the *Maestoso* goes beyond its role in the first movement: like the opening motto of op. 110, it prefigures momentous events to come, pointing towards the symbolic climax of the *Adagio*, one of the weightiest and most perfectly conceived of all Beethoven's slow movements.

The following *Scherzando vivace* strikes a note of ironic detachment and grim humour after the contemplative experience of the variations. The transition from the end of the *Adagio* is reminiscent of the shift in op. 101 from the opening *Allegretto ma non troppo* to the *Vivace alla Marcia*—a movement similar in its rhythm and counterpoint to this scherzo. One is reminded as well of the scherzo of the *Hammerklavier* Sonata, and still more of that of the Ninth Symphony. After the opening pizzicato fanfare—as Kerman notes, 'there are no timpani in a string quartet!'[7]—the movement unfolds contrapuntally, even fugally. Beethoven originally sketched the principal motifs in even eighth-notes, only later introducing the jagged upbeat rhythm that permeates the scherzo sections. The fugal texture is interrupted periodically by sudden fits and starts, massive unison passages, and recitative-like gestures; a strong disruptive energy infuses the whole. The *Scherzando vivace* assumes a

---

[7] *The Beethoven Quartets*, p. 230.

crucial role in the whole quartet by bringing together forces of rhythmic tension and dramatic qualities that are largely absent from the other movements.

The trio arises out of an acceleration of the rhythm of the scherzo. This whirlwind *Presto* contains the swiftest and hardest-driven music in the quartet and exposes some of its sharpest contrasts. The shadowy opening section in E♭ minor soon yields to a loud, somewhat coarse dance parody over a heavily accented pedal in D♭ major; this juxtaposition is then repeated to lead through different keys, three times in all. The alternation could seemingly continue indefinitely, but Beethoven breaks the pattern by repeating a melodic figure from the dance parody in the first violin in the high register. The trio dissolves into silence before the scherzo re-emerges softly in the same high register. As in the Ninth Symphony Beethoven recalls the trio in curtailed form just before the end of the movement. Rhetorically, the device is handled with special subtlety: after cutting short the beginning of the *Presto*, he first restates the *pianissimo* transition to the trio and then caps the movement with an emphatic *fortissimo* cadence based on the seminal upbeat rhythm.

As we have seen, Beethoven made sketches for an introductory slow movement in E major preceding the finale. In the end, he reduced the introduction to four unison bars, which preface the principal theme and return in somewhat extended form at the beginning of the development. The crux of the gesture is the semitone G–A♭, an interval of outstanding importance. The main theme is characterized by a linear motion passing from G through A♭ to an A♮, an expressive dissonance that is resolved through the further rising step B♭–C that forms the peak of the melody. The ambiguity in Beethoven's phrasing—two occurrences of the initial triadic motif are joined to A♭, while the third statement contains the climactic A♮—lends tension to the tune. Its expressive character, however, is relaxed, even folk-like. As in the first movement, a lyrical rather than a dramatic sensibility permeates the whole.

The broad first subject-group shows a ternary design; in the quiet thematic restatement beginning in the cello the opening phrases are absorbed into a contrapuntal texture. The humorous character of the second subject-group arises from repeated detached notes, surprising accents, and massive *fortissimo* chords, accompanied by triplet figuration in the first violin. In the following transition Beethoven emphasizes motifs containing a *falling* semitone, repeatedly using the step A♭–G, the inversion of the crucial G–A♭ semitone. At this point the introductory gesture is recalled, and its unison assertion of G–A♭ marks the beginning of a concise development based on a contrapuntal combination of the two main themes.

The most remarkable formal aspect of Beethoven's finale is surely its recapitulation in the subdominant, A♭ major. Indeed, the length of this 'false' reprise—32 bars—must exceed any other in the entire Classical quartet

repertoire, as Kerman has observed.[8] Its effect, however, is completely different from the familiar device of a 'false' recapitulation. Beethoven showed a
general tendency during his last decade to reshape the traditional relationship
between development and recapitulation in his sonata forms, and his use of
non-tonic recapitulations is but one aspect of this tendency. The finale of op.
127 is not an isolated example. The first movement of the A minor Quartet op.
132, for instance, contains a recapitulation in the dominant, as does the Credo
of the *Missa solemnis*.

In op. 127, by contrast, placement of the recapitulation in the subdominant
has a softening effect, casting the theme in a new light, and the procedure
might also be heard as a vast formal expansion of the subdominant stress
within the theme itself. At the subdominant reprise the tune begins in the
highest register of the viola, above a trill in the first violin. As the theme
unfolds Beethoven introduces subtle changes and new touches in scoring. The
material of the ensuing 'true' recapitulation in the tonic is also treated in ever
new ways. The repetition of the opening phrase, for instance, is heard doubled in the second violin and viola, with motivic imitations and decorations in
the first violin in an ethereal high register. The second subject-group, on the
other hand, is transposed in virtually unchanged form to the tonic.

What follows is one of Beethoven's most magical codas. This *Allegro com-
modo* in 6/8 time is reached through a transformation of the repeated notes
from the end of the recapitulation, which coalesce into trills. Transformed as
well is the main theme itself: stripped of the repetition of its first bar and
broadened in rhythmic contour, it becomes less droll and more expressive,
even coyish. It is now enhanced by an accompanying texture of triplet
sixteenth-notes (Ex. 98). Remarkable is the series of key changes through
falling major thirds, from C major to A♭ major to E major. The harmonic
energy for these modulations comes from the semitone motif in the theme.
Indeed, the entire series results directly from Beethoven's development of
these rising semitones (the last group is extended to effect the return of the
tonic, E♭ major):

C major:	F–F♯–G–A♭
A♭ major:	D♭–D♮–E♭–E♮
E major:	A–B♭–B–C–D♭–D♮–E♭

The keys of these modulations are of much importance in the work as a
whole. C major and E major were, of course, the keys of the additional movements that Beethoven sketched, and they are prominent in the finished quartet as well. One recalls the C major *Maestoso* in the first movement, the A♭
Adagio with its memorable central variation in E major, and the enormous A♭

---

[8] *The Beethoven Quartets*, pp. 236–7.

Ex. 98 String Quartet op. 127/IV

recapitulation in the finale. But entirely apart from their relationship with earlier movements, these tonal excursions through the circle of major thirds represent new and extraordinary aesthetic ramifications that derive strictly from the thematic structure. This is one of those passages in late Beethoven in which we can *hear* structure as we can in the work of no other composer.

In the remainder of the coda Beethoven sounds echoes of the rising semitone, accompanied by the pulsating triplet sixteenth motion. He had employed a similar suspended texture over pedal points in some of his last piano works, such as the Arietta movement of op. 111 and the coda of the Diabelli Variations. In no other quartet, however, had he achieved this kind of closing transfiguration of the basic thematic substance. By contrast, the brilliant, exhilarating coda in the major mode of the finale in the *Quartetto serioso* in F minor op. 95 is problematic, since it blithely ignores the dramatic tensions of the work up to that point.

The coda of the finale in op. 127 is most deeply grounded in the musical structure precisely when it appears most visionary and fantastic. There is no contradiction here between imagination and reason, but an irreducible synthesis of feeling and thought. Out of this tensional balance between expression and structure arises a spirit of high comedy that is neither Haydnesque nor Mozartian but close to a blend of both. In the closing moments of the quartet finale Beethoven conveys this quality of refined gaiety above all through his treatment of the mischievous, unsettling A♮. The thematic outline is distilled one last time, as the music reaches A♭ in the cello, and A♮ in the first violin, before the rising semitone to B♭ sets the stage for the emphatic final cadence.

Op. 127 was one of the last compositions whose performance Beethoven witnessed, and its early performance history is of special interest. The first hearing, led by Schuppanzigh on 6 March 1825, was not satisfactory, producing only a 'weak *succès d'estime*', in the words of the violinist Joseph Böhm, the leader of the quartet concerts in Vienna during Schuppanzigh's long absence from the city. Böhm reported:

When Beethoven learned of this—for he was not present at the performance—he became furious and let both performers and the public in for some harsh words. Beethoven could have no peace until the disgrace was wiped off. He sent for me first thing in the morning—In his usual curt way, he said to me. 'You must play my quartet'—and the thing was settled.—Neither objections nor doubts could prevail; what Beethoven wanted had to take place, so I undertook the difficult task.—It was studied industriously and rehearsed frequently under Beethoven's own eyes: I said Beethoven's *eyes* intentionally, for the unhappy man was so deaf that he could no longer hear the heavenly sound of his compositions. And yet rehearsing in his presence was not easy. With close attention his eyes followed the bows and therefore he was able to judge the smallest fluctuations in tempo or rhythm and correct them immediately. At the close of the last movement of this quartet there occurred a *meno vivace*, which seemed to me to weaken the general effect. At the rehearsal, therefore, I advised that the original tempo be maintained, which was done, to the betterment of the effect.

Beethoven, crouched in a corner, heard nothing, but watched with strained attention. After the last stroke of the bows he said, laconically, 'Let it remain so', went to the desks and crossed out the *meno vivace* in the four parts.[9]

Böhm performed the quartet several times subsequently, with notable success. His own report about the initial performance by Schuppanzigh was reaffirmed in an article on 28 April in Bäuerle's *Theaterzeitung*, which included the following words of praise for Böhm's interpretation:

. . . then a steadfast patron of art and noble connoisseur brought about a new performance of this quartet by the above named man [Schuppanzigh] with the substitution for first violin of Herr Prof. Böhm, since this group in the meantime had played the new quartet for a small group of art lovers with particular success. This professor now performed the wonderful quartet, twice over on the same evening, for the same very numerous company of artists and connoisseurs in a way that left nothing to be desired, the misty veil disappeared and the splendid work of art radiated its dazzling glory.[10]

*   *   *

This was but the first of several successful performances of the 'Galitzin' quartets during Beethoven's final years. These works did not come into existence as wholly isolated endeavours of the solitary deaf composer but were heard by

[9] Thayer-Forbes, pp. 940–1.   [10] Ibid., p. 941.

small yet devoted audiences. The broader public interest in such challenging music was severely limited, and few performances of the last quartets followed during the next decades. As with the *Hammerklavier* Sonata and the Diabelli Variations, appreciation and critical recognition of the quartets has grown through a long and gradual process.

The second quartet, in A minor, occupied Beethoven until July 1825; it was eventually published with the deceptively high opus number 132. This work has often been regarded as forming a 'triptych' together with the two quartets that followed it, op. 130 in B♭ major and op. 131 in C♯ minor. Paul Bekker advanced this notion in 1912, arguing that the three middle quartets differ strikingly from the preceding work in E♭ and the final Quartet in F major op. 135.[11] The justification for such a grouping rests not in the increasing number of movements in each quartet (five in op. 132, six in op. 130, seven in op. 131) but rather in their motivic structure: for each prominently displays intervallic relationships highlighting the semitones from the leading-note to the tonic and from the lowered sixth degree to the dominant. This configuration is heard in the cello at the outset of op. 132, and variants of these intervals appear in the fugue subject that begins op. 131 and in the *Grosse Fuge*, the original finale of op. 130.

Deryck Cooke traced such patterns in all five of the last quartets, but he tended to overemphasize the 'unifying' role of these relationships in pieces in which sharp individuality of character is the most prominent feature.[12] Curiously, Beethoven's engagement with this intervallic pattern in his sketches surfaces in entries for the slow introduction to a projected piano sonata for four hands that he never completed; the motivic material and sequential pattern, transposed from C minor to E♭ major, found its way into the scherzo of op. 127 (Ex. 99*a* and *b*). This sketch, from about August 1824, reveals that the basic intervallic configuration so prominent in the last quartets arose during Beethoven's reflection on another project altogether, in a different key. The *topos* in question stems from the Baroque, and it was familiar to Beethoven in part from some of Mozart's C minor works, such as the Fugue for two pianos that Beethoven had copied out in score many years earlier.

Most important is, of course, the aesthetic context within which such patterns take on a distinctive expressive meaning. The A minor Quartet is a work laden with pathos of a particularly painful, agonized quality, and the semitone F–E assumes special significance in this respect. Profound contrasts are exposed at the outset, in the juxtaposition of a remotely objective, contrapuntal elaboration of a cantus firmus motif in long note values (*assai sostenuto*) with an impassioned violin arpeggio that prolongs the dissonant note F in an

---

[11] *Beethoven*, pp. 532–4.
[12] 'The Unity of Beethoven's Late Quartets', pp. 30–49.

Ex. 99 (*a*) Autograph 11/2, fol. 5ᵛ

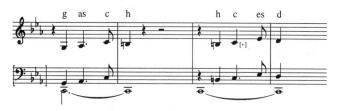

(*b*) String Quartet op. 127/III, bars 2–4

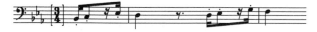

unstable, piercing gesture (*allegro*). The conflict revealed here casts a shadow not only over the first movement but over the quartet as a whole; and a later transformation of the violin arpeggio that prolongs the F forms the end of the recitative prefacing the fifth and final movement, marked *Allegro appassionato*. This recitative brings to mind the one that introduces the choral finale of the Ninth Symphony. As we have seen, the two works were indeed related in Beethoven's compositional process: as Nottebohm first pointed out, the main theme of the finale of op. 132 was originally conceived as part of a contemplated instrumental finale to the Ninth, comprising material that Beethoven rejected once he had settled on a choral finale for the symphony but later used in the quartet.

At the centre of the quartet, flanked by shorter dance movements in A major in second and fourth position, is the great slow movement, the 'Heiliger Dankgesang eines Genesenen an die Gottheit, in der lydischen Tonart' ('Holy Song of Thanks to the Godhead from a Convalescent, in the Lydian Mode'—i.e. in F, but without B♭). The programmatic title relates to Beethoven's own recovery from illness in April 1825. In its form this movement resembles the slow movement of the Ninth Symphony, with three appearances of the principal theme, treated in variation and alternating with a subsidiary theme in another key. The thematic contrast in the 'Heiliger Dankgesang' movement is more far-reaching than in the symphony, however, and pits a strictly modal hymn setting evoking a mystic, archaic aura against a vigorous, dance-like *Andante* in D major, which luxuriates in elaborate textures and decorative trills. Beethoven marked the *Andante* 'Neue Kraft fühlend' ('feeling new strength'); it seems to represent a vision of new strength that, as Kerman points out, 'has not been attained, and which perhaps never will be attained'.[13]

---

[13] *The Beethoven Quartets*, p. 254.

We have observed other instances of Beethoven's juxtaposing modal and tonal passages, notably in the Incarnatus of the Credo in the *Missa solemnis*, while the *Adagio con molto sentimento d'affetto* of the Cello Sonata op. 102 no. 2 more closely foreshadows the 'Heiliger Dankgesang'. But no other slow movement in Beethoven exploits such radical contrasts as this. One thinks in this connection of the pairing of *Arioso dolente* and lyrical fugue in op. 110, a work similarly associated with a recovery from serious illness. Instead of evoking Baroque models, as in op. 110, in the quartet Beethoven captures an even more remote or timeless ethos, yet the impulse is not antiquarian but modernistic; older models are sought in order to be tested and strained to their limits.

The initial presentation of the lydian chorale is austere and unearthly, but each return brings a deepening in sensibility. At the first recall the contrapuntal phrases that previously served only as interludes are merged with the hymn as a continuous, flowing accompaniment. Then, at its final appearance a new synthesis is achieved, forging the climax of the slow movement and of the entire quartet: Beethoven selects only the first phrase of the chorale melody, combining its pitches with the faster note values of the original interlude, which has now become a fugal countersubject. The enhanced subjectivity of the music is reflected in Beethoven's indication 'mit innigster Empfindung'. At the powerful stretto climax a vast gap in register opens between the instruments, and the countersubject briefly disappears as the hymn is asserted with astonishing intensity (Ex. 100). The atmosphere of rapt contemplation is sustained in the following passage, leading to the hushed conclusion of the movement on F, the lydian cadence that had been withheld from the earlier sections based on the modal hymn.

In its role as symbolic culmination of the entire work, this passage is comparable to the sublime E major variation at the heart of the *Adagio* of op. 127. The overall design of the A minor Quartet is largely symmetrical, with the finale returning to elements that were conspicuous in the opening movement, such as the emphasis on the semitone F–E. That motivic step is dramatized with operatic rhetoric in the recitative that prefaces the finale, and Beethoven underscores the narrative gesture by deriving the rhythmic ostinato figure on F–E in the ensuing rondo theme from the last notes of the recitative. Motivic echoes of this recitative are heard throughout the closing *Allegro appassionato*, reminding us that in the quartet Beethoven has inverted the function of the recitative in the Ninth: instead of opening up utopian possibilities, this recitative forces a renewed confrontation with the music of pathos that was ignored in the fourth movement, the *Alla marcia, assai vivace*.

It is fascinating that Beethoven originally intended to use the *Alla danza tedesca* of the next quartet, op. 130 in B♭, as the fourth movement of op. 132. As Brandenburg has shown, the *Alla danza tedesca* was removed from op. 132

Ex. 100 String Quartet op. 132/III, bars 179–95

only at the autograph stage; Beethoven transposed it from A major to G major before incorporating it into op. 130.[14] The complex expressive character of this piece, which J. W. N. Sullivan described as 'gay melancholy',[15] may have seemed inappropriate to Beethoven in a context following the 'Heiliger Dankgesang'; the *Alla marcia* offers a sharper contrast—a brief return to innocence or to the commonplace. The removal and re-use of the *Alla danza tedesca* is comparable with Beethoven's replacement of the finale of the Violin Sonata op. 30 no. 1, or the slow movement of the *Waldstein* Sonata, but it is quite different from the substitution of the original finale of the B♭ Quartet— the *Grosse Fuge*—as we shall see.

In the finale of the A minor Quartet Beethoven employs the rondo form for the last time in his career, apart from the substitute finale of the B♭ Quartet op. 130. The dominating role of the principal theme contributes to the character of sombre, impassioned obsession. As in the *Quartetto serioso* op. 95, the finale of op. 132 contains a coda in the major mode, but the conclusion is now far more integrated with the work as a whole than it was in the earlier quartet. The sound-texture of this *Presto* conclusion recalls the trio of the second

[14] 'The Autograph of Beethoven's Quartet in A minor, Opus 132', pp. 278–300.
[15] *Beethoven: His Spiritual Development*, p. 151.

movement, while its stress on F♮ in the cadential phrase recalls not only the ostinato accompaniment of the main theme of the finale but the expressive poignancy of this note in the first movement. The inflections of pain in the opening *Assai sostenuto* are not entirely forgotten, and even the prominent tonal stress on F throughout the quartet—from the second subject of the first movement to the lydian 'Dankgesang'—resonates faintly in this telling melodic detail.

In its character, the most difficult movement to grasp is the opening one, on account of its frequent changes in tempo and texture. So rich in contrast is this movement that Beethoven can treat the second half of the development as a recapitulation in the dominant preceding the 'true' recapitulation, a procedure that somewhat simplifies the formal design. As in some other works of these years, the dissociated character of the first movement is connected with its role in prefiguring the work as a whole: the initial *Assai sostenuto*, with its imitations of the cantus firmus in half-notes, foreshadows something of the rhythm and texture of the 'Heiliger Dankgesang'. The ensuing disruptive violin gesture in the *Allegro* has a somewhat parenthetical effect; it collapses onto the pitches F–E drawn from the *Assai sostenuto* and sustains the E, allowing us to hear this long note as a direct continuation from the solemn initial music. Time and again the drastic contrasts of this music harbour deeper unifying relationships.

The first movement of the following Quartet in B♭ major op. 130 carries the potential of such binary oppositions into the realm of paradox. We have discussed paradoxical features in earlier comic movements, such as the scherzo of op. 2 no. 3 and the scherzando of op. 59 no. 1; in op. 130, by contrast, Beethoven's ironic wit engages an expressive environment shaped not by comic rhetoric but by strong contrasts in tempo and character—a general procedure that first surfaces in the quartets in 'La Malinconia' of op. 18 no. 6. The term 'paradox' derives from the Greek *paradoxon*, meaning 'unbelievable' or 'beyond what is thought'; its Latin equivalent, *paradoxia*, denotes 'an apparent contradiction'.[16] Whereas in op. 132 the contrasts are clearly subordinated to the overall expressive character, in op. 130 they seem to be pursued for their own sake to create a condition of paradox. The themes may in themselves seem tame, even somewhat bland; but Beethoven's treatment of them is anything but predictable. The interplay of the opening *Adagio ma non troppo* in 3/4 metre and the following *Allegro* in 4/4 defies conventional expectations. The *Adagio* is no mere slow introduction; the ensuing *Allegro* is broken off after only five bars, bringing a return of the music in the slower tempo. Only then does the *Allegro* establish itself as the basic tempo of the remainder of the

---

[16] For a detailed discussion of these issues, see Imeson, *'The time gives it proofe': Paradox in the Late Music of Beethoven.*

exposition. The apparent incompatibility of these themes lies at the heart of the movement, and forms its central compositional idea.

Particularly impressive here is Beethoven's manipulation of temporality through the use of parenthetical structures. Kerman has commented, for instance, on the almost parodistic effect of the lyrical second subject in G♭ in the exposition, and on the over-deliberate, even mechanistic chromatic ascent leading up to it.[17] Beethoven places this theme on a pedestal, but instead of elevating it into the sublime he treats it as a subject of ironic enquiry. The artificial, even naked approach to its key prepares for the abrupt dissipation of the theme after only two phrases. In turn, the long note values of this lyrical subject and the rapid sixteenth-note motifs of the continuation correspond to the two contrasting tempos exposed at the beginning of the movement.

Even more extraordinary is the development. Beethoven had experimented with static music in some earlier development sections, notably the first movement of op. 110, but the 28-bar passage that precedes the recapitulation of this movement is quite unprecedented. At the outset of the development he repeatedly juxtaposes short fragments of the music in the two contrasting tempos. The continuation then brings an uncanny motivic dialogue played against an ostinato in the middle voices that is derived from an appoggiatura figure in the *Adagio* (Ex. 101). This dialogue highlights both the head-motif from the *Allegro*, with its rising fourth, and a variant of the lyrical second subject, with its initial ascending interval now widened to an octave and the continuation compressed into eighth-notes instead of quarters. These motifs communicate in a weirdly inconsistent fashion, reserving the right to disappear at will into the ostinato background. The lyrical octave ascent in the cello in the third bar of the *Allegro* seems to influence the rising head-motif in the first violin three bars later, where the fourth is expanded to an octave. Just after the change in key signature to G major the corresponding bass entry is blended into the ostinato figure. Curiously, the direction of resolution of these motifs into the ostinato background can initiate an inversion in the direction of the prevailing appoggiatura figure: the F♯–G ostinato of bars 11–12 thus becomes G–F♯ three bars later. Such relationships heighten the effect of temporal stasis—the trance-like suspension characteristic of this remarkable episode—which reveals one possible synthesis of apparently incompatible themes.

Beethoven reserves his supreme exercise in paradox for the coda. After recalling the beginning of the *Adagio ma non troppo* in slightly varied form, he dovetails the *Allegro* and *Adagio* phrases into one another to form a new continuity (Ex. 102). The chromatic ascent that originates in the *Adagio* as A–B♭ rises to B–C and C♯–D in the following *Adagio* excerpts, before finding a

17 *The Beethoven Quartets*, pp. 308–9.

Ex. 101 String Quartet op. 130/I, Development, bars 104–27

further continuation in the *Allegro* tempo of the cadential passage. These interdependent *Adagio* and *Allegro* sections which make up the coda are held in perfect balance, and Beethoven's manipulation of the music in contrasting tempos creates a mutually interlocking parenthetical structure. The excerpts interrupt one another, and are themselves interrupted. It becomes difficult, if not impossible, to say what is actually 'parenthetical' under such circumstances. The apparent contradiction is transcended (*aufgehoben*) in the achievement of the composite theme.

This most radically dissociated movement introduces Beethoven's most controversial single work: the original, or 'Galitzin', version of the B♭ Quartet with the *Grosse Fuge* ('Great Fugue') as finale. The *Grosse Fuge* is the largest and most difficult of all Beethoven's quartet movements, dubbed 'das

Ex. 102 String Quartet op. 130/I, coda, bars 214–end

Monstrum aller Quartett-Musik' in Schindler's derogatory formulation. As is well known, Beethoven eventually decided at the urgings of Karl Holz and the publisher Matthias Artaria to write a substitute finale for this quartet, separating the *Grosse Fuge* for publication as op. 133. Consequently, the B♭ Quartet has usually been performed without the *Grosse Fuge*, and debate about the virtues of the two finales has continued to this day without any clear resolution. In 1963 Warren Kirkendale argued for an interpretation of the *Grosse Fuge* as Beethoven's 'Art of the Fugue', as a compendium of fugal devices presumably inspired in part by one of Beethoven's teachers from his early Vienna years, Johann Georg Albrechtsberger.[18] In accordance with this view, Kirkendale found it entirely fitting to regard the *Grosse Fuge* as a work in its own right, divorced from the quartet. Other writers have found Kirkendale's argument overstated and have stressed the character of the *Grosse Fuge* as a finale, as well as pointing to the many motivic and textural threads that connect it with the earlier movements.

In his book *Beethoven and the Creative Process* Barry Cooper has concluded on the basis of sketch sources that since the *Grosse Fuge* can

be seen as something of an intrusion into the quartet, rather than the germ from which the work sprang, Beethoven's decision to replace it with a different movement, more in line with the others and with the finale he had intended while writing them, must seem entirely justified.[19]

Curiously, neither Cooper nor Nicholas Marston—in a recent analysis of 'interpretative process' in Beethoven sketch studies[20]—has taken proper account of the probing study of the *Grosse Fuge* and the genesis of the B♭ Quartet by Klaus Kropfinger.[21] Kropfinger points out that Beethoven regarded the first movement of the evolving quartet as an 'arduous introduction' (*schwergängige Einleitung*), and he indicates how the fugue came to serve as culmination to the diverse succession of movements. The principal fugue subject was actually sketched earlier, during Beethoven's labours on op. 132.

Kropfinger also addresses the complex biographical context surrounding Beethoven's replacement of the finale, a situation entirely different from the straightforward removal of the *Andante favori* from the *Waldstein* Sonata, for instance. The B♭ Quartet was actually first published with the *Grosse Fuge* as finale, before the substitute finale was composed. Karl Holz wrote to Beethoven in a conversation book of September 1826: 'You could easily have made two [quartets] from the B♭ Quartet';[22] and there is evidence that the piano arrangement of the *Grosse Fuge* that Beethoven made was originally intended to have formed part of a transcription of the entire quartet. In short, Beethoven's composition of the substitute rondo finale cannot be equated with a renunciation of the quartet in its original, 'Galitzin' version, with the *Grosse Fuge* as finale. Beethoven's fondness for the B♭ Quartet in its original

[18] 'The "Great Fugue" Op. 133: Beethoven's "Art of the Fugue" ', pp. 14–24.
[19] p. 214.   [20] 'Beethoven's Sketches and the Interpretative Process'.
[21] 'Das gespaltene Werk—Beethovens Streichquartett Op. 130/133'.
[22] *Ludwig van Beethovens Konversationshefte*, x, p. 185.

form is documented in the conversation books of early 1826, where it is referred to as his 'Leibquartett' ('favourite quartet').

Various reasons have been proposed to explain Beethoven's willingness to provide a new finale: they include the extra fee; his recognition of the difficulties experienced by the players and listeners (in spite of his comment 'Cattle! Asses!', when he heard the fugue had not been well received); his depressed and possibly conciliatory state of mind by the autumn of 1826, when the substitute finale was written; and even the changing aesthetic perspective brought about by his experience in composing the last two quartets, opp. 131 and 135. No one of these explanations seems compelling in itself; a proper assessment of the issue must rest primarily on aesthetic grounds, on our analysis of the music. Still, it is worth noting that Beethoven once before had authorized puzzling changes in a piece that culminates similarly in an astonishing and extremely difficult fugue—the *Hammerklavier* Sonata. In a letter to Ries of 1819 Beethoven suggested that, 'should the sonata not be suitable for London', it might be published without the *Largo*, or without the fugue but with the scherzo as finale, or even that the first movement and scherzo might form the entire sonata.[23] This patently destructive attitude towards the sonata can be at least partly explained as a willingness to allow arrangement for additional profit of a work that was being properly printed in Vienna. The motive of arrangement for additional profit would seem to apply as well to the case of the third 'Galitzin' Quartet.

One problem with Cooper's evaluation of the genesis of op. 130 is his tendency to identify selected preliminary sketches with the composer's 'intention' without taking sufficient account of the larger aesthetic context. Beethoven's sketches often represent the barest shorthand for very much more; one challenge in interpreting them is to conjure something of this missing context, and not to take them merely at face value, which risks conveying a misleading impression of their function and content. Cooper's 'completion' of the first movement of Beethoven's Tenth Symphony displays some shortcomings of his approach: the outcome might more accurately be described as an elaboration by the editor on motifs from Beethoven's sketchbooks than as Beethoven's 'symphony', since too little material survives to permit a proper realization.

By identifying Beethoven's 'intention' in op. 130 with unrealized finale sketches that are 'not unlike the substitute finale', Cooper comes to regard the *Grosse Fuge* as 'something of an intrusion into the quartet', but this reasoning fails to take sufficient account of the provisionary nature of the sketches and the evolving nature of intention as commitment to an artistic process. For another example, let us consider Beethoven's sketches for the Arietta theme

[23] Anderson, ii, L. 939.

in the final movement of his sonata op. III. Many of these sketches contain dance-like entries in 3/8 time akin to the world of Diabelli's waltz; the slow, chorale-like setting of the Arietta theme surfaces only in advanced sketches.[24] Would it then be correct to speak of the Arietta theme as representing 'something of an intrusion into the sonata'? On the contrary, the work of art we know as op. III first came into existence only after very extensive sketching by Beethoven. The existence of sketches does not guarantee *ipso facto* the existence of the work.

The aesthetic problems raised by the 'Galitzin' version of the B♭ Quartet have been reassessed recently by Richard Kramer, who looks beyond the analysis of thematic relationships to address the narrative implications of Beethoven's pairing of the Cavatina and the *Grosse Fuge*. For all its radical features, the B♭ Quartet bears comparison with a number of other compositions from Beethoven's later years. A sequence of shorter inner movements—two dance movements surrounding the exquisite *Andante con moto*—leads up to the Cavatina in penultimate position. Then, in direct juxtaposition to the heartfelt, lyrical, even operatic expression of the Cavatina, the transition to the finale annihilates this frame of reference. As Kramer points out, the moment of narrative intervention is the octave G that begins the 'Ouverture' to the fugue, a note that does not yet belong to the preview of themes to follow (Ex. 103): 'Wrenched from the pathos of the Cavatina, its graceless grace notes wrest the two middle-register Gs from that famous simultaneity with which the Cavatina expires and inflate them to an expanse of four octaves'.[25] As in the Ninth Symphony or the *Hammerklavier* Sonata, we encounter here a turning-point in the work as a whole, a moment of crucial narrative significance.

According to Holz, Beethoven said that the mere thought of the Cavatina brought him to tears; the ensuing 'Ouverture' seems to reject such sentiment in a way somewhat reminiscent of Czerny's report, many years earlier, about Beethoven's mocking laughter in response to the listeners who wept at his improvisations. An analogous moment is perhaps the passage from the 20th to the 21st variation—from the *Andante* to the *Allegro con brio*—in the Diabelli Variations, where an inward sanctuary of reflection is rudely flooded by the glaring light of ordinary reality. The transition to the *Grosse Fuge* lacks the parodistic dimension of the Diabelli Variations, but it dispels the preceding lyrical music with equal vehemence.

The parade of fugal themes in the 'Ouverture' anticipates the main sections of the great finale in reverse order. As Kramer points out, this sequence proceeds from the clearest thematic statement to the most obscure—the gapped

---

[24] The sketches for the Arietta movement are discussed and transcribed by William Drabkin in 'A Study of Beethoven's opus III and its Sources'.
[25] 'Between Cavatina and Ouverture', p. 178.

Ex. 103 (a) String Quartet op. 130/V, bars 61–end

(b) Grosse Fuge op. 133

form of the subject that serves as countersubject in the huge opening section in B♭. Conversely, the main sections of the fugue unfold with a sense of progress from the obscure to the coherent; the most basic form of the subject is withheld until the final passages. The most emphatic assertion of this principal fugue subject in the tonic B♭ occurs only in the closing section marked *Allegro molto e con brio*, where it is prefaced by brief reminiscences of two of the other main sections (now recalled in the proper order). In the *Grosse Fuge* Beethoven combines smaller movements into a composite form using variation technique, while employing unusually elaborate rhetorical devices of premonition and reminiscence. In these respects the quartet finale bears comparison to the choral finale of the Ninth Symphony.

Various thematic, harmonic, and structural relationships link the *Grosse Fuge* to the earlier movements of op. 130, but these do little to negate the impression of powerful, even bewildering contrasts. As with some of Beethoven's comic pieces, the integrity of this quartet resides in a tension between eccentricity and normality. The music shows us that more lurks behind the surface of things than might appear. Near the end of the fourth movement, the *Alla danza tedesca*, for instance, Beethoven juggles the measures of the dance in a free retrograde pattern, delightfully subverting our expectations. In the first movement, the most balanced, integrated, and hence 'normal' thematic presentation proves to be the coda—paradoxically, the passage that shifts gears most of all. In this context the *Grosse Fuge* provides a much more compelling culmination than the substitute rondo finale. The rondo, with its milder manners and Haydnesque character, sounds anticlimactic after the extraordinary chain of movements leading up to the Cavatina, whereas the fugue opens new territory, heightening the character of unpredictability that had invested the quartet from the outset, while broadening its expressive range to the utmost. As Kramer writes, the *Grosse Fuge* both reconciles and renounces 'all those disparate musics in op. 130'.[26]

Beethoven's severing of the *Grosse Fuge* from op. 130 raises fundamental questions about the role of the finale in his late style. Solomon compares the removal of the quartet fugue to Beethoven's concern, as reported by Czerny, that to close the Ninth Symphony with a choral finale was a mistake. A principle of 'alternative narrativity' may be at work here. In the choral finale or the *Grosse Fuge*, though not in the substitute finale, the modalities of earlier movements seem to be superseded and annulled; an organic relationship is thereby overstepped. Yet, as Solomon writes about the Ninth Symphony, 'The earlier movements are not wholly rejected; they are found insufficient to stand unsupported against evil'.[27] Beethoven's doubts about his most radical finales may have been connected to the ultimately unfulfilled nature of their depiction of the sublime, whose tensional structure harbours an ethical core.

[26] 'Between Cavatina and Ouverture', p. 188.
[27] 'Beethoven's Ninth Symphony: the Sense of an Ending', p. 151.

The Last Phase

1826–1827

W ITH the completion of the B♭ Quartet in November 1825 Beethoven at last fulfilled Galitzin's commission. As so often, his artistic response followed his own laws, quite apart from Galitzin's request for three quartets. For near the end of the year he began to sketch yet another quartet: this was the work in C♯ minor op. 131, which he reportedly considered his greatest, because 'there is less lack of fantasy than ever before'. Beethoven laboured on the C♯ minor Quartet until July 1826. It was followed by only two pieces: the final Quartet in F major op. 135 and the substitute rondo finale of the B♭ Quartet op. 130, both completed at Gneixendorf during the autumn of 1826.

The Quartet in C♯ minor is perhaps the most fully realized of all Beethoven's intrinsically musical narrative designs. In op. 131 he merges tendencies from some of his earlier works to forge a unique seven-movement sequence without any breaks between movements. The large-scale rhythmic continuity is only one aspect of the integrated network of relationships that holds together these seven movements, which are explicitly numbered in the score. In approaching this quartet it is helpful to recall some of the compositional strategies from Beethoven's earlier pieces that have been brought into play.

As early as the fantasy sonatas op. 27 Beethoven had shifted the overall dramatic weight from the first to the last movements of the sonata cycle, and in the E♭ Sonata he had recalled the slow movement in the finale. His later compositional style tends to explore further this reversal of the classic aesthetic sequence, in part through his resourceful use of anticipation, quotation, recitative, and other rhetorical devices. In both the C major Cello Sonata and

A major Piano Sonata op. 101, as we have seen, the lyrical opening movement is recalled at the threshold of the finale. In the *Hammerklavier* Sonata and Ninth Symphony a series of musical possibilities is glimpsed or reviewed before the discovery of the finale. Such directional tendencies also surface in the last sonatas, as well as in the original version of the B♭ Quartet, with the *Grosse Fuge* as finale.

In several pieces, including the D major Cello Sonata, the *Hammerklavier* Sonata, the A♭ Sonata op. 110, the Gloria and Credo of the *Missa solemnis*, and of course the B♭ Quartet, fugue is treated as the culmination of an extended cyclic form rich in contrast. The fugal subjects often display a unified structure elaborating a single crucial interval. In the Gloria and in op. 110 these themes are based on a series of ascending fourths; the Credo fugue subject elaborates a chain of descending thirds, a framework that also lurks beneath the surface of the fugal subject in the *Hammerklavier* Sonata.

In the C♯ minor Quartet, by contrast, Beethoven inverts the position of the fugue, treating it as the point of departure instead of the outcome of the work. The fugue subject in op. 131 is more dissonant and harmonically ambiguous than the subjects of his fugal finales, including even the *Grosse Fuge*, a fact only partly explained by its being in the minor mode. An extraordinary feature of this fugue subject is the way Beethoven has adapted the basic trope recorded in his early C minor sketch for the four-hand sonata: the motivic figure outlining 5–♭6–1–7 (G–A♭–C–B). In op. 131 he arranges these steps so as to emphasize the drooping flat sixth degree, A in C♯ minor: 5–7–1–♭6 (G♯–B♯–C♯–A) (Ex. 104). A is heard as crux of the theme, partly on account of its strong rhythmic position and accent, which are underscored as well by the crescendo; the second half of the phrase responds to the primacy of this sensitive pitch by gently decorating the downward resolution of the A to G♯.

This dissonance contributes to the atmosphere of bleak melancholy at the outset of the fugue, and to the expressive tension throughout. But most impressive are the far-reaching consequences that the initial gesture and its fugal development hold for the quartet as a whole. Beethoven infuses a profound instability into his fugue subject, and follows up the implications with

Ex. 104 String Quartet op. 131/I

sure instinct. Because of the stress on A♮ and the positioning of the turn-figure in bar 3 on F♯, the subject displays a strong drift to the subdominant; it is poised, as Kerman notes, half in the subdominant, half in the tonic.[1] Beethoven sustains this tension by placing the fugal answer in the subdominant, so that its sensitive accented pitch becomes D, the Neapolitan degree a semitone above the tonic C♯. In the closing moments of the fugue this semitone D–C♯ is emphasized in the most striking manner, with a subdominant entry in the cello answered in stretto in the first violin, which then returns to the crucial D in the following bar for added emphasis (Ex. 105).

Why does Beethoven single out these pitches, even deleting the turn-figure from the original subject in order to further highlight the Neapolitan degree, D? An answer to this question is supplied moments later, as he first distils the content of the music to a soft, *pianissimo* octave on C♯, before shifting the octave motif up a semitone to D to initiate the second movement, the gentle *Allegro molto vivace*. The music carries its own continuity within itself; the expressive tension within the fugue implies a further musical continuity that lies paradoxically beyond its confines, one that is to inhabit the tonality so clearly prepared by the opening movement: D major.

This is an unusually resourceful example of Beethoven's practice in some earlier intermovement transitions of anticipating the music to come. Several of the closest parallels are found in the piano sonatas. In the *Waldstein*, for example, the high G that forms the melodic peak of the rondo theme has already been sounded at the very end of the slow *Introduzione* and serves as a harmonic and melodic pivot between the two movements. Structurally, an even closer comparison can be made in the *Hammerklavier* Sonata, with the B major modulation in the development of the first movement; here the preceding series of harmonic descending thirds is followed by a modulation to the key a third below, as the energy generated by the chain of falling thirds is transferred to the level of the *tonal* plan. In op. 131 there is an analogous pivotal shift from harmonic to tonal structure in service of the first transition between movements; yet much more is at work here than an application of the structural intensity forged in the *Hammerklavier* Sonata to the problem of a transition between movements. A more revealing analogy is offered by the first movement of the A♭ Sonata op. 110, which shows some surprising latent similarities to op. 131. That comparison, in turn, offers a context in which to survey the broader significance of the narrative designs in many of Beethoven's compositions.

An analysis of the final six bars of the first movement of op. 110 entails consideration of threads of connection that reach across the entire work. The passage is at once a reminiscence and a foreshadowing (Ex. 106). The motif in

---

[1] *The Beethoven Quartets*, p. 296.

Ex. 105 String Quartet op. 131/I–II

Ex. 106 Piano Sonata op. 110/I, bars 110–end

thirds in the left hand five bars from the end, for instance, recalls a passage
near the beginning of the recapitulation. At the cadence Beethoven retains
the original polyphonic texture, register, and upper melodic outline of the
motto from the very beginning of the sonata—now reduced to the rising and
falling semitones C–Db and Db–C—while simultaneously preparing the
sonority and spacing that is to begin the *Allegro molto*, namely the third C–Ab,
which is about to be reharmonized in F minor in the ensuing scherzo-like
movement. At the same time, the penultimate dissonant diminished-seventh
chord containing Fb (bar 115) foreshadows the climactic dissonant sonority
that will be resolved into the closing Ab chord at the very end of the concluding fugue.

But we have not yet considered the aspect of Beethoven's coda that points
most provocatively towards what is to come. In the alto voice, three bars from
the close, he prefigures the fugue subject on the dominant, with the succession of ascending fourths—Eb–Ab and F–Bb—broken off at the dissonant Fb
of the penultimate chord. The rhythmic configuration of this foreshadowing,
with the first note augmented, corresponds to the *fortissimo* bass entry beginning on the dominant of C minor in the middle of the first fugue, where the
pattern is written in longer note values. This incomplete presentation of the
fugal subject is in keeping with the general character of the first movement—
suggestive of expectation or unfulfilled yearning. But such verbal formulations
are not in themselves precise enough to do justice to the music. Beethoven's
anticipation of the fugue is not confined to a single passage in it, and therein
lies much of the special poetic power of his coda. This foreshadowing relates
specifically, though not literally, to the C minor passage in the fugue; at the
same time, the dissonant breaking-off of the thematic allusion is connected to
the final cadence of the entire work.

In one concentrated gesture, therefore, Beethoven recalls two earlier passages of the first movement, while preparing the transition into the scherzo

and also prefiguring at least three passages to be heard much later in the finale. These relationships are not speculative, but specific; to a great extent they are empirically verifiable and can be confirmed through analysis and conveyed in adequate performance. The character of this passage evokes both closing and preparation, anticipation and reminiscence, promise and failure. But any of these pairs of concepts describes the music only partially; what is involved here is a single moment whose content forces us to contemplate the entire design.

The interdependence of form and psychology, or of structure and expression, in such passages draws attention to a narrative dimension in music, the existence of which some scholars have sought to deny. Carolyn Abbate has discussed the 'collapse of the analogy between music and narrative', arguing that music has no past tense and is mimetic, 'trap[ping] the listener in present experience and the beat of passing time, from which he cannot escape'. In her view, temporally separated recurrences of musical units, whether as motivic recall or large-scale recapitulation, form part of what in literature would be described as the 'artifice of discourse', not the 'story'; such repetition, seen in terms of formalist aesthetics, is 'structure, architecture, hence stasis: time frozen'.[2] In Beethoven's later works, however, the progression of musical events often creates tension between a linear, temporal unfolding on the one hand and a cyclic juxtaposition of contrasting modalities in successive movements on the other. The former is largely teleological in character, the latter immanent, based more on complementarity than on resolution or transformation. In the finale of the Ninth Symphony, for instance, the recitative passages and recall of earlier movements take on such a twofold temporal function: they operate teleologically, to underscore the role of the choral finale as a transcendence of the preceding movements, and they also serve immanently, to affirm the continuing, valid presence of earlier modalities at the threshold of the finale. The subsequent allusions to the first movement later in the choral finale contribute vitally to its 'dynamically open' quality and to its symbolic, archetypal import. We cannot consign such relationships to an abstract, atemporal status or regard them as mere 'artifice'; they are too fundamental to the artistic meaning. On the other hand, use of the narrative concept in no way denies the immediacy of music, although it does encourage attention to musical relationships that transcend a linear, temporal succession, thereby liberating the listener from mere confinement to 'present experience and the beat of passing time'.

In the present study I have attempted to explore not only successive musical events and their expressive connotations but also the precise nature of their interconnection. It is regarding the linkage or integration of a series of

[2] 'What the Sorcerer Said', pp. 230, 228, 229; material from this article has been incorporated into her *Unsung Voices: Opera and Musical Narrative in Nineteenth-Century Music*, pp. 30–60.

musical modalities that certain recent writers, such as Jean-Jacques Nattiez, have underestimated the possibilities of music. For Nattiez, an 'instrumental work is not *in itself* a narrative'; the narrative is regarded as inevitably a construction by the listener, who imaginatively fills in gaps left between the musical events. With pieces such as Beethoven's op. 110 or op. 131, however, the situation is actually the opposite: it is the work that seems more fully integrated than any single hearing or interpretation of it, and the work's structure that embodies the narrative thread. Nattiez's view that 'in the discourse of music, it is only a question of a play of forms and the reactions which they provoke' betrays the severely reductionist attitude underlying his position. What I have termed a 'narrative design' embracing the musical process as a whole does not arise from '*the plot imagined and constructed by the listeners* from functional objects', as in Nattiez's model, but involves instead the recognition of a configuration of audible elements inherent in the work of art, a configuration whose relationships are to a great extent empirically verifiable and which need to be assessed in context. Nattiez confesses that 'on the level of the strictly musical discourse, I recognize returns, expectations and resolutions, but of what, I do not know'.[3] But this is an evasion of the central critical task: to confront the work of art on its own terms. By assuming *a priori* an excessively abstract concept of music, Nattiez erects an illegitimate ontological barrier between the listener or interpreter and the work, prematurely closing the investigation into artistic meaning.

Closely connected to these questions is the issue of musical analysis involving an assumption of organic unity or artistic autonomy, an issue that has come under attack recently for its alleged 'tautology'.[4] In principle, there is no reason why the analysis of artistic unity should divorce works from their contexts or impose conventional strictures on the music. The problem lies rather in a failure to distinguish between a rich, synthetic unity, whereby perceived relationships are carefully tested against the sound of a work, and a merely schematic, analytical unity, whereby a piece is made to conform to a system external to it.[5] There is no problem with the concept of musical unity, provided that what is involved is a synthetic unity embracing contrast and diversity and not merely the reduction of a work to conform to an analytical system. Such reduction is a mere caricature of analysis. Some recent critiques directed

[3] 'Can One Speak of Narrativity in Music?', pp. 249, 244, 249, 245; this article also appears in French as 'Peut-on parler de narrativité en musique?'
[4] See the introduction to *Analyzing Opera: Verdi and Wagner*, ed. Abbate and Parker, esp. pp. 2–3; and Abbate and Parker, 'Dismembering Mozart', pp. 187–95.
[5] The difference between such synthetic and analytical concepts of unity might be compared to Kant's famous distinction between synthetic and analytic judgments in sec. 4 of the introduction to the *Critique of Pure Reason*: the former predicates something connected to, yet not contained in, the subject; in the latter, the predicate is already contained in the subject, yielding a tautology.

at this simplified notion of analysis risk what Milan Kundera, in his book *Immortality*, has dubbed 'imagology'—the easy, up-to-date fashioning of systems of ideals and anti-ideals. The severing of structure from expression points in this same unpromising direction. Recognition of the interdependence of structure and expression is essential if we are to appreciate the narrative continuity in Beethoven and to confront aesthetic dimensions that reach into the symbolic, mythic, or paradoxical.

This brings us back at last to Beethoven's C♯ minor Quartet, one of the richest of all narrative musical designs. For the opening *Adagio* of op. 131 not only presages the key of the ensuing *Allegro molto vivace* and supplies its initial octave motif; it also plots the tonal plan for the entire sequence of following movements and offers harmonic and motivic substance that is reincarnated in the powerful, raging *Allegro* finale, in sonata form. The opening fugue surveys keys directly related to C♯ minor—E major, A major, and B major—while also touching on the dominant minor and emphasizing the Neapolitan and subdominant, as we have seen. The tonalities of the succeeding movements, passing from D major in no. 2 to B minor, A major, E major, and G♯ minor in nos. 3–6 respectively, roughly correspond to the tonal regions explored in the fugue. The diversity of keys is thus integrated, and may even be heard to follow from the restless, searching melancholy of the opening fugue.

Only two of Beethoven's earlier quartets had gone beyond the standard Classical practice of confining the tonic keys of movements to a pair of tonalities. The E♭ Quartet op. 74 of 1809 introduces a third key (C minor) in the scherzo. The B♭ Quartet op. 130 employs three main tonalities in addition to the tonic: D♭ major in the *Andante*, G major in the *Alla danza tedesca*, and E♭ major in the Cavatina. The use of six keys in op. 131 represents a significant innovation, yet this expansion of tonal resource is grounded more than ever in the structure and character of music heard at the outset of the work. The opening fugue sets into motion a process that reaches its climax and resolution only after the cyclic return to the original key of C♯ minor in the final movement.

The end of the *Adagio ma non troppo e molto espressivo* in op. 131 thus assumes a narrative significance no less impressive than the corresponding coda in op. 110. This passage foreshadows the ensuing *Allegro molto vivace*, while simultaneously distilling essential relationships from the outset of the fugue that re-emerge with a vengeance in the finale. The projection here of harmonic tensions into the tonal structure has no counterpart in op. 110, and represents one of the most profound aspects of Beethoven's conception.

Each of the following movements adapts itself in different ways to the larger musical continuity. Beethoven's modification of sonata procedure in the *Allegro molto vivace*, and especially the disruptive gestures in the coda, act to undercut the formal autonomy of this scherzo-like movement. A short recitative-like transition then introduces the central set of variations in A major, marked *Andante ma non troppo e molto cantabile*. Like the variations in op. 109, these transformations of the theme take the form of a brilliant chain of revelations; some of the variations even undergo a change in character as they proceed. Thus it is that Beethoven links this slow movement with the sharply contrasting scherzo in *presto* tempo that follows. At the heart of the *Andante*, and the entire quartet, is the hymn-like sixth variation, the *Adagio ma non troppo e semplice*. In the midst of this contemplative music, at the beginning of the second half of the variation, the cello intrudes with a lively motif in sixteenth-notes in the bass (Ex. 107). Initially this cello figure threatens to disrupt the discourse of the other instruments; when the passage is repeated in varied form, the intrusive motif is echoed by the first violin and then continued without pause as an ostinato in the cello. What follows is an elaborate cadenza-like passage for each of the four instruments in turn (reminiscent of the vocal cadenzas for four soloists in the Credo of the *Missa solemnis* and the Ninth Symphony!), as well as a compressed but glorified recapitulation of the original theme preceded by thematic excerpts in C major and F major (the most distant tonal relations from C♯ minor in the entire quartet).

Ex. 107 String Quartet op. 131/IV, Variation 6, bars 195–206

[Adagio ma non troppo e semplice]

The final bars of this movement are delicately poised, enveloped in a mood of reminiscence; there is no strong sense of closure. Beethoven laboured on this passage more than any other in the quartet, sketching it over and over.[6] What he achieved is yet another moment of pregnant narrative significance: the repeated pizzicato As in the first violin allude to the hymn-like sixth variation, but the rising octaves in the middle instruments recall the end of the first movement, while the E octave in the second violin very subtly foreshadows the register of the opening treble phrase of the comic scherzo that follows. The scherzo theme is anticipated by a cello figure played *forte*, in the same register—and with almost the same notes—as the earlier intrusion of the cello motif in the *Adagio* variation. As Kerman has pointed out, these two gestures are related to one another.[7] The situation is somewhat reminiscent of the apparent quotation of 'Ich bin lüderlich' in the double-diminution passage in the second fugue of op. 110. An attitude of rapt contemplation in the hymn-variation is infused with a raw but vital energy that enriches the music as it is assimilated into it.

In the scherzo we can discern another thread of connection pointing to the penultimate movement, the G# minor lament. For this naively playful scherzo sports one exceptionally curious feature: a propensity to backtrack from its dominant, B major, and guide the music instead into G# minor (Ex. 108). Hence the thematic fourth F#–B is repeated in all four instruments, and G–B is tried out as well. Only at the *Molto poco adagio* does Beethoven reach the

Ex. 108 String Quartet op. 131/V, bars 20–39

[6] Cf. Winter, *The Compositional Origins of Opus 131*, pp. 232–8.
[7] *The Beethoven Quartets*, p. 327.

goal of this little episode: at the restoration of the *presto* tempo each of the instruments gingerly takes up the head of the theme in G♯ minor, *pianissimo*, and a proper continuation is ventured for four bars before the passage is discontinued and the theme reasserted *forte* in the tonic E major. In all, Beethoven takes us through this striking passage five times, impressing it on the memory and sensibility. Towards the end of the *presto*, both the scherzo and trio seem to fade into a rarefied ether. The trio is curtailed on its third appearance to just a pair of phrases, whereas the scherzo migrates into the highest register, *sul ponticello* and *pianissimo*. A sudden shift back to earth, marked *da capo per l'ordinario*, initiates the abrupt concluding passage, with its shocking and yet subtly prepared pivot from the scherzo's close on E to the heavy bald octaves on G♯ (Ex. 109). It is this turn to G♯ that those hesitating phrases in the scherzo had been hinting at.

Ex. 109 String Quartet op. 131/V, bars 489–end

Every movement of this quartet yields up a part of its own autonomy in the interest of the work as a whole. The sombre *Adagio quasi un poco andante* is even positioned parenthetically, for the *fortissimo* octaves on G♯ actually serve to prepare the *Allegro* finale more than the *Adagio*. For that reason the slow movement requires a pedestal, a soft G♯ minor chord which sounds like an intake of breath before the lyrical, recitative-like phrases that follow. The music has a retrospective air that harks back to the opening fugue. Now, after the enormous detour of the four intervening movements, Beethoven can finally reapproach head-on the tonal foundations of the quartet, with the slow music of no. 6 placed in a normal dominant cadential relationship to the tonic key. This last juncture between movements brings the tonal and formal process full circle, and it signals that fact at the powerful structural downbeat on a unison C♯ that begins the *Allegro*.

The link between the fugue and closing *Allegro* is direct and tangible, involving a massive reinterpretation of musical substance in the new environment of the finale. In this respect some earlier critics, such as Tovey, have been rather too cautious in assessing the extent of the kinship. Beethoven's own compositional model for this kind of transformation was his C♯ minor Sonata op. 27 no. 2, in which the primary theme of the finale arises from a drastic reinterpretation of the placid arpeggios of the *Adagio*—the substance of one movement is virtually transformed into another. The first movement of the *Tempest* Sonata shows how Beethoven could absorb such a technique into a single movement, by juxtaposing a slow, suspended, harmonically ambiguous version of the triadic figure with a decisive reinterpretation of it in a faster tempo, wherein formal expansion is achieved by means of sequential repetition of the motif.

If no other work realizes this principle quite so impressively as the C♯ minor Quartet, the reason may lie in a unique combination of factors. One is Beethoven's postponement, as in op. 101, of the first forceful cadence in the tonic key until the beginning of the finale. Another is his delaying of the most energetic rhythmic activity until the last movement; for in spite of its swift, vivacious character, the *presto* scherzo is too light in tone and straightforward in its formal construction to rival the finale in this respect. Beethoven holds in reserve an arresting anapaestic rhythm in *alla breve* time and allows it to dominate broad expanses of the finale. Yet another resource that has been held back is the sonata form itself, which is crowned by an overpowering recapitulation and a weighty coda.

At the outset of the final *Allegro* the silences are hardly less important than the notes (Ex. 110). The music unfolds in two-bar units, and the strong downbeats fall initially on the *fortissimo* unison C♯s and the corresponding unison octaves that follow on B♯ in bar 3 and on C♯ in bar 5. These unisons stand like a forbidding arch commanding the gateway to the finale, brutally contradicting the soft unison octaves on C♯ and D that had opened the dreamlike path from the fugue to the inner movements. Pauses place these octaves into high relief, even as Beethoven begins to reinterpret the seminal motivic material from the fugue in this new context. Out of the C♯ unison shoots the broken triad spanning G♯–C♯; the outward expansion of these notes to A–B♯ generates the rhythmic motif in bars 2–3 which is restated to close on C♯ two bars later. The same notes that formed the head of the fugue subject are now reshaped into a fierce cadential gesture. In turn, the impact of that gesture

Ex. 110 String Quartet op. 131/VII

seems to set into motion the stamping anapaestic rhythmic ostinato that
begins in bar 5. Even the head of the ensuing theme in the first violin is a
strict, stepwise elaboration of the ascending fanfare spanning C♯ to A.

Beethoven settles any doubts about a relationship with the fugue by soon
making direct allusion to the entire fugue subject, including its turn-figure, in
an expansive passage of 19 bars. The theme is repeated in double counterpoint
and resolved firmly into C♯ minor. This referential passage is introduced by a
pair of legato phrases in the first violin that act as transition from the driving
rhythmic opening of the *Allegro* to the explicit reference to the fugue.

In this finale the allusions to the fugue are not merely retrospective; they
bring a drastic transformation in character based on structural reinterpretation. In the coda, for instance, where Beethoven refers to the fugue subject for
the last time, he provides a powerful new *fortissimo* continuation that derives
the anapaestic rhythm from that thematic allusion (Ex. 111). A large number

Ex. 111 String Quartet op. 131/VII, bars 288–95

of such correspondences exist in the finale. In the development Beethoven
exploits musical relationships identical to those of the fugue to produce an
effect of fiery brilliance. The first half of the development is based on contrapuntal sequences in which an enormously extended rising bass is divided
between the instruments. At the midpoint of the development the powerful
drift of this ascending bass is transferred to the fanfare motif from the beginning of the movement. The fanfare is thereby destabilized, and rises to reach
D major, the Neapolitan degree so important in the fugue. But most unforgettable is Beethoven's treatment of the recapitulation, which emerges out of
a protracted measured trill in all four instruments (Ex. 112).

As in the corresponding passage in the first movement of the *Appassionata*
Sonata, the rhythmic drive from the development is concentrated into a kind
of stationary vibration. The stark effect of the beginning of the movement is
left far behind, as the tonal space is now filled out by the multiple trill. The
effect is spectacular, and involves more than rhythmic pulsation and textural
embellishment, since the double trill in the two violin parts prolongs G♯–A
and B♯–C♯, those crucial pitches from the fugue that dominate the finale as

Ex. 112 String Quartet op. 131/VII, bars 145–62

well. Nowhere else in the work do these notes sound so brilliantly. As in the last sonatas, the trill has here become a structural device and a radical means of heightening the musical tension.

In the recapitulation inherited traits from the fugue—the harmonic colour of the subdominant and Neapolitan—become increasingly prominent. The subject that alludes to the fugue is recapitulated in F♯ minor; the soaring, lyrical second subject returns in D major (an unprecedented yet eminently fitting procedure in this special case). The coda, on the other hand, opens a window on a specific moment in the fugue, namely the concluding passage we have discussed in connection with the transition to the second movement. At this point Beethoven is no longer so much concerned to emphasize D; it is the diminished-seventh harmony supporting A that becomes the focus of the reminiscence (Ex. 113). The diminished sonority appeared repeatedly in the last moments of the first movement, as the final harmonization of the pivotal note of the fugue subject; and while the A at the end of the fugue was about to be reinterpreted in D major, this A must now be resolved downwards to G♯ as part of the imminent cadence in C♯ minor.

Beethoven grants the resolution from A to G♯ very reluctantly. The music lingers wistfully over the A, as the referential theme is extended through

Ex. 113 String Quartet op. 131/VII, bars 352–67

an entire octave and brought to rest on this pitch for no less than five full bars. Moments later the descending fourth outlined by C♯–B–A–G♯ is reiterated in the anapaestic rhythm in slightly decorated form as C♯–B–A–G♯–A–F♯–G♯. That motif, in turn, is repeated seven times, passing from voice to voice as the tempo slows to *Poco Adagio*; Beethoven writes *semplice* and *espressivo* over the final entries in the first and second violins. Only at the 'Tempo I' indication six bars before the close is the resolution to G♯ firmly accomplished, inasmuch as the stable fifth G♯–C♯ is sustained for four bars in the first violin and viola, balancing and resolving the protracted diminished seventh supporting A that was heard earlier in the coda.

The final six-bar segment provides the completion of a vehement cadential progression that had been broken off 35 bars earlier to make room for the final reminiscence of the fugue. For the cadence had already been fully prepared, fortified by exciting rhythmic strettos on the Neapolitan—the ultimate assimilation of that important harmonic inflection into the tonic key of C♯. The 35-bar passage beginning at 'Ritmo di tre battute' is parenthetical. This last important example of parenthetical enclosure in Beethoven's music undercuts the triumphant conclusion and considerably deepens the expressive power of the coda.

In his excellent study of this quartet Kerman suggested that 'the mood of the C♯-minor Finale heightens and purifies the famous C-minor mood of Beethoven's early years'.[8] It is interesting in this regard that one basic motivic quarry for Beethoven's last quartets relates to the sketch for the abandoned four-hand sonata—a sketch actually notated in C minor. Beethoven's unique

---

[8] *The Beethoven Quartets*, p. 341.

design in the C♯ minor Quartet is framed by a double cycle of paired movements. The impressive gravity of the slow fugue yields to a seemingly
unbounded flight of imagination in the *Allegro molto vivace* and the following
inner movements, whereas the second *Adagio* prefaces a defiant reconfrontation in the finale with the strife-ridden C♯ minor tonality. By holding fast to
the memory of the fugue Beethoven's closing *Allegro* brings about a synthesis
of contemplation and action; in Schiller's terms, an unblinkered awareness of
suffering is merged with a capacity to resist these feelings and therefore not
accept them as permanent and irremediable. The note of triumph at the end
of the C♯ minor Quartet is momentary, however, and scarcely conceals the
profound duality of the coda, which reflects in turn the deep tensional interdependence of the outer movements.

The fugue and finale thus act like stern outer columns framing a fantastic
range of diverse inner episodes; of these, the scherzo, with its apotheosis of
play, represents the most extreme contrast, the humorous antipode to the serious and perhaps even tragic character of the C♯ minor music. It is revealing
that Beethoven contemplated but then rejected an additional closing passage
to the finale that would have unambiguously resolved the basic motivic complex to D♭ major, thereby replacing the notes C♯–B♯–A–G♯ by the enharmonic equivalents in the major, D♭–C–B♭–A♭. As Robert Winter has pointed
out, he used the sketched theme as the basis for the *Lento assai* of his last quartet, op. 135.[9] He even gave the tune a title in his sketchbook: 'sweet song of
peace'. In the passionate finale of the C♯ minor Quartet this serene inspiration could find no place.

*   *   *

Beethoven's artistic explorations of the 1820s have often captured the imagination of commentators, stimulating much discussion of the challenging aesthetic and moral issues encapsulated in the title of J. W. N. Sullivan's 1927
centennial study, *Beethoven's Spiritual Development*. With the passage of time,
a consensus has emerged that sees Beethoven's later sonatas and quartets not
as wayward productions of a deaf eccentric, as some early critics had seen
them, but as some of the richest contributions ever made to musical art. The
startling innovations of the last quartets may be said to centre on musical symbolism in the A minor quartet, paradoxical contrast in the B♭ major, and narrative design in the C♯ minor. The individuality of these works is just as
marked as that of Beethoven's early opuses of piano sonatas and the op. 18 and
'Razumovsky' Quartets, regardless of the presence of shared motivic figures.
The uniqueness of the last quartets is outwardly manifested in the growing
number of movements, culminating in the seven-movement design of op. 131.

---

[9] *The Compositional Origins of Beethoven's Opus 131*, pp. 121–4, 167–74, 206–9; see also
Bumpass, *Beethoven's Last Quartet*, i, pp. 222–4.

But no less striking is their expressive scope, which embraces moods ranging from whimsy and mocking humour to the sublime interiority of the slow movements—the *Adagio* of op. 127, the Cavatina of op. 130, and the 'Heiliger Dankgesang'. The last quartets are bold, visionary works that seem to open a new creative period rather than close an old one.

The relationship of this superb artistic production to Beethoven's biography, on the other hand, is more contradictory than ever. A safe, neatly rounded portrait of Beethoven's last year can be purchased only at the cost of truth, and we shall be compelled to settle for an 'open' conclusion, not unlike those compositions whose endings point provocatively into the silence beyond. Disorder, conflict, and misery in his life were on the ascent just as his artistic development was attaining new heights. The tragic climax in his biography coincided almost exactly with the completion of his splendid Quartet in C$\sharp$ minor: in the middle of the summer of 1826, in a desperate act of misguided self-assertion, his beloved nephew Karl attempted suicide.

Problems had been brewing for years and were doubtless connected to Beethoven's caring yet stubborn, overbearing, and suspicious conduct towards his young relative, whom he regarded as his 'son'. His possessiveness towards his nephew was coupled with hostility towards Karl's mother, Johanna van Beethoven, whom Beethoven dubbed 'The Queen of the Night'. As Karl grew to maturity, conflict with his uncle became more frequent. Part of this escalating tension may have been connected to Beethoven's reluctance to recognize Karl's need for independence. Matters came to a head during the first half of 1826, when Karl was living in separate lodgings and attending the Polytechnic Institute. Thayer writes that 'there were violent scenes, evidently in Karl's rooms, which deeply embittered him', and he quotes Karl's response to Beethoven's reproaches: 'You consider it insolence if, after you have upbraided me for hours undeservedly, this time at least, I cannot turn from my bitter feeling of pain to jocularity'.[10] Karl's behaviour towards his uncle may have been manipulative; according to Holz, he said he could wrap his uncle around his finger. Karl seems also to have fallen into debt, though apparently not to a very serious extent.

On 6 August 1826 Beethoven's distraught nephew discharged two bullets towards his head, wounding himself with the second shot, which grazed the bone. When asked by the police why he shot himself, Karl said that Beethoven 'tormented him too much'. According to Schindler and Holz, the impact on Beethoven of Karl's suicide attempt was shattering; Schindler wrote that 'he soon looked like a man of seventy'. From this point, the concern with Karl assumed an even more dominating role in Beethoven's affairs. Since suicide was an offence against the Church, there were penal aspects to

[10] Thayer-Forbes, p. 993.

be reckoned with after Karl's release from the hospital, and these especially distressed Beethoven. At the same time Beethoven's friends had persuaded him to enrol Karl in the military, a solution that inevitably meant separation from the boy, which Beethoven found very difficult to accept.

An interim solution was for Beethoven to accept the invitation of his brother Johann to visit the latter's Wasserhof estate at Gneixendorf, near Krems, one day's journey from Vienna. Johann had invited him previously, and Beethoven had always refused to come, partly because of his dislike of Johann's wife Therese. Beethoven's relationship with his brother showed strains resulting from their very different outlooks on life. When Johann had a calling-card printed with the word 'Gutsbesitzer', or 'landowner', Beethoven retorted by dubbing himself 'Hirnbesitzer', or 'brainowner' (Beethoven's description of his brother as a 'brain eater', on the other hand, touches on a common trait, since brain soup was one of Beethoven's favourite dishes). In any event, Beethoven had long hesitated to visit his brother. Even very shortly before, he had replied to Johann:

> I will not come.
> Your brother??????!!!!
> Ludwig

Now, however, with the pressing need to find a haven of refuge where Karl would be put at a distance from both the authorities and his mother, Beethoven consented to travel to Gneixendorf. The visit was supposed to be brief but was prolonged at Beethoven's insistence throughout the autumn. His conflicts with Karl continued there; even more bitter disputes ensued with his brother. Already seriously ill at Gneixendorf and faced with the prospect of losing close contact with his nephew, Beethoven may have sensed that his options were closing, time growing short. Finally, on 28 November 1826, he set out with Karl for Vienna in an open wagon. Inadequately clothed in the inclement weather, he arrived at his apartment in the Schwarzspanierhaus with pneumonia.

During December Beethoven's condition deteriorated rapidly, with worsening symptoms of jaundice due to the progress of liver disease, swollen feet, and dropsy. The accumulating fluid in his body was tapped and drained four times. After the last operation on 27 February 1827, the end was near. When Beethoven's physician Dr Wawruch promised him relief with the coming of spring, Beethoven replied, 'My day's work is finished. If there were a physician who could help me "his name shall be called Wonderful!"'. Wawruch confessed that 'This pathetic allusion to Handel's *Messiah* touched me so deeply that I had to confess its correctness to myself with profound emotion'.[11] Beethoven survived in agony for one more month; he died during a thunderstorm on 26 March 1827.

[11] Ibid., p. 1038.

*   *   *

The Quartet in F major op. 135 is the last work Beethoven finished, apart from
the substitute finale of op. 130; both pieces were begun at Vienna and completed at Gneixendorf. Some writers have perceived in these works a weakening in Beethoven's creative powers or at least in his ambition and have
associated this perceived decline with the depressing impact of Karl's suicide
attempt. Yet the musical quality of both pieces, and especially the F major
Quartet, remains very high. There is admittedly a retrospective character to
the last quartet: it is mainly an essay in Haydnesque wit, not a bold, expansive
composition like the other late quartets. As we have seen, such humorous
pieces were a lifelong interest with Beethoven, and F major was quite often
the chosen key, at least in other genres: one thinks of the piano sonatas op. 10
no. 2 and op. 54, the middle movement of the *Pastoral* Symphony, and the
Eighth Symphony. In 1826, with his third quartet in this key, Beethoven
capped his musical legacy with another masterpiece in the same vein.

It is just possible that this was indeed his artistic response to the grim events
of 1826: Beethoven's way was to respond to adversity with humour. Even his
nephew Karl referred to this reflex in complaining that he could not turn from
his 'bitter feeling of pain to jocularity', as his uncle wished. In his last years
Beethoven's passion for verbal puns took on a new and poignant intensity
which frequently found musical expression in the form of canons. Beethoven
and his colleagues were alert to punning opportunities, ranging from the
typical B–A–C–H *topos* to Karl Holz's jokes on Handel as 'Hendel' (roast
chickens) in 'Zäh-Dur' ('tough-major', or 'very tough', but sounding like
'C major').[12] While at work on the *Missa solemnis* Beethoven used the rhythm
of the 'Credo' motif for a canon concluding 'Weidmann, Weidmännchen,
Eselchen!' ('Huntsman, little hunter, little ass!').[13] The Danish composer
Friedrich Kuhlau was honoured by a canon to the words 'kühl, nicht lau'
('cool, not lukewarm'), a piece that begins with the notes B–A–C–H and is
linked in turn to the genesis of motivic configurations important in the last
quartets.[14] In 1825 Beethoven even published in the journal *Cäcilia* a satirical
'Lebensbeschreibung' ('biographical sketch') of Tobias Haslinger that
describes Haslinger's fictitious study with the theorist Albrechtsberger, culminating in the loftiest achievements in the art of making 'musical skeletons'.
Beethoven appended to his story two humorous canons, the second of which,
with its text 'Hoffmann! Hoffmann! Sei ja kein Hofmann, ja kein Hofmann!'

[12] The references to 'Hendel' in 'Zäh-Dur' and to 'Kühl, nicht lau' (see below) are discussed
in Platen, 'Über Bach, Kuhlau und die thematisch-motivische Einheit der letzten Quartette
Beethovens', pp. 152–3.

[13] See Schmidt-Görg, ed., *Ludwig van Beethoven: Ein Skizzenbuch aus den Jahren 1819/20*, p.
45.

[14] Platen, op. cit., pp. 152–3.

('Hoffmann! Hoffmann! Don't be a courtier, indeed not a courtier!', i.e. an obsequious person), is apparently his homage to E. T. A. Hoffmann.[15]

Quite possibly it was Holz's sense of humour that helped endear him to Beethoven, who by 1825 had tired of the company of the more dreary and sometimes surly Schindler. Holz's name, meaning 'wood', became the subject of numerous jokes by the composer. Beethoven dubbed him 'Best Mahogany', 'Best Splinter from the Cross of Christ', and 'Best lignum crucis'. He once observed to Holz that 'wood is a neuter noun', adding: 'So what a contradiction is the masculine form, and what other consequences may be drawn from *personified wood*?' Holz occasionally ventured jokes on his own name and was known to others in Beethoven's circle, such as Kanne and Schuppanzigh, as 'der Hölzerne' ('the wooden one').[16]

Characteristic of such humour is delight in the incongruous pairing of apparently incompatible elements: the sacred and the profane, the serious and the absurd, the obvious and the obscure. Pretensions are mocked; an unexpected depth and significance is perceived in seemingly trivial circumstances. The readiness to draw connections knows no bounds and no taboos; a free association of ideas is the point. This Shandian streak in Beethoven surfaces as early as the 1790s, in his descriptions of his friend Zmeskall as 'dearest Baron Muck-cart Driver' or 'garbage man', but it is most generously documented near the end of his life, which is filled with little episodes worthy of *Tristram Shandy*.

1826 was a year particularly rich in jokes and humorous canons. Early that year Beethoven met the old-fashioned Abbé Maximilian Stadler—who had no use for any music after Mozart—at Steiner's music shop. Before departing Beethoven knelt before the abbé and asked for his blessing, which Stadler granted, mumbling 'Nutzt's nicht, so schadt's nix' ('If it does no good, 'twill do no harm'). Beethoven kissed the abbé's hand to complete the solemn farce, to the great amusement of the bystanders. He tossed off a canon presumably in connection with this event, with the following text:

Signor Abbate! I'm ailing I'm ailing I'm ailing I'm ailing!
Holy Father hasten, give to me thy benediction, give me thy blessing, thy blessing!
Go to the devil, unless you hasten, go to the devil, unless you hasten, go to the devil![17]

Shortly thereafter, on 6 February, Beethoven wrote to Stadler alluding to 'your blessing very soon'. In the same letter he praises the abbé for publishing a letter defending the authenticity of Mozart's *Requiem*, adding, 'I have always counted myself among the greatest admirers of Mozart and shall remain so

[15] See Canisius, *Beethoven*, pp. 146–53.
[16] Cf. *Ludwig van Beethovens Konversationshefte*, viii, pp. 122, 172, and the facsimile after p. 176; and ix, p. 300.
[17] Thayer-Forbes, p. 988.

until my last breath ———'. Beethoven's unusual punctuation here recalls similar devices in Laurence Sterne. For the protracted dash following the words 'letzten LebensHauch' (literally, 'life's last breath') is no ordinary mark of punctuation but acts as a symbol for Beethoven's very last breath, a breath drawn for Mozart![18]

A recently discovered letter from the same year contains further examples of Beethoven's fun with puns, as Küthen has observed. In it Beethoven addresses his physician Dr Anton Braunhofer in grandiose terms as 'honoured master and practitioner of the cure'; his expression 'Ausüber der Aeskulapsie' plays on the expression 'ausübender Arzt' ('practising physician'), while adapting the term 'Aesculapian' ('healer') as a noun, meaning 'healing' or 'cure'. In the same paragraph Beethoven asks 'what else you have decided about my corpse', continuing 'my back is still not entirely in its old condition, I hope meanwhile it will still not be *necessary* to bend it, *indeed never*'.[19] His allusion to 'bending' does not refer merely to a physical condition. It is an assertion of his proud refusal to defer to royalty, recalling the famous incident at Teplitz in 1812 when Goethe supposedly bowed to the royal carriage while Beethoven refused to make any such gesture of servility. The German word 'beugen' means not only to bend but to humble oneself, to submit. Beethoven underscores his principled position by first expressing the hope that he need not yield, before then rejecting the mere possibility of submission through the underlined words '*ja nie*' ('indeed never').

In the summer of 1826 an incident occurred that is bound up with the genesis of the F major Quartet op. 135. After the première of the B♭ Quartet by Schuppanzigh's quartet on 21 March 1826, interest arose in arranging a performance by a different quartet at the house of a certain Ignaz Dembscher. Dembscher, however, had not subscribed for Schuppanzigh's concert, and he was subsequently forced by Beethoven to pay up in order to receive performance parts for the work. Dembscher queried 'Muss es sein?' ('Must it be?'), and Beethoven, highly amused, sketched a canon to the words 'Es muss sein! ja ja ja ja! Heraus mit dem Beutel!' ('It must be! yes yes yes yes! Out with your wallet!');[20] the canonic motif, in turn, found its way into the finale of Beethoven's last quartet.

[18]   See Küthen, 'Mozart—Schiller—Beethoven: Mozarts Modell für die Freudenhymne und die Fusion der Embleme im Finale der Neunten Symphonie', pp. 110–12; a facsimile of the letter of 6 February 1826 (Anderson L. 1468) is reproduced on p. 111. Beethoven omits the grammatically essential verb 'bleiben' from the end of his sentence to underscore his symbolic breath for Mozart.

[19]   This letter was published by Anna Maria Russo in *Nuova rivista musicale italiana*, xxv (1991), pp. 74–82, and in *The Beethoven Newsletter*, vi (1991); Küthen's important corrections to the transcription of the letter, with their clarification of Beethoven's puns, appear in *The Beethoven Newsletter*, vii (1992), p. 30.

[20]   This story stems from Karl Holz and is related in Thayer-Forbes, pp. 976–7, which also reproduces the canon. It dates from the beginning of August 1826 (cf. *Ludwig van Beethovens*

This canon predates Beethoven's main work on the quartet. In the meantime, around the second week of August, Beethoven submitted the C♯ minor Quartet to the publisher Schott, writing on the copy 'Zusammengestohlen aus Verschiedenem diesem und jenem' ('Put together from pilferings from one thing and another'). This is yet another example of his ironic humour. He entered the inscription in response to the publisher's requirement that the quartet be an original one. What may have amused Beethoven is the thought that this most integrated of compositions would appear to the uninitiated as a confused potpourri, particularly with the suggestion to that effect from himself. Such a misunderstanding did indeed ensue. Beethoven was obliged to write reassuringly to the alarmed publisher on 19 August that 'as a joke I wrote on the copy that it was put together from pilferings. Nevertheless, it is *brand new*'.[21]

A financial dispute arose around this time between Beethoven and Moritz Schlesinger, the publisher of op. 135. When the fee seemed smaller than expected, Beethoven remarked, in reference to the religion of the publisher and the modest length of the piece, that he would send a 'circumcised quartet'. This triple pun unexpectedly associates publisher, fee, and quartet under the category of 'circumcision', meaning the removal of a piece: Schlesinger's sending of 'circumcised ducats' meant that 'he shall have a circumcised quartet. That's the reason why it is so short'.[22] On 13 October Beethoven announced the completion of the work in yet another humorous letter to Haslinger, whom he addressed in music as 'First of all Tobiasses'.

Beethoven was doubtless guided in his composition of the F major Quartet by the pre-existing material that he took into its third and fourth movements: the theme of the *Lento assai* sketched for op. 131; and 'Der schwergefasste Entschluss' ('The Difficult Decision') motto, inspired by Ignaz Dembscher's earlier discomfiture, with the related canon on 'Muss es sein?', 'Es muss sein!' The urbane wit of the first movement neatly complements the unbuttoned humour of the finale. The animated scherzo, on the other hand, represents an antipode to the serenely unified slow movement, especially in its trio, which contains one of the most startling climaxes in all Beethoven's music.

The subtlety of the first movement is readily illustrated by comparison of

Konversationshefte, x, pp. 63, 317, 353. Schindler's account that the phrases 'Must it be?', 'It must be!' arose from the exchange between Beethoven and his housekeeper (*Beethoven As I Knew Him*, pp. 337–8) is supported by a forged entry in a conversation book (Beck and Herre, 'Anton Schindlers fingierte Eintragungen', p. 83) and must be dismissed. The connection to the Dembscher canon does not exclude other interpretations of Beethoven's motto, however. Rainer Cadenbach, editor of the forthcoming edition of the quartet for the new *Gesamtausgabe*, proposes that 'Must it be?' questions the need for a finale to follow the *Lento assai*. For another interpretation, see the study by Christopher Reynolds cited in note 25, below.

[21] Thayer-Forbes, p. 983, note 21.
[22] Thayer-Forbes, p. 1009, note 44; cf. also *Ludwig van Beethovens Konversationshefte*, x, pp. 49, 354⁻5.

the opening theme and its subsequent appearances in the recapitulation and coda. Beethoven begins with the Haydnesque device of an off-balance, harmonically ambiguous gesture, followed by a lucid continuation; the end of the first theme is so fashioned that it can act in slightly varied form as the final cadence at the end of this *Allegretto*. He exploits the ambiguous opening motif, on the other hand, to introduce a sly, 'false' recapitulation in the development section. All ambiguity seems to vanish as the stable phrases of the theme are played in the tonic F major, but a harmonic detail is then reinterpreted to facilitate modulation to A minor, opening up a new dramatic section of development.

The scherzo opens with a kind of triple rhythmic counterpoint between syncopated voices whose registral position is shuffled in subsequent phrases. Within this unusual texture melodic considerations are of secondary importance, and the primary voice simply glides over the major third spanning F–G–A. An interruption of uncouth, repeated Ebs is pitted against these rhythmic phrases, and the voices gradually converge to move in step as they approach the cadence in F major. In the trio a rising turn-figure spanning a third launches shooting scales into the high register in the first violin. The dance gains in intensity as these gestures are successively repeated in the keys of F major, G major, and A major, tonalities corresponding to the melodic steps of the scherzo, as Roger Sessions has observed.[23] Then comes the shattering climax (Ex. 114). The turn becomes a revolving cam, repeated

Ex. 114 String Quartet op. 135/II, bars 133–91

[23] *The Musical Experience*, pp. 49–50.

incessantly and *fortissimo* in the lower instruments and second violin; above this the first violin plays a rustic dance parody with sharp accents and enormous skips in register. There is an almost frightening character to the passage; an apocalyptic vision emerges, supplanting the rustic humour of the earlier music. Normality is restored only very gradually, as the revolving configuration softens to an almost inaudible triple *pianissimo* after nearly 50 repetitions of the motif. Beethoven then lowers the pitches F♯ and G♯ of the turn-figure to F and G, pointing ominously to the derivation of the turn, and hence the entire disruptive episode, from the smooth, gliding pitches heard at the outset of the scherzo.

After this unusually dynamic scherzo with its explosive trio, the 'sweet song of peace' is all the more moving; the two inner movements form a contrasting pair and share a thematic profile that features conjunct stepwise motion. In this *Lento assai, cantante e tranquillo*, Beethoven retains the key of D♭ major from his sketch and develops the theme as a series of variations that are so closely integrated that the form is often overlooked. The first two bars belong to the pedestal that accomplishes the change in key and provides the tonal foundation for the sublime theme that follows. The theme consists of eight bars, with two bars of cadential echoes. Each of the four variations adheres strictly to this design, whereby the last variation is extended into a coda of two bars to balance the pedestal at the beginning. Beethoven merges this scheme with aspects of sonata form: the theme and first variation are joined organically into a continuity, while the second variation, with its unison motion, turn to the minor, and brief modulation to E major, brings a marked contrast. The third variation is a decorated recapitulation of the theme, with canonic imitation between cello and first violin, and the last variation brings an exquisite climax in the highest register, while subtly resolving aspects of the variation in the minor. This is the most delicate and unified of all Beethoven's variation movements.

Then comes the finale, 'The Difficult Decision', whose double motto, 'Must it be?', 'It must be!', is printed at the head of the score. Beethoven had employed a pairing of interrogative and declarative motifs before, though without providing verbal cues such as are given here. A notable example is the rondo finale of his D major Piano Sonata op. 10 no. 3, where the ascending motivic figure of a semitone and third is eventually resolved into a descending form in the coda. According to an account by Schindler which may not be historically trustworthy but still merits critical consideration in this context, Beethoven is supposed to have associated the movement with the overcoming of melancholy; Richard Rosenberg implausibly extended this notion by underlaying the main form of the motif, in its interrogative, ascending version, with the words 'Noch traurig?' ('Still sad?').[24] In view of its source, this account must be regarded with utmost scepticism; still, the general association seems not atypical of Beethoven. In any event, the fact that the verbal formula proposed by Rosenberg does not apply to the coda underlines its very limited relevance to the specific musical context.

In op. 135 there is no such ambiguity; Beethoven seems to spell out the association in specific terms. Nevertheless, the movement offers pitfalls for interpretation. The almost operatic, exaggerated, parodistic treatment of the interrogative motif in the *Grave, ma non troppo tratto* is one such trap. To hear this music merely literally, as an expression of tragic pathos, may be tantamount to mistaking Beethoven's entreaty of a blessing from Abbé Stadler for an earnest gesture. The relation of the motifs to Dembscher's discomfiture is not binding for an interpretation, of course, but in this case the character of the *Allegro* seems very much like gaiety and quite remote from philosophical

---

[24] *Die Klaviersonaten Ludwig van Beethovens*, i, p. 108.

quandary. This is not to deny the possibility of multiple interpretations, which are sometimes at the heart of Beethoven's comic impulse, as we have seen. Christopher Reynolds, for instance, has argued for a reading of 'Muss es sein?', 'Es muss sein!' as a pun on the note 'Es', or E♭, an important pitch in this finale and in the quartet as a whole. Such an interpretation is plausible but partial; it does not come close to exhausting the associations of the music.[25] For Paul Bekker, writing in 1912, the movement conveys 'less an intrinsic gaiety than a humour won through reflection'.[26] But Bekker takes the mock pathos of the *Grave* sections too seriously, missing the parodistic dimension that surfaces at once in the opening *Grave* and even more clearly when Beethoven brings back the *Grave* at the end of the development. The blustering character is reinforced there through unusually crude scoring and exaggerated dynamics, before Beethoven once again dissolves the question into the unbridled high spirits of the *Allegro*.

As Kerman rightly observed, Beethoven captured 'something like the essence of gaiety' in this last movement of his last quartet.[27] Confirmation of this view can be sought through analysis of the one main theme for which Beethoven did not supply a verbal tag. This is the second subject, the ethereal 'fairy march', which appears in A major in the exposition and in F major in the recapitulation, before it is played *pianissimo* and pizzicato in the coda (Ex. 115).

Ex. 115 String Quartet op. 135/IV

[25] See Reynolds, 'The Representational Impulse in Late Beethoven, II: String Quartet in F major, Op. 135'. As we have seen, Beethoven sometimes indulged in compound musical puns such as the canon on 'Kühl, nicht lau' WoO 191, employing the opening notes B–A–C–H (see note 12 above); another example is the variant 'lau es', a veiled allusion to the name 'Laura Esther' employing the interval A–E♭ ('A' and 'Es' in German musical terminology).

[26] *Beethoven*, p. 555.   [27] *The Beethoven Quartets*, p. 367.

Ex. 115 *cont.*

In the passage just preceding it, the affirmative 'It must be!' motif reaches a crisis, as the music slows to *poco adagio* and comes to rest on ambiguous chromatic harmonies reminiscent of 'Must it be?' The 'fairy march' then carries the day, allowing the revitalized motto 'It must be!' to bring the quartet to its joyous conclusion. Significant in this respect is the rhythmic and intervallic kinship between 'Must it be?' and the head of the ethereal march. Beethoven's musical question consists of a falling third in dotted rhythm followed by a diminished fourth—F–D–Gb, as it appears most emphatically in the opening *Grave*. What he has done is to absorb this configuration into the contour and rhythm of his second subject, whose controlling intervals correspond audibly to 'Must it be?', though notated in a different tempo. A comparison of the two motifs is shown in Fig. 5. The rhythmic shape of the melodic progression from F through the repeated Cs to D in the second half of the second bar recalls the falling third F–D in dotted rhythm from the *Grave*; the ensuing turn-figure leading to G in the *Allegro* replaces the dissonant diminished fourth D–Gb from the *Grave* with a stable rising fourth leading from D through F to G. Beethoven goes beyond his own verbal tags in resolving the musical tensions in this enchanting closing passage.

Thus closes the F major Quartet, a fitting end to Beethoven's career and one of the finest examples of his humour in music. The study of Beethoven's biography has abundantly confirmed his propensity to regard the world around him in an ironic or comic light. This capacity may have been reinforced by the increasing discrepancy between his artistic sensibility and his

Fig. 5   Motifs in the String Quartet op. 135

ability to function in the everyday world. Already in the Bonn period, Helene von Breuning commented on Beethoven's 'raptus'; in 1801 Beethoven described himself as 'absentminded'; his self-absorption and disregard of the outer social world became appreciably greater in his period of depression after 1812, and after the complete erosion of his hearing around 1818. His 'penchant for sarcastic wit' and 'withdrawal from the world around him' were also noted by Gerhard von Breuning, who was in frequent contact with the composer during the last months of his life.[28] By 1821, as we have seen, it was possible for Beethoven to be arrested as a tramp. Some of the most colourful stories illustrating the perception of him by ordinary citizens stem from his stay at Gneixendorf. On one occasion an avid music lover who encountered him at a business office mistook him for an 'idiot' ('Trottel') and was shocked to learn of his error. Beethoven's habit of shouting and wildly gesticulating while composing on his outings was reason enough for him to be taken as a madman. One farmer related how Beethoven's behaviour twice frightened a pair of young oxen, causing them to stampede.

None of the absurdities in Beethoven's jokes could quite mirror the precarious dialectic of his own art and life, an experience that may account in part for his love of the dictum 'art is long, life is short'. Art offered something seemingly permanent, a bulwark of enduring meaning posited against the inevitable transience of life. At the same time, even trivial events could be transformed into artistic coinage, opening nourishing lines of connection between life and art. It is this quality of universality and challenging breadth of experience that must explain in part the continued vitality of Beethoven's music today.

Beethoven's artworks are above all vessels of tensional synthesis, whose ultimate task remains ever unfulfilled. The challenge to criticism lies in the need to apprehend this uneasy blend of the rational and sensuous while curbing schematic methodology or arbitrary speculation. A network of internal relationships sustains, modifies, or even defines the expressive character; form and psychology become interdependent, if not indistinguishable. An engagement with the immanent temporality of the work is the prerequisite not only of satisfactory performance but also of adequate analysis, which properly resembles an imagined performance, not merely an exercise in structural dismemberment or the mechanical rehearsal of *a priori* percepts. Useful analysis may build on the results of such systematic investigations, but it cannot end with them. For the real purpose of talking about music is to hear more in the music. What is to be heard is often underestimated; slick, technically fluent performances frequently fail to convey adequately the character of the works. In some cases, as in Beethoven's humorous pieces, for instance, such dynamic

---

[28] *Memories of Beethoven*, ed. Solomon, p. 44.

qualities as surprise, imbalance, and even disorientation need to be felt and communicated. An excessively literalistic approach, which pays homage to the notation but fails to probe its contextual meaning, is hopelessly inadequate here. It is more appropriate to stress the humanity of this music—those elements of dramatic character and narrative symbolism that inspire so many of these pieces, from the *Joseph* Cantata to the last quartets. As we have seen, Beethoven's art does not stand aloof from concerns of life, it does not lose itself in abstraction. On the contrary, the principle of self-determination embodied in this music gives it the strength to confront provocatively the boundary separating the potential from the actual, or art from life.

The same resilient, life-affirming attitude characterized Beethoven's response to the inevitability of death, as reflected, for instance, in his canon of 11 May 1825 on 'Doctor bar[s] the door to death. A note helps too in time of need', with its pun on *Note* ('note') and *Noth* ('need', as in extreme emergency, before impending death).[29] A conversation book from about this time records a variant of the idea: 'My doctor helped me, for I could write no more notes [*Noten*], but now I write notes [*Noten*] which help me out of my need [*Nöthen*]'.[30] Less than two years later notes could no longer help him, but Beethoven retained his taste for comic irony until the end. It is entirely typical, and deserving of respect, that the composer on his deathbed recited the common closing line of classical comedy: 'Plaudite, amici, comoedia finita est' ('Applaud, friends, the comedy is over').[31]

[29] In addition to its publication in standard editions of Beethoven's letters, this canon is reproduced with a facsimile of the manuscript in *Ludwig van Beethoven*, ed. Joseph Schmidt-Görg and Hans Schmidt, p. 30; and in Hans Bankl and Hans Jesserer, *Die Krankheiten Ludwig van Beethovens, Pathographie seines Lebens und Pathologie seiner Leiden*, pp. 42–3.

[30] *Ludwig van Beethovens Konversationshefte*, vii, pp. 256, 405.

[31] See Breuning, *Memories of Beethoven*, ed. Solomon, p. 102.

SELECTED BIBLIOGRAPHY

(For 'Bibliography of Works Cited' see below, pp. 351–60; for a more detailed annotated survey of writings on Beethoven up to 1977, see the bibliography in Maynard Solomon's *Beethoven* (New York: Schirmer, 1977). The following list is highly selective and emphasizes studies that have appeared since the 1980s.)

I. Basic Sources

A new complete edition was begun in 1961 (*Beethoven-Werke* [Munich: G. Henle Verlag]) but has been slow to reach publication, with many volumes and critical reports still outstanding. The standard collected edition thus remains *Beethovens Werke: Vollständige, kritische durchgesehene Gesamtausgabe*, 25 vols. (Leipzig: Breitkopf & Härtel, 1862–5; 1888). Works omitted from the old *Gesamtausgabe* are listed in Willy Hess, *Verzeichnis der nicht in der Gesamtausgabe veröffentlichten Werke Ludwig van Beethovens* (Wiesbaden: Breitkopf & Härtel, 1957). Hess subsequently edited the *Supplemente zur Gesamtausgabe*, 14 vols. (Wiesbaden: Breitkopf & Härtel, 1959–71).

The most comprehensive published collection of Beethoven's letters remains Emily Anderson, trans. and ed., *The Letters of Beethoven*, published in three volumes in 1961 (reprinted in 1985). Two editions are in press at the time of writing: the long-awaited complete edition of letters issued through the Beethoven-Haus at Bonn, *Ludwig van Beethoven: Briefwechsel: Gesamtausgabe*, 7 vols., ed. Sieghard Brandenburg and others; and an abridged practical edition in English, edited by Theodore Albrecht, that will supplement the Anderson edition (Lincoln and London: University of Nebraska Press, forthcoming).

The standard catalogue of Beethoven's works is Georg Kinsky and Hans Halm, *Das Werk Beethovens: Thematisch-bibliographisches Verzeichnis* (Munich: Henle, 1955). Also see Kurt Dorfmüller, ed., *Beiträge zur Beethoven-Bibliographie* (Munich: Henle, 1978).

The comprehensive edition of the conversation books used by the deaf composer during his last decade is Karl-Heinz Köhler, Grita Herre, and Dagmar Beck, eds., *Ludwig van Beethovens Konversationshefte*, 10 vols. (Leipzig: VEB Deutscher Verlag für Musik, 1968–93; two volumes are forthcoming). An earlier collected publication edited by Georg Schünemann (Berlin: Max Hesses Verlag) was broken off after three volumes in 1943; its readings often differ from the Leipzig edition.

Another important primary source is Beethoven's *Tagebuch*, or diary, from the years 1812–18. Maynard Solomon published an edition of the *Tagebuch* in German and in English translation, with commentary, in *Beethoven Studies*, iii, ed. Alan Tyson (Cambridge: Cambridge University Press, 1982). This edition was reprinted in Solomon's *Beethoven Essays* (Cambridge, Mass.: Harvard University Press, 1988); the German text was recently reissued as *Beethovens Tagebuch* in a handsome volume with additional editing by Sieghard Brandenburg (Mainz: v. Hase & Koehler Verlag, 1990).

The standard catalogue of Beethoven's musical sketchbooks is Douglas Johnson, Alan Tyson, and Robert Winter, *The Beethoven Sketchbooks: History, Reconstruction, Inventory* (Berkeley and Los Angeles: University of California Press, 1985). Since this study does not survey all of Beethoven's sketches on loose papers, it is supplemented by Hans Schmidt, 'Verzeichnis der Skizzen Beethovens', *Beethoven-Jahrbuch*, vi (1969), pp. 7–128.

The famous biography by Anton Schindler was most recently edited by Donald W. MacArdle and translated by Constance S. Jolly as *Beethoven As I Knew Him* (London and Chapel Hill: University of North Carolina Press, 1966). Research has shown Schindler to be an unreliable witness and has exposed a substantial number of entries in the conversation books as Schindler's forgeries. The forged entries are listed in Dagmar Beck and Grita Herre, 'Anton Schindlers fingierte Eintragungen in den Konversationsheften', in *Zu Beethoven*, i, ed. Harry Goldschmidt (Berlin: Verlag Neue Musik, 1979), pp. 11–89. Some well-known studies, such as Arnold Schmitz's influential book *Beethovens 'Zwei Prinzipe': ihre Bedeutung für Themen- und Satzbau* (Berlin and Bonn: Ferd. Dümmlers Verlagsbuchhandlung, 1923), are seriously undermined by their reliance on the dubious interpretations offered by Schindler.

The classic biography by the nineteenth-century American scholar Alexander Wheelock Thayer appeared in editions by Deiters and Riemann (1866–1917) and Krehbiel (1921); a revised and updated edition appeared as *Thayer's Life of Beethoven*, edited by Elliot Forbes (Princeton: Princeton University Press, 1964). Thayer's work served as a foundation for the important interpretative biography *Beethoven* by Maynard Solomon (New York: Schirmer, 1977), whose originality and high scholarship distinguish it from most other general studies available on Beethoven. An excellent concise survey of the life and works is *The New Grove Beethoven* by Joseph Kerman and Alan Tyson (London: Macmillan, 1981).

II. Yearbooks, Journals, Collections of Criticism

Three important scholarly series issued since the 1970s are the *Beethoven-Jahrbuch*, issued by the Beethoven-Haus at Bonn; *Beethoven Studies*, edited by Alan Tyson; and *Zu Beethoven*, edited by Harry Goldschmidt. The last issue of the *Beethoven-Jahrbuch* appeared in 1983; a resumption of this series is planned, and periodic collections of essays have continued to be issued by the Beethoven-Haus under other titles, such as *Beiträge zu Beethovens Kammermusik* (1987), *Beethoven und Böhmen* (1988), and *Beethoven: Zwischen Revolution und Restauration* (1989). The three volumes of *Beethoven Studies* appeared between 1973 and 1982; the three volumes of *Zu Beethoven* were published between 1979 and 1988. *The Beethoven Newsletter*, published since 1986 by the American Beethoven Society, contains shorter articles but not the longer, detailed studies characteristic of primary research.

The 1990s have seen the emergence of several new scholarly publications devoted to Beethoven. A new monograph series issued by the University of Nebraska Press, *North American Beethoven Studies*, began in 1991 with the appearance of *Beethoven's Compositional Process*, edited by the present writer. A new yearbook, *Beethoven Forum*, published by Nebraska and edited by Christopher Reynolds and others, first appeared in 1992; several volumes are in preparation. A series of sketchbook editions is planned. A major current German publication project on Beethoven is *Beethoven: Interpretationen seiner Werke*, edited by Carl Dahlhaus, Albrecht Riethmüller, and Alexander Ringer, and published by Laaber Verlag. This two-volume work includes detailed essays on virtually all of Beethoven's works.

III. BEETHOVEN'S SKETCHES, CREATIVE PROCESS

The valuable pioneering source studies by Gustav Nottebohm, and the interpretations of Paul Mies (*Beethoven's Sketches*, London: Oxford University Press, 1929, based entirely on Nottebohm's work) are now largely superseded by research done since the 1960s. Some of these works are listed in the bibliographies of *The Beethoven Sketchbooks* by Douglas Johnson, Alan Tyson, and Robert Winter; in addition to these three scholars, the studies by Sieghard Brandenburg, Barry Cooper, William Drabkin, Joseph Kerman, Richard Kramer, and Lewis Lockwood among others are worthy of mention. Brandenburg's uncollected studies have examined the sources of a number of Beethoven's major works. Lockwood's collected essays appeared as *Beethoven: Studies in the Creative Process* (Cambridge, Mass.: Harvard University Press, 1992); he is also general editor of the series Studies in Musical Genesis and Structure, published by Oxford University Press, which has issued studies of the Diabelli Variations, by the present writer (1987), and of the *Appassionata* Sonata, by Martha Frohlich (1991). Also see the aforementioned collection of essays, *Beethoven's Compositional Process*, published by the University of Nebraska Press (1991). Another recent study is Barry Cooper's book *Beethoven and the Creative Process* (Oxford: Clarendon, 1990). The Beethoven-Haus is committed to a series of sketchbook editions, but no such publications were issued between 1978 and 1993, when the *Landsberg 5* Sketchbook, transcribed and edited by Clemens Brenneis, appeared. On the sketches for Beethoven's Tenth Symphony, see Barry Cooper, 'Newly Identified Sketches for Beethoven's Tenth Symphony', *Music and Letters*, lxvi (1985), pp. 9–18; and Robert Winter, 'Of Realizations, Completions, Restorations and Reconstructions: from Bach's *The Art of Fugue* to Beethoven's Tenth Symphony', *Journal of the Royal Musical Association*, cxvi (1991), pp. 96–125.

Most recent Beethoven scholarship has been done in English- and German-speaking countries, but an influential contribution to Beethoven sketch research was the edition of the so-called 'Wielhorsky' Sketchbook by Natan L'vovich Fishman that was published in Moscow in 1962 (*Kniga eskizov Betkhovena za 1802–1803 gody*). For a discussion of the Beethoven studies of Fishman and some other scholars in the former Soviet Union, see Larissa Kirillina, 'Recent Russian Beethoven Scholars', *The Beethoven Newsletter*, vii (1992), pp. 10–16.

IV. ANALYSIS AND CRITICISM

For a collection of early reviews of Beethoven's music up to 1830, see Stefan Kunze, ed., *Ludwig van Beethoven: Die Werke im Spiegel seiner Zeit: Gesammelte Konzertberichte und Rezensionen bis 1830* (Laaber: Laaber Verlag, 1987). Also see Robin Wallace, *Beethoven's Critics* (Cambridge: Cambridge University Press, 1986), and the bibliographical overview of writings compiled by Donald W. MacArdle (*Beethoven Abstracts* [Detroit: Information Coordinators, 1973]). Recent discussions of Beethoven's relations with aesthetic currents of early Romanticism include Dahlhaus's *Ludwig van Beethoven* and the review of his book by John Daverio, 'Dahlhaus's Beethoven and the Esoteric Aesthetics of the Early Nineteenth Century', in *Beethoven Forum*, ii (1993), as well as Scott Burnham's article on A. B. Marx in *19th Century Music*, xiii (1990), and Maynard Solomon, 'Beethoven: Beyond Classicism', in *The Beethoven Quartet Companion*, ed. Robert Winter and Robert Martin (Berkeley: University of California Press, 1994), pp. 59–75. On Beethoven's attitudes towards nature, religion, and freemasonry, see Arnold Schmitz, *Das romantische Beethovenbild: Darstellung und Kritik* (Berlin and Bonn: Dümmler, 1927), esp. pp. 86–93, among other studies. Among many works devoted to aspects of Beethoven reception, a classic study is Leo Schrade, *Beethoven in France: The Growth of an Idea* (New Haven: Yale University Press, 1942). Hans Heinrich Eggebrecht's *Zur Geschichte der Beethoven Rezeption* has been republished in a volume containing two additional essays (Laaber: Laaber Verlag, 1994). See also Ruth A. Solie, 'Beethoven as Secular Humanist: Ideology and the Ninth Symphony in Nineteenth-Century Criticism', in *Explorations in Music, the Arts and Ideas:*

Essays in Honor of Leonard B. Meyer, ed. Eugene Narmour and Ruth A. Solie (Stuyvesant: Pendragon Press, 1988), pp. 1–42. The Beethoven myth has attracted attention in various recent studies, including Rainer Cadenbach, *Mythos Beethoven: Ausstellungskatalog* (Laaber: Laaber Verlag, 1986), Alessandra Comini, *The Changing Image of Beethoven: A Study in Mythmaking* (New York: Rizzoli, 1987), and Elisabeth Eleonore Bauer, *Wie Beethoven auf den Sockel kam: Die Entstehung eines musikalischen Mythos* (Stuttgart and Weimar: Metzler, 1992).

An outstanding older critical survey of Beethoven's music is Walter Riezler's *Beethoven*, trans. G. D. H. Pidcock (London: M. C. Forrester, 1938). The valuable critical commentaries by Donald Francis Tovey are scattered in part through the volumes of his *Essays in Musical Analysis*; also see his unfinished posthumous *Beethoven* monograph (London: Oxford University Press, 1944) and his somewhat schematic *Companion to Beethoven's Piano Sonatas* (London: Associated Board of the Royal Schools of Music, 1931), as well as Joseph Kerman's essay 'Tovey's Beethoven' in *Beethoven Studies*, ii, ed. Alan Tyson. A stimulating discussion of Beethoven's style focusing on the *Hammerklavier* Sonata is found in Charles Rosen's *The Classical Style: Haydn, Mozart, Beethoven* (London: Faber, 1971). Dieter Rexroth's *Beethoven: Monographie* (Mainz: Schott, 1982) consists mainly of a biographical summary, reprinting familiar documents bearing on Beethoven's life and work, although some original commentary is offered in the last chapters, devoted to the piano sonatas, variations, and *Fidelio*.

1. Beethoven's Creative Periods

An excellent summary of critical thought about Beethoven's evolving style periods from Wilhelm von Lenz to recent scholarship is found in Solomon's chapter 'Beethoven's Creative Periods' in his *Beethoven Essays*.

Early Years: Since Ludwig Schiedermair's *Der junge Beethoven* of 1925, the most intensive research has been done by Kerman and Johnson. Kerman's edition of the so-called 'Kafka' Sketchbook (*Ludwig van Beethoven: Autograph Miscellany from Circa 1786 to 1799 (The 'Kafka' Sketchbook)*, London, 1970) and Johnson's edition of the 'Fischhof' Miscellany in *Beethoven's Early Sketches* (PhD dissertation, 1978; Ann Arbor, 1980) have made most of Beethoven's early working papers available in transcription, offering a new platform for criticism. There is a shortage of good analytical writing on many of the early works, however, and some important music—like the *Joseph* Cantata—is still unavailable in adequate recordings.

Middle Years: A substantial analytical literature has accumulated on individual movements that have been interpreted as reflecting a turning-point in

Beethoven's compositional style. See, for instance, Dahlhaus's discussion of the first movement of the *Tempest* Sonata op. 31 no. 2 in his *Ludwig van Beethoven* monograph and other publications, or the various studies of the first movement of the *Eroica* Symphony cited below. The notion of Beethoven's 'new way' risks being overworked in some commentaries. Numerous earlier scholars, including Romain Rolland and Arnold Schmitz, have written about the relationship of Beethoven's 'heroic' style to French revolutionary currents; certain of these ideas are absorbed into Michael Broyles, *The Emergence and Evolution of Beethoven's 'Heroic' Style* (New York: Excelsior, 1987). Beethoven's stylistic evolution at the threshold of the nineteenth century still poses challenges to analytical criticism. The indispensable balance between normative categories of musical form and character on the one hand, and the particular qualities of individual works on the other, was grasped more surely in the nineteenth-century writings of E. T. A. Hoffmann or A. B. Marx than in those later studies from Hugo Riemann to the present in which either the allure of theory pursued for its own sake or an indulgence in programmatic interpretation has predominated. For a discussion of Marx's analyses and their later reception see Wulf Arlt, 'Zur Geschichte der Formenlehre und zur Beethoven-analyse im 19. Jahrhundert: Adolph Bernhard Marx', in *Beethoven '77: Beiträge der Beethoven-Woche 1977 veranstaltet von der Musik-Akademie Basel,* ed. Friedhelm Döhl (Zürich: Amadeus, 1979), pp. 21–44.

Later Years: Insightful discussions of Beethoven's 'late style' are found in Riezler's *Beethoven* and Martin Cooper's *Beethoven: The Last Decade* (London: Oxford University Press, 1970). Concise summaries of his late style are found in Brendel's 'Beethoven's New Style' in *Music Sounded Out* (London: Robson, 1990) and in chapter 4 of my *Beethoven's Diabelli Variations* (Oxford: Clarendon, 1987). Also see Kevin Korsyn, *Integration in Works of Beethoven's Final Period* (PhD dissertation, Yale University, 1983), and 'J. W. N. Sullivan and the Heiliger Dankgesang: Questions of Meaning in Late Beethoven', *Beethoven Forum*, ii (1993), pp. 133–74.

2. Selected Critical Studies by Genre

Symphonies: For a listing of older surveys by Grove and others, see Solomon's *Beethoven* (New York: Schirmer, 1977). *The Nine Symphonies of Beethoven* by Anthony Hopkins (London: Heinemann, 1981) is a clear but very basic guide. The *Eroica* Symphony has received very intense analytical attention, from Heinrich Schenker, 'Beethovens Dritte Sinfonie zum erstenmal in ihrem wahren Inhalt dargestellt', *Das Meisterwerk in der Musik: ein Jahrbuch von Heinrich Schenker*, iii (Munich, 1930; repr. Hildesheim and New York: Georg Olms Verlag, 1974); Walter Riezler, *Beethoven*, pp. 247–81; Ernest

Newman, *The Unconscious Beethoven* (London: Leonard Parsons, 1927), pp. 120–36; and David Epstein, *Beyond Orpheus* (Cambridge, Mass.: MIT Press, 1979), pp. 111–38, among others. Especially important are the four essays by Lewis Lockwood brought together in his *Beethoven: Studies in the Creative Process*.

Recent discussions of the Fifth Symphony are offered by Lawrence Kramer, *Music and Poetry: The Nineteenth Century and After* (Berkeley and Los Angeles: University of California Press, 1984), pp. 234–41; and Kerman, 'Taking the Fifth', *Das musikalische Kunstwerk: Geschichte—Ästhetik—Theorie: Festschrift Carl Dahlhaus zum 60. Geburtstag*, ed. Hermann Danuser, Helga de la Motte-Haber, S. Leopold and N. Miller (Laaber: Laaber Verlag, 1988), pp. 483–91, who offers a critique of Schenker's analysis. On the Sixth Symphony, see Rudolf Bockholdt, *Ludwig van Beethoven: VI. Symphonie F-Dur, op. 68 Pastorale* (Munich: Fink Verlag, 1981). One of many new publications on the Ninth Symphony is Solomon's outstanding essay 'The Ninth Symphony: A Search for Order', in *Beethoven Essays*. Leo Treitler offers a pair of articles on this work in his *Music and the Historical Imagination* (Cambridge, Mass.: Harvard University Press, 1989): 'History, Criticism, and Beethoven's Ninth Symphony' and '"To Worship that Celestial Sound": Motives for Analysis'. A challenging older study is Otto Baensch, *Aufbau und Sinn des Chorfinales in Beethovens neunter Symphonie* (Berlin and Leipzig: Walter de Gruyter, 1930); also see Johannes Bauer, *Rhetorik der Überschreitung: Annotationen zu Beethovens Neunter Symphonie* (Pfaffenweiler: Centaurus, 1992). The design of the choral finale is given renewed scrutiny in 'The Form of the Finale in Beethoven's Ninth Symphony' (*Beethoven Forum*, i, pp. 25–62) by James Webster, who finds that the analyses of Schenker and Tovey, far from being opposed, 'ideally complement each other' (p. 44).

String Quartets: The best overall critical study is Kerman, *The Beethoven Quartets* (New York: Norton, 1966); also see Philip Radcliffe's useful volume, *Beethoven's String Quartets* (London: Hutchinson, 1965, 2/1978). More recent analytical studies include Bruce Campbell, *Beethoven's Quartets Opus 59: An Investigation into Compositional Process* (PhD dissertation, Yale University, 1982); Lini Hübsch, *Ludwig van Beethoven: Rasumowsky-Quartette* (Munich: Fink Verlag, 1983); David L. Brodbeck and John Platoff, 'Dissociation and Integration: The First Movement of Beethoven's Opus 130', *19th Century Music*, vii (1983), pp. 149–62; Robert Winter, *The Compositional Origins of Beethoven's Opus 131* (Ann Arbor: UMI Research Press, 1982); and John Edward Crotty, *Design and Harmonic Organization in Beethoven's String Quartet, Opus 131* (PhD dissertation, University of Rochester, 1986). Also see *The Beethoven Quartet Companion*, ed. Robert Winter and Robert Martin (Berkeley: University of California Press, 1994). The entire first version of

Beethoven's Quartet op. 18 no. 1 is printed in Hans Josef Wedig, *Beethovens Streichquartett Op. 18 Nr. 1 und seine erste Fassung* (Bonn: Beethovenhaus, 1922). Mozart's influence on Beethoven's op. 18 no. 5 and op. 132 is assessed in Jeremy Yudkin, 'Beethoven's "Mozart" Quartet', *Journal of the American Musicological Society* xlv (1992), pp. 30–74.

Solo Piano Music: For an overview of earlier writings, see William S. Newman, *The Sonata in the Classic Era* (2nd ed., New York: Norton, 1972), who counted more than 50 books devoted to the sonatas alone. More recent contributions to this vast and ever growing literature include Newman's *Beethoven on Beethoven: Playing his Piano Music his Way* (New York: Norton, 1988) and my chapter 'Beethoven' in *Nineteenth-Century Piano Music*, ed. R. Larry Todd (New York: Schirmer, 1990), pp. 55–96. Critical evaluation of recordings, together with analytical description, is offered in Joachim Kaiser's *Beethovens 32 Klaviersonaten und ihre Interpreten* (Frankfurt: Fischer, 1975). For a discussion of rhetorical features of Beethoven's piano music, see George Barth, *The Pianist as Orator: Beethoven and the Transformation of Keyboard Style* (Ithaca: Cornell University Press, 1992). Schenker prepared critical editions with analysis of all the last sonatas except the *Hammerklavier* in *Die letzten Sonaten von Beethoven: Kritische Ausgabe mit Einführung und Erläuterung*, 4 vols. (Vienna: Universal, 1913–21; new ed. 1971). The best detailed survey of all the piano music is Jürgen Uhde, *Beethovens Klaviermusik*, 3 vols. (Stuttgart: Reclam, 1968–74), a work unfortunately overlooked in some recent bibliographies in English. Also see Uhde's collaborative book with Renate Wieland, *Denken und Spielen* (Kassel and New York: Bärenreiter, 1988), which is important as well for its discussion of Adorno's Beethoven criticism. This book is reviewed by the present author in *19th Century Music*, xv (1991), pp. 64–8. Uhde and Wieland offer detailed discussion of Adorno's stimulating writings on Beethoven that reached publication only in 1993 (Theodor W. Adorno, *Beethoven: Philosophie der Musik: Fragmente und Texte: Fragment gebliebener Schriften*, i, ed. Rolf Tiedemann (Frankfurt: Suhrkamp).

There is no adequate modern survey in English of Beethoven's numerous sets of piano variations. For a recent overview of classical variation procedures, see Elaine Sisman, *Haydn and the Classical Variation* (Cambridge, Mass.: Harvard University Press, 1993), who devotes her final chapter to Beethoven's transformation of the classical variation. Intense scrutiny of the genesis of the op. 35 Variations is offered by Christopher Reynolds in 'Beethoven's Sketches for the Variations in E♭ Op. 35', *Beethoven Studies*, iii, pp. 47–84. On the Diabelli Variations, see my aforementioned study and Brendel's essay 'Must Classical Music Be Entirely Serious? 2: Beethoven's Diabelli Variations' in *Music Sounded Out*.

Chamber Music with Piano: For an overview of the genre of the piano trio, see Basil Smallman, *The Piano Trio: Its History, Technique, and Repertoire* (Oxford: Clarendon, 1990). The most recent study of Beethoven's trios is the German conference report *Beethovens Klaviertrios: Symposion München 1990*, ed. Rudolf Bockholdt and Petra Weber-Bockholdt (Munich: Henle, 1992), which includes valuable essays by Stefan Kunze on op. 70 no. 1, and by Peter Cahn on op. 70 no. 2. A discussion of the violin sonatas is contained in Max Rostal, *Ludwig van Beethoven: Die Sonaten für Klavier und Violine* (Munich: Piper, 1981; Eng. trans. by Horace and Anna Rosenberg, New York and Gloucester, 1985).

Fidelio: Noteworthy are the studies of Willy Hess, most recently *Das Fidelio-Buch: Beethovens Oper Fidelio, Ihre Geschichte und Ihre Drei Fassungen* (Winterthur: Amadeus, 1986); Winton Dean, 'Beethoven and Opera', in *The Beethoven Companion*, ed. Denis Arnold and Nigel Fortune (London: Faber, 1971; and New York: Norton, 1971, as *The Beethoven Reader*), pp. 331–86; and articles by Tyson, Lühning, and most recently Michael Tusa, 'The Unknown Florestan: The 1805 Version of "In des Lebens Frühlingstagen"', *Journal of the American Musicological Society*, xlvi (1993), pp. 175–220.

Works for the Congress of Vienna: Especially useful is the collection of essays *Beethoven: Zwischen Revolution und Restauration* (Bonn: Beethovenhaus, 1989), with contributions by Küthen, Michael Ladenburger ('Der Wiener Kongress im Spiegel der Musik', pp. 275–306), and Thomas Röder ('Beethovens Sieg über die Schlachtenmusik, Opus 91, und die Tradition der Battaglia', pp. 229–58).

Missa solemnis: See the Cambridge Handbook *Beethoven: Missa solemnis* by William Drabkin, published in 1991, and studies by Drabkin, Kirkendale, and others listed in the 'Bibliography of Works Cited'. Wilfrid Mellers's *Beethoven and the Voice of God* (London: Oxford University Press, 1983) contains an extensive but highly speculative discussion. Also see Theodor W. Adorno, 'Alienated Masterpiece: The *Missa Solemnis*', *Telos*, xxviii (1976), pp. 113–24.

Lieder: A valuable overview is contained in Hans Boettcher, *Beethoven als Liederkomponist* (Augsburg: Benno Filser, 1928). A classic essay is Kerman's 'An die ferne Geliebte', in *Beethoven Studies*, i, pp. 123–57; also see Lockwood's 'Beethoven's Sketches for *Sehnsucht* (WoO 146)', in the same volume, pp. 97–122.

3. Specialized Analytic Approaches

Many analyses of Beethoven's music focus on motivic relationships, thematic structure, rhythmic and metrical phenomena, or harmonic and tonal structure; the most convincing studies do not lose sight of the relations of these and other musical elements to one another. The method of analysing motivic relationships and derivations in Beethoven's music has a venerable tradition; the studies of Walter Engelsmann, Rudolph Réti, and Deryck Cooke, among others, illustrate this approach. Also see Kurt von Fischer, *Die Beziehungen von Form und Motiv in Beethovens Instrumentalwerken* (Strasbourg and Zürich: Heity, 1948). Authors who have seen in Beethoven a continuation of older rhetorical traditions include Erich Schenk, 'Barock bei Beethoven', *Beethoven und die Gegenwart: Festschrift Ludwig Schiedermair zum 60. Geburtstag* ed. Arnold Schmitz (Berlin and Bonn: Dümmler, 1937), pp. 177–219; and Warren Kirkendale, 'New Roads to Old Ideas in Beethoven's *Missa solemnis*', *Musical Quarterly*, lvi (1970), pp. 665–701. See also Wolfgang Osthoff, 'Das "Sprechende" in Beethovens Instrumentalmusik', in *Beiträge zu Beethovens Kammermusik: Symposion Bonn 1984*, ed. Sieghard Brandenburg and Helmut Loos (Munich, 1987), pp. 11–40.

Erwin Ratz, in his *Einführung in die musikalische Formenlehre* (Vienna: Universal, 1968), emphasizes phrase structure and form, an approach adapted by William E. Caplin in recent studies, such as 'Structural Expansion in Beethoven's Symphonic Forms', in *Beethoven's Compositional Process*, pp. 27–54. Rhythmic and metrical relations have fascinated many writers, from Heinrich Christoph Koch in the eighteenth century to the recent work of Edward Cone and others. For a stimulating and lucid analysis of rhythmic and metrical tension in the Sonata op. 10 no. 3 and the Fifth Symphony, see Andrew Imbrie, ' "Extra" Measures and Metrical Ambiguity in Beethoven', *Beethoven Studies*, i, pp. 45–66. A discussion of the controversial problems of tempo and interpretation in Beethoven is offered by Rudolf Kolisch, *Tempo und Charakter in Beethovens Musik*, ed. Regina Busch, in *Musik-Konzepte 76/77* (Munich, 1992); a version in English, as 'Tempo and Character in Beethoven's Music', is appearing in *The Musical Quarterly*, lxxvii (1993), pp. 90–131 (only part 1 was published at the time of writing; an earlier version appeared in *The Musical Quarterly* of 1943). For an alternative to Kolisch's system concerning the relationship of tempo and character see Uhde and Wieland, *Denken und Spielen*, pp. 231–45, esp. pp. 232 and 242, where Uhde asks 'Why shouldn't certain analogous structural details take on a qualitatively different character in different works?' Also see on this point Peter Gülke, 'Zum Verhältnis von Intention und Realisierung bei Beethoven', *Musik-Konzepte 8: Beethoven: Das Problem der Interpretation* (Munich, 1979), pp. 34–53.

The most influential analyses that emphasize linear, harmonic, and tonal coherence in Beethoven's music are those of Heinrich Schenker. Some analysts, including Roger Kamien and Carl Schachter, have offered revealing studies along these lines; a convincing application of principles derived from

Schenker is found in Kevin Korsyn's *Integration in Works of Beethoven's Final Period* (PhD dissertation, Yale University, 1983). Leo Treitler and Joseph Kerman have drawn attention to the risk, in the work of Schenker and some of his followers, of a totalizing attitude that locates the artwork in a self-contained matrix of relationships, while downgrading other important features of artistic character and meaning. Some of the attendant ideological problems are discussed by Michael Russ, 'On Schenkerism: A Closed Circle of Elite Listeners?', *Music Analysis*, xii (1993), pp. 266–85. As Russ observes (p. 271), analysts such as Patrick McCreless have been able to absorb Treitler's critique, acknowledging the limited and potentially limiting scope of Schenker's approach. The notion of the work of art as a merely closed and unified system is decidedly un-Beethovenian and needs to be balanced against the richly dramatic, rhetorical, and contrast-laden elements of his musical style. Thrasybulos Georgiades was not wrong to perceive in the discontinuities of the Viennese Classical style an embodiment of human freedom (*Musik und Sprache*, Berlin, Göttingen, and Heidelberg: Springer Verlag, 1954, pp. 90 ff., 115 ff.); clearly, an adequate critical system needs to take proper account not merely of 'structure' but of the wit, spontaneity, and spirit of this music.

4. Other Critical Approaches

Humour, Irony, and Paradox: A worthy older study of Beethoven's musical humour is Theodor Veidl, *Der musikalische Humor bei Beethoven* (Leipzig: Breitkopf & Härtel, 1929); also see Arnold Schering, *Humor, Heldentum, Tragik bei Beethoven: Über einige Grundsymbole der Tonsprache Beethovens*, ed. Helmuth Osthoff (Strasbourg/Kehl: Librairie Heitz, 1955). The topic of paradox is explored by Sylvia Imeson, *'The time gives it proofe': Paradox in the Late Music of Beethoven* (PhD dissertation, University of Victoria, 1993); other relevant studies include Brendel's 'Must Classical Music be Entirely Serious?', in *Music Sounded Out*, and the present author's article (with its paradoxical title) 'Beethoven's High Comic Style in Piano Sonatas of the 1790s' or 'Beethoven, Uncle Toby, and the Muck-Cart Driver', *Beethoven Forum*, v (in German in *Beethoven-Jahrbuch*, xi, both forthcoming). Critical evaluation of Beethoven's verbal humour is offered by, among others, Martin Cooper, in *Beethoven: The Last Decade*. See also Rey M. Longyear, 'Beethoven and Romantic Irony', *The Musical Quarterly*, 56 (1970), pp. 647–64; reprinted in *The Creative World of Beethoven*, ed. Paul Henry Lang (New York: Norton, 1971), pp. 145–62.

Symbolism, Myth, and Narrative: Critical studies touching on issues of myth, symbolism, and narrative include the aforementioned essays by Solomon and Treitler on the Ninth Symphony and Floros's book on *Beethovens Eroica und Prometheus-Musik* (Wilhelmshaven: Heinrichshofen's Verlag, 1978). Recent debate on the subject of narrative in music has been intense. See my discussion of studies of music and narrative by Anthony Newcomb, Carolyn Abbate, and Jean-Jacques Nattiez in 'Integration and Narrative Design in Beethoven's Piano Sonata in A♭ major, Opus 110', *Beethoven Forum*, i, pp. 111–45; and Richard Kramer's essay 'Between Cavatina and Ouverture: Opus 130 and the Voices of Narrative' in the same volume, pp. 165–89. Also see the ongoing discussion concerning the Orpheus 'programme' in the *Andante con moto* of Beethoven's Fourth Concerto: Owen Jander, 'Beethoven's "Orpheus in Hades"', *19th Century Music*, viii (1984), pp. 195–212; Edward T. Cone, 'Beethoven's Orpheus—or Jander's?', *19th Century Music*, viii (1984), pp. 283–6; and Joseph Kerman, 'Representing a Relationship: Notes on a Beethoven Concerto', *Representations*, xxxix (1992), pp. 80–101. A stimulating symposium on music and narrative with contributions by Lawrence Kramer, Fred Everett Maus, Patrick McCreless, and others appeared in the *Indiana Theory Review*, xii (1991); many examples discussed in that volume are drawn from Beethoven.

BIBLIOGRAPHY OF WORKS CITED

Abbate, Carolyn, 'What the Sorcerer Said', *19th Century Music*, xii (1989), pp. 221–30
——, *Unsung Voices: Opera and Musical Narrative in Nineteenth-Century Music* (Princeton: Princeton University Press, 1991)
—— and Roger Parker, eds., *Analyzing Opera: Verdi and Wagner* (Berkeley and Los Angeles: University of California Press, 1989)
—— and Roger Parker, 'Dismembering Mozart', *Cambridge Opera Journal*, ii (1990), pp. 187–95
Anderson, Emily, ed., *The Letters of Beethoven*, 3 vols. (London: Macmillan, 1961, repr. 1985)
Árnason, Vilhjálmur, 'Morality and Humanity', *Journal of Value Inquiry*, xxii (1988), pp. 3–22
—— 'The Discourse of Freedom', *Rechtstheorie*, xix (1988), pp. 491–501
Badura-Skoda, Paul, 'Noch einmal zur Frage Ais oder A in der Hammerklaviersonate Opus 106 von Beethoven', *Musik—Edition—Interpretation: Gedenkschrift Günter Henle* (Munich: Henle, 1980), pp. 53–81
Baensch, Otto, *Aufbau und Sinn des Chorfinales in Beethovens neunter Symphonie* (Berlin and Leipzig: Walter de Gruyter, 1930)
Bankl, Hans, and Hans Jesserer, *Die Krankheiten Ludwig van Beethovens: Pathographie seines Lebens und Pathologie seiner Leiden* (Vienna: Verlag Wilhelm Maudrich, 1987)
Beck, Dagmar, and Grita Herre, 'Anton Schindlers fingierte Eintragungen in der Konversationsheften', *Zu Beethoven*, i, ed. Harry Goldschmidt (Berlin: Verlag Neue Musik, 1979), pp. 11–89
Ludwig van Beethovens Konversationshefte, 10 vols., ed. Karl-Heinz Köhler, Grita Herre, and Dagmar Beck (Leipzig: VEB Deutscher Verlag für Musik, 1968–93; 2 vols. forthcoming)
Beethovens Werke: vollständige, kritisch durchgesehene Gesamtausgabe, 25 vols. (Leipzig: Breitkopf & Härtel, 1862–5; 1888)
Bekker, Paul, *Beethoven* (Berlin: Schuster & Loeffler, 1912)
Berlin, Isaiah, *Four Essays on Liberty* (London: Oxford University Press, 1969)
Berlioz, Hector, *À travers chants* (Paris: Michel Lévy Frères (Libraires Éditeurs), 1862, and Guichard, 1971; Eng. trans., 1913–18)
Blom, Eric, *Beethoven's Pianoforte Sonatas Discussed* (London: J. M. Dent & Sons, and New York: E. P. Dutton, 1938)
Boettcher, Hans, *Beethoven als Liederkomponist* (Augsburg: Benno Filser Verlag, 1928)
Brandenburg, Sieghard, 'Bemerkungen zu Beethovens op. 96', *Beethoven-Jahrbuch*, ix (1977), pp. 11–25
Brandenburg, Sieghard, 'Ein Skizzenbuch Beethovens aus dem Jahre 1812: Zur

Chronologie des Petterschen Skizzenbuches', *Zu Beethoven: Aufsätze und Anno-tationen*, ed. Harry Goldschmidt (Berlin: Verlag Neue Musik, 1979), pp. 117–48

—— 'The Autograph of Beethoven's Quartet in A minor, Opus 132: The Structure of the Manuscript and its Relevance for the Study of the Genesis of the Work', *The String Quartets of Haydn, Mozart, and Beethoven: Studies of the Autograph Manuscripts*, ed. Christoph Wolff (Cambridge, Mass.: Harvard University Department of Music, 1980), pp. 278–300

—— 'Die Quellen zur Entstehungsgeschichte von Beethovens Streichquartett Es-Dur Op. 127', *Beethoven-Jahrbuch*, x (1983), pp. 221–76

—— 'Die Skizzen zur Neunten Symphonie', *Zu Beethoven 2: Aufsätze und Dokumente*, ed. Harry Goldschmidt (Berlin: Verlag Neue Musik, 1984), pp. 88–129

Brendel, Alfred, *Musical Thoughts and Afterthoughts* (London: Robson, and Princeton: Princeton University Press, 1976)

—— *Music Sounded Out: Essays, Lectures, Interviews, Afterthoughts* (London: Robson, and New York: Farrar Straus Giroux, 1990) [page references in this book are to the British edition]

—— *Musik beim Wort genommen* (Munich: Piper, 1992)

Breuning, Gerhard von, *Memories of Beethoven: From the House of the Black-Robed Spaniards*, ed. Maynard Solomon (Cambridge: Cambridge University Press, 1992); first pubd as *Aus dem Schwarzspanierhaus* (Vienna: Rosner, 1874)

Broch, Hermann, *Schriften zur Literatur 2: Theorie*, ed. Paul Michael Lützeler (Frankfurt am Main: Suhrkamp Verlag, 1975) [contains both 'Das Böse im Wertsystem der Kunst' and 'Einige Bemerkungen zum Problem des Kitsches']

—— 'Notes on the Problem of Kitsch', *Kitsch: The World of Bad Taste*, ed. Gillo Dorfles (New York: Bell), pp. 49–76

Broyles, Michael, *The Emergence and Evolution of Beethoven's Heroic Style* (New York: Excelsior, 1987)

Bruner, Carol, 'The Genesis and Structure of Beethoven's Overture "Die Weihe des Hauses", Op. 124' (MA thesis, University of Victoria, 1990)

Bülow, Hans von, ed., *Beethovens Werke für Pianoforte Solo von op. 53 an in kritischer und instruktiver Ausgabe*, i (Stuttgart: Cotta, 1877); and *Beethoven Sonatas for Pianoforte Solo* (New York: Schirmer, 1894)

Bumpass, Laura Kathryn, *Beethoven's Last Quartet* (PhD dissertation, University of Illinois, Urbana-Champaign, 1982)

Burnham, Scott, 'Criticism, Faith, and the *Idee*: A. B. Marx's Early Reception of Beethoven', *19th Century Music*, xiii (1990), pp. 183–92

Burton, Anthony, notes to recording of the Beethoven piano trios by Wilhelm Kempff, Henryk Szering, and Pierre Fournier (Deutsche Grammophon)

Butor, Michel, *Dialogue avec 33 variations de Ludwig van Beethoven sur une valse de Diabelli* (Paris: Gallimard, 1971)

Canisius, Claus, *Beethoven: 'Sehnsucht und Unruhe in der Musik'* (Munich: Piper, 1992)

Caplin, William E., 'Structural Expansion in Beethoven's Symphonic Forms', *Beethoven's Compositional Process*, ed. William Kinderman (Lincoln and London: University of Nebraska Press, 1991), pp. 27–54

Chytry, Joseph, *The Aesthetic State: A Quest in Modern German Thought* (Berkeley, Los

Angeles, and London: University of California Press, 1989)

Cooke, Deryck, 'The Unity of Beethoven's Late Quartets', *Music Review*, xxiv (1963), pp. 30–49

Cooper, Barry, *Beethoven and the Creative Process* (Oxford: Clarendon, 1990)

—— *Beethoven's Folksong Settings: Chronology, Sources, Style* (Oxford: Clarendon, 1994)

Cooper, Martin, *Beethoven: The Last Decade 1817–1827* (London and New York: Oxford University Press, 1970)

—— *Judgements of Value: Selected Writings on Music*, ed. Dominic Cooper (Oxford and New York: Oxford University Press, 1988)

Czerny, Carl, *Über den richtigen Vortrag der sämtlichen Beethoven'schen Klavierwerke*, ed. Paul Badura-Skoda (Vienna: Universal, 1963); Eng. trans. as *On the Proper Performance of All Beethoven's Works for the Piano* (Vienna: Universal, 1970)

Dahlhaus, Carl, *Ludwig van Beethoven und seine Zeit* (Laaber: Laaber Verlag, 1987); Eng. trans. by Mary Whittall as *Ludwig van Beethoven: Approaches to his Music* (Oxford: Clarendon Press, 1991)

Danuser, Hermann, *Musikalische Prosa* (Regensburg: Gustav Bosse Verlag, 1975)

Dische, Irene, *Ein fremdes Gefühl oder Veränderungen über einen Deutschen*, Ger. trans. by Reinhard Kaiser (Berlin: Rowohlt, 1993); Eng. version as *Sad Strains of a Gay Waltz* (London: Bloomsbury, 1994)

Drabkin, William, *The Sketches for Beethoven's Piano Sonata in C Minor, Opus 111*, 2 vols. (PhD dissertation, Princeton University, 1977)

—— 'The Agnus Dei of Beethoven's *Missa solemnis*: The Growth of its Form', *Beethoven's Compositional Process*, ed. William Kinderman (Lincoln and London: Nebraska, 1991), pp. 131–59

—— *Beethoven: Missa solemnis* (Cambridge: Cambridge University Press, 1991)

Einstein, Alfred, 'Beethoven's Military Style', *Essays on Music* (New York: Norton, 1956), pp. 243–49

Floros, Constantin, *Beethovens Eroica und Prometheus-Musik* (Wilhelmshaven: Heinrichshofen's Verlag, 1978)

Forbes, Elliot, ed., *Thayer's Life of Beethoven* (Princeton: Princeton University Press, 1964)

Forte, Allen, *The Compositional Matrix* (New York: Baldwin, 1961)

Frimmel, Theodor von, 'Beethovens Spaziergang nach Wiener Neustadt', *Beethoven-Forschung: Lose Blätter*, ix (1923), pp. 2–12

Frohlich, Martha, *Beethoven's 'Appassionata' Sonata* (Oxford: Clarendon, 1991)

Gadamer, Hans-Georg, 'Ende der Kunst?', *Ende der Kunst—Zukunft der Kunst* (Munich: Deutscher Kunstverlag, 1985), pp. 16–33

Goldschmidt, Harry, *Um die Unsterbliche Geliebte: Eine Bestandsaufnahme* (Leipzig: VEB Deutscher Verlag für Musik, 1977)

—— ed., *Zu Beethoven* (Berlin: Verlag Neue Musik), i (1979); ii (1984); iii, ed. with Georg Knepler (1988)

—— ' "Und wenn Beethoven selber käme . . .": Weitere Aspekte zum Mälzelkanon', *Zu Beethoven*, ii (Berlin: Verlag Neue Musik, 1984), pp. 185–204

Göllner, Theodor, 'Beethovens Ouvertüre "Die Weihe des Hauses" und Händels

Trauermarsch aus "Saul"', *Festschrift Heinrich Hüschen*, ed. D. Altenburg (Cologne: Gitarre und Laute Verlagsgesellschaft, 1980), pp. 181–9

Gülke, Peter, *Zur Neuausgabe der Sinfonie Nr. 5 von Ludwig van Beethoven: Werk und Edition* (Leipzig: Peters, 1978)

—— *Franz Schubert und seine Zeit* (Laaber: Laaber, 1991)

Harrington, Michael, *Socialism: Past and Future* (New York: Mentor, 1992; 1st pubd 1989)

Hertzmann, Erich, 'The Newly Discovered Autograph of Beethoven's *Rondo à Capriccio*, Op. 129', *Musical Quarterly*, xxxii (1946), pp. 171–95

Howell, Standley, 'Der Mälzelkanon—eine weitere Fälschung Schindlers?', *Zu Beethoven*, ii, ed. H. Goldschmidt (Berlin: Verlag Neue Musik, 1984), pp. 163–71

Hübsch, Lini, *Ludwig van Beethoven: Rasumowsky-Quartette* (Munich: Fink Verlag, 1983)

Imeson, Sylvia, *'The time gives it proofe': Paradox in the Late Music of Beethoven* (PhD dissertation, University of Victoria, 1993)

Jander, Owen, 'Beethoven's "Orpheus in Hades"', *19th Century Music*, viii (1984), pp. 195–212

John, Kathryn, 'Das Allegretto-Thema in op. 93, auf seine Skizzen befragt', *Zu Beethoven*, ii, ed. Harry Goldschmidt (Berlin: Verlag Neue Musik, 1984), pp. 117–48

Johnson, Douglas, '1794–95: Decisive Years in Beethoven's Early Development', *Beethoven Studies*, i, ed. Alan Tyson (New York: Norton, 1973), pp. 1–28

—— *Beethoven's Early Sketches in the 'Fischhof Miscellany'* (PhD dissertation, University of California, Berkeley, 1978)

—— *Beethoven's Early Sketches in the 'Fischhof Miscellany', Berlin Autograph 28* (Ann Arbor: UMI Research Press, 1980)

—— ed., *The Beethoven Sketchbooks: History, Reconstruction, Inventory* [with Alan Tyson and Robert Winter] (Berkeley and Los Angeles: University of California Press, 1985)

Kant, Immanuel, *Kritik der reinen Vernunft* (Stuttgart: Reclam, 1966; 1st pubd 1781); Eng. trans. by N. K. Smith as *Critique of Pure Reason* (London: Macmillan, 1968)

Kastner, Emerich, and Julius Kapp, eds., *Ludwig van Beethovens sämtliche Briefe* (Leipzig: Hesse & Becker, 1923)

Kerman, Joseph, *The Beethoven Quartets* (New York: Norton, 1966)

—— 'An die ferne Geliebte', in *Beethoven Studies*, i, ed. Alan Tyson (New York: Norton, 1973), pp. 123–57

—— 'Representing a Relationship: Notes on a Beethoven Concerto', *Representations*, xxxix (Berkeley: University of California Press, 1992)

Kinderman, William, 'Beethoven's Symbol for the Deity in the *Missa solemnis* and the Ninth Symphony', *19th Century Music*, ix (1985), pp. 102–18

—— *Beethoven's Diabelli Variations* (Oxford: Clarendon, 1987); my recording of the Diabelli Variations was issued by Hyperion Records in 1995 (Hyperion CDA 66763)

—— 'Tonality and Form in the Variation Movements of Beethoven's Late Quartets', in *Beiträge zu Beethovens Kammermusik: Symposion Bonn 1984*, ed. Sieghard Brandenburg and Helmut Loos (Munich: Henle, 1987), pp. 135–51.

—— 'Thematic Contrast and Parenthetical Enclosure in Beethoven's Piano Sonatas, Opp. 109 and 111', *Zu Beethoven*, iii, ed. Harry Goldschmidt and Georg Knepler (Berlin: Verlag Neue Musik, 1988), pp. 43–59

—— 'Beethoven', in *Nineteenth-Century Piano Music*, ed. R. Larry Todd (New York: Schirmer, 1990), pp. 55–96

—— ed., *Beethoven's Compositional Process* (Lincoln and London: University of Nebraska Press, 1991)

—— Review of William S. Newman, *Beethoven on Beethoven*, and Jürgen Uhde and Renate Wieland, *Denken und Spielen*, *19th Century Music*, xv (1991), pp. 64–8

—— 'Integration and Narrative Design in Beethoven's Piano Sonata in A♭ major, Opus 110', in *Beethoven Forum*, i, ed. Christopher Reynolds (Lincoln and London: University of Nebraska Press, 1992), pp. 111–45

—— Essays on the sonatas opp. 109, 110, 111 and on the String Quartet in E♭ op. 127, *Beethoven: Interpretationen seiner Werke, ii*, ed. Carl Dahlhaus, Albrecht Rieth-müller, and Alexander Ringer (Laaber: Laaber Verlag, 1994), pp. 162–81; 278–91

—— 'Beethoven's High Comic Style in Piano Sonatas of the 1790s' or 'Beethoven, Uncle Toby, and the Muck-Cart Driver', *Beethoven Forum*, v (forthcoming); Ger. version in *Beethoven-Jahrbuch*, xi (forthcoming)

Kirkendale, Warren, 'The "Great Fugue" Op. 133: Beethoven's "Art of the Fugue"', *Acta musicologica*, xxxv (1963), pp. 14–24

—— 'New Roads to Old Ideas in Beethoven's *Missa solemnis*', *Musical Quarterly*, lvi (1970), pp. 665–701; rpt. in *The Creative World of Beethoven*, ed. Paul Henry Lang (New York: Norton, 1971), pp. 163–99

Klein, Hans-Günter, *Ludwig van Beethoven: Autographe und Abschriften*, Staatsbibliothek Preussischer Kulturbesitz, Kataloge der Musikabteilung, ed. Rudolf Elvers, 1st series, *Handschriften*, ii (Berlin, 1975)

Köhler, Karl-Heinz, 'The Conversation Books: Aspects of a New Picture of Beethoven', in *Beethoven, Performers and Critics. The International Beethoven Congress Detroit, 1977*, ed. Robert Winter and Bruce Carr (Detroit: Wayne State University Press, 1980), pp. 147–61

Kolodin, Irving, *The Interior Beethoven* (New York: Alfred A. Knopf, 1975)

Korsyn, Kevin, *Integration in Works of Beethoven's Final Period* (PhD dissertation, Yale University, 1983)

Kramer, Lawrence, *Music and Poetry: The Nineteenth Century and After* (Berkeley, Los Angeles, London: University of California Press, 1984)

Kramer, Richard, 'Ambiguities in *La Malinconia*: What the Sketches Say', *Beethoven Studies*, iii, ed. Alan Tyson (Cambridge: Cambridge University Press, 1982), pp. 29–46

—— Review of Robert Winter and Bruce Carr, eds., *Beethoven, Performers, and Critics: The International Beethoven Congress, Detroit, 1977, Journal of Music Theory*, xxvii (1983), pp. 299–306

—— 'Counterpoint and Syntax: On a Difficult Passage in the First Movement of Beethoven's String Quartet in c minor, Opus 18 No. 4', *Beiträge zu Beethovens Kammermusik: Symposion Bonn 1984*, ed. Sieghard Brandenburg and Helmut Loos (Munich: Henle, 1987), pp. 111–24

Kramer, Richard, 'Between Cavatina and Ouverture: Opus 130 and the Voices of Narrative', *Beethoven Forum*, i, ed. Christopher Reynolds (Lincoln and London: University of Nebraska Press, 1992), pp. 165–89

Kretzschmar, Hermann, *Führer durch den Konzertsaal* (Leipzig: Breitkopf & Härtel, 1921; 1st pubd 1887–90; rev. edns to 1939)

Kropfinger, Klaus, 'Das gespaltene Werk—Beethovens Streichquartett Op. 130/133', *Beiträge zu Beethovens Kammermusik: Symposion Bonn 1984*, ed. Sieghard Brandenburg and Helmut Loos (Munich: Henle, 1987), pp. 296–335

Kundera, Milan, *Immortality*, trans. Peter Kussi (London: Faber & Faber, 1991) [discussion of imagology on pp. 126–31]

Kunze, Stefan, ed., *Ludwig van Beethoven: Die Werke im Spiegel seiner Zeit: Gesammelte Konzertberichte und Rezensionen bis 1830* (Laaber: Laaber Verlag, 1987)

Küthen, Hans-Werner, ed., *Ludwig van Beethoven: Klavierkonzert Nr. 3 in c*, Studienpartitur (Kassel, London, New York: Bärenreiter, 1987)

—— 'Beethovens "wirklich ganz neue Manier"—Eine Persiflage', *Beiträge zu Beethovens Kammermusik: Symposion Bonn 1984*, ed. Sieghard Brandenburg and Helmut Loos (Munich: Henle, 1987), pp. 216–24

—— ' "Wellingtons Sieg oder die Schlacht bei Vittoria': Beethoven und das Epochenproblem Napoleon', *Beethoven: Zwischen Revolution und Restauration*, ed. Sieghard Brandenburg and Helga Lühning (Bonn: Beethovenhaus, 1989), pp. 259–73

—— 'Schöpferische Rezeption im Finale der 9. Symphonie von Beethoven', in *Probleme der symphonischen Tradition im 19. Jahrhundert*, ed. Siegfried Kross (Tutzing: Schneider, 1990), pp. 41–65

—— 'Pragmatic Instead of Enigmatic: "The Fifty-First Sonata" of Beethoven', *The Beethoven Newsletter*, vii (1992), pp. 68–73

—— 'Mozart—Schiller—Beethoven: Mozarts Modell für die Freudenhymne und die Fusion der Embleme im Finale der Neunten Symphonie', *Hudební věda*, ii (1993), pp. 90–128

Ladenburger, Michael, ed., *Eine Brüsseler Beethoven-Sammlung: Das Beethoven-Porträt von Ferdinand Georg Waldmüller: Die Originalausgaben der Klaviersonaten Beethovens* (Exhibition catalogue, Bonn: Beethovenhaus, 1991)

Langer, Susanne, *Philosophy in a New Key: A Study in the Symbolism of Reason, Rite, and Art* (New York: Mentor, 1961; 1st pubd 1942)

Larsen, Jens Peter, 'Beethovens C-dur-Messe und die Spätmessen Joseph Haydns', *Beiträge '76–78: Beethoven-Kolloquium 1977: Dokumentation und Aufführungspraxis* (Kassel: Bärenreiter, 1978), pp. 12–19

Lenz, Wilhelm von, *Beethoven et ses trois styles* (St Petersburg: Bernard, 1852–3)

—— *Kritischer Katalog sämtlicher Werke Ludwig van Beethovens mit Analysen derselben* (Hamburg: Hoffmann & Campe, 1860)

Levy, Janet, *Beethoven's Compositional Choices: The Two Versions of Opus 18, No. 1, First Movement* (Philadelphia: University of Pennsylvania, 1982)

Lockwood, Lewis, 'Beethoven's Unfinished Piano Concerto of 1815: Sources and Problems', *Musical Quarterly*, lvi (1970), pp. 624–46 [also see Nicholas Cook, 'Beethoven's Unfinished Piano Concerto: A Case of Double Vision?', *Journal of the*

American Musicological Society, xlii (1989), pp. 338–74; and the exchange between Lockwood and Cook in *JAMS*, xliii (1990), pp. 376–82, 382–5]

—— 'Beethoven and the Problem of Closure', *Beiträge zu Beethovens Kammermusik: Symposion Bonn 1984*, ed. Sieghard Brandenburg and Helmut Loos (Munich: Henle, 1987), pp. 254–72

—— 'The Compositional Genesis of the *Eroica* Finale', *Beethoven's Compositional Process*, ed. William Kinderman (Lincoln and London: University of Nebraska Press, 1991), pp. 82–101

—— *Beethoven: Studies in the Creative Process* (Cambridge, Mass., and London: Harvard University Press, 1992)

Loos, Helmut, and Sieghard Brandenburg, eds., *Beiträge zu Beethovens Kammermusik: Symposion Bonn 1984* (Munich: Henle, 1987)

Lühning, Helga, and Sieghard Brandenburg, eds., *Beethoven: Zwischen Revolution und Restauration* (Bonn: Beethovenhaus, 1989)

—— Facsimile edition of *Ludwig van Beethoven: Nur wer die Sehnsucht kennt* (Bonn: Beethovenhaus, 1986)

Mann, Thomas, *Doktor Faustus: Das Leben des deutschen Tonsetzers Adrian Leverkühn, erzählt von einem Freunde* (Frankfurt am Main: Fischer, 1991; 1st pubd 1947)

Marcuse, Herbert, *Eros and Civilisation* (Boston: Beacon Press, 1955)

Marston, Nicholas, 'Beethoven's Sketches and the Interpretative Process', *Beethoven Forum*, i, ed. Christopher Reynolds (Lincoln and London: University of Nebraska Press, 1992), pp. 225–42

Marx, Adolf Bernhard, *Ludwig van Beethoven: Leben und Schaffen* (Berlin, 1859; rpt. Hildesheim and New York: Georg Olms, 1979)

Matthews, Denis, *Beethoven* (London: J. M. Dent & Sons, 1985)

Mellers, Wilfrid, *Beethoven and the Voice of God* (London: Oxford University Press, 1983)

Meredith, William, 'The Origins of Beethoven's op. 109', *The Musical Times*, cxxvi (1985), pp. 713–16

Misch, Ludwig, *Beethoven-Studien* (Berlin: Walter de Gruyter, 1950; Eng. trans., Norman: University of Oklahoma Press, 1953)

Moore, Julia, 'Beethoven and Inflation', *Beethoven Forum*, i, ed. Christopher Reynolds (Lincoln and London: University of Nebraska Press, 1992), pp. 191–223

Nattiez, Jean-Jacques, 'Can One Speak of Narrativity in Music?', *Journal of the Royal Musical Association*, cxv (1990), pp. 240–57 [also in French as 'Peut-on parler de narrativité en musique?', *Canadian University Music Review*, x (1990), pp. 68–91]

Newman, Ernest, *The Unconscious Beethoven: An Essay in Musical Psychology* (London: Leonard Parsons, 1927)

—— notes to the recording of Beethoven's symphonies conducted by Otto Klemperer with the Philharmonia Orchestra (Angel)

Nietzsche, Friedrich, *Menschliches, Allzumenschliches I und II*, ed. Giorgio Colli and Mazzino Montinari (Berlin and New York: Walter de Gruyter, 1988; first published Chemnitz, 1880)

Nohl, Ludwig, *Beethovens Leben*, 3 vols. (Vienna and Leipzig, 1864–1906); Eng. trans. John J. Lalor (Chicago: A. C. McClurg, 1892)

Nottebohm, Gustav, *Beethoveniana* (Leipzig: Peters, 1872)

—— *Ein Skizzenbuch von Beethoven aus dem Jahre 1803* (Leipzig: Peters, 1880); Eng. trans. in *Two Beethoven Sketchbooks* (London: Gollancz, 1979), pp. 47–125

—— *Zweite Beethoveniana: nachgelassene Aufsätze* (Leipzig: Peters, 1887)

Plantinga, Leon, 'When Did Beethoven Compose His Third Piano Concerto?', *The Journal of Musicology*, vii (1989), pp. 275–307

Platen, Emil, 'Über Bach, Kuhlau und die thematisch-motivische Einheit der letzten Quartette Beethovens', *Beiträge zu Beethovens Kammermusik: Symposion Bonn 1984*, ed. Sieghard Brandenburg and Helmut Loos (Munich: Henle, 1987), pp. 152–64

—— '"Voilà Quelque Chose aus dem alten Versatzamt": Zum Scherzo des Klaviertrios B-Dur opus 97', *Beethovens Klaviertrios: Symposion München 1990*, ed. Rudolf Bockholdt and Petra Weber-Bockholdt (Munich: Henle, 1992), pp. 168–84

Plato's Republic, ed. and trans. I. A. Richards (Cambridge: Cambridge University Press, 1966); German trans. Friedrich Schleiermacher (Munich: Wilhelm Goldmann, 1972)

Radcliffe, Philip, *Beethoven's String Quartets* (London: Hutchinson, 1965; New York: E. P. Dutton, 1968; Cambridge: Cambridge University Press, 2/1978)

Ratz, Erwin, *Einführung in die musikalische Formenlehre* (Vienna: Universal, 1968)

Reynolds, Christopher, 'The Representational Impulse in Late Beethoven, I: *An die ferne Geliebte*', *Acta musicologica*, lx (1988), pp. 43–61

—— 'The Representational Impulse in Late Beethoven, II: String Quartet in F Major, Op. 135', *Acta musicologica*, lx (1988), pp. 180–94

Riemann, Hugo, *Beethovens Streichquartette* (Berlin: Schlesinger'sche Buch- und Musikhandlung, and Vienna: C. Haslinger, 1912)

Ries, Ferdinand, and Franz Gerhard Wegeler, *Biographische Notizen über Ludwig van Beethoven* (Coblenz: K. Badeker, 1838); suppl. by Wegeler (Coblenz, 1845); Eng. trans. Frederick Noonan (Arlington, Va.: Great Ocean, 1987; London: Deutsch, 1988)

Riezler, Walter, trans. G. D. H. Pidcock, *Beethoven* (London: M. C. Forrester, 1938); first pubd Berlin: Atlantis, 1936; frequent reprintings of German edition

Rolland, Romain, *Beethoven: Les grandes époques créatrices*, 6 vols. (Paris: Sablier, 1928–45)

Rosen, Charles, *The Classical Style: Haydn, Mozart, Beethoven* (London: Faber, and New York: Norton, 1971)

—— *Sonata Forms* (New York: Norton, 1980)

Rosenberg, Richard, *Die Klaviersonaten Ludwig van Beethovens* (Olten/Lausanne: Urs Graf Verlag, 1957)

Russo, Anna Maria, 'Una lettera sconosciuta di Beethoven', *Nuova rivista musicale italiana*, xxv (1991), pp. 74–82

Schenker, Heinrich, *Beethovens Neunte Sinfonie* (Vienna: Universal, 1912: rpt. 1969); Eng. trans. by John Rothgeb (New Haven: Yale University Press, 1992)

Scherf, Horst, 'Die Legende vom Trinker Beethoven', *Münchener Beethoven-Studien*, ed. Johannes Fischer (Munich and Salzburg: Emil Katzbichler, 1992), pp. 236–48

Schering, Arnold, *Beethoven und die Dichtung* (Berlin: Junker & Dünnhaupt, 1936)

Schiller, Friedrich, *Über die ästhetische Erziehung des Menschen in einer Reihe von Briefen* [Aesthetic Letters] (Stuttgart: Reclam, 1965; 1st pubd 1795)

—— *Über naive und sentimentalische Dichtung* (Stuttgart: Reclam, 1978; 1st pubd 1795)

Schindler, Anton, *Biographie von Ludwig van Beethoven* (Münster, 1840, 3/1860); ed. Donald W. MacArdle, trans. Constance S. Jolly, *Beethoven As I Knew Him* (London and Chapel Hill: University of North Carolina Press, 1966)

Schmidt-Görg, Joseph, ed., *Ludwig van Beethoven: Ein Skizzenbuch aus den Jahren 1819/20* (Bonn: Beethovenhaus, facsimile 1968; transcription 1970)

—— and Hans Schmidt, eds., *Ludwig van Beethoven: Bicentennial Edition 1770–1970* (Bonn: Beethoven-Archiv and Hamburg: Polydor International, 1974)

Schmitz, Arnold, *Das romantische Beethovenbild: Darstellung und Kritik* (Berlin and Bonn: Dümmler 1927; repr. 1978)

Scott, Marion, *Beethoven* (London: J. M. Dent & Sons, 1934; 4th ed. 1943)

Sessions, Roger, *The Musical Experience of Composer, Performer, Listener* (Princeton: Princeton University Press, 1950)

Solomon, Maynard, *Beethoven* (New York: Schirmer, 1977)

—— 'Beethoven's Tagebuch of 1812–1818', *Beethoven Studies*, iii, ed. Alan Tyson (Cambridge: Cambridge University Press, 1982), pp. 193–288

—— 'Beethoven's Ninth Symphony: A Search for Order', *19th Century Music*, x (1986), pp. 3–23

—— *Beethoven Essays* (Cambridge, Mass.: Harvard University Press, 1988) [reprints Solomon's essay 'Beethoven's Ninth Symphony: A Search for Order', pp. 3–32, as well as his edition of the *Tagebuch*]

—— 'Beethoven's Ninth Symphony: the Sense of an Ending', *Probleme der symphonischen Tradition im 19. Jahrhundert: Internationales Musikwissenschaftliches Colloquium Bonn 1989 Kongressbericht*, ed. Siegfried Kross (Tutzing: Hans Schneider, 1990), pp. 145–56; and in *Critical Inquiry*, xvii (1991), pp. 289–305

—— *Beethovens Tagebuch*, ed. Sieghard Brandenburg (Mainz: v. Hase & Koehler Verlag, 1990)

—— ed., Gerhard von Breuning, *Memories of Beethoven* (Cambridge: Cambridge University Press, 1992)

Sonneck, O. G., ed., *Beethoven: Impressions of Contemporaries* (New York: Schirmer, 1926)

Staehelin, Martin, ed., *Ludwig van Beethoven: Sonate für Klavier und Violine G-dur Opus 96*, facsimile edition of the autograph manuscript (Munich: Henle, 1977)

Sterne, Laurence, *The Life and Opinions of Tristram Shandy Gentleman*, ed. Graham Petrie, with an introduction by Christopher Ricks (Harmondsworth, Mddx: Penguin, 1967; 1st pubd 1759–67)

Sullivan, J. W. N., *Beethoven: His Spiritual Development* (London, and New York, 1927; frequent reprintings)

Tarnas, Richard, *The Passion of the Western Mind: Understanding the Ideas that have Shaped our World View* (New York: Harmony, 1991)

Tellenbach, Marie-Elisabeth, *Beethoven und seine 'Unsterbliche Geliebte' Josephine Brunswick: ihr Schicksal und der Einfluss auf Beethovens Werk* (Zürich: Atlantis, 1983)

Thayer, Alexander Wheelock, *Ludwig van Beethovens Leben*, ed. Hermann Deiters, 3 vols. (Berlin, 1866–79); 2nd edn by Hugo Riemann (Berlin: Breitkopf & Härtel, 1907–15); Eng. edn by H. E. Krehbiel from Thayer's notes, 3 vols. (New York: Beethoven Association, 1921); rev. edn by Elliot Forbes as *Thayer's Life of Beethoven* (Princeton: Princeton University Press, 1964)

Tolstoy, Leo, *What is Art? and Essays on Art*, Eng. trans. by Aylmer Maude (London: Oxford University Press, 1955) [includes *The Kreutzer Sonata*]

Tovey, Donald Francis, *A Companion to Beethoven's Pianoforte Sonatas* (London: Associated Board of Royal Schools of Music, 1931)

—— *Beethoven* (London: Oxford University Press, 1944)

—— *Essays and Lectures on Music* (London: Oxford University Press, 1949) [contains Tovey's detailed essay on the C# minor Quartet op. 131, 'Some Aspects of Beethoven's Art Forms']

Tyson, Alan, 'Beethoven's Heroic Phase', *The Musical Times*, cx (1969), pp. 139–41

—— ed., *Beethoven Studies*, i (New York: Norton, 1973); ii (Oxford: Oxford University Press, 1977); iii (Cambridge: Cambridge University Press, 1982)

—— 'The Authors of the Op. 104 String Quintet', *Beethoven Studies*, i, pp. 158–73

—— facsimile editions of Quartets op. 59 nos. 1 and 2 (London: Scolar, 1980)

—— 'The "Razumovsky" Quartets: Some Aspects of the Sources', *Beethoven Studies*, iii, pp. 107–40

—— with Douglas Johnson and Robert Winter, *The Beethoven Sketchbooks: History, Reconstruction, Inventory* (Berkeley and Los Angeles: University of California Press, 1985)

Uhde, Jürgen, *Beethovens Klaviermusik*, 3 vols. (Stuttgart: Reclam, 1968–74)

—— and Renate Wieland, *Denken und Spielen: Studien zu einer Theorie der musikalischen Darstellung* (Kassel and New York: Bärenreiter, 1988)

Ulibischeff, Alexander, *Beethoven—ses critiques et ses glossateurs* (Paris: Gavelot, 1857); Ger. trans. (Leipzig: Brockhaus, 1859)

Wagner, Richard, 'Ouvertüre zu "Koriolan"', *Sämtliche Schriften und Dichtungen*, v (Leipzig: Siegel, 1872), pp. 173–6

Wallace, Robin, *Beethoven's Critics* (Cambridge: Cambridge University Press, 1986)

Weber, Gottfried, 'Über Tonmalerei', *Cäcilia*, iii (1825), pp. 154–72; repr. in *Ludwig van Beethoven: die Werke im Spiegel seiner Zeit*, ed. Stefan Kunze (Laaber: Laaber Verlag, 1987), pp. 279–88 [this review originally appeared in the *Jenaische Allgemeine Literatur-Zeitung*, 13 (1816)]

Welsch, Wolfgang, *Ästhetisches Denken* (Stuttgart: Reclam, 1990)

Winter, Robert, 'The Sketches for the "Ode to Joy"', *Beethoven, Performers, and Critics: The International Beethoven Congress, Detroit, 1977* (Detroit: Wayne State University Press, 1980), pp. 191–209

—— *The Compositional Origins of Beethoven's Opus 131* (Ann Arbor: UMI Research Press, 1982)

—— with Douglas Johnson and Alan Tyson, *The Beethoven Sketchbooks: History, Reconstruction, Inventory* (Berkeley and Los Angeles: University of California Press, 1985)

INDEX OF BEETHOVEN'S COMPOSITIONS

~~~~~~

This list includes all Beethoven's works with opus numbers, and those without opus numbers (WoO or Hess) that are mentioned in the book. Opus and WoO ('Werk ohne Opuszahl') numbers are taken from Georg Kinsky and Hans Halm, *Das Werk Beethovens: Thematisch-bibliographisches Verzeichnis* (Munich: Henle, 1955). Hess numbers refer to works not contained in the old complete edition; they are listed in Willy Hess, *Verzeichnis der nicht in der Gesamtausgabe veröffentlichten Werke Ludwig van Beethovens* (Wiesbaden: Breitkopf & Härtel, 1957).

Page numbers in bold type indicate detailed discussion. For a list of works by categories, see Beethoven, Works, in the general index.

Opus

GENERAL INDEX

DATE DUE

06/02/97			
MAR 1 4 1997			
01/18/99			
APR 1 0 2001			
DEC 0 5 2001			
APR 1 8 2002			
FEB 2 5 2010			
WITHDRAWN			
GAYLORD			PRINTED IN U.S.A.